D0765595

Evaluating and Treating Adolescent Suicide Attempters

From Research to Practice

Evaluating and Treating Adolescent Suicide Attempters

From Research to Practice

Edited by

Anthony Spirito
Brown Medical School
Providence, Rhode Island

James C. Overholser
Case Western Reserve University
Cleveland, Ohio

ACADEMIC PRESS
An imprint of Elsevier Science

Amsterdam   Boston   London   New York   Oxford   Paris
San Diego   San Francisco   Singapore   Sydney   Tokyo

Academic Press
An imprint of Elsevier Science.
525 B Street, Suite 1900, San Diego, California 92101-4495, USA
http://www.academicpress.com

Academic Press
84 Theobalds Road, London WC1X 8RR, UK
http://www.academicpress.com

Library of Congress Catalog Card Number: 2002107987

International Standard Book Number: 0-12-657951-2

PRINTED IN THE UNITED STATES OF AMERICA
03   04   05   06   07   MM   9   8   7   6   5   4   3   2   1

Contents

3   Predisposing Factors in Suicide Attempts: Life Stressors

James Overholser

4   Mood States: Depression, Anger, and Anxiety

Barbara A. Wolfsdorf, Jennifer Freeman, Kristen D'Eramo, James Overholser, and Anthony Spirito

5   Cognitive Factors: Hopelessness, Coping, and Problem Solving

Christianne Esposito, Benjamin Johnson, Barbara A. Wolfsdorf, and Anthony Spirito

6 *Behavioral Factors: Substance Use*

Robyn Mehlenbeck, Anthony Spirito, Nancy Barnett,
and James Overholser

7 *Behavioral Factors: Impulsive and Aggressive Behavior*

C. Esposito, A. Spirito, and J. Overholser

8 *Social Factors: Family Functioning*

Jamie Hollenbeck, Jennifer Dyl, and Anthony Spirito

9 Social Factors: Peer Relationships

Mitchell J. Prinstein

10 Social Factors: Isolation and Loneliness versus Social Activity

Sylvia M. Valeri, PhD

11 High-Risk Populations

Julia M. DiFilippo, Cristianne Esposito, James Overholser, and Anthony Spirito

Contributors

Numbers in parenthesis indicate the page numbers on which authors' contributions begin.

Nancy Barnett (113), Brown University, Providence, Rhode Island.

Julie Boergers (261), Rhode Island Hospital, Brown Medical School, Providence, Rhode Island.

Kristen D'Eramo (53), Bradley Hospital, Brown Medical School, East Providence, Rhode Island.

Julia M. DiFilippo (229), Case Western Reserve University, Cleveland, Ohio.

Diedre Donaldson (295), Saint Anne's Hospital, Brown Medical School, Fall River, Massachusetts.

Jennifer Dyl (161), Bradley Hospital, Brown Medical School, East Providence, Rhode Island.

Christianne Esposito (89, 147, 229), Brown Medical School, Providence, Rhode Island.

Jennifer Freeman (53), Rhode Island Hospital, Brown Medical School, Providence, Rhode Island.

Jamie Hollenbeck (161), Bradley Hospital, Brown Medical School, East Providence, Rhode Island.

Benjamin Johnson (89), Rhode Island Hospital, Brown Medical School, Providence, Rhode Island.

Jayne Kurkjian (277), Providence VA Medical Center, Brown Medical School, Providence, Rhode Island.

Robyn Mehlenbeck (113), Rhode Island Hospital, Brown Medical School, Providence, Rhode Island.

James Overholser (19, 41, 53, 113, 147, 229, 295, 323), Case Western Reserve University, Cleveland, Ohio.

Mitchell J. Prinstein (191), Yale University, New Haven, Connecticut.

Anthony Spirito (1, 19, 53, 89, 113, 147, 161, 229, 261, 277, 295, 323), Brown Medical School, Providence, Rhode Island.

Sylvia M. Valeri (215), Brown Medical School, Providence, Rhode Island.

Barbara A. Wolsdorf (53, 89,), Boston VA Healthcare System, Boston, Massachusetts.

Preface

Attempted suicide in adolescence is a significant health problem. Although only a small portion of adolescents who attempt suicide will go on to kill themselves, they almost all continue to experience a variety of emotional and behavioral difficulties. This is true no matter how medically benign the attempt. Indeed, adolescents attempt suicide for a number of different reasons, many of which seem relatively trivial to adults. Yet, the reason for the attempt simply represents the "final straw" for these adolescents. They arrive at this event with a history of difficulties. Some adolescents are lonely, isolated and depressed, seeing little hope for the future. Other adolescents present with both depressed mood and behavioral difficulties, with the depression often arising secondary to the longstanding conduct problems. Still others make impulsive attempts in response to what is perceived as an unbearable stressor. These very different pathways to an attempt make it clear that no two suicide attempters are alike. Thus, thoroughly understanding the reasons for an adolescent's suicide attempt and the constellation of factors which led up to the attempt, are important in laying the groundwork for effective treatment. This book was designed to provide clinicians with a thorough understanding of these important background factors.

The topics for each of the chapters in this book were based on a comprehensive review of the literature which we published in 1989. In each chapter, we update the literature since the publication of the review article in order to provide the most relevant data for clinicians. Most chapters follow a specific format. First, a review of the empirical literature on each topic is presented. Then, measures commonly used to assess each of the areas of functioning are described. Both clinical experience and psychometric qualities determined the selection of measures for each chapter. The interview questions and suggestions for practice which are offered in many of the chapters are derived from both our clinical experience and empirical data.

The audience for this book includes mental health practitioners from all relevant disciplines. We have tried to make the text useful for psychologists, psychiatrists, social workers, school counselors, and pastoral ministers. We hope to provide material for any professional who might have supportive contact with suicidal individuals. The use of self-report measures in most chapters was designed to maximize the usefulness of the book for all clinicians. We include one chapter that describes the limited empirical research database on the treatment of adolescent suicide attempters. Description of treatment approaches that we have used with this population are described but await empirical verification. Nonetheless, we hope that this volume will prove useful for guiding therapy, will help update front-line clinicians on research findings, and inform clinical practice.

Most of this book has derived from the integration of our research experience and our clinical practice. Since 1987, we have collaborated on research projects designed to improve our understanding of adolescents who attempt suicide. These research studies have examined many facets of suicidal behavior such as emotional distress, risk factors, coping styles, and social support available to the suicidal teen. Also, we have conducted several studies to examine the reduction / prevention of suicidal behavior in high schools. All of our studies have tried to retain a strong focus on assessment and therapy issues that are relevant when working with suicidal teens.

We value the scientist-practitioner model, and appreciate the many complexities when trying to integrate research and practice. The research side of our work provides us with facts, statistics, and "objective" evidence to support or refute our ideas about suicide risk. However, an emphasis on pure research can neglect many of the subtle nuances that guide clinical work. In clinical practice, it is important to treat each individual as unique, and work to understand the idiographic patterns of vulnerability factors and coping resources. An emphasis on pure clinical practice is likely to prevent the clinician from appreciating broad patterns across individuals. Hence, it seems essential to integrate the science and practice of suicidology.

We often give presentations on strategies for suicide risk assessment and suicide prevention. After many presentations, at least one participant is likely to ask about some of the discouraging aspects of this work. From a realistic perspective, there are many difficulties trying to predict whether or not a specific individual will commit suicide. Furthermore, many aspects of the treatment of suicidal individuals become complicated by long-standing stressors, comorbid conditions, persistent vulnerability factors, and the stigma surrounding suicide. In addition, concerns about legal liability have discouraged many mental health professionals and researchers from working with suicidal clients. If our work encourages more clinical research or helps to prevent the suicidal death of even one adolescent, we will have accomplished much.

Anthony Spirito, Providence RI
James Overholser, Cleveland OH

To my father Anthony L. Spirito, M.D.

Anthony Spirito

To Patti, Kate, and Nick,

I want to express my gratitude for the many ways you show your understanding of the demands of my work, for tolerating my never-ending task of writing and revising the written word, and showing your love and compassion whenever I need the warmth and comfort of our family relationships.

Also, I would like to thank the many patients, research participants, research assistants, and hospital administrators who have been supportive with our work on suicidal teens. Without their time and openness, we could not have gained some of our limited insights into the problem of suicidal crisis and its management.

James C. Overholser

CHAPTER 1

Understanding Attempted Suicide in Adolescence

Anthony Spirito

This book focuses on adolescents who attempt suicide. Its goal is to provide an up-to-date empirical review of adolescent suicide attempters and to use research data to inform clinical practice. In this introductory chapter, we first describe the epidemiology of completed suicide and suicide attempts, including the demographic risk factors associated with suicidal behavior in teens. We then briefly review the clinical formulation guidelines advocated by leading practitioners in the field and the conceptual models used to determine factors that precede a suicide attempt by an adolescent. The remainder of the book reviews the empirical literature on the precursors to suicide attempts with implications for the evaluation of adolescent suicide attempters outlined in each chapter. The final chapter outlines treatment guidelines based on the current state of the empirical literature.

COMPLETED SUICIDE IN ADOLESCENCE

Suicide is currently the third leading cause of death for adolescents between the ages of 15 and 19 years and the fourth leading cause of death

Evaluating and Treating Adolescent Suicide Attempters
Copyright 2003, Elsevier Science (USA). All rights reserved.

for children between 10 and 14 years (Centers for Disease Control; CDC 1995). In 1960, the rate of suicide completion by adolescents aged 15 to 19 years old was 3.6 per 100,000 persons; by 1991, this rate increased to 11.1 per 100,000 (Holinger, Offer, Barter, & Bell, 1994). Rates of completed suicide among U.S. adolescents increased 28.3% from 1980 to 1992 (CDC, 1995). Males have much higher rates than females. International suicide rates vary, but in most developed countries, youth suicide has increased dramatically and is one of the leading causes of death among youth (Diekstra & Golbinat, 1993).

INCIDENCE OF ADOLESCENT SUICIDE ATTEMPTS

Although there are differences between adolescents who attempt and complete suicide, a previous suicide attempt is one of the best predictive risk factors for eventual completed suicide by an adolescent (Shaffer, Garland, Gould, Fisher, & Trautman, 1988). In a recent study (Lecomte & Fornes, 1998), one-third of youth who died by suicide had previously attempted suicide at least once. In the WHO:EURO Study on Parasuicide in European countries, rates of attempted suicide and completed suicide in the 15-to-24-year-old age group were correlated, especially among males (Hawton *et al.*, 1998). Based on their review of existing studies, Bell and Clark (1998) estimated that there are 15 to 20 nonfatal suicide attempts for each completed suicide.

Adolescent attempters are at risk for eventual completed suicide because the previous suicidal experience may sensitize a person to suicide-related thoughts and behaviors (Beck, 1996). Beck conceptualized these thoughts and behaviors as orienting schema and suicidal models. Suicidal behavior makes the suicidal schema more easily accessible and easily triggered in future stressful situations. Once the taboo against suicide has been broken, it becomes easier to view suicide as a viable solution to life's problems. Thus, the importance of understanding the factors that lead to a suicide attempt cannot be underestimated.

Rates of attempted suicide rise precipitously during adolescence (Kessler, Borges, & Walters, 1999). Borst, Noam, and Bartok (1991) postulated that with the advent of puberty, social-cognitive reorganization leads to more internal attribution of unhappiness from previous external attributions. This shift in attributional style leads to more self-blame in response to interpersonal stressors, and in some adolescents it results in suicidal behavior. A prior suicide attempt in turn increases the likelihood of another attempt (Wichstrom, 2000). In a community sample in the United States, a prior suicide attempt increased the chance of a future attempt eight-fold (Lewinsohn, Rohde, & Seeley, 1994).

Over the past 40 years, the rate of adolescent suicide attempts has increased dramatically (CDC, 1995). For example, in the Oxford region of Great Britain, suicide attempts increased almost 200% in 15- to 24-year-old males (Hawton, Fagg, Simkin, Bale, & Bond, 1997) between 1985 and 1995. Within a 12-month period, approximately 20.5% of adolescents in the United States seriously consider attempting suicide, 15.7% develop a suicide plan, 7.7% attempt suicide, and 2.6% of adolescents attempt suicide in a manner that requires emergency medical treatment (CDC, 1998). Table 1 shows 1997 national data percentages of suicide attempts that did not require medical attention and those that were medically serious by sex and race.

Brener, Krug, and Simon (2000) examined nationally representative data from high school students collected in 1991, 1993, 1995, and 1997. The data were collected using the Youth Risk Behavior Surveillance survey. The number of students reporting that they are seriously considering suicide and making a suicide plan decreased significantly over this time period. However, the number of students reporting a suicide attempt that required medical attention increased over this time period. The increase was strongest for students in the 9th grade compared to 10th through 12th grade. Andrews and Lewinsohn (1992) reported on the rates found in a representative sample of 1700 primarily white high school students in Oregon. The initial data for this study were collected in 1985. The Andrews and Lewinsohn (1992) rates per 100,000 are comparable to

TABLE 1   Percentage of Adolescents Reporting a Suicide Attempt on the 1997 Youth Risk Behavior Surveillance Survey Conducted by the Centers for Disease Control (1998)

	Females		Males	
	Any attempt %	Medically serious %	Any attempt %	Medically serious %
White	10.3	2.6	3.2	1.5
African-American	9.0	3.0	5.6	1.8
Hispanic	14.9	3.8	7.2	2.1

the CDC (1998) findings with white adolescents. Lifetime history of suicide attempts for the 14 to 18-year-old adolescents was 7.1%; 10.1% for girls and 3.8% for boys. This gender difference, with much higher rates in girls than boys, is found consistently in clinical and community samples. Of these attempts, 31% occurred between 16 and 17 years of age, 44% between 14 and 15 years of age, 19% between 12 and 13 years of age, and 5% between 10 and 11 years of age.

Safer (1997) reviewed 29 studies of anonymous surveys of suicidal behavior from nine countries. Consistent with the studies reviewed here, a median of 7 to 10% of adolescents reported having made one or more suicide attempts. When studies ($n = 7$) using structured interviews were reviewed, a 3 to 4% lifetime prevalence of attempted suicide was found. Safer (1997) concluded that the rate of attempted suicide is two to three times more prevalent when assessed under conditions of anonymity, probably due to concerns about confidentiality. Thus, anonymous survey research may provide the best estimate of suicidal urges in the general community.

INCIDENCE AMONG YOUNG ADOLESCENTS

Young adolescents have lower rates of attempts than older adolescents. Younger adolescents may be less likely to act on suicidal feelings due to a mixture of developmental, psychological, and family factors. In a sample of 1542, primarily white, young adolescents 12 to 14 years of age who were surveyed in 1986, 1.9% of males and 1.5% of females reported at least one suicide attempt in their lifetime (Garrison, Jackson, Addy, McKeown, & Waller, 1991). In a more recent study of 5000 children in sixth, seventh, and eighth grade (11 to 14 years old), Roberts, Roberts, and Chen (1998) found 8.3% of these young adolescents reported a suicide attempt in their lifetime, suggesting that the rate in young adolescents may be increasing.

ETHNIC DIFFERENCES

The majority of information on ethnic differences in suicide attempts has been collected with Hispanic and African-American adolescents. Hispanics consistently report higher rates of suicide attempts than other ethnic groups. In the CDC (1998) survey, 6.3% of white adolescents reported having attempted suicide in the prior year compared to 7.3% of African-American adolescents and 10.7% of Hispanic adolescents. Suicide attempts that required medical attention were more consistent with comparable suicide rates across ethnic groups: white (2%), African-American (2.4%), and Hispanic (2.9%) adolescents. In other studies, however, members of Hispanic families have been found twice as likely as those from African-American and Caucasian families to make suicide attempts that require medical attention (Feldman & Wilson, 1997; Lester & Anderson, 1992; Roberts & Chen, 1995). In one study (Razin O'Dowd, Nathan, & Rodriquez, 1991), Hispanic adolescents represented more than 25% of all patients hospitalized for suicidal behavior, the highest rate for any age or ethnic group, even though adolescent Hispanic families accounted for only 1.4% of the community served by the hospital.

Multiethnic studies (e.g., Lester & Anderson, 1992; Vega, Gil, Zimmerman, & Warheit, 1993) suggest that acculturation and other sociocultural factors account for these higher rates among Hispanic adolescents. Zayas, Kaplan, Turner, Romano, and Gonzalez-Ramos (2000) proposed an integrative model in which sociocultural, familial, and particularly mother-daughter relationship issues interact with developmental issues to lay the groundwork for Hispanic adolescent suicide attempts. More specifically, Zayas *et al.* (2000) believe that disparities between adolescent and parent acculturation, socioeconomic disadvantage, traditional gender-role socialization, cultural, developmental, and intergenerational conflict tend to converge and create conditions that lead to suicidal behavior in adolescent Hispanic families. Dysfunction in these families may be related to sociocultural factors, specifically the degree of traditionalism in the family. Traditionally structured Hispanic families often have restrictive, authoritarian parents, which may affect the development of adolescent females moving toward autonomy, even when the father is absent (Zayas *et al.*, 2000). In addition, extended family supports to help parents manage these issues are limited due to immigration. The mother-daughter relationship is often characterized by low tolerance for differentiation and over-involvement of the mother with the daughter.

Another group at high risk for suicidal behavior are Native American youth. The 1990 National American Indian Adolescent Health Survey (Borowsky, Resnick, Ireland, & Blum, 1999) sampled more than 11,000 Native American students in schools on reservations in eight Indian Health Service areas. The overall rate of lifetime suicide attempts was

16.8%, almost twice the average reported in other surveys (Safer, 1997). The rate for girls was 21.8%. The rates also varied considerably across tribes.

Studies with other ethnic and racial groups are rare. In a school sample of more than 5000 ethnically diverse young adolescents consisting of Anglo, Mexican, Vietnamese, and Pakistani children, the Pakistani children had a three-fold elevated risk for a recent suicide attempt (Roberts, Chen, & Roberts, 1997) using the Anglo group as the reference. For suicidal plans in the prior two weeks, there was a two-fold increased risk for mixed-ancestry adolescents and a three-fold increase for Pakistani children.

ASSESSMENT OF THE ADOLESCENT IMMEDIATELY FOLLOWING A SUICIDE ATTEMPT

Assessment of the mental state experienced by the adolescent during the acute suicidal crisis is critical in formulating an adequate treatment plan. The first goal of this evaluation is to determine the risk of an immediate reattempt and whether the adolescent requires a psychiatric admission. The decision to hospitalize an adolescent is usually based on (1) continued suicidal ideation, (2) a major psychiatric disorder that cannot be treated initially as an outpatient, or (3) psychological/family factors that may place the adolescent at continued risk for immediate self-harm or reattempt. Also, the clinician must investigate the adolescent's suicidal ideation preceding the attempt, as well as the reasons for the suicide attempt.

Some of the leading clinical researchers have reviewed the areas they believe should be assessed at the time of an attempt. Hawton (1986) listed the following areas as important: suicidal intent or reason for the suicide attempt; current coexisting stressors; preexisting psychiatric disorders; family history, particularly of suicidal behavior; and self-stated coping strategies and social support. Attitudes of the adolescent and family toward mental health treatment are also important to assess prior to discharge (Hawton, 1996) in order to gauge the likelihood of follow-through with recommendations for outpatient care.

In developing the Measure of Adolescent Potential for Suicide, Eggert, Thompson, and Herting (1994) outlined the following suicide risk factors: suicide exposure, attitudes/beliefs, ideation (frequency and intensity), suicide plans/preparation, number of prior attempts and their lethality, and present versus past threat. Eggert and colleagues (1994) also assessed related risk factors in three areas: emotional distress (depression, hopelessness, anxiety, anger, and perceived stress), level of stress (number of stressful events and violence/victimization), and deviant behaviors (drug involvement, school status, likelihood of dropout, and risky behaviors). The final area assessed is protective factors: personal resources (self-esteem, personal control, and coping strategies) and social support (availability, amount of support, and satisfaction with support). This comprehensive framework guides the clinician through an assessment of many relevant factors.

Rudd and Joiner (1998) proposed three domains that need to be assessed when evaluating adolescent and young adult suicide attempters. The first domain includes predisposing factors such as age, gender, previous psychiatric history, previous history of suicidal behavior in self and family, and history of abuse, familial violence, or punitive parenting. The second domain includes acute and chronic risk factors such as current stressors, losses, or health problems; current Axis I diagnoses; current Axis II diagnoses; current dysphoria characterized by anger, depression, helplessness, hopelessness, guilt, anxiety/panic, anhedonia, insomnia, diminished attention/concentration; cognitive rigidity and poor problem-solving; social isolation and limited social support; impulse control problems, such as substance abuse, aggressive behavior, or risk-taking tendencies; nature of suicidal thinking and behaviors such as active versus passive ideation; frequency, intensity, and duration of suicidal ideation; specificity of plans; availability of methods; preparatory behaviors; self-control; and reasons for dying. The third domain consists of protective factors including being actively engaged in treatment, good physical health, cognitive flexibility and good problem-solving abilities, available and amenable social support, supportive family, and hopefulness (i.e., reasons for living).

Hendin (1991) believes the psychodynamic meaning of suicide stems from both cognitive and affective states. Rage, hopelessness, despair, and guilt are common in adolescents who made suicide attempts. Rage, which often arises secondary to early exposure to violence, is perceived as uncontrollable while the suicide attempt itself is seen as a means of controlling rage. Despair and hopelessness result from failure to perceive any significant interpersonal relationships. Guilt, often excessive and inappropriate, lies behind the depressive symptomatology. The cognitive component refers primarily to conscious and unconscious meanings given to death. These include rebirth or reunion with a lost loved one, retaliatory abandonment, revenge, and self-punishment or atonement. These meanings are often interrelated and can be viewed as responses to loss, separation, or abandonment.

Suicide assessment can be organized in terms of types of attempters. Drawing on theoretical formulations and empirical data, Orbach (1997) postulated the existence of three different types of suicidal behavior: depressive-perfectionistic, impulsive, or disintegrating. Underlying these three typologies are different clusters of risk factors. These risk factors are similar to those already presented and include psychiatric diagnoses (depression, substance use, conduct disorder, panic attacks), phenomenological states (hopelessness, shame, guilt, loneliness, anger, irritability, lability, anxiety), self-destructive processes (e.g., intropunitiveness, high expectations, self-negativity, self-devaluation, self-abnegation), personality traits (e.g., rigidity, impulsivity, aggression, oversensitivity), stress (e.g., loss/separation, rejection, family violence and conflict, physical illness), suicide facilitators (e.g., family history of suicide, firearm availability, exposure to suicide), background factors (age, gender, biological factors), and symptomatic behavior (preoccupation with death, suicide threats, attempts, and completed suicide).

Orbach's (1997) taxonomy has the advantage of differentiating the underlying causes that may result in suicidal behavior. For example, in the depressive-perfectionist suicide, depression or substance abuse (psychiatric diagnoses) lead to hopelessness, guilt, and loneliness (phenomenological states), which in turn result in self-negativity and intra-punitiveness (self-destructive process). In the impulsive suicide, on the other hand, conduct disorder (diagnosis) lead to anger and irritability (phenomenological states) and result in self-entrapment or self-hate (self-destructive process). Finally, in the disintegrating suicide, schizophrenia or panic attacks (diagnosis) lead to lability or anxiety (phenomenological states) and result in self-abnegation (self-destructive process). Conflicting findings in the literature may be related to having patients from the different clusters in different studies. Orbach admitted that his model is preliminary, may omit certain risk factors and suicidal patterns, and that the pathways to suicidal behavior may not be as direct as postulated in the model. Despite the need for research examining this theory and its pathways, the model provides guidelines by which clinicians can assess suicide potential in adolescents. Also, the model helps to explain the process of suicide risk as it evolves over time.

Suicide assessment can be organized in terms of stages. Stoelb and Chiriboga (1998) proposed a process model for understanding suicide risk in adolescents. This model examines primary risk factors (mood disorder, hopelessness, prior suicide attempt), secondary risk factors (substance abuse, personality disorder), and situational risk factors (life stress, social support, prior exposure to suicide). The model culminates in four stages of suicide assessment, beginning with the primary risk factors. Second, the individual should be assessed for suicidal thoughts and degree of planning. Third, when an individual has displayed some degree of suicide risk, the secondary risk factors should be evaluated. Finally, the situational risk factors can be evaluated and may help guide treatment.

As can be seen, many investigators have shared their views on the proper assessment of suicidal adolescents. There is much overlap across the suicide risk factors proposed by Hawton (1996), Eggert *et al.* (1994), Orbach (1997), Rudd and Joiner (1998), and Stoelb and Chiriboga (1998). The major areas to address in an assessment can be extrapolated from these clinical researchers as follows: suicidal history/behavior, psychological/psychiatric functioning and psychosocial stressors, attitudes toward mental health treatment, and individual/family strengths that facilitate treatment. Each of these areas will be discussed in detail throughout this book.

MODELS OF ATTEMPTED SUICIDE

Although the factors listed above are important to consider when evaluating an adolescent who has recently attempted suicide, it is helpful for clinicians to organize their clinical decision making around a theoretical model. King (1998) noted that any model must be transactional—that is, the factors and their interrelationships change over time and combine to create both multiple pathways to suicidal behavior and changing risk over time. Due to the complexity of transactional models, King (1998) suggested that models that illustrate developmental pathways for subgroups of individuals may be most helpful for clinicians.

Brent (1997) presented a general model of the pathways to adolescent suicidal behavior. This model is designed to assist clinicians in identifying areas that need to be assessed and then targeted in treatment. Brent believes that a precipitant leads to intense affect and poor affect regulation through one of three pathways: lack of assertiveness, cognitive distortion, or perceived ineffectiveness in interpersonal relationships. This intense affect in turn leads to impulsive decision making, difficulties generating alternative solutions, and an inability to evaluate consequences of actions, which eventually results in suicidal behaviors. This model has practical utility for therapists, as each of these problem areas can be addressed in individual or group therapy.

Shaffer and Pfeffer (2001) presented a model that combines some of the underlying factors postulated previously as well as areas for prevention and intervention. Shaffer and Pfeffer noted that an adolescent with an active disorder, such as substance abuse, anxiety, or an affective disorder, often experiences suicidal ideation as part of the disorder. Alternatively, adolescents with psychiatric disorders may experience an acute mood change in response to a stressor. The mood change, such as anxiety, hopelessness, or anger, in turn leads to suicidal ideation. This suicidal ideation may result in suicidal behavior if certain facilitators are present, such as an underlying trait (impulsivity, serotonin abnormality), social risk factors (exposure, social isolation), mental state (agitation), and method availability. Suicide dampeners, on the other hand, decrease the possibility of suicidal behavior as an outcome. Dampeners include social inhibitors (strong taboo against suicide, available social support, presence of others, limited access to method) and a "slowed down" mental state.

Only one assessment model to date has been tested empirically. Based on data collected with a large sample of high school students, Lewinsohn, Rohde, and Seeley (1996) postulated a model that includes the constructs of psychopathology, environmental factors, interpersonal problems, and physical illness. These four domains can influence the person's cognitions/coping, leading to suicidal behavior. Using structural equation modeling, results showed that psychopathology had the strongest direct effect on suicidal behavior. Physical health and environmental factors had small, but statistically significant, direct effects. All four constructs had statistically significant indirect effects on suicidal behavior. Tests of this model with clinical populations have not been conducted.

PSYCHOLOGICAL CHARACTERISTICS VERSUS PSYCHIATRIC DIAGNOSIS

This book focuses on the cognitive, behavioral, emotional, and environmental factors associated with adolescent suicide attempts. These various factors also make up the symptoms that constitute psychiatric diagnoses. We have chosen to focus the chapters in this book on psychological characeristics, rather than diagnoses, because the implications for an individual adolescent can be more prescriptive without negating the treatment course necessary for the underlying psychiatric disorder. The focus on psychological characteristics may help the clinician more clearly identify those factors—such as impulsivity, anxiety, aggression—which result in the suicide attempt, even among persons with the same diagnosis, such as depression. Alternatively, certain characteristics, such as impulsivity, may be risk factors for some psychiatric diagnoses, such as alcohol abuse, but not others, such as depression.

Despite our de-emphasis of psychiatric diagnosis, it is important for clinicians to understand that most suicide attempters meet the criteria for underlying psychiatric disorders. The most common diagnosis associated with attempted suicide in adolescence is depression. However, it should be emphasized that risk for suicidal behavior increases when depression is comorbid with another psychiatric disorder (Fergusson & Lynskey, 1995; Kerfoot, Dyer, Harrington, Woodham, & Harrington, 1996; Kovacs, Goldston, & Gatsonis, 1993; Laederach, Fischer, Bowen, & Ladame, 1999). Conduct disorder is common in suicidal adolescents (Feldman & Wilson, 1997; Trautman, Rotheram-Borus, Dopkins, & Lewin, 1991), as is substance abuse (see Chapter 6). Personality disorders, with or without comorbid diagnoses, also increase the risk for attempted and completed suicide (Brent, Johnson, *et al.*, 1993; Brent *et al.* 1994). Andrews and Lewinsohn (1992), in a community sample, found that depression, substance use, and disruptive behavior disorders, but not panic disorder, were most strongly related to suicide attempts. Post-traumatic stress disorder (PTSD) has received less attention in empirical studies than the other diagnostic categories, but a recent study (Mazza, 2000) of high school students found that after controlling for gender and depression, PTSD symptomatology was significantly related to suicidal ideation and showed a trend toward being related to suicide attempts.

These diagnoses in attempted suicide can be compared to several psychological autopsy studies on completed suicide in adolescence (Brent, Perper, *et al.*, 1993; Marttunen, Hillevi, Henriksson, & Longvist, 1991; Shaffer *et al.*, 1996). These studies found that 80 to 90% of adolescents who complete suicide have a psychiatric disorder. About one-half have a mood disorder (particularly prevalent in females), and one-third have a substance use disorder (especially older males). Conduct disorder varied across the three studies (17%, 31%, and 50%), as did anxiety disorder (4%, 14%, and 27%). Thus, suicide risk is not specific to depression, and clinicians must be aware of several psychiatric diagnoses that are related to elevated suicide risk.

ORGANIZATION OF THIS BOOK

We previously presented a model of attempted suicide (Spirito, Overholser, & Vinnick, 1995) that is designed to facilitate an assessment of the adolescent who attempts suicide. Our model also indicates interventions that are most appropriate based on the individual adolescent's presentation. The revised model (see Figure 1) presented here combines factors from the other models reviewed in this chapter and is based on the assumption that suicide attempters display cognitive, behavioral, and emotional characteristics that affect their risk of repeated suicidal behavior. The topic areas specified in Table 2 are meant to provide a review of the most important areas of functioning seen among adolescent suicide attempters. In so doing, we hope this model serves as a means of organizing clinical data collected in a thorough assessment of an adolescent who has attempted

TABLE 2   Specific Factors to Be Assessed in Model of Attempted Suicide

---

I.   Specific predisposing factors
    A. Family
        1. Family composition
        2. Family conflict/violence
        3. Family history of suicidal behavior
        4. Family models of suicidal behavior
        5. Family violence
    B. Individual
        1. Impulse control deficits
        2. Negative self-concept
        3. Prior suicide attempt
        4. Attraction to death/meaning attributed to dying
        5. Preexisting psychiatric disorders, including personality disorders
        6. Physical health
    C. Environmental
        1. Peer models of suicidal behavior
        2. Access to suicide methods
    D. Biological
II. Stressors
    A. Number
    B. Perceived or real
    C. Temporal factors
    D. Perceived controllability
    E. Type
        1. Family

FIGURE 1   Model of attempted suicide.

suicide. In addition, given the high-risk nature of this group, we hope that this book provides information regarding future risk for continued suicidal behavior. The conceptual model presented is not all inclusive. Most notably, biological markers are not reviewed. However, as proposed, the model is consistent with Kazdin's (1988) contention that the most promising conceptualizations of child dysfunction are those designed to

TABLE 2   (*continued*)

---

      2. Interpersonal
         • Loss/separation
         • Rejection/disappointment
         • Peer conflict
      3. Personal failures, e.g., academic
III. Emotions
    A. Depression
      1. Loneliness
    B. Anger
    C. Anxiety
    D. Shame/guilt
    E. Mood lability
IV. Behavior
    A. Social withdrawal/isolation
    B. Substance use
    C. Conduct disturbance/risky behavior
    D. Adaptive behaviors: seeking and receiving support from peers and family
V. Cognitions
    A. Hopelessness
    B. Cognitive distortions/rigidity
    C. Negative attributional style
    D. Poor problem-solving skills
    E. Self-blame, intropunitiveness
    F. Adaptive cognitions: coping, positive attitudes toward mental health treatment, reason for living

---

"explain a circumscribed set of influences and their effects. By being more restricted in scope, mini-theories are more likely to be directly testable and to be subject to refutation and revision" (p. 108).

In the chapters that follow, we cover the research literature relevant to each of these areas and the implications for the assessment and treatment of adolescent suicide attempters. We primarily review the empirical literature over the past decade pertinent to each of the components of the model presented in Figure 1. At times, we compare the findings of the past decade to our knowledge base at the time we presented a previous review paper on the risk factors for attempted suicide in adolescence (Spirito, Brown, Overholser, & Fritz, 1989) in order to give the reader a better sense of the direction the field has been taking.

In drawing conclusions from the literature, it is important to keep in mind the many methodological issues related to this research. Perhaps of primary importance is the choice of populations under study. Samples may be clinical (i.e., psychiatric inpatient, medical inpatient, psychiatric outpatient) or nonclinical (i.e., community, high school) samples. The differences among these populations may have important implications for translating results into interventions with suicidal adolescents.

When selecting studies to cover in each area, we first reviewed the studies that were conducted with clinical samples of adolescent suicide attempters. For some areas, especially those with fewer clinical studies, we also reviewed findings obtained from community samples in which adolescents identified themselves as having made a suicide attempt. However, in many studies, definitions of attempted suicide were not very specific. Also, some studies focus on attempted suicide, while others examined suicidal ideation. Suicidal ideation is an important precursor to suicide attempts and may lead to an increased risk for suicide attempts (Pelkonen, Marttunen, Pulkinen, Laippala, & Aro, 1997). However, the comparability of ideators and attempters is uncertain. Some studies suggest that there may be important differences between adolescents who attempt suicide and those who just think about it (Kovacs, Goldston, & Gatsonis, 1993; Pinto & Whisman, 1996). Studies also varied by site. There are studies with children and adolescents in outpatient (Kosky, Silburn, & Zubrick, 1990; Wetzler, Asnis, Hyman, Virtue, Zimmerman, & Rathus, 1996) and inpatient (Brent, Kolko, *et al.*, 1993; Marciano & Kazdin, 1994) psychiatric settings indicating few differences between ideators and attempters on a number of measures psychological functioning. Given this discrepancy, we did include studies of clinical, but not community, samples of adolescent suicide ideators when the available literature on attempters was sparse or there was a particularly interesting study with clear implications for suicide attempters.

Because this book focuses on attempted suicide, we do not systematically review the literature on completed suicide in adolescence but do discuss studies with clear implications for attempters or those comparing suicide attempters to suicide completers. Finally, developmental differences are clearly evident between adolescents and adults who attempt suicide. Consequently, we only mention studies with adults if there is an important clinical or conceptual finding with clear implications for the care of adolescent suicide attempters or future research with this group. In addition, although most studies use a wide age range in their samples of adolescents, whenever possible we distinguish between findings with younger versus older adolescents.

REFERENCES

Andrews, J. A., & Lewinsohn, P. M. (1992). Suicidal attempts among older adolescents: Prevalence and co-occurrence with psychiatric disorders. *Journal of the American Academy of Child and Adolescent Psychiatry, 31*, 655–662.

Beck, A. (1996). Beyond belief: A theory of modes, personality, and psychopathology. In P. Salkovkis (Ed.), *Frontiers of cognitive therapy* (pp. 1–25). New York: Guilford Press.

Bell, C., & Clark, P. (1998). Adolescent suicide. *Pediatric Clinics of North America, 34*, 365–380.

Borowsky, I., Resnick, M., Ireland, M., & Blum, R. (1999). Suicide attempts among American Indian and Alaska Native Youth. *Archives of Pediatric and Adolescent Medicine, 153*, 573–580.

Borst, S., Noam, G., & Bartok, J. (1991). Adolescent suicidality: A clinical developmental approach. *Journal of the American Academy of Child and Adolescent Psychiatry, 30*, 796–803.

Brener, N., Krug, E., & Simon, T. (2000). Trends in suicide ideation and suicidal behavior among high school students in the United States, 1991–1997. *Suicide and Life-Threatening Behavior, 30*, 304–312.

Brent, D. (1997). Practitioner review: The after care of adolescents with deliberate self-harm. *Journal of Child Psychology and Psychiatry, 38*, 277–286.

Brent, D., Johnson, B., Bartle, S., Bridge, J., Rather, C., Matta, J., Connolly, J., & Constantine, D. (1993). Personality disorder, tendency to impulsive violence, and suicidal behavior in adolescents. *Journal of the American Academy of Child and Adolescent Psychiatry, 32*, 69–75.

Brent, D., Johnson, B., Perper, J., Connolly, J., Bridge, J., Bartle, S., & Rather, C. (1994). Personality disorder, personality traits, impulsive violence and completed suicide in adolescents. *Journal of the American Academy of Child and Adolescent Psychiatry, 33*, 1080–1086.

Brent, D., Kolko, D., Wartella, M., Boylan, M., Moritz, G., Baugher, M., & Zelenak, J. (1993). Adolescent psychiatric inpatients' risk of suicide attempt at 6-month follow-up. *Journal of the American Academy of Child and Adolescent Psychiatry, 32*, 95–105.

Brent, D., Perper, J., Moritz, G., Allman, C., Friend, A., Roth, C., Schweers, J., Balach, L., & Baugher, M. (1993). Psychiatric risk factors for adolescent suicide: A case-control study. *Journal of the American Academy of Child and Adolescent Psychiatry, 32*, 521–529.

Centers for Disease Control. (1995). Suicide among children, adolescents, and young adults—United States, 1980–1992. *Morbidity and Mortality Weekly Report, 44*, 239–291.

Centers for Disease Control. (1998). Youth-risk behavior surveillance—United States, 1997. *Morbidity and Mortality Weekly Report, 47*, 239–291.

Diekstra, R. F., & Golbinat, W. (1993). The epidemiology of suicidal behavior: A review of three continents. *World Health Statistics Quarterly, 46*, 52–68.

Eggert, L., Thompson, E., & Herting, J. (1994). A Measure of Adolescent Potential for Suicide (MAPS): Development and preliminary findings. *Suicide and Life-Threatening Behavior, 24*, 359–381.

Feldman, M., & Wilson, A. (1997). Adolescent suicidality in urban minorities and its relationship to conduct disorders, depression, and separation anxiety. *Journal of the American Academy of Child and Adolescent Psychiatry, 36*, 75–84.

Fergusson, D., & Lynskey, M. (1995). Childhood circumstances, adolescent adjustment, and suicide attempts in a New Zealand birth cohort. *Journal of the American Academy of Child and Adolescent Psychiatry, 34*, 612–622.

Garrison, C., Jackson, K., Addy, C., McKeown, R., & Waller, J. (1991). Suicidal behaviors in young adolescents. *American Journal of Epidemiology, 133*, 1005–1014.

Hawton, K. (1986). *Suicide and attempted suicide among children and adolescents*. Beverly Hills, CA: Sage.

Hawton, K., Arensman, E., Hulten, A., Wasserman, D., Schmidtke, A., Bille-Brahe, U., DeLeo, D., Kerkhof, A., Bjerke, T., Crepet, P., Haring, C., Lonngvist, J., Michel, K., Querejeta, Philllipe, I., Salander-Renberg, E., & Temesvary, E. (1998). The relationship between attempted suicide and suicide rates among young people in Europe. *Journal of Epidemiology and Community Health, 52*, 191–194.

Hawton, K., Fagg, J., Simkin, S., Bale, E., & Bond, A. (1997). Trends in deliberate self-harm in Oxford, 1985–1995, and their implications for clinical services and the prevention of suicide. *British Journal of Psychiatry, 171*, 556–560.

Hendin, H. (1991). Psychodynamics of suicide, with a particular reference to the young. *American Journal of Psychiatry, 148*, 1150–1158.

Holinger, P., Offer, D., Barter, J., & Bell, C. (1994). *Suicide and homicide among adolescents.* New York: Guilford.

Kazdin, A. (1988). Child psychotherapy: Developing and identifying effective treatments. New York: Pergamon Press.

Kerfoot, M., Dyer, E., Harrington, V., Woodham, A., & Harrington, R. (1996). Correlates and short-term course of self-poisoning in adolescents. *British Journal of Psychiatry, 168*, 38–42.

Kessler, R., Borges, G., & Walters, E. (1999). Prevalence of and risk factors for lifetime suicide attempts in the National Comorbidity Survey. *Archives of General Psychiatry, 56*, 617–626.

King, C. (1998). Suicide across the lifespan: Pathways to prevention. *Suicide and Life-Threatening Behavior, 28,* 328–337.

Kosky, R., Silburn, S., & Zubrick, S. R. (1990). Are children and adolescents who have suicidal thoughts different from those who attempt suicide? *Journal of Nervous and Mental Disease, 178,* 38–43.

Kovacs, M., Goldston, D., & Gatsonis, C. (1993). Suicidal behaviors and childhood onset depressive disorders: A longitudinal investigation. *Journal of the American Academy of Child and Adolescent Psychiatry, 32,* 8–20.

Laederach, J., Fischer, W., Bowen, P., & Ladame, F. (1999). Common risk factors in adolescent suicide attempters revisited. *Crisis, 20,* 15–22.

LeComte, D., & Fornes, P. (1998). Suicide among youth and young adults, 15 through 24 years of age: A report of 392 cases from Paris, 1989–1996. *Journal of Forensic Sciences, 43,* 964–968.

Lester, D., & Anderson, D. (1992). Depression and suicidal ideation in African-American and Hispanic American high school students. *Psychological Reports, 71,* 618.

Lewinsohn, P. M., Rohde, P., & Seeley, J. R. (1994). Psychosocial risk factors for future adolescent suicide attempts. *Journal of Consulting and Clinical Psychology, 62,* 287–305.

Lewinsohn, P. M., Rohde, P., & Seeley, J. R. (1996). Adolescent suicidal ideation and attempts: Prevalence, risk factors, and clinical implications. *Clinical Psychology: Science and Practice, 3,* 25–46.

Marciano, P. L., & Kazdin, A. E. (1994). Self-esteem, depression, hopelessness, and suicidal intent among psychiatrically disturbed inpatient children. *Journal of Clinical Child Psychology, 23,* 151–160.

Marttunen, M., Hillevi, M., Henrikson, M., & Lonqvist, J. (1991). Mental disorders in adolescent suicide: DSM-III diagnoses in Axis 1 and II diagnoses in suicides among 13-to-19 year olds in Finland. *Archives in General Psychiatry, 48,* 834–839.

Mazza, J. (2000). The relationship between post-traumatic stress symptomatology and suicidal behavior in school-based adolescents. *Suicide and Life-Threatening Behavior, 30,* 91–103.

Orbach, I. (1997). A taxonomy of factors related to suicdal behavior. *Clinical Psychology: Science and Practice, 4,* 208–224.

Pelkonen, M., Marttunen, M., Pulkinen, E., Laippala, P., & Aro, H. (1997). Characteristics of outpatient adolescents with suicidal tendencies. *Acta Psychiatrica Scandinavica, 95,* 100–107.

Pinto, A., & Whisman, M. (1996). Negative affect and cognitive biases in suicidal and non-suicidal hospitalized adolescents. *Journal of the American Academy of Child and Adolescent Psychiatry, 35,* 158–165.

Razin, A. M., O'Dowd, M. A., Nathan, A., & Rodriquez, I. (1991). Suicidal behavior among inner-city Hispanic adolescent females. *General Hospital Psychiatry, 13,* 45–58.

Roberts, R. E., & Chen, R. (1995). Depressive symptoms and suicidal ideation among Mexican-origin and Anglo adolescents. *Journal of the American Academy of Child and Adolescent Psychiatry, 37,* 1294–1300.

Roberts, R. E., Chen, Y. R., & Roberts, C. R. (1997). Ethnocultural differences in prevalence of adolescent suicidal behaviors. *Suicide and Life-Threatening Behavior, 27,* 208–217.

Roberts, R. E., Roberts, C. R., & Chen, Y. R. (1998). Suicidal thinking among adolescents with a history of attempted suicide. *Journal of the American Academy of Child and Adolescent Psychiatry, 37,* 1294–1300.

Rudd, M. D., & Joiner, T. (1998). The assessment, management, and treatment of suicidality: Toward clinically informed and balanced standards of care. *Clinical Psychology: Science and Practice, 5,* 135–150.

Safer, D. (1997). Self-reported suicide attempts by adolescents. *Annals of Clinical Psychiatry, 9,* 263–269.

Shaffer, D., Garland, A., Gould, M., Fisher, P., & Trautman, P. (1988). Preventing teenage suicide: A critical review. *Journal of the American Academy of Child and Adolescent Psychiatry, 27,* 675–687.

Shaffer, D., Gould, M. S., Fisher, P., Trautman, P., Moreau, D., & Flory, M. (1996). Psychiatric diagnosis in child and adolescent suicide. *Archives of General Psychiatry, 53,* 339–348.

Shaffer, D., & Pfeffer, C. (2001). Practice parameters for the assessment and treatment of children and adolescents with suicidal behavior. *Journal of the American Academy of Child and Adolescent Psychiatry, 40,* Suppl. 7, 245–515.

Spirito, A., Brown, L., Overholser, J., & Fritz, G. (1989). Attempted suicide in adolescence: A review and critique of the literature. *Clinical Psychology Review, 9,* 335–363.

Spirito, A., Overholser, J., & Vinnick, L. (1995). Psychological evaluation of adolescent suicide attempters in the general hospital. In L. Siegel & J. Wallander (Eds.), *Adolescent health problems: Behavioral perspectives* (pp. 97–116). New York: Guilford.

Stoelb, M., & Chiriboga, J. (1998). A process model for assessing adolescent risk for suicide. *Journal of Adolescence, 21,* 359–370.

Trautman, P., Rotheram-Borus, M., Dopkins, S., & Lewin, N. (1991). Psychiatric diagnoses in minority female adolescent suicide attempters. *Journal of the American Academy of Child and Adolescent Psychiatry, 30,* 617–622.

Vega, W. A., Gil, A. G., Zimmerman, R. S., & Warheit, G. J. (1993). Risk factors for suicidal behavior among Hispanic, African-American, and non-Hispanic white boys in early adolescence. *Ethnicity and Disease, 3,* 229–241.

Wetzler, S., Asnis, G., Hyman, R., Virtue, C., Zimmerman, J., & Rathus, J. (1996). Characteristics of suicidality among adolescents. *Suicide and Life-Threatening Behavior, 26,* 37–45.

Wichstrom, L. (2000). Predictors of adolescent suicide attempts. A nationally representative longitudinal study of Norwegian adolescents. *Journal of the American Academy of Child and Adolescent Psychiatry, 39,* 603–610.

Winger, P., Offer, D., Barton, J., & Bell, C. (1994). *Suicide and homicide among adolescents.* New York: Guilford.

Zayas, L., Kaplan, C., Turner, S., Romano, K., & Gonzalez-Ramos, G. (2000). Understanding suicide attempts in adolescent Hispanic females. *Social Work, 45,* 53–63.

CHAPTER 2

Precursors to Adolescent Suicide Attempts

James Overholser and Anthony Spirito

When examining suicidal behavior among adolescents, it is important to consider a broad range of factors that may be involved in the suicidal act. There are numerous precursors to suicidal behavior. Perhaps a useful starting point is an examination of factors that are directly involved in the suicidal process. Factors related to suicidal behavior include prior suicidal ideation, the method used, the degree of suicidal intent, and various precipitants that may have triggered the suicidal act. These factors obviously play a central role in understanding the suicidal act and greatly influence the outcome (i.e., self-inflicted injury or death by suicide). Thus, clinicians should be prepared to conduct a thorough evaluation of these precursors to the suicide attempt.

SUICIDAL IDEATION

Suicidal ideation is an important precursor to attempted suicide. However, only a small proportion of adolescents who think about suicide actually

Evaluating and Treating Adolescent Suicide Attempters
Copyright 2003, Elsevier Science (USA). All rights reserved. **19**

go on to attempt it. Adolescents who have attempted suicide report more frequent thoughts about both death and suicide than do their nonsuicidal peers (Kienhorst, DeWilde, Van Den Bout, Diekstra, & Wolters, 1990). One study documented that 90% of a community sample of adolescents that reported a suicide attempt also reported suicidal ideation (Andrews & Lewinsohn, 1992). As the severity of suicidal ideation increases, the adolescent becomes more likely to make a suicide attempt (Dubow, Kausch, Blum, Reed, & Bush, 1989). Of the small group of students in the Dubow *et al.* study who reported extremely troubling suicidal ideation, 49% had made a suicide attempt.

Attitudes toward death, dying, and suicide can play an important role in the suicide process. Adolescents who have thought about killing themselves have a more positive and less shameful view of suicide (Stein, Witztum, Brom, DeNour, & Elizur, 1992). Adolescent suicide attempters also report lower levels of fear of death than psychiatric controls or high school comparison groups (Orbach, Kedem, Gorchover, Apter, & Tyano, 1993). These findings led Orbach and colleagues to hypothesize that fear of death is experienced differently by suicide attempters and therefore may not serve the inhibitory function it appears to play among nonsuicidal adolescents. Furthermore, when a friend or close family member dies by suicide, adolescents are likely to report a stronger attraction to death and a weaker attraction to life (Gutierrez, King, & Ghaziuddin, 1996). When adolescents have a friend die by suicide, their own thoughts of death and suicide tend to increase in frequency and intensity (Brent *et al.*, 1993). Currently, we do not have good evidence documenting how long these reactions last. However, these reactions could push a vulnerable adolescent closer toward suicide.

Suicidal ideation can include thoughts about reasons for dying, specific plans to make an attempt, consideration of the availability of the intended method, and attitudes toward accepting the suicidal thoughts (Beck & Steer, 1993). There is increased likelihood of an actual attempt when adolescents display the spectrum of suicidal cognitions and verbalizations, including ideation, plans, and threats (Pearce & Martin, 1994). Perhaps most important, suicidal ideation is closely related to hopelessness (Steer, Kumar, & Beck, 1993), a cognitive factor that has been found to be closely related to suicide risk.

Some suicide attempts are preceded by very little suicide ideation. Two surveys of high school students in Oregon (Andrews & Lewinsohn, 1992) and South Carolina (Garrison, McKeown, Valois, & Murray, 1993) found 13% and 18% of the students, respectively, reported having attempted suicide but did not report suicidal ideation over the same time period. In a sample of adolescent suicide attempters in a general medical hospital (Spirito, unpublished data), scores on the Suicide Ideation Questionnaire (Reynolds, 1987), which assesses ideation in the prior two weeks, ranged from the 31st percentile to 99th percentile. Thus, adolescent suicide attempters report a broad range of suicidal ideation prior to their attempt. These data suggest that some suicide attempts are impulsive acts. Alternatively, adolescents may be reluctant to admit to their suicidal thoughts after the fact, due to shame or regret over their previous suicidal urges or concerns it may result in psychiatric hospitalization. One study of a sample of adolescents who were psychiatrically hospitalized in Israel revealed a moderate correlation between suicidality and impulsivity (Horesh, Gothelf, Ofek, Weizman & Apter, 1999), with a stronger relationship noted for boys than girls. Horesh *et al.* (1999) speculated that impulsivity may be related to serotonin levels, and therefore impulsive adolescents might respond to SSRI medications. Brown, Overholser, Spirito, and Fritz (1991) categorized 86 adolescent suicide attempters as impulsive or nonimpulsive according to the degree of premeditation prior to their attempt. The nonimpulsive attempters were more depressed and hopeless than the impulsive group. Thus, it seems prudent for clinicians to distinguish between impulsive suicide attempts and planned suicide attempts when evaluating an adolescent who has recently made a suicide attempt. This distinction is also helpful in disposition planning with different interventions focused on impulse control versus depression and despair. Finally, adolescents who report continued suicidal ideation following an attempt are of particular concern to clinicians. Continued suicidal ideation, especially with continued plans or high suicidal intent, places an adolescent at increased risk for a reattempt (Lewinsohn, Rohde, & Seeley, 1994).

Assessment of Suicidal Ideation

The assessment of suicidal ideation in adolescents has been conducted with several different instruments. Many of these measures, for example, the Scale for Suicidal Ideation and Suicide Ideation Items, Suicide Ideation Questionnaire (SIQ), have been reviewed by Garrison, Lewinsohn, Marsteller, Langhinrichsen, and Lann (1991). The Suicide Ideation Questionnaire (SIQ: Reynolds, 1987) is probably the most widely used measure with adolescents. The SIQ is a 30-item self-report measure designed to assess frequency of thoughts about suicide in junior and senior high school students. The SIQ items are rated on a 7-point scale ranging from "never having had the thought" to "having the thought almost every day." The SIQ was developed in field testing of more than 2400 adolescents. Construct validity (Reynolds, 1987) has been demonstrated via substantial correlations with related constructs such as depression and hopelessness. The SIQ and other self-report measures are easily administered, and there are data, at least with adults (Kaplan *et al.*, 1994), suggesting that the agreement between clinician interview and patient self-report for suicidal ideation is very high. Clinicians can check the individual items to determine not only the presence of suicidal thoughts but their duration and intensity.

METHOD OF SUICIDE ATTEMPT

The method used in a suicidal act can sometimes play a determining role in the outcome. Suicide completers typically use more violent and more lethal methods than suicide attempters (Otto, 1972). Nonetheless, adolescents who attempt suicide should be taken seriously because even nonlethal suicide attempts increase the likelihood of subsequent attempts and eventual death by suicide. Furthermore, suicidal ideation is predictive of suicidal acts. In one follow-up study (McKeown *et al.*, 1998), adolescents who reported suicidal behaviors at the baseline assessment were significantly more likely than their nonsuicidal peers to report both suicidal plans and actual attempts occurring during a 12-month follow-up. McKeown *et al.* (1998) speculated that planning of future attempts may increase after a nonfatal attempt, again emphasizing the high-risk status of attempters. Other studies have also found that adolescents who attempt suicide once are likely to attempt again (Lewinsohn, Rohde, & Seeley, 1994; Pfeffer *et al.*, 1993), perhaps using a more lethal method on the second occasion.

In our previous review (Spirito, Overholser, & Stark, 1989), drug overdoses were by far the most common method of suicide attempt among adolescents. Research in the past decade has consistently found a limited range of methods used by adolescents, with drug overdose the most frequent method, at least in part because most adolescents have limited access to highly lethal methods. For example, of 296 adolescents who attempted suicide in one study (Nakamura, McLeod, & McDermott, 1994), 85% did so by drug overdose. The limited range of methods is especially noticeable among adolescent females who attempt suicide. In a study of 19 adolescent females from a low-income, urban area who had attempted suicide (King, Raskin, Gdowski, Butkus, & Opipari, 1990), 17 of the 19 (89%) females had attempted suicide by drug overdose while the remaining two females had slashed their wrists. In a large school-based sample of older adolescents (grades 9 to 12), 121 adolescents had attempted suicide (Andrews & Lewinsohn, 1992). Of these attempts, the most common methods included drug overdose (53%), cutting wrists or other tissue (27%), and hanging (6%). The vast majority of these attempts were rated as low lethality. We believe the lethality of attempt may be determined more by the adolescent's access to methods than by their intent to die.

In Britain, the same pattern of suicide attempt method holds as for the United States. Hawton and colleagues reported that self-poisoning was found in 87% of 10- to 19-year-old attempters seen for hospital care between 1976 and 1989 (Hawton & Fagg, 1992). Self-poisoning was used by 95% of those attempters under 16 years old between 1976 and 1993 (Hawton, Fagg, & Simkin, 1996). Research has been conducted in New Zealand (Beautrais, Joyce, & Mulder, 1996) that also supports the prevalence of drug overdoses. Beautrais and colleagues examined 129 youth (aged 13 to 24) who had attempted suicide by medically serious methods that involved a high risk of fatality and that required medical hospitalization to treat the resulting medical problems that were incurred because of the suicide attempt. Results showed that even among medically serious attempters, adolescents often used drug overdose (76.7%), with fewer attempters using carbon monoxide poisoning (10.9%), and hanging (2.3%). Gunshot wounds were rare, even in this sample of medically serious suicide attempters. Thus, even with a limited access of methods, suicidal behavior by teens can cause serious injury or death.

Suicide Attempts by Different Age Adolescents

There are some age differences in the method used to attempt suicide. When young adolescent psychiatric inpatients (ages 12 to 13) who reported suicidal ideation were asked what method they would use to commit suicide, the most common method they reported involved suffocation by impractical means such as choking themselves, holding their breath, or drowning (Asarnow & Guthrie, 1989). In addition, of those young adolescents who had previously attempted suicide, the most common methods actually used involved suffocation, drug overdose, and hitting their head. When investigators examine suicide attempts by older adolescents (mean age = 17.5), the majority reported taking an overdose of medications or toxic substances (deWilde, Kienhorst, Diekstra, & Wolters, 1993). Thus, the medical lethality of suicide attempts among young adolescents is likely to be low, often due to misconceptions about the lethality of various methods and limited access to more lethal methods.

Even when a suicide attempt creates a strong medical risk, young adolescents may misconstrue the expected lethality of the act. Indeed, Harris and Myers (1997) found that adolescents have easy access to acetaminophen and use it in suicide attempts. However, 50% of adolescents surveyed significantly underestimated the dose of acetaminophen that would be required to cause death and lacked knowledge regarding the dangerousness and side effects of acetaminophen use (Harris & Myers, 1997). Because adolescents often overestimate the lethality of their own—and others—attempts, highly suicidal adolescents may attempt suicide by an apparently nonlethal method. Thus, low lethality overdoses do not necessarily imply low risk adolescents. As we concluded in 1989, other than the small minority of attempts that involve unusual or extremely lethal methods, other factors beyond method need to be considered in evaluating suicide risk during suicide attempts.

Method Differences in Attempters versus Completers

When adolescent suicide attempters and completers are compared, significant differences emerge between the method used by these two groups. Because of the imminent lethality of most firearms, guns are used infrequently in suicide attempts, but sometimes are used in completed suicide by youth. A study in Oregon (Andrus et al., 1991) examined 137 adolescents who died by suicide compared with 644 adolescents who had attempted suicide. The strongest variable differentiating attempters from completers was the method used in the suicidal act. Among adolescent suicide attempters, the most common methods were drug overdose (75.5%), laceration or stabbing (10.4%), and poisons (6.5%). Among adolescents who died by suicide, the most common methods were the use of firearms (72.3%), hanging (16.8%), and other methods (5.8%) such as jumping, drowning, or motor vehicle crash. Extremely little overlap was seen between attempters and completers in the method used during the suicidal act.

When examining youth who died by suicide, a recent study conducted in Norway found that 41% used hanging, 39% used firearms, 8% used carbon monoxide, and 5% used drug overdose (Groholt, Ekeberg, Wichstrom, & Haldorsen, 1997). Among these completers, significant gender differences were found in the type of method used. Firearms were more likely to be used by males (43%) than females (23%), whereas hanging was more common in females (50%) than males (38%). Drug overdose was a relatively uncommon method to result in death for both males (3%) and females (13%). There is some evidence that the use of firearms is influenced by the availability of guns (Marzuk *et al.*, 1992). Thus, restricting access to guns may help to reduce the risk of suicide, especially among adolescents who are less likely to have access to other highly lethal methods (Brent *et al.*, 1991).

LETHALITY OF ATTEMPT

In the adult suicide literature, medical lethality of attempt is associated with the psychological seriousness of the attempt in most, but not all, studies (Plutchik, van Praag, Picard, Conte, & Korn, 1989). At the time of our previous review article, studies examining lethality of attempt did not find medical lethality to discriminate among adolescent suicide attempters very well (Spirito *et al.*, 1989), and these findings remain true a decade later. For example, impulsive behavior may result in a suicide attempt of relatively high lethality with relatively low intent (Brent, 1997).

In a recent study of 108 adolescent suicide attempters (Nasser & Overholser, 1999), all suicidal acts were rated for the degree of lethality of method. Adolescents were then classified as attempting suicide using high, medium, or low lethal methods. Very few differences were observed across these three groups, suggesting that severity of suicidal method may not be a useful dimension for rating suicidal adolescents. Nonetheless, suicide attempts of high lethality, especially those methods associated with completed suicide, such as hanging or firearms, need to be taken seriously by clinicians (Brent, 1997).

Assessment of Lethality of Attempt

The Lethality of Suicide Attempt Rating Scale (Smith, Conroy, & Ehler, 1984) was designed to assess the objective lethality as well as the circumstances surrounding a suicide attempt by an adult. The 11-point scale has scores that range from 0 (death is an impossible result) to 10 (death is almost a certainty). An example of a behavior receiving a rating of 0 would be light scratches that do not break the skin or ingestion of fewer than 10 acetaminophen. An example of behavior receiving a score of 10 would be jumping from a tall building or any action involving firearms. This scale provides a standardized way of rating the lethality of suicide attempts.

Clinical Implications: Method and Lethality of Attempt

Among adolescents, the choice of method for attempting suicide seems to be largely dictated by opportunity and availability. Drug overdoses predominate in most suicide attempts during adolescence, at least in part because of the easy access and opportunity to choose this method. There are local, preferred methods, however, and these need to be kept in mind when evaluating a suicide attempter (Shaffer & Pfeffer, in press). Attempts other than by overdose or superficial cutting may be predictive of higher likelihood of repeat suicide attempts and ultimately completed suicide (Shaffer & Pfeffer, in press). The mental health professional should assess the availability of means for a serious suicide attempt. When firearms or lethal prescription medication are available, steps should be taken to remove them from the home. This recommendation is not routinely made by medical personnel (e.g., Wislar et al., 1998) and thus it falls upon the psychiatric consultant to make sure these simple strategies are implemented.

SUICIDAL INTENT

For clinicians who evaluate adolescents following a suicide attempt, one of the main goals of the interview is to determine the risk for further suicidal behavior. A key piece of clinical information that clinicians use to help in the prediction of further suicidal risk is the adolescent's suicide intent at the time of the attempt—that is, the extent an attempter wished to die. Prior to 1990, relatively little research had examined suicidal intent in adolescents. In the past decade, however, several studies have been conducted using the Suicide Intent Scale (SIS; Beck, Schuyler, & Herman,

1974) with adolescents (e.g., Brown *et al.*, 1991). The SIS was designed to quantify the degree of suicidal intent based on objective circumstances related to the index suicide attempt and the attempter's own perception of the intent of the suicidal behavior. One reason for its use is that the SIS measures subjective suicidal intent rather than *actual* lethality of the attempt. Studies have shown that there is no significant correlation between intent to die and the lethality of the attempt (Plutchik, van Praag, Picard, Conte, & Korn, 1989). However, it is unclear whether adolescents are able to assess the lethality of their suicide methods in a reliable manner (Rotheram-Borus & Trautman, 1988). Further evidence for measuring subjective intent includes studies indicating that repeat attempts are positively correlated with the adolescents' belief that death was a likely result of their attempt, despite the actual medical lethality (Spirito, Lewander, Levy, Kurkjian, & Fritz, 1994).

Suicide intent among adolescent suicide attempters is composed of several dimensions. A factor analysis conducted on 150 adolescent suicide attempters' SIS responses identified four SIS factors labeled expressed intent, planning, concealment, and communication (Kingsbury, 1993). Spirito, Sterling, Donaldson, and Arrigan (1996) conducted factor analyses of the SIS with two different samples of adolescent suicide attempters and concluded that the most meaningful factor structure was represented by a forced three-factor solution. The three factors that emerged were labeled expected outcome (e.g., lethality conceptions, ambivalence about living, and concept of reversibility of the attempt), isolation behavior (e.g., precautions against discovery, acting to gain help, overt communication before the act), and planning activities (e.g., degree of planning, final acts, presence of a suicide note). Expected outcome was associated with depression and suicidal ideation; planning activities were related to depression, suicidal ideation, and hopelessness; but isolation behavior was not related to any of the clinical constructs measured.

There appear to be important differences in suicidal intent between adolescents who attempt suicide and those who complete it. Of youth who committed suicide in Norway, 48% had expressed their suicidal intent prior to their death, 36% had written a farewell note, and 24% had attempted suicide at least once previously (Groholt *et al.*, 1997). Using a psychological autopsy methodology, Brent and colleagues (1988) used the Suicide Intent Scale to evaluate 27 adolescents who had completed suicide and 38 suicide attempters. Results suggested that the suicide completers displayed higher levels of suicidal intent as compared to attempters. Adolescents who died by suicide were found to be isolated from others during the suicidal act, had taken greater precautions against discovery, showed more planning of the suicidal act, and were more likely to have communicated their suicidal intent to others prior to the act. Thus, adolescents who die by suicide tend to display very high levels of suicidal intent. It is clear that mental health professionals need to identify the suicidal intent of adolescents in order to intervene in a timely manner.

Assessment of Suicidal Intent

An adolescent's expectation regarding the outcome of a suicide attempt may be difficult to determine because his or her concept and understanding of death is different from that of an adult. This has also been found to be true in relation to ratings of medical lethality and severity of suicidal behavior (Spirito, Brown, Overholser, Fritz, & Bond, 1991). The SIS has the most empirical support for use with adolescents. The Spirito *et al.* (1996) study suggests that the portion of the SIS that might be most useful with adolescents is the planning activities factor because these items are correlated most strongly with other pertinent clinical constructs.

Reynolds (1991) has developed a measure called the Suicidal Behaviors Interview (SBI) that clinicians might also find useful. The first section of the SBI examines general psychological distress, major and minor life events, and social support. The second part of the SBI assesses history of suicidal intention and attempts as well as self-injurious behavior. The SBI was designed to evaluate the history of suicidal behavior. The SBI is psychometrically sound (Reynolds, 1991) and may be adaptable for an adolescent who has just attempted suicide. The Schedule for Affective Disorders and Schizophrenia for School-Age Children (K-SADS; Orvachel, Puig-Antich, Chambers, Tabrizi, & Johnson, 1982) has a scale to rate intent of a suicide attempt into one of six categories, ranging from no intent to extreme intent, based on the adolescent's description of the attempt.

PRECIPITANTS AND REASONS FOR THE SUICIDE ATTEMPT

Suicidal acts are usually triggered by a recent disruption in the person's daily functioning. In our 1989 review article, family problems were the most common precipitants, followed by difficulty with peers and then school problems. These precipitants have remained consistent over the past decade. In New Zealand, among adolescents who made a medically serious suicide attempt, the most common precipitants included the termination of a relationship (24%) or other interpersonal problems (26%) such as arguments with friends or family members (Beautrais, Joyce, & Mulder, 1997). Other precipitants were less common, but included financial difficulties (9%), legal problems (7%), difficulties at school (6%), and difficulties at work (4%). In Britain, the stressors most commonly encountered involved difficulties in current relationships with family members, friends, and boyfriends/girlfriends, with the younger adolescents reporting more family/parent problems and fewer peer or boyfriend/girlfriend problems (Hawton & Fagg, 1992; Hawton, Cole, O'Grady, Osborne, 1996). Arguments with parents often precede adolescent suicide attempts (Spirito, Overholser, & Stark, 1989; Wilson *et al.*, 1995) and completed suicide (Hoberman & Garfinkel, 1988). However, it must be kept in mind that conflict with parents is also common among high school students who do not attempt suicide (Adams, Overholser, & Spirito, 1994). Nonetheless, interpersonal conflict was the most common precipitant of the suicidal act reported by these adolescents, which was also true of studies reported in our previous review article. Thus, interpersonal conflict is common during adolescence and can create a vulnerable period during which depression and suicidal risk are elevated.

Suicidal acts are usually not well-conceived notions reflecting a fully determined attitude. Instead, most suicidal adolescents would prefer to stay alive but they feel unable or unwilling to endure the physical or emotional pain that has encumbered their life. In a sample of 50 British adolescents (Hawton *et al.*, 1982), the most frequently endorsed motives for the suicide attempt were relief, escape, or death. Kienhorst and colleagues (1995) interviewed 48 adolescent suicide attempters about the factors that led up to their suicidal act. Adolescent suicide attempters reported several common themes as the reason for their suicide attempt, including a feeling that their situation was unbearable (80%), impossible (71%), and they desperately wanted to stop feeling the emotional pain (75%). Consistent with Hawton *et al.* (1982), these suicide attempts did not appear to be manipulative acts designed to obtain help or attention from others but appeared to be desperate acts caused by emotional distress and feelings of helplessness. Despite this finding, clinicians tended to attribute adolescents' suicide attempts to more manipulative motives, such as determining whether they are loved or drawing attention to themselves (Hawton *et al.*, 1982). It should be noted that adolescents in the Kienhorst deWilde, Diekstra, &

Wolters (1995) study were interviewed retrospectively, and the time elapsed since their suicide attempt varied considerably, from 1 week to 1 year. It is possible that personal explanations for one's suicide attempt could vary over time. For example, some adolescents may gain more insight into their attempt with time and treatment. Conversely, as time passes, other adolescents may not accurately recall the emotions or the cognitions that preceded their attempt.

Boergers, Spirito, and Donaldson (1998) examined self-reported reasons for suicide attempts and psychological functioning in 120 adolescent suicide attempters who were hospitalized on the pediatric floor of a general medical hospital. Consistent with prior research, the most frequently endorsed motives for self-harm were a desire to die (28%), to escape (13%), and to obtain relief (18%). Manipulative reasons for the drug overdose (such as making people sorry, 9%) were endorsed less frequently. Correlations with other measures provided evidence of the validity of these self-reports. Adolescents who cited a desire to die as a reason for their suicide attempt reported more hopelessness, depression, tendencies for perfectionism, and difficulties with anger expression.

Assessment of Reasons for Attempts and Precipitants

The Reasons for Overdose Scale (Hawton et al., 1982) has been used in several studies to assess adolescent motivation. It consists of nine items tapping reasons for the attempt such as wanting to die, trying to escape from an impossible situation, making others feel sorry for you, and so on. It has been used in both European (Hawton et al., 1982; Kienhorst et al., 1995) and American (Boergers et al., 1998) studies.

The precipitants to adolescent suicide attempts are typically everyday stressors, particularly interpersonal conflict. These apparently minor stressors are often perceived as "the last straw" for individuals who are struggling with other risk factors. Thus, clinicians should not underestimate the seriousness of an adolescent's suicide attempt based on the nature of the suicide precipitant. More detailed questioning about the reasons for an attempt can be helpful in clarifying the current stressors and the adolescent's motive. It is also important to determine whether the precipitating stressor has been resolved and to evaluate if conflictual interpersonal relationships may have been altered by the suicidal act itself.

Although interpersonal problems are the most common precipitants for suicide attempts, the research described above suggests that interpersonal motivations, such as escape or relief, are the most common reasons for adolescent suicide attempts (Boergers *et al.*, 1998). Adolescents' cognitive constructions of the reasons for their suicide attempt have important implications for clinicians who need to make disposition decisions and to engage the adolescent in treatment. Clinicians can gain a better understanding of the meaning the adolescent attaches to the attempt by inquiring directly about the reasons for the attempt and offering the adolescent a variety of options. An understanding of the patient's own cognitions about the attempt is critical for establishing a trusting therapeutic alliance and for tailoring the type of treatment that is offered. For example, clinicians and families often view adolescent suicide attempts as a cry for help. However, relatively few adolescents in the Boergers *et al.* (1998) study acknowledged help-seeking as a motivation for their attempt. This suggests that many adolescent suicide attempters may bristle at the notion that their attempt was a cry for help and might engage in treatment more easily if emphasis is placed on helping them to obtain some sense of relief from an unbearable situation. Thus, if the treatment is focused on the situational problems rather than the suicidal person, engagement in the treatment process may improve.

REASONS FOR LIVING

As important as it is to assess the reasons for a suicide attempt, it may be more important to assess reasons for living when making a disposition on an adolescent suicide attempter. The Reasons for Living Scale-Adolescent Version (RFL-A) and its counterpart The Brief Reasons for Living Inventory for Adolescents (BRFL-A; Osman *et al.*, 1996) may be useful instruments in this regard. The latter measure consists of five subscales, four of which were shown by Osman *et al.* (1996) to discriminate between suicidal and nonsuicidal adolescents: survival and coping beliefs, responsibility to family, moral objections, and fear of suicide. Fear of social disapproval, the fifth subscale, did not discriminate suicidal from nonsuicidal adolescents. In one of the first studies using the RFL-A with adolescents, Cole (1989) demonstrated that the subscales of the measure were related to suicidal thoughts and behaviors after controlling for depression and hopelessness. Gutierrez, Osman, Kopper, and Barrios (2000) found that the RFL-A was able to discriminate suicide attempters from nonsuicidal adolescent psychiatric inpatients better than a measure of hopelessness. Gutierrez *et al.* (2000) noted that the different subscales of the RFL-A can help clinicians target interventions to more specific beliefs. Chan (1995) reported data with adolescents supporting the cross-cultural suitability of the scale.

The Survival and Coping Beliefs subscale has the most empirical support. Strosahl, Chiles, and Linehan (1992) examined reason for living, hopelessness, and depression as predictors of suicidal intent in 51 adolescents and young adults hospitalized for suicidal behavior. The Survival and Coping Beliefs subscale of the RFL-A was the strongest predictor of suicidal intent. Goldston, Daniel, Reboussin, Rebousin, Frazier, and Harris (2001), in a follow-up study of adolescent psychiatric inpatients, found that among adolescents who attempted suicide at baseline, high scores on the Survival and Coping Beliefs subscale decreased the risk for repeat suicide attempts during the follow-up period. Pinto, Whisman, and Conwell (1998) found that suicidal and nonsuicidal adolescents were most strongly differentiated by the degree of survival and coping beliefs, reflecting the suicidal tendency to hold negative expectations for the future. Because the Survival and Coping Beliefs Scale has been shown to be highly correlated with social desirability (Osman *et al.*, 1996), it is unclear whether coping per se is the adaptive characteristic being measured by the scale.

PREDICTION OF FUTURE SUICIDAL RISK: STANDARDIZED MEASURES

A number of standardized measures are used to predict risk for suicidal behavior among adolescents. Although these measures have not been used specifically to predict risk of a repeat attempt, they are reviewed here because they may have potential to shed light on those factors that put an adolescent suicide attempter at risk for future suicide attempts. There is some value in having at-risk adolescents complete measures of suicidal behavior, because clinicians may overestimate suicidality in patients (Joiner, Rudd, & Rajab, 1999) making it more difficult to discriminate high risk individuals.

The Measure of Adolescent Potential for Suicide (MAPS; Eggert, Thompson, & Herting, 1994) was developed to assess suicide potential for teenagers between 14 and 18 years of age. The MAPS measures three different areas: direct suicide risk factors, related risk factors, and protective factors. The direct suicide risk factors subscale includes questions related to exposure to suicidal behavior, attitudes/beliefs about suicide, suicide ideation, plans, and prior attempts. Related risk factors has items pertinent to emotional distress (anger, anxiety, depression, and hopelessness), stressors, and deviant behaviors, such as substance use, risky behaviors, and school status. The protective factors measure refers to constructs such as support, self-esteem, coping, and personal control. The MAPS has good psychometric properties and is advocated as a means of identifying high-risk youth in need of future intervention.

The Multi-Attitude Suicide Tendency Scale (MAST, Orbach *et al.*, 1991) is a 30-item scale developed in Israel and designed to tap four attitudes among adolescents: attraction to death, attraction to life, repulsion by death, and repulsion by life. The MAST scale has been shown to differentiate between suicidal and nonsuicidal groups, suicide ideators from attempters, and suicidal inpatients from outpatients. The profile most commonly exhibited by suicidal adolescents was low on attraction to life, high on repulsion by life, and high on attraction to death. The Multi-Attitude Suicide Tendency Scale correlated highly with another measure of suicidal tendencies. A study of American college students essentially replicated the factor structure and confirmed that the repulsion by death scale was most poorly related to suicidal behavior (Osman, Barrios, Hymann, & Osman, 1992). The MAST scale appears useful for clinicians, but additional psychometric studies are necessary.

A study in Australia attempted to differentiate suicide attempters from nonattempters using the Revised Adolescent Suicide Questionnaire (Pearce & Martin, 1994). This scale consists of yes or no questions about suicide ideation, plans, threats, attempts, and deliberate self-harm. Adolescents who respond yes to an item are asked further questions, including how often they have acted this way in the prior six months and how likely they perceive themselves to engage in this behavior in the near future. A composite index was found to differentiate attempters and nonattempters.

The Life Attitudes Schedule (LAS) was developed by Lewinsohn *et al.* (1995) to assess a broad spectrum of suicidal behavior on a unidimensional continuum ranging from positive life-enhancing acts to negative life-threatening behaviors. The LAS measures four content areas: death related, health related, injury related, and self related. There are 24 items for each content area, half of which are positive and half of which are negative. In addition, the 24 items of each valence are equally divided into three behavior types: thoughts, findings, and actions. Positive items are reverse-scored so that higher scores are indicative of suicidality. Three different forms of the LAS were created so the measures could be used in repeated measures designs. One-month test-retest reliability was high, as were internal consistency coefficients for the entire scale.

CLINICIAN'S SUMMARY

When interviewing an adolescent shortly after a suicide attempt, it is important to understand four related aspects of the attempt: suicidal ideation, the method of the attempt, the precipitants of the attempt, and the suicidal intent underlying the attempt. Finally, a review of reasons for living should be included as part of the assessment.

Preexisting and Continuing Suicidal Ideation

Suicidal ideation can be assumed to underlie almost all suicidal acts. However, the duration and complexity of the suicidal ideation can vary across adolescents. Some adolescents attempt suicide after lengthy thought and detailed plans, whereas others behave in a more impulsive manner. The Suicide Ideation Questionnaire (Reynolds, 1987) gives norms and critical items, which can be reviewed with the adolescent. Structured scales, like the SIQ, help ensure that all relevant areas are covered. If a scale is not available to be administered, questions are recommended to tap the frequency (How often did you have these thoughts of hurting yourself?), intensity (How strong were these thoughts?), duration (How long ago did you first start to have these thoughts?), and specificity of suicidal plans (Did you think how you would do it and when you would do it?).

Method of Attempt

Methods used in suicide attempts are often limited by the adolescent's limited access to prescription drugs or guns. Most adolescents attempt suicide by over-the-counter medications taken in overdose. The method used by suicidal adolescents does not necessarily reflect the degree of desperation experienced by the adolescent. It is most important to understand how upset the adolescent is about the precipitant of the attempt rather than to make a judgment about its seriousness. Therefore, when evaluating an attempt of low lethality, clinicians need to consider other aspects of the attempt, particularly intentionality, and not be misled by the low-risk nature of an attempt method. More important, attempts of high lethality associated with completed suicide, such as attempts by hanging and firearms, need to be considered very seriously. Access to potentially lethal methods for another attempt (such as firearms, knives, and even driving) must be restricted, at least until this episode of suicidality resolves.

Attempt Precipitants

Precipitants often involve common forms of interpersonal conflict. Do not assume that an adult's perception of the seriousness of the precipitant matches the adolescent's view of the magnitude of the problem. Sometimes, severe emotional reactions can be "ignited" by a rather small "fire." It is important to understand the emotional upset experienced as a result of the precipitant rather than making a judgment about the seriousness of the precipitant.

Reasons for Attempt

In addition to the attempt precipitants, there is also a specific reason for the suicide attempt. Many adolescents may be unable to articulate a reason for the attempt beyond the precipitant. Thus, it is useful for clinicians to present various options to adolescents after first asking an open-ended question about the reason for the attempt. The reasons articulated by Hawton *et al.* (1982) are useful here and include wanting to die, wanting to get relief from a terrible state of mind, wanting to escape for awhile from an impossible situation, wanting to make people understand how desperate the adolescent was feeling, wanting to make people sorry for the way they had treated the adolescent, wanting to frighten or get someone back, wanting to influence someone or get someone to change his or her mind, wanting to show how much the adolescent loved someone, wanting to find out whether someone really loved the adolescent or not, and wanting to seek help from someone.

Suicide Intent

Suicidal intent is a key factor in understanding the suicidal adolescent. Manipulative intent is rare. Instead, most adolescents become suicidal when their problems appear overwhelming and their coping resources seem inadequate. Clinicians should question the adolescent about at least two major aspects of suicidal intent: expected outcome and planning of the attempt. Questions related to the expected outcome of the attempt include expectations regarding the fatality of the attempt, the reversibility of the attempt, ambivalence about living, and the purpose of the attempt. Questions about planning should be used to determine degree of planning and premeditation of the attempt, as well as any final actions made in anticipation of death. If the adolescent remains suicidal after the attempt, the clinician should ask specific questions about a future plan (how, when, and where).

Reasons for Living

The assessment of suicidal thoughts and behaviors should conclude with a review of the adolescent's reasons for living. It will often be the case that the adolescent is unable to generate such hopeful thoughts spontaneously, in which case the use of a measure such as the Brief Reasons for Living is useful. Contrasting a potential positive future with the adolescent's suicidal state may help diminish the adolescent's suicidal thinking. The types of questions that might be asked include the following: Do you think things can improve and your future will be happier? Are there things you want to do that you haven't done yet? Do you have future plans that you want to carry out?

Conclusions

A thorough assessment of an adolescent following a suicide attempt is important. The guidelines provided here will cover the areas with the greatest implications for the management of the adolescent following a suicide attempt.

REFERENCES

Adams, D., Overholser, J. C., & Spirito, A. (1994). Stressful life events associated with adolescent suicide attempts. *Canadian Journal of Psychiatry, 39*, 43–48.

Andrews, J. A., & Lewinsohn, P. M. (1992). Suicidal attempts among older adolescents: Prevalence and co-occurrence with psychiatric disorders. *Journal of the American Academy of Child and Adolescent Psychiatry, 31*, 655–662.

Andrus, J. K., Fleming, D. W., Heumann, M. A., Wassell, J. T., Hopkins, D. D., & Gordon, J. (1991). Surveillance of attempted suicide among adolescents in Oregon, 1988. *American Journal of Public Health, 81*, 1067–1069.

Asarnow, J. R., & Guthrie, D. (1989). Suicidal behavior, depression, and hopelessness in child psychiatric inpatients: A replication and extension. *Journal of Clinical Child Psychology, 18*, 129–136.

Beautrais, A. L., Joyce, P. R., & Mulder, R. T. (1996). Risk factors for serious suicide attempts among youths aged 13 through 24 years. *Journal of the American Academy of Child and Adolescent Psychiatry, 35*, 1174–1182.

Beautrais, A. L., Joyce, P. R., & Mulder, R. T. (1997). Precipitating factors and life events in serious suicide attempts among youths aged 13 through 24 years. *Journal of the American Academy of Child and Adolescent Psychiatry, 36*, 1543–1551.

Beck, A. T., Schuyler, D., & Herman, I. (1974). Development of suicidal intent scales. In A. T. Beck, H. Resnick, & D. Lettieri (Eds.), *The prediction of suicide* (pp. 45–56). Bowie, MD: Charles Press.

Beck, A. T., & Steer, R. A. (1993). *Beck Scale for Suicide Ideation Manual.* San Antonio, TX: Psychological Corporation.

Boergers, J., Spirito, A., & Donaldson, D. (1998). Reasons for adolescent suicide attempts: Associations with psychological functioning. *Journal of the American Academy of Child and Adolescent Psychiatry, 37*, 1287–1293.

Brent, D. (1997). Practitioner Review: The aftercare of adolescents with deliberate self-harm. *Journal of Child Psychology and Psychiatry, 38*, 277–286.

Brent, D., Perper, J., Allman, C., Moritz, G., Wartella, M., & Zelenak, J. (1991). The presence and availability of firearms in the homes of adolescent suicides: A case-control study. *Journal of the American Medical Association, 266*, 2989–2995.

Brent, D. A., Perper, J. A., Mortiz, G., Allman, C., Schweers, J., Roth, C., Balach, L., Canobbio, R., & Liotus, L. (1993). Psychiatric sequelae to the loss of an adolescent peer to suicide. *Journal of the American Academy of Child and Adolescent Psychiatry, 32*, 509–517.

Brown, L., Overholser, J., Spirito, A., & Fritz, G. (1991). The correlates of planning in adolescent suicide attempts. *Journal of the American Academy of Child and Adolescent Psychiatry, 30*, 95–99.

Chan, D. (1995). Reasons for Living among junior and senior high school youth. *Suicide and Life-Threatening Behavior, 25*, 347–357.

Cole, D. (1989). Validation of the Reasons for Living Inventory in general and delinquent adolescent samples. *Journal of Abnormal Child Psychology, 17*, 13–27.

deWilde, E. J., Kienhorst, I., Diekstra, R. F., & Wolters, W. H. (1993). The specificity of psychological characteristics of adolescent suicide attempters. *Journal of the American Academy of Child and Adolescent Psychiatry, 32*, 51–59.

Dubow, E. F., Kausch, D. F., Blum, M. C., Reed, J., & Bush, E. (1989). Correlates of suicidal ideation and attempts in a community sample of junior high and high school students. *Journal of Clinical Child Psychology, 18*, 158–166.

Eggert, L., Thompson, E., & Herting, J. (1994). A Measure of Adolescent Potential for Suicide (MAPS): Development and preliminary findings. *Suicide and Life-Threatening Behavior, 24*, 359–381.

Garrison, C., Lewinsohn, P., Marstellar, F., Langhinrichsen, J., & Lann, I. (1991). The assessment of suicidal behavior in adolescents. *Suicide and Life-Threatening Behavior, 21*, 217–230.

Garrison, C. Z., McKeown, R. E., Valois, R., & Murray, V. (1993). Aggression, substance use, and suicidal behaviors in high school students. *American Journal of Public Health*, *83*, 179–184.

Goldston, D., Daniel, S., Reboussin, B., Reboussin, D., Frazier, P., & Harris, A. (2001). Cognitive risk factors and suicide attempts among formerly hospitalized adolescents: A prospective naturalistic study. *Journal of the American Academy of Child and Adolescent Psychiatry*, *40*, 91–99.

Groholt, B., Ekeberg, O., Wichstrom, L., & Haldorsen, T. (1997). Youth suicide in Norway, 1990–1992: A comparison between children and adolescents completing suicide and age and gender-matched controls. *Suicide and Life-Threatening Behavior*, *27*, 250–263.

Guiterrez, P., King, C., & Ghaziuddin, N. (1996). Adolescent attitudes about death in the relation to suicidality. *Suicide and Life-Threatening Behavior*, *26*, 8–18.

Gutierrez, P., Osman, A., Kopper, B., & Barros, F. (2000). Why young people do not kill themselves: The Reason for Living Inventory for Adolescents. *Journal of Clinical Child Psychology*, *29*, 177–187.

Harris, H. E., & Myers, W. C. (1997). Adolescents' misperceptions of the dangerousness of acetaminophen in overdose. *Suicide and Life-Threatening Behavior*, *27*, 274–277.

Hawton, K., Cole, D., O'Grady, J., & Osborne, M. (1982). Motivational aspects of deliberate self-poisoning in adolescents. *British Journal of Psychiatry*, *141*, 286–291.

Hawton, K., & Fagg, J. (1992). Deliberate self-poisoning and self-injury in adolescents: A study of characteristics and trends in Oxford, 1976–89. *British Journal of Psychiatry*, *161*, 816–823.

Hawton, K., Fagg, J., & Simkins, S. (1996). Deliberate self-poisoning and self-injury in children and adolescents under 16 years of age in Oxford, 1976–1993. *British Journal of Psychiatry*, *169*, 202–208.

Hoberman, H., & Garfinkel, B. (1988). Completed suicide in youth. *Canadian Journal of Psychiatry*, *33*, 495–504.

Horesh, N., Gothelf, D., Ofek, H., Weizman, T., & Apter, A. (1999). Impulsivity as a correlate of suicidal behavior in adolescent psychiatric inpatients. *Crisis*, *20*, 8–14.

Kaplan, M., Asnis, G., Sanderson, W., Keswani, L., Lecuona, J., & Joseph, S. (1994). Suicide assessment: Clinical interview vs. self-report. *Journal of Clinical Psychology*, *50*, 294–298.

Kienhorst, J., deWilde, E., Diekstra, R., & Wolters, W. (1995). Adolescents' image of their suicide attempt. *Journal of the American Academy of Child and Adolescent Psychiatry*, *34*, 623–628.

Kienhorst, W. M., deWilde, E. J., van Den Bout, J., Diekstra, R. F., & Wolters, W. H. (1990). Characteristics of suicide attempters in a population-based sample of Dutch adolescents. *British Journal of Psychiatry*, *156*, 243–248.

King, C. A., Raskin, A., Gdowski, C. L., Butkus, M., & Opipari, L. (1990). Psychosocial factors associated with urban adolescent female suicide attempts. *Journal of the American Academy of Child and Adolescent Psychiatry*, *29*, 289–294.

Kingsbury, S. J. (1993). Clinical components of suicidal intent in adolescent overdose. *Journal of the American Academy of Child and Adolescent Psychiatry*, *32*, 518–520.

Lewinsohn, P., Langhinrichsen-Rohling, J., Langford, R., Rohde, P., Seeley, J., & Chapman, J. (1995). The Life Attitudes Schedule: A scale to assess adolescent life-enhancing and life-threatening behavior. *Suicide and Life-Threatening Behavior*, *25*, 458–474.

Lewinsohn, P. M., Rohde, P., & Seeley, J. R. (1994). Psychosocial risk factors for future adolescent suicide attempts. *Journal of Consulting and Clinical Psychology*, *62*, 287–305.

Marzuk, P. M., Leon, A. C., Tardiff, K., Morgan, E. B., Stajic, M., & Mann, J. J. (1992). The effect of access to lethal methods of injury on suicide rates. *Archives of General Psychiatry, 49*, 451–458.

McKeown, R., Garrison, C., Cuffe, S., Waller, J., Jackson, K., & Addy, C. (1998). Incidence and predictors of suicidal behaviors in a longitudinal sample of young adolescents. *Journal of the American Academy of Child and Adolescent Psychiatry, 37*, 612–619.

Nakamura, J. W., McLeod, C., & McDermott, J. (1994). Temporal variation in adolescent suicide attempts. *Suicide and Life-Threatening Behavior, 24*, 343–349.

Nasser, E., & Overholser, J. (1999). Assessing varying degrees of lethality in adolescent suicide attempters. *Acta Psychiatrica Scandinavica, 99*, 423–431.

Orbach, I., Kedem, P., Gorchover, O., Apter, A., & Tyano, S. (1993). Fears of death in suicidal and nonsuicidal adolescents. *Journal of Abnormal Psychology, 102*, 553–558.

Orbach, I., Milstein, I., Har-Even, D., Apter, A., Tiano, S., & Elizur, A. (1991). A Multi-Attitude Suicide Tendency Scale for adolescents. *Psychological Assessment, 3*, 398–404.

Orvaschel, H., Puig-Antich, J., Chambers, W., Tabrizi, M., & Johnson, R. (1982). Retrospective assessment of prepubertal major depression with the Kiddie-SADS-E. *Journal of the American Academy of Child Psychiatry, 21*, 392–397.

Osman, A., Barrios, F., Hymann, L., & Osman, J. (1992). The Multi-Attitude Suicide Tendency Scale: Psychometric characteristics in an American sample. *Journal of Clinical Psychology, 49*, 701–708.

Osman, A., Kopper, B., Barrios, F., Osman, J., Besett, S., & Linehan, M. (1996). The Brief Reasons for Living Inventory for Adolescents-BRFL-A. *Journal of Abnormal Child Psychology, 24*, 433–443.

Otto, V. (1972). Suicidal acts by Children and adolescents: A follow-up study. *Acta Psychiatrica Scandinavica—Supplement, 233*, 5–23.

Pearce, E., & Martin, G. (1994). Predicting suicide attempts among adolescents. *Acta Psychiatrica Scandinavica, 90*, 324–328.

Pfeffer, C., Klerman, G., Hurt, S., Kakuma, T., Peskin, J., & Siefker, C. (1993). Suicidal children grow up: Rates and psychosocial risk factors for suicide attempts during follow-up. *Journal of the American Academy of Child and Adolescent Psychiatry, 32*, 106–113.

Pinto, A., Whisman, M., & Conwell, Y. (1998). Reasons for living in a clinical sample of adolescents. *Journal of Adolescence, 21*, 397–405.

Plutchik, R., van Praag, H., Picard, S., Conte, H. R., & Korn, M. (1989). Is there a relation between the seriousness of suicidal intent and the lethality of the suicide attempt? *Psychiatric Research, 27*, 71–79.

Reynolds, W. (1987). *Suicide Ideation Questionnaire.* Odessa, FL: Psychological Assessment Resources.

Roberts, R., Roberts, C., & Chen, Y. (1998). Suicidal thinking among adolescents with a history of attempted suicide. *Journal of the American Academy of Child and Adolescent Psychiatry, 37*, 1294–1300.

Rotheram-Borus, M. J., & Trautman, P. D. (1988). Hopelessness, depression, and suicidal intent among adolescent suicide attempters. *Journal of the American Academy of Child and Adolescent Psychiatry, 27*, 700–704.

Shaffer, D., & Pfeffer, C. (in press). Practice parameters for the assessment and treatment of children and adolescents with suicidal behavior. *Journal of the American Academy of Child and Adolescent Psychiatry.*

Smith, K., Conroy, R., & Ehler, B. (1984). Lethality of Suicide Attempt Rating Scale. *Suicide and Life-Threatening Behavior, 14,* 215–242.

Spirito, A., Brown, L., Overholser, J., Fritz, G., & Bond, A. (1991). The use of the Risk-Rescue Scale with adolescents: A cautionary note. *Death Studies, 15,* 269–280.

Spirito, A., Lewander, W., Levy, S., Kurkjian, J., & Fritz, G. (1994). Emergency department assessment of adolescent suicide attempters: Factors related to short-term follow-up outcome. *Pediatric Emergency Care, 10,* 6–12.

Spirito, A., Overholser, J., & Stark, L. (1989). Common problems and coping strategies, II: Findings with adolescent suicide attempters. *Journal of Abnormal Child Psychology, 17,* 213–221.

Spirito, A., Sterling, C., Donaldson, D., & Arrigan, M. (1996). Factor analysis of the Suicide Intent Scale with adolescent suicide attempters. *Journal of Personality Assessment, 67,* 90–101.

Steer, R. A., Kumar, G., & Beck, A. T. (1993). Self-reported suicidal ideation in adolescent psychiatric inpatients. *Journal of Consulting and Clinical Psychology, 61,* 1096–1099.

Stein, D., Witztum, E., Brom, D., DeNour, A., & Elizur, A. (1992). The association between adolescents' attitudes toward suicide and their psychosocial background and suicidal tendencies. *Adolescence, 27,* 949–959.

Strosahl, K., Chiles, J., & Linehan, M. (1992). Prediction of suicide intent in hospitalized parasuicides: Reasons for living, hopelessness, and depression. *Comprehensive Psychiatry, 33,* 366–373.

Wilson, K., Stelzer, J., Bergman, J., Kral, M., Inayatullah, M., & Elliott, C. (1995). Problem solving, stress, and coping in adolescent suicide attempts. *Suicide and Life-Threatening Behavior, 25,* 241–252.

Wislar, J., Grossman, J., Kruesi, M., Fendrich, M., Franke, C., & Ignatowicz, N. (1998). Youth suicide-related visits in an emergency department serving rural counties: Implications for means restriction. *Archives of Suicide Research, 4,* 75–87.

CHAPTER 3

Predisposing Factors in Suicide Attempts: Life Stressors

James Overholser

Stressful life events can trigger a suicidal act, but perhaps only in individuals who already possess a vulnerability to suicide. The presence of stressful events may help explain when a suicidal crisis is likely to occur, but may not clarify why the individual acts in a suicidal manner. In general, the events that trigger a suicidal act may be perceived by the individual as reflecting their loss, humiliation, shame, or failure. Thus, the stressful event itself serves as a trigger to push the individual toward suicidal behavior as a desperate attempt to cope with these intense emotional reactions.

The stressful life events that are related to suicide vary over the life cycle. As compared to other age groups, adolescents who die by suicide are more likely to be struggling with issues related to identity formation and separating from their parents. Hence, they become more vulnerable to rejection from their peers (Rich, Warsradt, Nemiroff, Fowler, & Young 1991). The risk of suicide increases after the onset of puberty, and the biological, psychological, and social changes associated with adolescence may increase the degree of stress experienced by most adolescents (Aro, Marttunen, & Lonnqvist, 1993).

Suicidal acts are often triggered by recent stressors in the individual's life. However, many stressors build up gradually over time. Whereas precipitants refer to those events that immediately precede a suicidal act, stressors refer to the events that occur weeks or months prior to the suicidal behavior. When a loss or conflict disrupts the individual's daily life, the person may turn to suicidal acts as a desperate attempt to cope with severe life problems. A recent study (Huff, 1999) found that the number of stressful life events reported by 335 high school students accounted for 80% of the variance in suicidal ideation. Several of the most common stressors involved conflict with parents or siblings. In a similar study of 272 high school students (Rubenstein, Halton, Kasten, Rubin, & Stechler, 1998), suicide risk was closely related to life stress scores. Adolescents who reported attempting suicide in the previous year reported stress scores that were 62% higher than their nonsuicidal peers. Thus, stressful life events should be evaluated as potential triggers for suicidal thoughts and suicidal acts. When evaluating stressful events, it is useful to examine the number of stressors, different types of events, the perceived controllability of the events, and temporal factors involved in the stress-suicide relationship.

NUMBER OF STRESSFUL LIFE EVENTS

Many studies have simply examined the number of life events experienced by an adolescent for some specified period prior to the attempt. In one study, the overall number of life events discriminated adolescent female, low-income suicide attempters from a matched sample of nonsuicidal psychiatric patients (King, Raskin, Gdowski, Butkus, & Opipari, 1990). Similarly, Brent, Kolko, Allan, and Brown (1990) reported that suicidal affectively ill psychiatric inpatients reported more life events in the year prior to their hospitalization than nonsuicidal, psychiatrically hospitalized, affectively ill adolescents. de Wilde, Kienhorst, Diekstra, and Wolters (1992) also found that suicide attempters reported more negative life events before age 12 than nonsuicidal, depressed adolescents and a nonsuicidal comparison group. In addition, the suicide attempters were exposed to more change in residence than the comparison groups. Wagner, Cole, and Schwartzmen (1995) evaluated a large sample of adolescent students in order to identify a subset of 147 adolescents who had previously attempted suicide at least once, and 261 adolescents who reported depression or suicidal ideation. As compared to students who had experienced only suicidal ideation, students who had previously attempted suicide reported more stress in terms of conflict with parents, concerns about sexuality, problems with the police, and a lack of supportive adults at school. Thus, in this school-based research, higher levels of stress were seen among adolescent suicide attempters.

Other studies have not found such a clear relationship between life events and suicidal behavior. In one study, adolescents who were hospitalized because of suicide risk reported higher levels of negative life events than psychiatric controls and a high school comparison group (Fremouw, Callahan, & Kashden, 1993). However, only the difference between suicidal patients and high school students was significant. Furthermore, stressful life events were not a useful specific predictor of suicide risk when using multivariate analyses. Two studies of community samples found a relationship between life stressors and self-reported suicide attempts, but only after accounting for depression (Dubow, Kausch, Blum, Reed, & Bush, 1989; Garrison, Jackson, Addy, McKeown, & Waller, 1991).

It remains unclear whether stressful life events play a role in suicide risk beyond causing the general emotional distress that arises in most individuals. However, a recent study (Wetzler et al., 1996) examined levels of negative life stress in nonsuicidal adolescents as compared to three suicidal groups: adolescents reporting suicidal ideation, adolescents who attempted suicide but did not require medical treatment, and adolescents who required medical treatment following their suicide attempt. All three suicidal groups reported higher levels of negative life stress as compared to nonsuicidal controls. Thus, the presence of negative life stress may be a nonspecific risk factor that increases general emotional distress, or specifically depression (Adams & Adams, 1991), which in turn leads to suicidal behavior.

It is important to examine the impact of life stress on eventual completed suicide. In a study that compared 67 adolescents who died by suicide with 67 matched community controls (Brent, Perper, et al., 1993), suicide completers were found to experience a higher degree of life stress during the 12 months prior to their death. Thus, the potentially lethal effects of stress may not be immediately apparent but may accumulate over several months. Also, stressors may not refer to a single event but to several disruptive events that accumulate over time.

TYPES OF STRESSFUL LIFE EVENTS: INTERPERSONAL

Not all types of life stress are related to suicidal behavior. Some stressful events are positive (e.g., graduating from high school), some events are relatively minor (e.g., having a flat tire), some events are a common part of adolescence (e.g., conflict with parents), and some events don't typically affect teenagers (e.g., getting divorced). The types of stressors that seem to play an important role in the suicide process are usually major events that result in lasting, negative life changes. As compared to nonsuicidal controls, adolescent and young adult suicide attempters report an increased frequency of interpersonal conflict, work problems, legal problems, physical illness, and serious financial problems (Beautrais, Joyce, & Mulder, 1997).

Suicidal behavior is often related to interpersonal conflict or loss. Lewinsohn, Rohde, and Seeley (1994) found that a number of life events were associated with a future suicide attempt in a large high school sample. Most of these life events were interpersonal in nature, including arguments, fights, and a breakup with a boyfriend or girlfriend. Many of the other events were family related, such as psychopathology in a family member or family member relocating. In a recent study of self-poisoning cases by youth under age 16, the most common stressors included relationship problems with parents, conflict with friends, school problems, and social isolation (Hawton, Fagg, & Simkins, 1996). All of these events are fairly common during adolescence. However, as compared to nonsuicidal controls, adolescent suicide attempters were significantly more likely to report a recent breakup with a boyfriend or a girlfriend (Simonds, McMahon, & Armstrong, 1991). Compared to high school students, adolescent suicide attempters have reported higher levels of major negative events and more frequent exit events (Adams, Overholser, & Spirito, 1994). Brent *et al.* (1993) compared the six-month follow-up outcome of suicidal versus nonsuicidal adolescent psychiatric inpatients. Loss and parental financial concerns were associated with a suicide attempt at follow-up. Morano, Cisler, and Lemerond (1993) followed psychiatrically hospitalized suicide attempters and nonsuicidal adolescents with depression and found that experiencing a loss in the three months prior to hospitalization was much more common in the attempters (50%) than in nonattempters (5%).

Finally, in the Brent, Perper, *et al.* (1993) study of completed suicide, suicide completers were found to experience more interpersonal conflict with parents and with their romantic partners. Suicide completers experienced more interpersonal loss, typically the disruption of a romantic relationship. Gould, Fisher, Parides, Flory, and Shaffer (1996) conducted a case-control study of 120 adolescents who completed suicide and compared them to a matched community sample. For boys, the risk of suicide increased secondary to an interpersonal loss, such as a romantic relationship. Gould *et al.* (1996) speculate that girls are more likely to have more confiding relationships with both same-sex and opposite-sex peers than boys. Boys, on the other hand, who go on to complete suicide may become overdependent in the romantic relationship, which in turn results in overwhelming distress at the time of a breakup.

TYPES OF STRESSFUL LIFE EVENTS: DEATH AND SEPARATION/DIVORCE

Several retrospective studies have examined the relationship between death of a parent and suicide attempts. Prospective studies of psychiatrically hospitalized inpatients, some of whom had made a suicide attempt (Brent *et al.*, 1993), as well as community samples (Lewinsohn *et al.*, 1994; Reinherz *et al.*, 1995) have not found that the death of a parent predicted a subsequent suicide attempt. Similarly, retrospective studies have not found that parental death predicts a suicide attempt (Kienhorst, de Wilde, van Den bort, Diekstra, & Wolters, 1990; Lewinsohn, Rohde, & Seeley, 1993; Slap, Vorters, Chaudhuri, & Centor, 1989).

The findings are less definitive regarding the effects of separation and divorce on attempted suicide. Two prospective design studies with clinical (Kovacs, Goldston, & Gatsonis, 1993) and community (Reinherz *et al.*, 1995) samples did not find a relationship between separation/divorce and subsequent attempted suicide. Two retrospective studies of adolescents hospitalized in general medical hospitals (Paluszny, Davenport, & Kim, 1991; Slap *et al.*, 1989) also failed to demonstrate a relationship between separation/divorce and attempted suicide. Only deWilde *et al.* (1992), in their study comparing suicide attempters to depressed and nonsuicidal groups, found that parental separation/divorce before 12 years of age was more common in the suicide attempter group.

TYPES OF STRESSFUL LIFE EVENTS: PHYSICAL ILLNESS

Chronic physical illness can increase the risk of suicidal behavior. Hawton *et al.* (1996) identified concurrent physical disorders in 13.3% of the girls and 18.8% of the boys who attempted suicide; respiratory disorders were the most common illness (7.6%). Although most adolescents who attempt suicide are in good physical health, the presence and severity of a chronic physical illness can add to the emotional stress experienced by the adolescent. In addition, secondary problems may develop as an offshoot of the physical illness. Thus, an adolescent who suffers from severe asthma or chronic migraine headaches may find it difficult to engage in positive activities, such as sporting programs or social events. The reduced activity could in turn affect the adolescent's mood state.

LIFE EVENTS AND PERCEIVED CONTROLLABILITY

Another important factor related to the effects of life events is the perceived controllability over the event. In one study, suicidal adolescents described their stressors as having a more severe and influential effect on their emotions, but there was no significant difference between suicidal and nonsuicidal adolescents in terms of the perceived controllability of the events (Wilson et al., 1995). This may be due to the two-edged nature of perceived controllability. Perceived controllability can be helpful in situations where the individual can change the problem in order to prevent its recurrence. However, perceived controllability can be detrimental in cases where the individual feels guilty or deserving of blame for negative events that could have been avoided.

TEMPORAL FACTORS IN LIFE STRESS

Stressful life events may have their impact for a lengthy time period. Adolescent suicide attempters have been found to report higher levels of stress during the months preceding their suicide attempt (Brent, Kolko, Allan, & Brown, 1990). As compared to adolescents hospitalized for an acute medical illness, adolescent suicide attempters reported higher levels of life stress 3 months and 12 months prior to their attempt (Slap et al., 1989). Adolescents report an increased frequency of various life events during the year prior to a medically serious suicide attempt (Beautrais et al., 1997).

Although chronic stressors (e.g., ongoing family conflict) may play an important role in the mental health of adolescents, such long-standing problems are common even in nonpsychiatric controls (Adams *et al.*, 1994). Nonetheless, chronic stressors were correlated with higher levels of depression and suicidal ideation among female, but not male, adolescent suicide attempters (Adams *et al.*, 1994).

In addition to recent stressful events, some evidence suggests that early trauma can have long-lasting effects. In some cases, research has found that serious loss experienced in early childhood can increase the risk of death by suicide during adolescence (Kjelsberg, Neegard, & Dahl, 1994). Lewinsohn, Rohde, and Seeley (1996) found that death of a parent before age 12 was reported by 2.6% of the adolescents who had never made a suicide attempt, 4.1% of the one-time attempters, and 8.3% of the multiple attempters. In a study of adult suicide attempters (Wasserman & Cullberg, 1989), 52% had lost contact with one or both parents before the age of 18, due to death of the parent (25%) or divorce (27%). Thus, some negative events can have lasting impact that may predispose the individual toward depression and suicide.

STRESSFUL LIFE EVENTS AND MULTIPLE ATTEMPTS

There is one study (Joiner & Rudd, in press) of young adult psychiatric patients that suggests that negative life events may be particularly damaging for those who have made multiple suicide attempts. Negative life events may prolong a crisis situation for those who have multiple suicide attempts in the past, but not for first-time attempters. Clinicians, therefore, should be particularly sensitive to the occurrence of negative life events among multiple attempters.

CLINICAL IMPLICATIONS

In the past decade, data have accumulated supporting the notion that stressful life events may play an important role in the development of suicidal tendencies among adolescents by serving as a trigger to the suicidal act. However, stressful life events may have an indirect relationship on suicidal crises via their impact on the adolescent's feelings of depression and hopelessness. Studies testing the direct and indirect effects of life events and suicidality in adolescents have yet to be conducted.

The negative effects of life stress cannot be examined in isolation. Many psychosocial factors converge to determine the individual's ability to cope with the stressful life events. Although it is clear that more research on the mechanisms that protect adolescents from life stressors is needed, few studies have been conducted on mediators. One exception is a study that found the effects of stress on suicide ideation are mediated by social support and problem-solving skills (Yang & Clum, 1994), as well as other personal and social resources available to the individual. Other chapters will address these issues.

ASSESSMENT OF LIFE EVENTS

Various measures can be used to assess the presence and severity of life events, using different formats (i.e., interview versus questionnaire), different time frames (i.e., previous month, past year, or lifetime incidence), and different types of events (e.g., major stressors versus daily hassles). When examining life stress that precedes a nonfatal suicide attempt, ratings of life stress are usually obtained from the adolescent's self-report. Most studies assess life stress using a questionnaire (e.g., Adams et al., 1994), often modified from older, established scales (e.g., Coddington, 1972). Although questionnaires are efficient, they are usually not the most thorough method for evaluating the presence of stressful life events. Interview measures are more thorough but can be quite time consuming and are often impractical in many settings. However, even when using a simple 10-point scale derived from DSM Axis IV, higher levels of life stress are closely related to suicidality (Myers et al., 1991).

Several life event scales have been developed specifically for adolescents. The Adolescent Perceived Events Scale (APES; Compas, Davis, Forsythe, & Wagner, 1987) is a checklist of 159 daily hassles and major stressful events experienced by adolescents that requests participants to report if they have experienced particular events and if so, the frequency, desirability, and impact of the event. Johnson and McCutcheon (1980) developed the 46-item Life Events Checklist specifically for adolescents. Each event experienced in the prior year is rated as to its desirability (good or bad) and its effect on the adolescents' lives (more, some, moderate, great). In general, scales that were developed for adolescents are superior to general-use measures because they contain few items that are irrelevant to adolescents (e.g., divorce, retirement).

CLINICIAN GUIDELINES

Suicidal adolescents experience a number of stressful events during the months prior to their suicidal crisis. Although the subjective experience of stress can accumulate across different events, it is more useful to understand the type and impact of specific stressors.

Different types of events have been related to suicide risk, with the most common stressors involving interpersonal conflict or loss. When evaluating an adolescent who attempted suicide, clinicians should at least screen for the presence of minor, major, and chronic stressful life events in five key domains (Lewinsohn *et al.*, 1996): school (e.g., poor grades), parents/family (e.g., legal or financial problems, marital problems, parent-adolescent conflict, parental psychopathology or suicidal behavior), friends (e.g., peer arguments, fights), work (e.g., difficulties with supervisor, termination), and other personal stressors (e.g., health problems, relationship difficulties/breakup, interpersonal loss via death/divorce, leaving home, legal troubles).

Whenever an adolescent experiences suicidal urges in the aftermath of a significant interpersonal stressor, therapy must focus on the adolescent's ability to manage the situation and grow beyond it.

Suicidal tendencies may be mediated by perceptions of negative events. Suicidal adolescents should be helped to evaluate their life events from a realistic but positive view. When appropriate, adolescents should cultivate internal attributions for positive events and external or unstable attributions for negative events.

Although stressful life events can play an important role in suicidal behavior, stressors probably serve to aggravate the adolescent's feelings of distress and despair. Other factors, such as a major depressive disorder or persistent feelings of hopelessness, may play more central roles in understanding and treating suicidal adolescents. Focusing excessively on recent stressors may neglect important underlying variables (McKeown *et al.*, 1998). Several important moderating factors should be included in the evaluation, such as the individual's coping style, social support, and adaptive personality traits (Sandin, Chorot, Santed, Valiente, & Joiner, 1998).

REFERENCES

Adams, D., Overholser, J. C., & Spirito, A. (1994). Stressful life events associated with adolescent suicide attempts. *Canadian Journal of Psychiatry, 39*, 43–48.

Adams, M., & Adams, J. (1991). Life events, depression, and perceived problem-solving alternatives in adolescents. *Journal of Child Psychology and Psychiatry, 32,* 811–820.

Aro, H., Marttunen, M., & Lonnqvist, J. (1993). Adolescent development and youth suicide. *Suicide and Life-Threatening Behavior, 23,* 359–365.

Beautrais, A. L., Joyce, P. R., & Mulder, R. T. (1997). Precipitating factors and life events in serious suicide attempts among youths aged 13 through 24 years. *Journal of the American Academy of Child and Adolescent Psychiatry, 36,* 1543–1551.

Brent, D., Kolko, D., Allan, M., & Brown, R. (1990). Suicidality in affectively disordered adolescent inpatients. *Journal of the American Academy of Child and Adolescent Psychiatry, 29,* 586–593.

Brent, D., Kolko, D., Wartella, M., Boylan, M., Moritz, G., Baugher, M., & Zelenak, J. P. (1993). Adolescent psychiatric inpatients' risk of suicide attempt at 6-month follow-up. *Journal of American Academy of Child and Adolescent Psychiatry, 32,* 95–105.

Brent, D., Perper, J. A., Moritz, G., Baugher, M., Roth, C., Balach, L., & Schweers, J. (1993). Stressful life events, psychopathology, and adolescent suicide: A case control study. *Suicide and Life-Threatening Behavior, 23,* 179–187.

Coddington, R. (1972). The significance of life events as etiologic factors in the diseases of children. II. A study of a normal population. *Journal of Psychosomatic Research* (16), 205–213.

Compas, B. E., Davis, G. E., Forsythe, C. J., & Wagner, B. M. (1987). Assessment of major and daily stressful events during adolescence: The Adolescent Perceived Events Scale. *Journal of Consulting and Clinical Psychology, 55,* 534–541.

deWilde, E., Kienhorst, I., Diekstra, R., & Wolters, W. (1992). The relationship between adolescent suicidal behavior and life events in childhood and adolescence. *American Journal of Psychiatry, 149,* 45–51.

Dubow, E. F., Kausch, D. F., Blum, M. C., Reed, J., & Bush, E. (1989). Correlates of suicidal ideation and attempts in a community sample of junior high and high school students. *Journal of Clinical Child Psychology, 18,* 158–166.

Fremouw, W., Callahan, T., & Kashden, J. (1993). Adolescent suicidal risk: Psychological, problem solving, and environmental factors. *Suicide and Life-Threatening Behavior, 23,* 46–54.

Garrison, C., Jackson, L., Addy, D., McKeown, R., & Waller, J. (1991). Suicidal behaviors in young adolescents. *American Journal of Epidemiology, 133,* 1005–1014.

Gould, M., Fisher, P., Parides, M., Flory, M., & Shaffer, D. (1996). Psychosocial risk factors of child and adolescent completed suicide. *Archives of General Psychiatry, 53,* 1155–1162.

Hawton, K., Fagg, J., & Simkins, S. (1996). Deliberate self-poisoning and self-injury in children and adolescents under 16 years of age in Oxford, 1976–1993. *British Journal of Psychiatry, 16,* 202–208.

Huff, C. (1999). Source, recency, and degree of stress in adolescence and suicide ideation. *Adolescence, 34,* 81–89.

Johnson, J. H., & McCutcheon, S. (1980). Assessing life stress in older children and adolescents: Preliminary findings with The Life Events Checklist. In I. G. Sarason & C. D. Spielberger (Eds.), *Stress and anxiety* (Vol. 7, pp. 111–125). Washington, DC: Hemisphere.

Joiner, T., & Rudd, D. (in press). Intensity and duration of suicidal crises vary as a function of previous suicide attempts and negative life events. *Journal of Abnormal Psychology.*

Kienhorst, C. W. M., deWilde, E. J., van Den bort, J., Diekstra, R. F. W., & Wolters, W. H. G. (1990). Characteristics of suicide attempters in a population-based sample of Dutch adolescents. *British Journal of Psychiatry, 156*, 243–248.

King, C. A., Raskin, A., Gdowski, C. L., Butkus, M., & Opipari, L. (1990). Psychosocial factors associated with urban adolescent female suicide attempts. *Journal of the American Academy of Child and Adolescent Psychiatry, 29*, 289–294.

Kjelsberg, E., Neegard, E., & Dahl, A. (1994). Suicide in adolescent psychiatric inpatients: Incidence and predictive factors. *Acta Psychiatrica Scandinavica, 89*, 235–241.

Kovacs, M., Goldston, D., & Gatsonis, C. (1993). Suicidal behaviors and childhood-onset depressive disorders: A longitudinal investigation. *Journal of the American Academy of Child and Adolescent Psychiatry, 32*, 8–20.

Lewinsohn, P., Rohde, P., & Seeley, J. (1994). Psychosocial risk factors for future suicide attempts. *Journal of Consulting and Clinical Psychology, 62*, 297–305.

Lewinsohn, P., Rohde, P., & Seeley, J. (1996). Adolescent suicidal ideation and attempts: Prevalence, risk factors and clinical implications. *Clinical Psychology: Suicide and Practice, 3*, 25–46.

Lewinsohn, P. M., Rohde, P., & Seeley, J. R. (1993). Psychosocial characteristics of adolescents with a history of suicide attempts. *Journal of the American Academy of Child and Adolescent Psychiatry, 32*, 60–68.

McKeown, R., Garrison, C., Cuffe, S., Waller, J., Jackson, K., & Addy, C. (1998). Incidence and predictors of suicidal behaviors in a longitudinal sample of young adolescents. *Journal of the American Academy of Child and Adolescent Psychiatry, 37*, 612–619.

Morano, C., Cisler, R., & Lemerond, J. (1993). Risk factors for adolescent suicide behavior: Loss, insufficient familial support, and hopelessness. *Adolescence, 28*, 851–865.

Myers, K., McCauley, E., Calderon, R., Mitchell, J., Burke, P., & Schloredt, K. (1991). Risks for suicidality in major depressive disorder. *Journal of the American Academy of Child and Adolescent Psychiatry, 30*, 86–94.

Palusnzy, M., Davenport, C., & Kim, W. J. (1991). Suicide attempts and ideation: Adolescents evaluated on a pediatric ward. *Adolescence, 26*, 209–215.

Reinherz, H. Z., Giaconia, R. M., Silverman, A. B., Friedman, A., Pakel, B., Frost, A. K., & Cohen, E. K. (1995). Early psychosocial risks for adolescent suicidal ideation and attempts. *Journal of the American Academy of Child and Adolescent Psychiatry, 34*, 599–611.

Rich, C., Warsradt, G., Nemiroff, R., Fowler, R., & Young, D. (1991). Suicide, stressors, and the life cycle. *American Journal of Psychiatry, 148*, 524–527.

Rubenstein, J., Halton, A., Kasten, L., Rubin, C., & Stechler, G. (1998). Suicidal behavior in adolescents: Stress and protection in different family contexts. *American Journal of Orthopsychiatry, 68*, 274–284.

Sandin, B., Chorot, P., Santed, M., Valiente, R., & Joiner, T. (1998). Negative life events and adolescent suicidal behavior: A Critical analysis from the stress process perspective. *Journal of Adolescence, 21*, 415–426.

Simonds, J., McMahon, T., & Armstrong, D. (1991). Youth suicide attempters compared with a control group: Psychological, affective, and attudinal variables. *Suicide and Life-Threatening Behavior, 21*, 415–426.

Slap, G. B., Vorters, D. F., Chaudhuri, S., & Centor, R. M. (1989). Risk factors for attempted suicide during adolescence. *Pediatrics, 84*, 762–772.

Wagner, B., Cole, R., & Schwartzman, P. (1995). Psychosocial correlates of suicide attempts among junior and senior high school youth. *Suicide and Life-Threatening Behavior, 25,* 358–372.

Wasserman, D., & Cullberg, J. (1989). Early separation and suicidal behavior in the parental home of 40 consecutive suicide attempters. *Acta Psychiatrica Scandinavica, 79,* 296–302.

Wetzler, S., Asnis, G., Hyman, R., Virtue, C., Zimmerman, J., & Rathus, J. (1996). Characteristics of suicidality among adolescents. *Suicide and Life-Threatening Behavior, 26,* 37–45.

Wilson, K., Stelzer, J., Bergman, J., Kral, M., Inayatullah, M., & Elliott, C. (1995). Problem solving, stress, and coping in adolescent suicide attempts. *Suicide and Life-Threatening Behavior, 25,* 241–252.

Yang, B., & Clum, G. (1994). Life stress, social support, and problem-solving skills predictive of depressive symptoms, hopelessness, and suicide ideation in an Asian student population: A test of a model. *Suicide and Life-Threatening Behavior, 24,* 127–139.

CHAPTER 4

Mood States: Depression, Anger, and Anxiety

Barbara A. Wolfsdorf, Jennifer Freeman, Kristen D'Eramo, James Overholser, and Anthony Spirito

Suicidal behavior is the end result of a number of cognitive, behavioral, and emotional factors. Although depression is most commonly thought of as the primary emotion that accompanies suicidal behavior, not all adolescent suicide attempters are depressed, and not all depressed adolescents attempt suicide. Other emotional states may be equally important in understanding a suicide attempt. Anger, for example, has been shown to be common in many adolescents who attempt suicide, and anxiety has been evident in adolescents who complete suicide. In this chapter, we will review depressed mood, anger, and anxiety as potentially important emotional correlates of adolescent suicide attempts.

Although emotional states are sometimes investigated in isolation (e.g., Lehnert, Overholser, & Spirito, 1994), when researchers study adolescent suicidality, several emotions are usually examined within one investigation (e.g., Boergers, Spirito, & Donaldson, 1998; Marciano & Kazdin, 1994; Negron, Piacentini, Graae, Davies, & Shaffer, 1997). Unfortunately, the relation of each of these emotional states to adolescent suicidal behavior is often analyzed in isolation from other relevant emotional states (e.g.,

Evaluating and Treating Adolescent Suicide Attempters

53

Grossi & Violato, 1992; King, Raskin, Gdowski, Butkus, & Opipari, 1990; Negron *et al.*, 1997; Rotheram-Borus, Walker, & Ferns, 1996). Fewer researchers have evaluated the relative importance of each emotion within the context of other emotions or other psychosocial variables (e.g., Asarnow & Guthrie, 1989; Boergers *et al.*, 1998; Marciano & Kazdin, 1994; Myers, McCauley, Calderon, & Treder, 1991).

A number of approaches to assessing emotions and attempting to understand their relation to adolescent suicide attempts have been used. Researchers in the field have used self-report measures (e.g., Boergers *et al.*, 1998; Marciano & Kazdin, 1994; Negron *et al.*, 1997; Pinto & Whisman, 1996), interview assessments and ratings (e.g., Asarnow & Guthrie, 1989; Boergers *et al.*, 1998; Marciano & Kazdin, 1994), and parental perspectives (e.g., King *et al.*, 1990). Although overwhelmingly retrospective in nature (for exceptions, see Myers, McCauley, Calderon, & Treder, 1991; Pfeffer, Klerman, Hurt, Lesser, Peskin, & Siefker, 1991), data have been collected within 24 hours of an adolescent's suicide attempt (e.g., Boergers *et al.*, 1998) or as long as several years after the attempt (e.g., Rotheram-Borus *et al.*, 1996). These differences in methodology need to be considered when interpreting, and especially when comparing, the results of different research studies.

Because an exhaustive review of the literature on emotions and adolescent suicidality is beyond the scope of this chapter, we focused on the most recent literature that targeted adolescents most similar to those clinicians might see in practice. Therefore, here we review investigations of the emotional correlates of adolescent suicide attempts published in the past decade that meet several criteria. First, only empirical investigations of clinical populations were included. Investigations of community samples were excluded from this review. Second, studies that included *only* adolescents characterized by suicidal ideation or threats were not included in this review. We tried to focus on suicide attempts and completed suicide by adolescents. Third, investigations were included only if the focus was on suicidal behavior rather than a specific disorder. Fourth, studies that included nonsuicidal "self-harm" behaviors were excluded from this review.

Based on more than 25 published investigations that met these criteria, our general conclusion is that significant levels of depressed mood, anger, and anxiety are associated with adolescent suicide attempts. However, results are far from consistent. Disentangling the relations between suicidality and each of these emotional states is challenging. In an effort to more clearly elucidate these relations, we will address the literature relevant to each emotion in turn, highlighting the various populations under investigation.

DEPRESSION

Perhaps the most extensively studied emotional state seen in adolescents who attempt suicide is depression. In our discussion, we use the term *depression* broadly to refer to depressed mood as well as the full-blown syndrome of depression or a depressive disorder. Depressive disorder refers to adolescents demonstrating a constellation of symptoms that meet the criteria for a formal diagnosis of depression, whereas depressive symptoms refer to individual symptoms of the disorder. When possible, this distinction is made explicit. More than 25 published studies in the past decade have focused, at least in part, on depressed mood among adolescent suicide attempters in clinical settings. These samples were collected in a variety of settings, including emergency departments (ED), pediatric medical units, psychiatric inpatient programs, outpatient psychiatric care clinics, and residential treatment facilities. Overwhelmingly, this research supports the clinical observation that the majority of adolescents who attempt suicide suffer from depressed mood.

Emergency Department and Medical Patients

Although still retrospective in their investigation of the emotions that are associated with suicide attempts, studies of adolescents presenting to the ED or evaluated in a medical unit soon after an attempt may offer the most accurate information regarding depressed mood associated with an attempt. In general, these studies suggest that adolescent attempters seen in the context of the ED or pediatric unit are characterized by depressed mood (Negron et al., 1997; Paluszny, Davenport, & Kim, 1991; Trautman, Rotheram–Borus, Dopkins, & Lewin, 1991). In their study of suicidal adolescents presenting to a medical center ED, Negron and his colleagues (Negron et al., 1997) compared adolescent suicide attempters and ideators in an effort to understand the emotional course that surrounds a suicidal episode. They found that ideators and attempters reported similarly high levels of depressed mood prior to the suicidal episode, that depressed mood increased for both groups during the episode, and that their depressed mood returned to baseline levels following the episode. Thus, the findings suggest that time-limited surges of depression may be closely related to suicidal thoughts and acts.

Using a similar sample, Trautman and his collaborators (Trautman *et al.*, 1991) also found that suicide attempters were characterized by depressed mood. These researchers assessed attempters referred to a hospital specialty clinic from the pediatric ED, psychiatrically disturbed controls, and community controls. A high prevalence of depressive disorders was noted among suicide attempters (42%) and psychiatrically disturbed controls (48%), as well as high frequencies of depressive symptoms for both psychiatric groups. In addition, the rates of depressive disorders and symptoms among attempters were significantly greater than those among community controls. Although these rates did not differ between the two psychiatric groups, the authors assert that this may have been the result of inflated levels of depression among the psychiatric controls, many of whom were referred to a specialty clinic for depression. Nonetheless, these rates of depression are quite high. In Great Britain, Kingsbury, Hawton, Steinhardt, and James (1999) compared 33 adolescent suicide attempters, 30 psychiatric controls, and 30 community controls on a number of psychological variables, including anger, hopelessness, problem solving, and self-concept. Although the attempters had significantly higher scores on all the psychological measures, these differences were not significant after controlling for depression, with the exception of impulsivity, which remained higher in the attempters. The authors concluded that depression is the most important factor to assess in adolescents who attempt suicide.

In attempting to understand the emotional profile of suicidal adolescents, it is important to remember that attempters are not a homogeneous group. Thus, the emotional correlates of adolescent suicide attempts may vary as a function of other characteristics of the adolescent or the attempt (e.g., whether the attempt is premeditated or impulsive, or the extent to which the adolescent wishes to die). Therefore, some researchers have focused on specific types of attempters (e.g., Boergers *et al.*, 1998; Brown, Overholser, Spirito, & Fritz, 1991). For example, when they focused on the degree of planfulness of an attempt, Brown and associates (1991) found that adolescents who made premeditated suicide attempts were characterized by more depressed mood than adolescents who made impulsive attempts.

Unfortunately, research into these finer distinctions is extremely limited. Results from a study conducted by Boergers and colleagues (1998) indicated that attempters with a wish to die demonstrate an emotional profile that is distinct from those who do not report a wish to die. Among other things, those attempters with a wish to die were significantly more depressed than those without a wish to die. In fact, these researchers found that depressed mood was the most reliable predictor of a desire to die. In contrast, Paluszny and associates (1991) found that depressed mood did *not* differentiate adolescents who made more lethal suicide attempts from those who made less lethal attempts. However, as noted in Chapter 2, medical lethality may not be a very good indicator of suicidal intent in adolescents, and this may explain the divergent findings. There were also differences in how the researchers evaluated depressed mood (e.g., Boergers *et al.* used an established self-report inventory, whereas Paluszny and colleagues interviewed patients following diagnostic guidelines but did not report using established measures of depressed mood).

Thus, studies of suicide attempters seen in general hospitals do indicate that a significant proportion of these adolescents report depressed mood. Nonetheless, in this heterogeneous population, the presence of a large number of adolescents who do not report depressed mood indicates the need to assess other mood states as well.

Psychiatric Inpatients

Investigations of psychiatric inpatient samples are consistent with findings from studies of ED patients. In general, this literature suggests that depressed mood is associated with suicidal behavior, and that depressed mood is higher in suicide attempters than in community controls or nonsuicidal psychiatric inpatients (Apter *et al.*, 1995; Asarnow, 1992; Brent, Kolko, Allan, & Brown, 1990; Dori & Overholser, 1999; Feldman & Wilson, 1997; Marciano & Kazdin, 1994; Ohring, Apter, Ratzoni, Weizman, Tyano, & Plutchik, 1996; Overholser, Freihert, & DiFilippo, 1997; Stein, Apter, Ratzoni, Har-Even, & Avidan, 1998). However, results of research within this population are not entirely uniform. For example, Pinto and Whisman (1996) did not find a difference between hospitalized ideators versus attempters in depressed mood. Discrepancies in results exist both within individual studies and between different studies.

Within individual studies, findings have differed based on how depression is measured (i.e., self-reported mood versus diagnostic status). For example, Marciano and Kazdin (1994), in a study of children and young adolescents, found that although self-reported depressed mood predicted suicidality within their sample, a formal diagnosis of depression did not. In contrast, results from other studies have demonstrated higher rates of affective disorders among suicide attempters than among nonsuicidal inpatients (i.e., Asarnow & Guthrie, 1989; Pinto & Whisman, 1996). These same investigators did not find a significant relationship between self-reported depressed mood and suicidality. Based on these discrepant results, Marciano and Kazdin (1994) concluded that "self-report and diagnostic assessment provide separate but informative means of assessing depression in suicidal children" (p. 158).

Brent *et al.* (1993) followed adolescent inpatients, with and without a history of suicidal ideation and attempts, six months after their discharge from the hospital. More than 90% of those who attempted suicide at follow-up were suicidal during their baseline psychiatric hospitalization, and 71% of those had made a prior suicide attempt. Other risk factors for a suicide attempt at follow-up included a diagnosis of major depression at their first psychiatric hospitalization, the presence of an affective disorder with comorbidity, and the presence of a depressive disorder that persisted through the follow-up period.

Although most researchers have investigated the relation between depression and adolescent suicide attempts in general, some have made finer distinctions within groups of attempters and evaluated youngsters with histories of multiple suicide attempts. The characteristics of multiple attempters are discussed in greater detail elsewhere in this volume (see Chapter 11). However, it should be noted here that adolescent suicide attempters with histories of multiple attempts are characterized by high rates of affective disorders and depressive symptoms (Asarnow & Guthrie, 1989; Goldston, Daniel, Reboussin, Kelley, Ievers, & Brunstetter, 1996; Stein *et al.*, 1998).

Goldston and colleagues (1996) found higher levels of depressive symptoms among repeat suicide attempters and patients with a history of attempts than among patients with no history of suicide attempts. However, these investigators did *not* find a difference between levels of depressive symptoms among first-time attempters and patients with no history of attempts. Thus, multiple suicide attempts may be related to severe depression, whereas a single suicide attempt may be related to other mood states, as well as cognitive and behavioral factors. This discrepancy in the Goldston *et al.* (1996) study did not seem to be related to the age or gender of participants, method of assessment, or absolute level of depressed mood.

Other Clinical Populations

Additional studies have been conducted with other populations, including psychiatric outpatients, individuals in residential treatment facilities, crisis center patients, and samples that mix these groups. These studies are of high-risk samples, but not all patients have attempted suicide. Within outpatient populations, results indicate that mood disorders are more common among suicidal adolescents than nonsuicidal outpatients, that as many as 87% of attempters exhibit symptoms of depression (Kosky, Silburn, & Zubrick, 1990), and that outpatient attempters may be as much as 10 times more likely than nonsuicidal outpatients to have a mood disorder (Pelkonen, Marttunen, Pulkkinen, Laippala, & Aro, 1997).

However, results from other samples are less consistent. For example, Rotheram-Borus and colleagues (Rotheram-Borus et al., 1996) investigated adolescents from a large community-based agency that included both nonresidential crisis counseling and residential shelters. These researchers found that adolescent suicide attempters were more frequently depressed than nonattempters. In addition, attempters in this sample were two to three times more likely to report certain depressive symptoms (i.e., trouble concentrating, sleep disturbance) than their nonattempting counterparts. In contrast, Grossi and Violato (1992) found no differences in depressed mood when they compared adolescent suicide attempters and nonsuicidal adolescents in residential treatment centers. It seems likely that these discrepant findings may be attributed to the inclusion of patients in crisis in the Rotheram-Borus study. Almost 25% of those adolescents made their attempt within one month of the assessment. In contrast, the time between attempt and assessment is unknown (but probably longer) for the sample used by Grossi and Violato. Their adolescents may have been more stable after spending time in a residential treatment center. This suggests the time-limited nature of high levels of depressive symptoms in some of these adolescents and the likely ability of these patients to benefit from treatment.

Still other investigations have combined clinical samples to include adolescents receiving treatment from hospitals and clinics or crisis centers (e.g., Hollis, 1996; King et al., 1990), adolescents in mental health institutions and schools (e.g., Kienhorst, de Wilde, Diekstra, & Wolters, 1992), and individuals who were previously hospitalized on a psychiatric inpatient unit (e.g., Pfeffer et al., 1991). In general, these studies add support to the assertion that adolescents who attempt suicide suffer from depressed mood. Results from one investigation suggested that compared to non-depressed adolescents, the risk of suicidal behavior (including ideation, threats, and attempts) is more than four times greater among adolescents with a depressive syndrome (Hollis, 1996). Furthermore, in a prospective investigation, Pfeffer and colleagues assessed community adolescents and adolescents who had previously been assessed when they were psychiatric inpatients six to eight years earlier. Combining these groups for analyses, Pfeffer *et al.* found that 80% of adolescents who attempted suicide during the follow-up period had a mood disorder, and that having a mood disorder within the year prior to the attempt was the strongest risk factor for a first suicide attempt during the follow-up period (Pfeffer *et al.*, 1991).

In another prospective study, Kovacs, Goldstone, and Gatsonis (1993) also found that major depressive disorder and dysthymia were associated with significantly higher rates of suicide attempts at follow-up, especially in the presence of comorbid conduct and substance abuse disorders. Lewinsohn, Rohde, and Seeley (1996) examined the psychological characteristics of 115 depressed adolescents who participated in two group therapy outcome studies and then divided their sample into depressed subjects with and without a past suicide attempt. After controlling for gender and baseline level of depression upon entry into treatment, the adolescents with a history of a suicide attempt demonstrated lower self-esteem, poorer coping skills, more loneliness, less enjoyment of pleasant activities, and experienced more major life events than the depressed adolescents with no history of suicide attempt.

Although some studies fail to find absolute differences between adolescent suicide attempters and nonattempters, these investigations still demonstrate important differences between the groups. For example, King and associates (1990) found no differences between attempters' and non-attempters' self-reported depressed mood *at the time of their evaluation*. However, these investigators did find that parents of adolescent attempters described their children as more depressed during the period of time *preceding and including* the attempt. In addition, Kienhorst and colleagues (1992) found no overall differences in degree of depressed mood between attempters and depressed nonattempters. However, these researchers found attempters to be more negative and hopeless than their nonattempting peers and found that attempters and depressed nonattempters where characterized by different symptoms of depression. Specifically, attempters were characterized by more emotional lability and withdrawal, whereas depressed nonattempters were characterized by more passivity, fatigue, and bipolarity. The important role of social isolation and withdrawal as a precursor to a suicide attempt is reviewed in Chapter 9.

Summary

Investigations of the relation between depression and adolescent suicide attempts use samples from a variety of clinical settings, including ED, medical units, psychiatric inpatient units, outpatient centers, crisis centers, and residential facilities. Although not universal in their findings, data from these studies provide strong evidence for the importance of depression as an emotional correlate of adolescent suicide attempts. For many but not all adolescents, depression is accompanied by suicidality. Evidence exists for this relation when depression is assessed in many ways, including depressive symptomatology, depressed mood state, and depression as a diagnostic syndrome. Furthermore, specific symptoms may be particularly important in thinking about suicidal adolescents. For example, adolescent attempters may be characterized by emotional lability and withdrawal. In addition, the influence of depression may be particularly important for adolescents with a strong wish to die and for those who make planned, deliberate attempts.

Our conclusions based on this review of clinical samples are consistent with Flisher's (1999) review of 11 cross-sectional studies of community samples (10 of which were based in high schools) that examined depressed mood and suicidal ideation/attempts. For example, Andrews and Lewinsohn (1992) found that two-thirds of the adolescent suicide attempters in their community sample had a diagnosis of major depression. In addition, these findings with attempters are consistent with the high rates of mood disorder found in adolescents who complete suicide. In his review of seven psychological autopsy studies, Flisher (1999) noted that rates of major depression ranged from 23 to 52%. Brent et al. (1988) reported very similar rates of affective disorders in both attempters and completers.

Assessment of Depression

Depression and depressed mood are clearly important to thoroughly assess whenever an adolescent attempts suicide. Diagnostic interviews, clinician rating scales, and self-report measures are all available to clinicians.

Diagnostic Interviews

The diagnostic interview represents one critical component of the clinician's assessment for depression and is particularly useful for assessing the broad set of symptoms of depression and for delineating comorbid diagnoses (Kazdin & Marciano, 1994). According to Hodges (1994), there is growing evidence that the diagnostic interview is more effective at determining depressive diagnoses than are symptom checklists or self-report measures. A number of general diagnostic interviews for children and adolescents include modules for assessing depressive disorders. Interviews vary in format, length, and psychometric properties. In determining which interview will be most useful, clinicians need to consider the benefits and limitations of all options available. Here we provide a brief description of five of the most frequently used diagnostic interviews and include comparative information when relevant and available. All five interviews include both child and parent versions.

Three of the diagnostic interviews are semistructured and allow the examiner to vary the questions used. These should be administered by a skilled clinician and include the *Child Assessment Schedule* (CAS; Hodges, McKnew, Cytryn, Stern, & Kline, 1982), the *Interview Schedule for Children* (ISC; Kovacs, 1985) and the *Schedule for Affective Disorders and Schizophrenia in School-Age Children* (K-SADS; Puig-Antich & Chambers, 1978). The CAS has three versions, the most recent of which (published in 1990) is most appropriate for adolescents. Approximately half of the items on the CAS are diagnostic and the other half assess general problems in daily functioning. The CAS has an accompanying manual and computer scoring program to help the examiner generate scale scores for the total interview, each diagnostically related symptom area, and 11 specific content areas (e.g., school, friends, family). Psychometric studies suggest adequate reliability and validity for diagnoses, symptom scales, and content area scores (see Hodges, 1994). The ISC was originally developed to provide current symptom ratings for depressive disorders, but it has since been modified to permit differential diagnosis. The interview requires administration by a highly skilled clinician who is capable of incorporating the symptom information from the interview with other information in order to make a diagnosis. The clinician first interviews the parent and then the child. Following both interviews, the clinician rates each item three times based on the parent's report, the child's report, and an overall summary rating across both informants. Very little psychometric data are available for the ISC (Hodges, 1994). The K-SADS is available in both the epidemiological version (K-SADS-E; Orvaschel, 1995) and in the present and lifetime version (K-SADS-PL; Kaufman *et al.*, 1997). The K-SADS-PL is a semistructured diagnostic interview that has been widely used by researchers to identify major depressive disorder (MDD) and dysthymia (DD) in youth samples. Because the K-SADS-PL is a more time-intensive evaluation than is generally permitted under current clinical practice parameters (Kaufman, Martin, King, & Charney, 1999), it is more commonly used by researchers than by clinicians.

The two remaining diagnostic interviews, the *Diagnostic Interview for Children and Adolescents* (DICA; Welner, Reich, Herjanic, Jung, & Amado, 1987) and the *Diagnostic Interview Schedule for Children* (DISC; Shaffer, Fisher, Lucas, Dulcan, & Schwab-Stone, 2000), are highly structured and can be administered by trained lay examiners as well as in paper-and-pencil and computerized versions. The most recent version of the DICA, the DICA-R, is based on DSM-III-R diagnoses and is divided into two forms, one for children ages 6 to 12 and another for adolescents ages 13 to 17. Both forms are similar in content but vary in terms of wording for age appropriateness. Psychometric data on the DICA-R suggested satisfactory reliability for MDD diagnosis. Researchers comparing the K-SADS-PL to the computerized version of the *Diagnostic Interview for Children and Adolescents-Revised* (cDICA-R; Reich, Cottler, McCallum, Corwin, & Van Eerdewegh, 1995) have reported relative strengths and weaknesses of the two instruments. Hamilton and Gillham (1999) reported findings based on data with preadolescents suggesting that the K-SADS-PL had a higher diagnostic threshold for MDD and double depresssion than the cDICA-R, which, the authors suggested, is more consistent with DSM-IV criteria. Other research suggests that the psychometric properties of the K-SADS-PL are superior to those of the cDICA-R (e.g., Kaufman *et al.*, 1997; Reich *et al.*, 1995).

The DISC, available in both child (DISC-C) and parent (DISC-P) versions, is a structured interview developed for use with children and adolescents ages 6 to 17. The NIMH-DISC contains items that assess current and past symptoms, behaviors, and emotions corresponding to DSM-IV diagnostic criteria. Items are grouped into separate diagnostic modules, each based on a set of related diagnoses for a number of Axis I diagnoses, including MDD. The NIMH-DISC has demonstrated good to excellent diagnostic sensitivity (e.g., Fisher *et al.*, 1993). The interrater reliability (e.g., Shaffer *et al.*, 1993), test–retest reliability (e.g., Jensen *et al.*, 1995; Schwab-Stone *et al.*, 1993), and construct validity (e.g., Costello, Edelbrock, & Costello, 1985; Weinstein, Noam, Grimes, Stone, Schwab-

Stone, 1990) of the NIMH–DISC are comparable to, or better than, other structured diagnostic interviews. Like the DICA-R, the NIMH–DISC is available in both pencil-and-paper and computerized versions. The computerized version (DISC-2.3; Costello *et al.*, 1985; Fisher *et al.*, 1993) takes approximately one to three hours to complete depending on the number of symptoms endorsed by the adolescent. It has demonstrated adequate reliability (Shaffer, Fisher, Lucas, Dulcan, & Schwab-Stone, 2000).

Clinicians need to think carefully about the benefits and limitations of using clinician-administered, computerized or pencil-and-paper versions of these interviews. There is some evidence to suggest that children and adults will reveal more sensitive information on a computerized test than they will in a personal interview (Turner, Ku, Lindberg, Pleck, & Sonestein, 1998). Reich and Cottler (1999) reported that many children revealed information about issues such as substance abuse using a computer that they would not otherwise disclose. On the other hand, clinicians may consider the importance of clinical skill and experience in diagnosing psychiatric disorders as a reason for using personal interviews.

Clinician Rating Scales

Clinician rating scales can be useful for providing a standardized format for recording clinical impressions of an adolescent's presentation. One rating scale that is frequently used in combination with a diagnostic interview is the *Children's Depression Rating Scale—Revised* (CDRS-R; Poznanski *et al.*, 1984). The CDRS-R is an adaptation of the widely used adult clinician scale, the *Hamilton Scale for Depression* (HRSD; Hamilton, 1967). On both scales, the clinician rates symptom areas of depression based on the adolescent's verbal report and nonverbal behavior. Depending on the developmental level of the child, the clinician may choose to use either the CDRS-R or the HRSD. The CDRS-R contains 15 items rated on the basis of verbal responses and 3 items rated on the basis of nonverbal behaviors. The following categories are rated by clinicians: schoolwork, capacity to have fun, social withdrawal, sleep, appetite, excessive fatigue, physical complaints, irritability, guilt, self-esteem, depressed feelings, morbid ideation, suicidal ideation, and weeping. Most items are rated on a 7-point scale. Total scores on the CDRS-R can range from 18 to 118 points, with scores greater than 40 generally indicating clinical depression. Despite its frequent use, little information on the psychometric properties of the scale is available (Hodges, 1994).

Self-Report Measures

Because many depressive symptoms reflect subjective feelings and self-perceptions, and because children are often considered better informants of their own internalizing symptoms than are parents (Kazdin, 1994), self-report measures of depressive symptoms are a critical part of assessing depression in children and adolescents. Although self-reports are not designed to be diagnostic, they do provide information about symptom severity. Several self-report measures of depressed mood and symptoms exist. Among the most prominent of these is the *Beck Depression Inventory* (BDI; Beck, Ward, Mendelson, Mock, & Erbaugh, 1961). The BDI is a 21-item inventory used to assess affective, cognitive, behavioral, and physiological aspects of depression. Each item consists of a series of four self-descriptive sentences, each of which describes a symptom of depression with increasing severity. Each description is assigned a score from 0 to 3. The BDI requires a fifth-grade reading level and has been shown to be appropriate for adolescents as young as age 13 (Steer & Beck, 1988). Research with adolescents indicates adequate internal consistency and test–retest reliability (Kashani, Sherman, Parker, & Reid, 1990; Reynolds, 1985; Roberts, Lewisohn, & Seeley, 1991; Strober, Green, & Carlson, 1981; Teri, 1982), as well as adequate validity (Lempers, Clarke-Lempers, & Simons, 1989; Steer, Beck, & Garrison, 1986). Scores between 0 and 9 are in the normal range, scores between 10 and 18 reflect mild to moderate depression, scores between 17 and 29 indicate moderate to severe depression, and scores between 30 and 63 suggest severe depression.

The *Children's Depression Inventory* (CDI; Kovacs, 1982) was developed as a downward extension of the BDI and may be used alternatively if the clinician has concerns about the developmental appropriateness of the BDI. The CDI contains 27 items addressing symptom severity through three increasingly severe alternative statements. The CDI, like the BDI, is a well-validated scale (see Reynolds, 1994) and very commonly used in clinical practice. A cutoff score of 19 has been reported to indicate a clinically significant level of depression.

The *Center for Epidemiological Studies Depression Scale* (CES-D; Radloff, 1977) is a 20-item scale developed by researchers at the National Institute of Health. The CES-D includes items extracted from previously validated measures of depression assessing depressed mood, feelings of guilt and worthlessness, feelings of helplessness and hopelessness, loss of energy, and sleep and appetite disturbances. Items are divided into four subscales (labeled Depressed Affect, Happy, Somatic, and Interpersonal). Respondents rate the frequency (over the past week) of 20 symptoms on a scale from 0 (*rarely or none of the time*) to 3 (*most or all of the time*). Although the CES-D was originally designed for use with adults, good psychometric data exist for its use with adolescents, including high internal consistency and a stable factor structure when readministered one month later (Roberts, Andrews, Lewinsohn, & Hops, 1990). Reynolds (1994) does, however, advise caution when using the CES-D as a diagnostic instrument with adolescents, citing evidence that the use of the recommended cutoffs (i.e., 16) results in an inflated number of false positives among adolescent samples.

The *Reynolds Adolescent Depression Scale* (RADS; Reynolds, 1987) is another well-established self-report measure designed specifically for use with adolescents between 12 and 17 years of age. The RADS requires a third-grade reading level and contains 30 items, each rated on a 4-point scale from *almost never* through *most of the time*. The RADS is designed to assess the presence and severity of somatic, motivational, cognitive, mood, and vegetative components of depressive symptoms. Scale development research has demonstrated adequate internal consistency, test-retest reliability, and convergent validity (Reynolds, 1987). The RADS includes percentile scores against which an adolescent's scores can be compared. A cutoff score of 77 indicates symptoms associated with clinical depression. In addition, the RADS includes critical items that may be useful for clinicians, including "I thought about killing myself," "I thought about how I would kill myself," "I thought about when I would kill myself," "I thought about what to write in a suicide note," "I thought about writing a will," "I thought about telling people I plan to kill myself," "I thought about how easy it would be to end it all," and "I thought if I had the chance I would kill myself."

Other relevant self-report measures include the *Children's Depression Scale* (CDS; Lang & Tisher, 1978), a 66-item modified card-sort response assessment, the *Depression Self-Rating Scale* (DSRS; Birleson, 1981), which assesses the frequency of 18 symptoms within the past week, the *Childhood Depression Assessment Tool* (DAT; Brady, Nelms, Albright, & Murphy, 1984), a 26-item yes/no format, the depression subscale of the *Youth Self-Report* (YSR; Achenbach & Edelbrock, 1987), and the 66-item *Depressive Experiences Questionnaire for Adolescents* (DEQ-A; Blatt, Schaffer, Bers, & Quinlan, 1992). The DEQ-A differs from the other scales in that it measures experiences related to depression whereas the other measures assess depressive symptomatology. Specifically, the DEQ-A assesses dependency (i.e., fears about interpersonal relationships, including loss of others), self-criticism (i.e., feelings of guilt, emptiness, failure, and inability to live up to self-expectations), and efficacy (i.e., goal-oriented strivings and feelings of personal accomplishment).

Parent and Teacher Report

As with the assessment of any disorder, information from multiple sources can be useful in making an accurate diagnosis and in treatment planning. Parent and teacher reports provide useful information about the severity and frequency of depressive symptoms. This is particularly important in younger and more cognitively limited adolescents for whom a limited capacity for judging symptom severity and frequency may impede an accurate clinical picture of the course and current presentation of the disorder (Clarizio, 1994). Furthermore, behavioral presentations may vary across situational domains and information about the child's presentation in each area can be invaluable in assessment and intervention planning.

Several general psychopathology scales contain depression subscales. The *Behavior Assessment Scale for Children* (BASC; Reynolds & Kamphaus, 1992) is a well-known instrument designed to evaluate the behaviors, thoughts, and emotions of children and adolescents. The BASC Parent and Teacher Rating Scales include 131 items of observable adaptive and maladaptive behaviors of children and adolescents ages 4 to 18 years in community and home settings. Composite scores are provided in the following areas: externalizing problems (aggression, hyperactivity, conduct problems), internalizing problems (anxiety, depression, somatization), attention problems, other problems (atypicality, withdrawal), and adaptive skills (adpatability, leadership, social skills). The BASC provides standardized scores and percentiles for all composites and subscales, based on general norms, gender-specific norms, and clinical norms. The authors have established adequate reliability and validity. The BASC also has a self-report form appropriate for adolescents. The *Child Behavior Checklist* (CBCL; Achenbach, 1991) is a parent-completed measure that includes 118 items rated on a scale from 0 to 2. The CBCL yields broad-band scales reflecting general types of behavior patterns (internalizing and externalizing behaviors), as well as specific symptom domains (e.g., anxious/depressed). There are also teacher- and adolescent-report versions of the scale, referred to as the CBCL Teacher Report Form (TRF; Achenbach, 1991) and the Youth Self-Report (YSR; Achenbach & Edelbrock, 1987). All three versions of the CBCL have been widely studied and are well validated in both clinical and general samples. Finally, the *Personality*

Inventory for Children (PIC; Wirt, Lachar, Klinedinst, & Seat, 1977), a parent-report form designed for assessment of children aged 3 to 16 years, contains several clinical subscales, including Depression, Anxiety/Withdrawal, and Social Skills. The depression subscale consists of 46 items and has been shown to have excellent test-retest reliability. However, researchers have criticized the PIC because of its outdated norms, cross-informant inconsistency, and lack of validity data (Clarizio, 1994).

The majority of the self-report measures of depression have also been modified for use as parent-report forms. For example, both the CDI and the CDS have been used as parent-rated measures of depressive symptomatology. Mostly, there are modest relations between parent and self-report forms of the same scales, and no single adapted measure has shown superior reliability or validity (Kazdin, 1990).

ANGER

Although depression is often highlighted as the critical factor in the study of adult suicidality, not all adolescent suicide attempters are depressed. For example, Feldman and Wilson (1997) found that less than half of the suicidal adolescents in their study met or exceeded the clinical cutoff of the Children's Depression Inventory (CDI, Kovacs, 1982; Kovacs & Beck, 1977). Other emotions are also critical for understanding the emotional profile of suicidal adolescents. Of particular importance for adolescent suicidality is the role of anger.

Most of the nine studies that in the past decade have investigated the relation between anger and adolescent suicide attempts were already mentioned in our discussion of depression (i.e., Boergers *et al.*, 1998; Brown *et al.*, 1991; Goldston *et al.*, 1996; Negron *et al.*, 1997; Pinto & Whisman, 1996; Rotheram-Borus *et al.*, 1996; Stein *et al.*, 1998). As noted previously, these investigations represent a range of clinical settings. Although results do not provide a clear delineation of the relative importance of anger in the lives of adolescents who attempt suicide, they demonstrate that anger is an important variable to consider when trying to understand the emotional life of adolescent suicide attempters.

ED and Medical Patients

In their investigation of the relations between various aspects of anger and adolescent suicide attempts, Lehnert *et al.* (1994) compared recent suicide attempters in a general medical hospital with high school students. Results indicated that, in comparison to the high school control group, the suicide attempters reported greater levels of internalized and externalized anger and a greater propensity to experience and express anger (i.e., trait anger). Results of the study by Negron and colleagues (Negron *et al.*, 1997) are consistent with the notion that anger may be an important emotional correlate of adolescent suicidal behavior. In their assessment of anger over the course of a suicidal episode, these researchers found that during the suicidal act, anger increased from pre-episode levels for both suicide ideators and attempters. Following the suicidal act, suicide attempters reported a greater decrease in anger than the ideators. Although few differences were reported between the ideating and attempting adolescents, the two groups had similar histories of suicide attempts. Therefore, distinctions between these two groups may have been obscured.

Spirito and colleagues (Boergers *et al.*, 1998; Brown *et al.*, 1991) have also included anger in their investigations of the planning and motivation for adolescent suicide attempts. Data from these investigations suggest that anger may be more relevant for understanding a patient's motivation for a suicide attempt than for differentiating type of attempt (i.e., impulsive versus premeditated). Specifically, results indicated anger expression was greater among adolescent attempters who reported a wish to die as a reason for their attempt, than among attempters who did not report this motivation (Boergers *et al.*, 1998). However, no differences in level of anger expression were found between premeditated and impulsive attempters (Brown *et al.*, 1991). Thus, anger appears to be distinct from impulsiveness of the suicidal act.

Psychiatric Inpatients

Interestingly, evidence for the importance of anger as an emotional correlate of adolescent suicide attempts is less strong within studies of adolescent attempters in psychiatric inpatient units. In their investigation of first-time and repeat attempters, Stein *et al.* (1998) found that all inpatients in the study (i.e., first-time attempters, repeat attempters, and nonsuicidal inpatient controls) reported more anger than community controls, but only repeat attempters reported more anger than nonsuicidal inpatients. Consistent with these findings, Pinto and Whisman (1996) found that suicide attempters did not differ from suicide ideators or nonsuicidal psychiatric inpatients with regard to levels of reported anger. Similarly, Goldston *et al.* (1996) found no differences in levels of state anger (i.e. anger at the time of the attempt) among adolescent inpatients who had recently made a first suicide attempt, recently made a repeat attempt, had a previous (but not current) attempt, and those who had never attempted suicide. Interestingly, results from the Goldston *et al.* investigation indicated that trait anger (anger more characteristic of the adolescent's typical functioning) was higher among previous (but not current) attempters than among all other inpatient groups in the study.

Other Clinical Populations

Data collected by Myers, McCauley, Calderon, and Treder (1991) provide strong evidence for the importance of anger in adolescent suicidal behavior. In their longitudinal investigation of recently depressed outpatients and inpatients, these researchers found that anger predicted suicidality over the 3-year follow-up period and that initial suicidality and anger best predicted later suicidality. These variables were analyzed in the context of a number of other psychosocial factors such as depressive symptomatology, hopelessness, anhedonia, and separation anxiety. Although this study has the methodological advantage of being longitudinal in nature, it should be noted that the "suicidal" adolescents in this investigation were predominantly mild to moderate ideators (less than 10% of adolescents in this sample made an actual suicide attempt). In addition, the sample was primarily an outpatient one because many of the more severe inpatients dropped out of the study early on. This dropout rate is likely to have implications for the generalizability of these results to adolescent suicide *attempters.* However, results from an investigation of "pure" suicide attempters lend support to these findings. In their investigation of adolescents in nonresidential crisis centers and residential shelters, Rotheram-Borus and associates (1996) found that more attempters reported feeling frequently angry (50.2%) than their nonattempting counterparts (27%).

Summary

Researchers investigating the relation of anger and adolescent suicide attempts have collected data in a variety of clinical settings, such as EDs, medical hospitals, psychiatric inpatient programs, outpatient clinics, and residential treatment facilities. Results of these investigations are some-what equivocal. Some data indicate that anger is an important emotional correlate of adolescent suicide attempts. However, other results suggest that anger may be less closely linked with suicide attempts per se and more closely related to severe psychological difficulties in general. When adolescent attempters are compared to adolescents in the community (e.g., Lehnert *et al.*, 1994; Stein *et al.*, 1998), differences in levels of anger emerge. However, when compared with other psychiatric patients (e.g., Negron *et al.*, 1997; Pinto & Whisman, 1996), these differences are greatly reduced. Still, evidence from longitudinal research bolsters the argument that anger is important for understanding adolescent suicide attempters.

Assessment of Anger

Assessing an adolescent suicide attempter's mode of anger expression is an important task for all clinicians. Although externalized anger may be more easily identified, internalized anger is important to assess given its close relation to depression and hopelessness (Lehnert *et al.*, 1994). Anger may be associated with both conduct and depressive disorders, and exter-nalizing disorders in the presence of depression increases the risk of suicide attempts (Kovacs *et al.*, 1993). The combination of angry outbursts and depressed mood should be a warning sign to clinicians (Lehnert *et al.*, 1994). High levels of aggressive behavior are also found in adolescents diagnosed with major depressive disorder (Knox, King, Hanna, Logan, & Ghaziuddin, 2000). The diagnostic interviews discussed under the assess-ment of depression all contain items assessing anger in the sections on depressive disorders and conduct disorders.

Self-Report Measures

A number of self-report measures are available for assessing various com-ponents of anger, aggressive behavior, and anger control in adolescents. One type of scale presents the child or adolescent with hypothetical anger-producing situations and asks the respondent to report his or her expected anger level. The *Anger Inventory* (Novaco, 1975) is a 90-item adult measure that presents hypothetical anger-evoking situations. A 5-point Likert scale indicating degree of anger is used for responses. The types of situations include being called a liar, being teased, being blamed for something you didn't do, and being talked about behind your back.

The *Children's Inventory of Anger* (CIA; Finch, Saylor, & Nelson, 1987) is a 71-item sample designed to measure children's possible anger responses to hypothetical situations using a 4-point Likert scale. Whereas more of the choices on the Anger Inventory may be more pertinent to adults than adolescents, many of the items on the CIA may be more pertinent to children than adolescents. The types of situations on the CIA include being stood up by a friend, being grounded by a parent, someone cheating in a game, someone breaking a promise, and being reported by a peer to a teacher for misbehavior. The *Problem Inventory for Adolescent Girls* (Gaffney & McFall, 1981) is a 52-item inventory of hypothetical interpersonal conflict situations rated on a 5-point scale indicating level of competence in handling this conflict. The *State-Trait Anger Expression Inventory-2* (STAXI; Spielberger, 1999) may be the most commonly used scaled to assess anger. The STAXI contains several subscales measuring state anger and trait anger, as well as anger expression and anger control. The trait anger subscale contains ten items and may be particularly useful as a screen of overall level of anger, given that trait anger has been shown to be related to suicide attempts. The items on the trait anger subscale inquire about having a fiery temper, being hotheaded, flying off the handle, and tending to make angry statements and actions.

ANXIETY

Another emotional state that has received significant attention by researchers as related to adolescent suicide attempts is anxiety. In the past decade, nine published research investigations have focused, at least in part, on anxiety. Many of the studies have been described in the descriptions of the literature addressing depression and anger (e.g., King *et al.*, 1990; Kosky *et al.*, 1990; Pinto & Whisman, 1996; Stein *et al.*, 1998; Trautman *et al.*, 1991). Therefore, the published research describing anxiety among adolescent suicide attempters is similar in its scope to the other populations under study addressing depression and anger among these adolescents. This literature suggests that anxiety, particularly trait anxiety, is an important emotional correlate of adolescent suicide attempts.

ED and Medical Patients

In the only recent evaluation of anxiety and suicide attempters within an ED population, Trautman and colleagues (1991) evaluated female patients referred from the ED to a hospital clinic. Their results suggest that anxiety may be an important variable in adolescent suicide attempts, but that it may not distinguish suicide attempters from other psychiatric populations. More specifically, these researchers found similarly high prevalence rates of anxiety disorders (i.e., sufficient symptoms to meet the criteria for a formal psychiatric diagnosis) among both attempters (43%) and nonattempting outpatients (44%), as well as similar levels of anxiety symptoms among these two groups. Suicide attempters reported greater levels of anxiety symptoms than community controls in the sample.

Psychiatric Inpatients and Outpatients

Most investigations of anxiety within adolescent psychiatric inpatient or outpatient populations are consistent with data from the Trautman study. Although not entirely uniform in their findings, this research indicates that a significant proportion of adolescent suicide attempters experience anxiety, and that they experience more anxiety than their nonattempting counterparts (for an exception, see Pinto & Whisman, 1996). For example, in their study of outpatient adolescent suicide attempters and ideators, Kosky and associates (Kosky *et al.*, 1990) found that similarly high proportions of attempters (77%) and ideators (73%) were characterized by anxiety.

Evidence in this area seems to be more strongly in support of the importance of trait anxiety (compared to state anxiety) in adolescent suicide attempts. Specifically, Stein and colleagues (1998) examined psychiatric inpatients and found that first-time attempters reported more trait anxiety than nonsuicidal inpatients and community controls, and that both first-time and repeat attempters reported more state anxiety than nonsuicidal inpatients and community controls. In addition, interviewers rated state and trait anxiety among first-time attempters as higher than that among community controls (Stein *et al.*, 1998). Similarly, Ohring *et al.* (1996) found that inpatient adolescent attempters demonstrated higher levels of state and trait anxiety than nonsuicidal inpatients. When controlling for depression, however, differences between the two groups remained only for *trait* anxiety.

In their study of psychiatric inpatients, Goldston and colleagues (1996) found stronger evidence for the relation between trait anxiety and suicidality than between state anxiety and suicidality. Although they found a tendency for first-time attempters, repeat attempters, previous attempters, and nonattempting controls to differ with regard to state anxiety, the differences among these groups were not significant. However, results showed that repeat attempters and previous attempters reported more trait anxiety than nonattempting adolescents. It should also be noted that interviewer ratings of anxiety did not differ between first-time attempters and nonsuicidal inpatients.

Other Clinical Populations

Researchers using mixed samples to explore the relation between anxiety and adolescent suicide attempts have failed to replicate the findings of investigations of more homogeneous samples. For example, in their investigation combining psychiatric outpatients and inpatients, Myers, McCauley, Calderon, Mitchell, Burke, and Schloredt (1991) found that within the sample as a whole, separation anxiety was not related to degree of suicidality. In addition, although results indicated an *inverse* relation between separation anxiety and degree of suicidality within patients diagnosed with major depressive disorder, this relation disappeared when separation anxiety was analyzed in context with depressive symptoms and conduct problems. Results from other mixed samples are similar. Specifically, King *et al.* (1990) found no significant differences in levels of anxiety between adolescent suicide attempters and community controls, and Kienhorst and associates (1992) found no differences between attempters and depressed nonattempters.

Summary

Research using homogeneous samples provides support for the importance of anxiety as an emotional correlate of adolescent suicide attempts and suggests that anxiety may be particularly problematic for adolescent suicide attempters specifically (as opposed to psychiatric patients in general). However, research using mixed samples for investigation has failed to find this relation. Furthermore, studies of community samples suggest that not all types of anxiety are equally important in the emotional lives of suicidal adolescents. Gould *et al.* (1998), examining data from the Methods for the Epidemiology of Child and Adolescent Mental Disorders (MECA), found that an anxiety disorder did increase the risk for a suicide attempt in this community sample. After taking into account other psychosocial variables, the one study that examined separation anxiety did not find it to be related to suicidality (Myers, McCauley, Calderon, Mitchell, et al., 1991). Pilowsky, Wu, and Anthony (1999) reported on a community-based sample of 13- and 14-year-old adolescents comprised mainly of African-American youth. After controlling for demographics, major depression, and alcohol/drug use, adolescents with a history of panic attacks were twice as likely to have made suicide attempts than those without a history of panic attacks. Thus, future research will need to be aware not only of anxious symptomatology but also different types of anxiety disorders, including panic and PTSD. For the clinician, it is important to assess anxiety symptoms as well as to be aware that other mood states beyond depression are related to suicidality. Indeed, Fawcett and Rosenblate (2000) reported on three cases of adults with severe anxiety who committed suicide within 24 hours of an evaluation in an ED.

Assessment of Anxiety

As in the evaluation of other adolescent disorders, the assessment of anxiety should include a history of the onset and development of the anxiety symptoms, associated stressors, family history, developmental history, school history, and medical history. In addition to these general areas of assessment, a comprehensive anxiety evaluation should pay careful attention to a number of specific issues. These include (1) whether the anxiety is stimulus specific, spontaneous, or anticipatory, (2) the degree of avoidance in daily life caused by the anxiety symptoms, (3) social and familial reinforcers of symptoms, (4) medications or medical disorders that may cause anxiety symptoms, and (5) family history of anxiety disorders (American Academy of Child and Adolescent Psychiatry, AACAP, 1997).

A complete assessment of anxiety should also include structured or semistructured psychiatric interviews to confirm anxiety diagnoses and other comorbid disorders. Additionally, clinician rating scales, self-report scales, and parent-report measures are useful to determine the specific nature and severity of anxiety symptoms. The overall goal of an assessment should be to (1) provide reliable and valid assessment of symptoms across multiple domains, (2) discriminate symptom clusters, (3) assess severity, (4) incorporate multiple observations (e.g., parent and child), and (5) be sensitive to treatment-related changes in symptoms (March, Parker, Sullivan, Stallings, & Conners, 1997; Stallings & March, 1995). The following discussion will review a number of commonly used and researched structured interviews, clinician–rating scales, and child–parent self-report measures with specific attention to the instrument's primary purposes and psychometric properties.

Diagnostic Interviews

A number of general diagnostic interviews for children and adolescents modules related to anxiety disorders. These include the Schedule for Affective Disorders and Schizophrenia for School Age Children-Epidemiologic Version (K-SADS-E; Orvaschel, 1995), the Schedule for Affective Disorders and Schizophrenia for School Age Children-Present and Lifetime Version (K-SADS-PL; Kaufman *et al.*, 1997), the Diagnostic Interview for Children and Adolescents-Revised (DICA-R; Reich, 1997), and the National Institute of Mental Health Diagnostic Interview Schedule for Children (DISC; Shaffer, Fisher, Duncan, & Davies, 1996). These interviews were discussed under the assessment of depression. Only the Anxiety Disorders Interview Schedule for DSM-IV- Child Version (ADIS-IV) (Silverman & Albano, 1996) is designed specifically to evaluate anxiety disorders in youth.

The *Anxiety Disorders Interview Schedule for DSM-IV-Child Version (ADIS for DSM-IV-C)* is a semistructured interview designed to assess DSM-IV anxiety disorders in children and adolescents ages 7 to 17 years. The instrument has both child and parent components and evaluates all DSM-IV anxiety diagnoses. The ADIS also assesses school refusal, mood, and externalizing disorders (e.g., dysthymia, major depressive disorder, ADHD, oppositional defiant disorder) and includes a screening for substance abuse, psychosis, selective mutism, eating disorders, somatoform disorder, and specific developmental and learning disorders.

Completion of the ADIS for DSM-IV-C requires one to 1.5 hours for each interview (child and parent). Assessment of situational and cognitive cues for anxiety, intensity of anxiety, nature and extent of avoidance, and precipitating events is included for each disorder. Although substantial overlap exists between the parent and child interviews, children are asked about their symptomatology in more detail and parents are questioned more heavily on history and effects of the anxiety, as well as on externalizing disorders. Composite diagnoses are derived by combining the results of the parent and child interviews.

With regard to psychometric properties of the ADIS for DSM-IV-C, reliability and validity have not been reported for this most recent edition.

However, reliability of both the child and parent versions of the earlier Anxiety Disorders Interview Schedule for Children (ADIS-C for DSM-III-R) is good. Interrater reliability is high for child and parent interviews and for the composite diagnosis (Silverman & Nelles, 1988) are adequate, as are kappas for specific diagnoses (Rapee, Barrett, Dadds, & Evans, 1994). Silverman and Eisen (1992) examined two-week test-retest reliability and found an adequate reliability. Finally, studies examining the validity of the ADIS-C have also been encouraging. Rabian, Ginsburg, and Silverman (1994) found that symptom scale scores of the interviews were significantly associated with scores on parent and child anxiety rating scales.

Clinician Rating Scales

A number of clinician rating scales have been developed to assess anxiety in children and adolescents. These measures allow for clinician ratings of symptoms of anxiety disorders (e.g., social phobia, specific phobia, generalized anxiety disorder). Symptoms of obsessive compulsive disorder and post-traumatic stress disorder are generally not included in these scales. Many of these instruments are based on composite interviews of both child and parent.

The *Hamilton Anxiety Rating Scale* (HARS; Hamilton, 1959) was developed for use with adults, but it has been adapted and validated for adolescents (Clarke & Donovan, 1994). It assesses both psychological and physiological symptoms of anxiety and has been shown to have adequate test-retest reliability. The *Children's Anxiety Rating Scale (CARS*; Riddle & Greenhill, 1997) is used to rate severity of anxiety in children and adolescents, ages 6 to 17 years. The measure combines a symptom checklist to determine presence or absence of symptoms in the previous week and seven severity items to determine the CARS total score. Psychometric properties of the CARS are currently being studied. The *Anxiety Rating Scale for Children-Revised* (Bernstein, Crosby, Perwien & Borchardt, 1996) was modeled after the HARS, with questions adapted for children and adolescents. It is reported to have high test-retest reliability and discriminates between children with and without an anxiety disorder (AACAP, 1997; Bernstein *et al.*, 1996). Finally, although specific to obsessive compulsive disorder, the *Child Yale-Brown Obsessive Compulsive Scale* (C-YBOCS; Scahill *et al.*, 1997) assesses the child's current OCD symptoms and severity with regard to both obsessions and compulsions. Adequate reliability and validity have been demonstrated, as well as sensitivity to change after treatment.

Self-Report Measures

A number of self-report measures have been developed to assess the severity of both generalized anxiety and fearfulness in children and adolescents. Additionally, many instruments exist that measure the severity of symptoms specific to individual disorders (e.g., social anxiety, post-traumatic stress reactions, obsessions, and compulsions).

The *Multidimensional Anxiety Scale for Children* (MASC; March, Parker, Sullivan, Stallings, & Conners, 1997) is a self-report measure designed to assess anxiety symptoms in children and adolescents ages 8 to 18 years. The MASC covers four domains: physical symptoms, social anxiety, harm avoidance, and separation anxiety. Psychometric properties of the MASC have been well studied (March *et al.*, 1997; March, Sullivan, and Parker, 1999). Adequate reliability has been reported. With regard to validity, the MASC factor structure has been shown to be invariant across gender and age and more strongly correlated with other measures of anxiety than measures of depression. The measure has also been effective in discriminating children with anxiety disorders from children with ADHD (March *et al.*, 1997).

The *Revised Children's Manifest Anxiety Scale* (RCMAS; Reynolds & Richmond, 1978) is designed to assess the level and nature of anxiety in children and adolescents ages 6 to 19 years. The RCMAS yields subscale scores for worry/oversensitivity, physiological symptoms, concentration anxiety, and lying. Overall, the RCMAS has strong psychometric properties. Internal consistency and test-retest reliabilities are good (Witt, Heffer, & Pfeiffer, 1990). The total score has also been shown to correlate highly with other measures of child anxiety (Reynolds & Paget, 1983). However, there have been concerns about the ability of the RCMAS to discriminate amongst anxiety disorders or between anxiety disorders and other diagnoses (e.g., ADHD, major depressive disorder; Stallings & March, 1995). As a result, the worry/oversensitivity index is considered to have the greatest diagnostic utility (Eisen & Kearney, 1995). The measure may be best used to assess general distress with an emphasis on anxiety in general psychiatric or normal populations (Stallings & March, 1995).

The *State-Trait Anxiety Inventory for Children* (STAIC; Spielberger, Edwards, Lushene, Monturi, & Platzek, 1973) measures state and trait anxiety in children between the ages of 8 and 12 years. Internal consistency and test-retest reliabilities are adequate (Spielberger *et al.*, 1973). Clinically anxious children have been shown to rate themselves higher than normals on both state and trait scales (Strauss, Lease, Last, & Francis, 1988). Like the RCMAS, the STAIC has not been shown to discriminate well between diagnostic groups (Hoehn-Saric, Maisami, & Weigand, 1987). As a result, the STAIC is also best used as a general screening tool or general change index for either state or trait anxiety (Stallings & March, 1995).

The *Screen for Child Anxiety Related Emotional Disorders* (SCARED; Birmaher *et al.*, 1997) is a more recently developed instrument designed to screen for symptoms of generalized anxiety disorder, separation anxiety disorder, panic disorder, social phobia, and school phobia in children and adolescents ages 9 to 18 years. Psychometric data are limited, but promising (Birmaher *et al.*, 1997). The scale comprises five identified factors: somatic/panic, generalized anxiety, separation anxiety, social phobia, and school phobia, with adequate internal consistencies. The SCARED also shows good discriminant validity between anxiety disorders as well as between anxiety and other disorders (although it is better at differentiating anxiety and disruptive disorders than anxiety and depressive disorders).

Finally, a number of more specific measures of anxiety deserve brief mention. The *Fear Survey Schedule for Children—Revised* (FSSC-R; Ollendick, 1983) measures general fears such as those that involve school, home, social or physical conditions, travel, and animals. *The Social Anxiety Scale for Children—Revised* (SASC-R; La Greca & Stone, 1993) focuses on fear of negative evaluation, social avoidance, and social distress. The *Social Phobia and Anxiety Inventory for Children* (SPAI-C; Beidel, Fink, & Turner, 1995) assesses specific symptoms, cognitions, and behavior in social situations. The *Leyton Obsessional Inventory-Child Version* (LOI-CU; Berg, Whitaker, Davies, Flament, & Rapoport, 1988) is a self-report measure of obsessional traits and symptoms. The *Post-traumatic Stress Disorder Reaction Index* (PTSD-RI; Pynoos *et al.*, 1987) and the *Kiddie Post-traumatic Symptomatology* (K-PTS; March, Amaya-Jackson, Murray, & Schulte, 1998) assess reexperiencing, avoidance, and arousal symptoms specific to post-traumatic stress disorder.

Parent and Teacher Report

Although anxiety symptoms are generally more accurately reported by children and adolescents than by their parents/caregivers, two rating scales can be administered to parents to obtain information about their child's anxiety. The SCARED, described earlier as a child self-report, includes a parent-report version. However, parent-child correlations are low to moderate for the total anxiety score and for the specific factors (Birmaher *et al.*, 1997). Finally, the Child Behavior Checklist (CBCL; Achenbach, 1991) also yields an overall measure of internalizing symptoms as well as an anxious/depressed subscale.

WHAT TO LOOK FOR

Suicidal adolescents experience a myriad of negative emotional states. Studies of these adolescents have found suicidal risk to be associated with depressed mood, anger, and sometimes anxiety. From both clinical and methodological perspectives, it seems useful to consider the negative emotional states that precede the suicidal crisis as distinct from the emotional states reported by the adolescent during the treatment and recovery stages. Adequate (but not entirely consistent) findings support the notion that suicide risk is increased by a combination of negative emotional states, especially when these negative emotions persist over time. Kovacs *et al.* (1993) have suggested that the inability to either tolerate or regulate emotional distress is the consistent hallmark of adolescents who attempt suicide and that the suicidal behavior itself represents one attempt to reduce this intolerable negative affect.

Assessment Guidelines

Depressed mood, anger, and anxiety are clearly important emotional states that should be thoroughly assessed in the adolescent who attempts suicide. The assessment strategy will differ according to the clinical setting and clinician preferences. Although diagnostic interviews are the gold standard and should be used routinely, we recognize that this is not always feasible. Therefore, we suggest the following stepped assessment approach be used as a minimum:

1. Administer self-report measures first in a brief self-guided assessment session conducted prior to the initial interview. Use measures that provide cutoff scores.
2. Review the adolescent's responses to the self-report measures and score measures to determine whether the adolescent reaches the clinical cutoff score.

3. Review individual items with the adolescent during the initial interview to gain a more thorough understanding of the adolescent's emotional state. Pay particular attention to critical items, if available.

4. If the adolescent reaches a clinical cutoff, administer the modules from a structured diagnostic interview corresponding to the relevant symptomatology (i.e., anxiety, mood disorder, and conduct disorder). If clinician time is limited, the computerized version of the DISC may be the interview of choice, if office space is available for the adolescent or his or her parents to answer the questions on the DISC. Alternatively, clinician rated scales, which cover the diagnostic criteria for the different disorders, might be used. Diagnostic interviews requiring clinician judgment, such as the KSADS or CAS, represent the most thorough integration of empirical and clinical practice.

REFERENCES

Achenbach, T. (1991). *Manual for the Child Behavior Checklist/4–18 and 1991 profile.* Burlington, VT: University of Vermont Department of Psychiatry.

Achenbach, T. M., & Edelbrock, C. (1987). *Manual for the Youth Self-Report and Profile.* Burlington: Department of Psychiatry, University of Vermont.

American Academy of Child and Adolescent Psychiatry. (1997). Practice parameters for the assessment and treatment of children and adolescents with anxiety disorders. *Journal of the American Academy of Child and Adolescent Psychiatry, 36 (Suppl.),* 69S–84S.

Andrews, J., & Lewinsohn, P. (1992). Suicide attempts among older adolescents: Prevalence and co-occurrence with psychiatric disorders. *Journal of the American Academy of Child and Adolescent Psychiatry, 27,* 655–662.

Apter, A., Gothelf, D., Orbach, I., Weizman, R., Ratzoni, G., Har-Even, D., & Tyano, S. (1995). Correlation of suicidal and violent behavior in different diagnostic categories in hospitalized adolescent patients. *Journal of the American Academy of Child and Adolescent Psychiatry, 34,* 912–918.

Asarnow, J. R. (1992). Suicidal ideation and attempts during middle childhood: Associations with perceived family stress and depression among child psychiatric inpatients. *Journal of Clinical Child Psychology, 21,* 35–40.

Asarnow, J. R., & Guthrie, D. (1989). Suicidal behavior, depression, and hopelessness in child psychiatric inpatients: A replication and extension. *Journal of Clinical Child Psychology, 18,* 129–136.

Beck, A. T., Ward, C. H., Mendelson, M., Mock, J., & Erbaugh, J. (1961). An inventory for measuring depression. *Archives of General Psychiatry, 4,* 561–571.

Beidel, D., Fink, C., & Turner, S. (1995). A new instrument for the assessment of social anxiety in children: The Social Phobia and Anxiety Inventory for Children. *Psychological Assessment, 7,* 73–79.

Berg, C. Z., Whitaker, A., Davies, M., Flament, M. F., & Rapoport, J. L. (1988). The survey form of the Leyton Obesssional Inventory-Child Version: Norms from an epidemiological study. *Journal of the American Academy of Child and Adolescent Psychiatry, 27*, 759–763.

Bernstein, G. A., Crosby, R. D., Perwien, A. R., & Borchardt, C. M. (1996). Anxiety rating scale for children-revised: Reliability and validity. *Journal of Anxiety Disorders, 10*, 97–114.

Birleson, P. (1981). The validity of depressive disorder in childhood and the development of a self-rating scale: A research report. *Journal of Child Psychology and Psychiatry, 22*, 73–88.

Birmaher, B., Khetarpal, S., Brent, D., Cully, M., Balach, L., Kaufman, J., & McKenzie-Neer, S. (1997). The Screen for Child Anxiety Related Emotional Disorders (SCARED): Scale construction and psychometric characteristics. *Journal of the American Academy of Child and Adolescent Psychiatry, 36*, 545–553.

Blatt, S. J., Schaffer, C. E., Bers, S. A., & Quinlan, D. M. (1992). Psychometric properties of the Depressive Experiences Questionnaire for Adolescents. *Journal of Personality Assessment, 59*, 82–98.

Boergers, J., Spirito, A., & Donaldson, D. (1998). Reasons for adolescent suicide attempts: Associations with psychological functioning. *Journal of the American Academy of Child and Adolescent Psychiatry, 37*, 1287–1293.

Brady, M. A., Nelms, B. C., Albright, A. V., & Murphy, C. M. (1984). Childhood depression: Development of a screening tool. *Pediatric Nursing, 10*, 222–225.

Brent, D., Kolko, D., Allan, M., & Brown, R. (1990). Suicidality in affectively disordered adolescent inpatients. *Journal of the American Academy of Child and Adolescent Psychiatry, 29*, 586–593.

Brent, D., Kolko, D. J., Wartella, M. E., Boylan, M. B., Moritz, G., Baugher, M., & Zelenak, J. P. (1993). Adolescent psychiatric inpatients' risk of suicide attempt at 6-month follow-up. *Journal of the American Academy of Child and Adolescent Psychiatry, 32*, 95–105.

Brent, D., Perper, J., Goldstein, C., Kolko, D., Allan, M., Allman, C., & Zelenak, J. (1988). Risk factors for adolescent suicide: A comparison of adolescent victims with suicidal inpatients. *Archives of General Psychiatry, 45*, 581–588.

Brown, L. K., Overholser, J., Spirito, A., & Fritz, G. K. (1991). The correlates of planning in adolescent suicide attempts. *Journal of the American Academy of Child and Adolescent Psychiatry, 30*, 95–99.

Clarizio, H. E. (1994). Assessment of depression in children and adolescents by parents, teachers, and peers. In W. M. Reynolds & H. F. Johnston (Eds.), *Handbook of Depression in Children and Adolescents* (pp. 235–248). New York: Guilford Press.

Clarke, D. B., & Donovan, J. E. (1994). Reliability and validity of the Hamilton Anxiety Rating Scale in an adolescent sample. *Journal of the American Academy of Child and Adolescent Psychiatry, 33*, 354–360.

Costello, E. J., Edelbrock, C. S., & Costello, A. J. (1985). Validity of the NIMH Diagnostic Interview Schedule for Children: A comparison between psychiatric and pediatric referrals. *Journal of Abnormal Child Psychology, 13*, 579–595.

Dori, G., & Overholser, J. (1999). Depression, hopelessness, and self-esteem: Accounting for suicidality in adolescent psychiatric patients. *Suicide and Life-Threatening Behavior, 29*, 309–318.

Eisen, A. R., & Kearney, C. A. (1995). Assessment of fear and anxiety related problems, *Practitioner's guide to treating fear and anxiety in children and adolescents: A cognitive behavioral approach* (pp. 77–96). Northvale, NJ: Jason Aronson, Inc.

Fawcett, J., & Rosenblate, R. (2000). Suicide within 24 hours after assessment in the Emergency Department: Look for and manage anxiety. *Psychiatric Annals, 30,* 229–231.

Feldman, M., & Wilson, A. (1997). Adolescent suicidality in urban minorities and its relationship to conduct disorders, depression, and separation anxiety. *Journal of the American Academy of Child and Adolescent Psychiatry, 36,* 75–84.

Finch, A. J., Saylor, C., & Nelson, M. (1987). Assessment of anger in children. In R. Prinz (Ed.), *Advances in behavioral assessment of children and families.* (pp. 235–265). New York: JAI Press, Inc.

Fisher, P. W., Shaffer, D., Piacentini, J. C., Lapkin, J., Kafantaris, V., Leonard, H., & Herzog, D. B. (1993). Sensitivity of the Diagnostic Interview Schedule for Children, 2nd Edition (DISC-2.1), for specific diagnoses of children and adolescents. *Journal of the American Academy of Child and Adolescent Psychiatry, 32,* 666–673.

Flisher, A. (1999). Annotation. Mood disorder in suicidal children and adolescents: Recent developments. *Journal of Child Psychology and Psychiatry, 40,* 315–324.

Gaffney, L., & McFall, R. (1981). A comparison of social skills in delinquent and non-delinquent adolescent girls using a behavioral role-playing inventory. *Journal of Consulting and Clinical Psychology, 49,* 959–967.

Goldston, D. B., Daniel, S., Reboussin, D. M., Kelley, A., Ievers, C., & Brunstetter, R. (1996). First-time suicide attempters, repeat attempters, and previous attempters on an adolescent inpatient psychiatry unit. *Journal of the American Academy of Child and Adolescent Psychiatry, 35,* 631–639.

Gould, M., King, R., Greenwald, S., Fisher, P., Schwab-Stowe, M., Kramer, R., Flisher, A., Goodman, S., Canino, G., & Shaffer, D. (1998). Psychopathology associated with suicidal ideation and attempts among children and adolescents. *Journal of the American Academy of Child and Adolescent Psychiatry, 37,* 915–923.

Grossi, V., & Violato, C. (1992). Attempted suicide among adolescents: A stepwise discriminant analysis. *Canadian Journal of Behavioural Science, 24,* 410–413.

Hamilton, J., & Gillham, J. (1999). The K-SADS and diagnosis of major depressive disorder. *Journal of the American Academy of Child and Adolescent Psychiatry, 38,* 1065–1066.

Hamilton, M. (1959). The assessment of anxiety states by rating. *British Journal of Medical Psychology, 32,* 50–55.

Hamilton, M. (1967). Development of a rating scale for primary depressive illness. *British Journal of Social and Clinical Psychology, 6,* 278–296.

Hodges, K. (1994). Evaluation of depression in children and adolescents using diagnostic clinical interviews. In W. M. Reynolds & H. F. Johnston (Eds.), *Handbook of depression in children and adolescents* (pp. 183–208). New York: Guilford Press.

Hodges, K., McKnew, D., Cytryn, L., Stern, L., & Kline, J. (1982). The Child Assessment Schedule (CAS) diagnostic interview: A report on reliability and validity. *Journal of the American Academy of Child Psychiatry, 21,* 468–473.

Hoehn-Saric, E., Maisami, M., & Weigand, D. (1987). Measurement of anxiety in children and adolescents using semi-structured interviews. *Journal of the American Academy of Child and Adolescent Psychiatry, 28,* 541–545.

Hollis, C. (1996). Depression, family environment, and adolescent suicidal behavior. *Journal of the American Academy of Child and Adolescent Psychiatry, 35,* 622–630.

Jensen, P., Roper, M., Fisher, P., Piacentini, J., Canino, G., Richters, J., Robio-Stipec, M., Dulcan, M., Goodman, S., Davies, M., Shaffer, D., Bird, H., Lahey, B., & Schwab-Stone, M. (1995). Test-retest reliability of the Diagnostic Interview Schedule for Children (DISC 2.1): Parent, child, and combined algorithms. *Archives of General Psychiatry, 52,* 61–71.

Kashani, J. H., Sherman, D. D., Parker, D. R., & Reid, J. C. (1990). Utility of the Beck Depression Inventory with clinic-referred adolescents. *Journal of the American Academy of Child and Adolescent Psychiatry, 29,* 278–282.

Kaufman, J., Birmaher, B., Brent, D., Rao, V., Flynn, C., Moreci, P., Williamson, D. & Ryan, N. (1997). Schedule for Affective Disorders and Schizophrenia for School-Age Children-Present and Lifetime versions (K-SADS-PL): Initial reliability and validity data. *Journal of the American Academy of Child and Adolescent Psychiatry, 36,* 980–988.

Kaufman, J., Martin, A., King, R., & Charney, D. (1999). The K-SADS and diagnosis of major depressive disorder: Comment. *Journal of the American Academy of Child and Adolescent Psychiatry, 38,* 1067–1068.

Kazdin, A. E. (1990). Assessment of childhood depression. In A. LaGreca (Ed.), *Through the eyes of the child: Obtaining self-reports from children and adolescents* (pp. 189–233). Boston: Allyn & Bacon.

Kazdin, A. E. (1994). Informant variability in the assessment of childhood depression. In W. M. Reynolds, H. F. Johnston, *et al.* (Eds.), *Handbook of depression in children and adolescents: Issues in clinical child psychology* (pp. 249–271). New York: Plenum Press.

Kazdin, A. E., & Marciano, P. L. (1998). Childhood and adolescent depression. In E. J. Mash & R. A. Barkley (Eds.), *Treatment of childhood disorders* (2nd ed., pp. 211–248). New York: Guilford Press.

Kienhorst, C. W. M., de Wilde, E. J., Diekstra, R. F. W., & Wolters, W. H. G. (1992). Differences between adolescent suicide attempters and depressed adolescents. *Acta Psychiatrica Scandinavica, 85,* 222–228.

King, C. A., Raskin, A., Gdowski, C. L., Butkus, M., & Opipari, L. (1990). Psychosocial factors associated with urban adolescent female suicide attempts. *Journal of the American Academy of Child and Adolescent Psychiatry, 29,* 289–294.

Kingsbury, S., Hawton, K., Steinhardt, K., & Jones, A. (1999). Do adolescents who take overdoses have specific psychological characteristics? A comparative study with psychiatric and community controls. *Journal of the American Academy of Child and Adolescent Psychiatry, 38,* 1125–1131.

Knox, M., King, C., Hanna, G., Logan, D., & Ghaziuddin, N. (2000). Aggressive behavior in clinically depressed adolescents. *Journal of the American Academy of Child and Adolescent Psychiatry, 39,* 611–618.

Kosky, R., Silburn, S., & Zubrick, S. R. (1990). Are children and adolescents who have suicidal thoughts different from those who attempt suicide? *The Journal of Nervous and Mental Disease, 178,* 38–43.

Kovacs, M. (1982). Children's Depression Inventory. Pittsburgh, PA: Western Psychiatric Institute and Clinic.

Kovacs, M. (1985). Interview Schedule for Children (ISC). *Psychopharmacology Bulletin, 21,* 991–994.

Kovacs, M., & Beck, A. T. (1977). An empirical clinical approach towards a definition of childhood depression. In J. G. Schulterbrandt & A. Raskin (Eds.), *Depression in Children.* New York: Raven Press.

Kovacs, M., Goldston, D., & Gatsonis, C. (1993). Suicidal behaviors and childhood-onset depressive disorders: A longitudinal investigation. *Journal of the American Academy of Child and Adolescent Psychiatry, 32*, 8–20.

LaGreca, A. M., & Stone, W. L. (1993). Social anxiety scale for children-revised: Factor structure and concurrent validity. *Journal of Clinical Child Psychology, 22*, 17–27.

Lang, M., & Tisher, M. (1978). *Children's Depression Scale*. Victoria: Australian Council for Educational Research.

Lehnert, K. L., Overholser, J. C., & Spirito, A. (1994). Internalized and externalized anger in adolescent suicide attempters. *Journal of Adolescent Research, 9*, 105–119.

Lempers, J., Clarke-Lempers, D., & Simons, R. L. (1989). Economic hardship, parenting, and distress in adolescence. *Child Development, 60*, 25–39.

Lewinsohn, P., Rohde, P., & Seeley, J. (1996). Adolescent suicidal ideation and attempts: Prevalence, risk factors, and clinical implications. *Clinical Psychology Science and Practice, 3*, 25–46.

March, J. S., Amaya-Jackson, L., Murray, M. C., & Schulte, A. (1998). Cognitive-behavioral psychotherapy for children and adolescents with posttraumatic stress disorder after a single-incident stressor. *Journal of the American Academy of Child and Adolescent Psychiatry, 37*, 585–593.

March, J. S., Parker, J. D. A., Sullivan, K., Stallings, P., & Conners, C. K. (1997). The Multidimensional Anxiety Scale for Children (MASC): Factor structure, reliability, and validity. *Journal of the American Academy of Child and Adolescent Psychiatry, 36*, 554–565.

March, J. S., Sullivan, K., & Parker, J. (1999). Test-retest reliability of the Multidimensional Anxiety Scale for Children. *Journal of Anxiety Disorders, 13*, 349–358.

Marciano, P. L., & Kazdin, A. E. (1994). Self-esteem, depression, hopelessness, and suicidal intent among psychiatrically disturbed inpatient children. *Journal of Clinical Child Psychology, 23*, 151–160.

Myers, K., McCauley, E., Calderon, R., Mitchell, F., Burke, P., & Schloredt, K. (1991). Risks for suicidality in major depressive disorder. *Journal of the American Academy of Child and Adolescent Psychiatry, 30*, 86–94.

Myers, K., McCauley, E., Calderon, R., & Treder, R. (1991). The 3-year longitudinal course of suicidality and predictive factors for subsequent suicidality in youths with major depressive disorder. *Journal of the American Academy of Child and Adolescent Psychiatry, 30*, 804–810.

Negron, R., Piacentini, J., Graae, F., Davies, M., & Shaffer, D. (1997). Microanalysis of adolescent suicide attempters and ideators during the acute suicidal episode. *Journal of the American Academy of Child and Adolescent Psychiatry, 36*, 1512–1519.

Novaco, R. (1975). *Anger control: The development and evaluation of an experimental treatment*. Lexington, MA: D. C. Health & Company.

Ohring, R., Apter, A., Ratzoni, G., Weizman, R., Tyano, S., & Plutchik, R. (1996). State and trait anxiety in adolescent suicide attempters. *Journal of the American Academy of Child and Adolescent Psychiatry, 35*, 154–157.

Ollendick, T. H. (1983). Reliability and validity of the Revised Fear Survey Schedule for Children (FSSC-R). *Behaviour Research and Therapy, 21*, 685–692.

Orvaschel, H. (1995). *Schedule for Affective Disorders and Schizophrenia for School-Age Children-Epidemiologic Version-5 (K-SADS-E-5)*. Fort Lauderdale, FL: Nova Southeastern University.

Overholser, J., Freiheit, S., & DiFilippo, J. (1997). Emotional distress and substance abuse as risk factors for suicide attempts. *Canadian Journal of Psychiatry, 42*, 402–408.

Paluszny, M., Davenport, C., & Kim, W. J. (1991). Suicide attempts and ideation: Adolescents evaluated on a pediatric ward. *Adolescence, 26*, 209–215.

Pelkonen, M., Marttunen, M., Pulkkinen, E., Laippala, P., & Aro, H. (1997). Characteristics of out-patient adolescents with suicidal tendencies. *Acta Psychiatrica Scandinavica, 95*, 100–107.

Pfeffer, C. R., Klerman, G. L., Hurt, S. W., Lesser, M., Peskin, J. R., & Siekfer, C. A. (1991). Suicidal children grow up: Demographic and clinical risk factors for adolescent suicide attempts. *Journal of the American Academy of Child and Adolescent Psyhciatry, 30*, 609–610.

Pilowsky, D., Wu, L., & Anthony, J. (1999). Panic attacks and suicide attempts in mid-adolescence. *American Journal of Psychiatry, 156*, 1545–1549.

Pinto, A., & Whisman, M. A. (1996). Negative affect and cognitive biases in suicidal and nonsuicidal hospitalized adolescents. *Journal of the American Academy of Child and Adolescent Psychiatry, 35*, 158–165.

Poznanski, E. O., Grossman, J. A., Buschbaum, Y., Banegas, M., Freeman, L., & Gibbons, R. (1984). Preliminary studies of the reliability and validity of the Children's Depression Rating Scale. *Journal of the American Academy of Child Psychiatry, 23*, 191–197.

Puig-Antich, J., & Chambers, W. (1978). *The Schedule for Affective Disorders and Schizophrenia for School-age Children (Kiddie-SADS)*. New York: New York State Psychiatric Institute.

Pynoos, R. S., Frederick, C. J., Nader, K., Arroyo, W., Steinberg, A., Eth, S., Nunez, F., & Fairbanks, L. (1987). Life threat and post traumatic stress in school-age children. *Archives of General Psychiatry, 44*, 1057–1063.

Rabian, B., Ginsburg, G. S., & Silverman, W. K. (1994). *ADIS-R for children*. Paper presented at the Anxiety Disorders Association of America, Santa Monica, CA.

Radloff, L. S. (1977). The CES-D Scale: A self-report scale for research in the general population. *Applied Psychological Measurement, 1*, 385–401.

Rapee, R. M., Barrett, P. M., Dadds, M., & Evans, L. (1994). Reliability of the DSM-III-R childhood anxiety disorders using structured interview: Interrater and parent-child agreement. *Journal of the American Academy of Child and Adolescent Psychiatry, 33*, 984–992.

Reich, W. (1997). *Diagnostic Interview for Children and Adolescents-Revised, DSM-IV Version*. Toronto: Multi-Health Systems.

Reich, W., Cottler, L., McCallum, K., Corwin, D., & Van Eerdewegh, M. (1995). Computerized interviews as a method of assessing psychopathology in children. *Comprehensive Psychiatry, 36*, 40–45.

Reich, W., & Cottler, L. B. (1999). The K-SADS and diagnosis of major depressive disorder; Comment. *Journal of the American Academy of Child and Adolescent Psychiatry, 38*, 1066–1067.

Reynolds, C. R., & Kamphaus, R. W. (1992*). BASC Manual*. Circle Pines, MN: American Guidance Service.

Reynolds, C. R., & Paget, K. D. (1983). National normative and reliability data for the Revised Children's Manifest Anxiety Scale. *School Psyhcology Review, 12*, 324–336.

Reynolds, C. R., & Richmond, B. O. (1978). What I think and feel: A revised measure of children's manifest anxiety. *Journal of Abnormal Child Psychology, 6*, 271–280.

Reynolds, W. M. (1985). Depression in childhood and adolescence: Diagnosis, assessment, intervention strategies, and research. In T. R. Kratochwill (Ed.), *Advances in school psychology* (Vol. 4, pp. 133–189). Hillsdale, NJ: Erlbaum Associates.

Reynolds, W. M. (1987). *Reynolds Adolescent Depression Scale: Professional Manual*. Odessa, FL: Psychological Assessment Resources.

Reynolds, W. M. (1994). Assessment of depression in children and adolescents by self-report questionnaires. In W. M. Reynolds & H. F. Johnston (Eds.), *Handbook of depression in children and adolescents* (pp. 209–234). New York: Guilford Press.

Riddle, M. A., & Greenhill, L. L. (1997). Children's Anxiety Rating Scale (CARS): Unpublished Manuscript.

Roberts, R. E., Andrews, J. A., Lewinsohn, P. M., & Hops, H. (1990). Assessment of depression in adolescents using the Center for Epidemiological Studies Depression Scale. *Psychological Assessment: A Journal of Consulting and Clinical Psychology, 2*, 122–128.

Roberts, R. E., Lewinsohn, P. M., & Seeley, J. R. (1991). Screening for adolescent depression: A comparison of depression scales. *Journal of the American Academy of Child and Adolescent Psychiatry, 30*, 58–66.

Rotheram-Borus, M. J., Walker, J. U., & Ferns, W. (1996). Suicidal behavior among middle-class adolescents who seek crisis services. *Journal of Clinical Psychology, 52*, 137–143.

Scahill, L., Riddle, M., McSwiggin-Hardin, M., Ort, S., King, R., Goodmand, W., Chicchetti, D., & Leckman, J. (1997). Children's Yale-Brown obsessive compulsive scale. *Journal of the American Academy of Child and Adolescent Psychiatry, 36*, 844–852.

Schwab-Stone, M., Fisher, P., Piacentini, J., Shaffer, D., Davies, M., & Briggs, M. (1993). The Diagnostic Interview Schedule for Children-Revised Version (DISC-R): II. Test-retest reliability. *Journal of the American Academy of Child and Adolescent Psychiatry, 32*, 651–657.

Shaffer, D., Fisher, P., Dulcan, M., & Davies, M. (1996). The NIMH Diagnostic Interview Schedule for Children (DISC 2.3): Description, acceptability, prevalences, and performance in the MECA study. *Journal of the American Academy of Child and Adolescent Psychiatry, 35*, 865–877.

Shaffer, D., Fisher, P., Lucas, C. P., Dulcan, M. K., & Schwab-Stone, M. E. (2000). NIMH Diagnostic Interview Schedule for Children, Version IV (NIMH DISC-IV): Description, differences from previous versions, and reliability of some common diagnoses. *Journal of the American Academy of Child and Adolescent Psychiatry, 39*, 28–38.

Shaffer, D., Schwab-Stone, M., Fisher, P., Cohen, P., Piacentini, J., Davies, M., Connors, C. K., & Regier, D. (1993). The Diagnostic Interview Schedule for Children—Revised Edition (DISC-R): I. Preparation, field testing, interrater reliability, and acceptability. *Journal of the American Academy of Child and Adolescent Psychiatry, 32*, 643–650.

Silverman, W. K., & Albano, A. M. (1996). *Anxiety Disorders Interview Schedule for DSM-IV: Child Version—Child Interview Schedule*. San Antonio, TX: The Psychological Corporation.

Silverman, W. K., & Eisen, A. R. (1992). Age differences in the reliability of parent and child reports of child anxious symptomatology using a structured interview. *Journal of the American Academy of Child and Adolescent Psychiatry, 31*, 117–124.

Silverman, W. K., & Nelles, W. B. (1988). The Anxiety Disorders Interview Schedule for Children. *Journal of the American Academy of Child and Adolescent Psychiatry, 27*, 772–778.

Spielberger, C. (1999). *The State-Trait Anger Expression Inventory-2*. Odessa, FL: Psychological Assessment Resources.

Spielberger, C. D., Edwards, C. D., & Lushene, R. E., Monturi, J., & Platzek, S. (1973). *STAIC: Preliminary manual for the State-Trait Anxiety Inventory for Children*. Palo Alto, CA: Consulting Psychologists Press.

Stallings, P., & March, J. S. (1995). Assessment. In J. S. March (Ed.), *Anxiety disorders in children and adolescents* (pp. 125–147). New York: Guilford Press.

Steer, R. A., & Beck, A. T. (1988). Use of the BDI, Hopelessness Scale, Scale for Suicide Ideation, and Suicidal Intent Scale with adolescents. In A. R. Stiffman & R. A. Feldman (Eds.), *Advances in adolescent mental health* (pp. 219–231). Greenwich, CT: JAI Press.

Steer, R. A., Beck, A. T., & Garrison, B. (1986). Applications of the BDI. In N. Sartorius & T. A. Ban (Eds.), *Assessment of depression* (pp. 121–142). Geneva, Switzerland: World Health Organization.

Stein, D., Apter, A., Ratzoni, G., Har-Even, D., & Avidan, G. (1998). Association between multiple suicide attempts and negative affects in adolescents. *Journal of the American Academy of Child and Adolescent Psychiatry, 37*, 488–494.

Strauss, C. C., Lease, C. A., Last, C. G., & Francis, G. (1988). Overanxious disorder: An examination of developmental differences. *Journal of Abnormal Child Psychology, 16*, 57–68.

Strober, M., Green, J., & Carlson, G. (1981). Utility of the Beck Depression Inventory with psychiatrically hospitalized adolescents. *Journal of Consulting and Clinical Psychology, 49*, 482–483.

Teri, L. (1982). The use of the Beck Depression Inventory with adolescents. *Journal of Abnormal Child Psychology, 10*, 277–284.

Trautman, P. D., Rotheram-Borus, M. J., Dopkins, S., & Lewin, N. (1991). Psychiatric diagnoses in minority female adolescent suicide attempters. *Journal of the American Academy of Child and Adolescent Psychiatry, 30*, 617–622.

Turner, C., Ku, L., Lindberg, L., Pleck, J., & Sonenstein, F. (1998). Adolescent sexual behavior, drug use, and violence: Increased reporting with computer survey technology. *Science, 280*, 867–873.

Weinstein, S. R., Noam, G. G., Grimes, K., Stone, R., & Schwab-Stone, M. (1990). Convergence of DSM-III diagnoses and self-reported symptoms in child and adolescent inpatients. *Journal of the American Academy of Child and Adolescent Psychiatry, 29*, 627–634.

Welner, Z., Reich, W., Herjanic, B., Jung, K., & Amado, H. (1987). Reliability, validity, and parent-child agreement studies of the Diagnostic Interview for Children and Adolescents (DICA). *Journal of the American Academy of Child and Adolescent Psychiatry, 26*, 649–653.

Wirt, R., Lachar, D., Klinedinst, J., & Seat, P. (1977). *Multidimensional description of personality*. Los Angeles: Western Psychological Services.

Witt, J. C., Heffer, R. W., & Pfeiffer, J. P. (1990). Structured rating scales: A review of self-report and informant rating processes, procedures, and issues. In C. R. R. R. W. Kamphaus (Ed.), *Handbook of psychological and educational assessment of children: Personality, behavior, and context* (pp. 364–394). New York: Guilford Press.

CHAPTER 5

Cognitive Factors: Hopelessness, Coping, and Problem Solving

Christianne Esposito, Benjamin Johnson, Barbara A. Wolfsdorf, and Anthony Spirito

Maladaptive cognitive processes frequently play an important role in suicidal behavior. Hopelessness is the cognitive state that often accompanies depression and has been found to be prominent in many adolescents who attempt suicide. Maladaptive cognitive coping strategies, such as wishful thinking, may also contribute to suicidal behavior and need to be addressed in psychotherapy to prevent or understand a suicide attempt. This chapter reviews those studies that have examined cognitive factors in adolescents who attempt suicide.

HOPELESSNESS

In their investigations of the characteristics associated with adolescent suicide attempts, many researchers have focused on hopelessness. Hopelessness has been defined as a lowered expectation of obtaining certain goals and a diminished belief in the likelihood of finding success (Melges & Bowlby, 1969). Hopelessness is accompanied by feelings of personal

Evaluating and Treating Adolescent Suicide Attempters

futility, loss of motivation, and the expectation that the future will hold either continued failure, suffering, or negative personal consequences (Beck, Weissman, Lester, & Trexler, 1974).

The study of hopelessness and suicidality exists both in conjunction with, and separate from, the study of depression and suicidality. Approximately 14 published studies in the past decade have examined the relation between hopelessness and adolescent suicide attempts. Like the studies of depression, these samples span a variety of settings, such as emergency departments (ED), pediatric medical units, psychiatric inpatient programs, and residential treatment facilities. Data support widespread clinical observations that adolescents who attempt suicide are characterized by hopelessness. Although this relationship consistently emerges when the relation between hopelessness and suicidal behavior is evaluated in isolation, a far more complex picture emerges when hopelessness is investigated in the context of other variables.

ED and Medical Patients

In a small study comparing adolescent suicide attempters hospitalized on a pediatric unit to a group of nonsuicidal, psychiatrically at-risk adolescents on a number of measures of psychosocial functioning, the groups differed only on degree of hopelessness, with the suicide attempters reporting significantly higher levels than the comparison group (Swedo et al., 1991). In another study evaluating hopelessness among adolescent suicide attempters presenting to an ED, Negron and colleagues tracked levels of adolescent hopelessness for ideators and attempters throughout the course of a suicidal episode (Negron, Piacentin, Graae, Davies, & Shaffer, 1997). These researchers attempted to understand the emotional course that surrounds a suicidal episode, including emotions experienced by adolescents before, during, and after the episode. Results indicated that adolescent suicide attempters reported greater levels of hopelessness than adolescent ideators only prior to the precipitating stressor. During and after the suicidal episode, adolescent attempters and ideators reported similar levels of hopelessness. Thus, hopelessness may be a time-limited risk factor for many suicidal adolescents.

Spirito and colleagues (Boergers, Spirito, & Donaldson, 1998; Brown, Overholser, Spirito, & Fritz, 1991) included hopelessness in their investigations of planning and motivation in adolescent suicide attempts. These studies found an important relation between hopelessness as measured by the Hopelessness Scale for Children (Kazdin, Rodgas, & Colbus, 1986) and degree of planning, as well as an association between hopelessness and death motivation. Adolescents who made premeditated suicide attempts were more hopeless than those who made impulsive attempts (Brown *et al.*, 1991). In addition, Boergers *et al.* (1998) found that although depression was a better predictor of this motivation, a wish to die was also associated with hopelessness. Thus, the combination of depression and hopelessness may be a potent mix that underlies many suicidal tendencies. Indeed, McLaughlin, Miller, and Warwick (1996) compared adolescents who had taken overdoses and were treated in an ED to psychiatric clinic and schoolchildren controls and found significantly higher scores on the Hopelessness Scale for Children in the overdose group. When they limited their analyses to only depressed adolescents, a much larger proportion of the suicide attempters reported higher hopelessness levels compared to the depressed adolescents in the control groups.

Psychiatric Inpatients

Most researchers have studied hopelessness in adolescent suicide attempters within inpatient psychiatric facilities (e.g., Asarnow & Guthrie, 1989; Marciano & Kazdin, 1994; Mitchell & Rosenthal, 1992; Morano, Cisler, & Lemerond, 1993; Pinto & Whisman, 1996). These investigations generally evaluate the importance of hopelessness as a psychosocial correlate of suicidal behavior relative to other variables. The results of these endeavors are inconsistent. Some researchers have failed to find a relation between hopelessness and adolescent suicide attempts (e.g., deWilde, Kienhorst, Diekstra, & Wolters, 1993; Mitchell & Rosenthal, 1992; Pinto & Whisman, 1996; Rotheram-Borus & Trautman, 1988). However, methodological problems in one of these investigations may have obscured the results (i.e., in Mitchell & Rosenthal, the groups were small and unequal in number).

Other investigators have found a complicated set of relations between hopelessness and adolescent suicidality. For example, Morano and colleagues (1993) investigated the relations of loss, insufficient family support, and hopelessness using the Hopelessness Scale (Beck *et al.*, 1974) among 40 adolescent psychiatric inpatients matched on level of depression. Adolescent suicide attempters reported feeling more hopeless prior to their attempt than their equally depressed but nonattempting, counterparts. Although these data provide support for the assertion that hopelessness may be a stronger predictor of suicidality than depression, it is important to note that when evaluated in relation to other variables (i.e., loss and family support), hopelessness no longer predicted suicidality.

In contrast to the results of Morano *et al.* (1993), Marciano and Kazdin (1994) found support for the importance of depression relative to hopelessness in the suicidal behavior of children and young adolescents. Although these researchers found that suicidal adolescents described greater hopelessness on the Hopelessness Scale for Children than their nonsuicidal counterparts, this relation was diminished when evaluated against the importance of depression. Consistent with Boergers *et al.* (1998), Marciano and Kazdin found that depressive symptomatology was the best predictor of suicide status and that hopelessness did not add to the discrimination of suicidal and nonsuicidal adolescents beyond the contribution of depression.

Even more complicated are the results of Asarnow, Carlson, & Guthrie, (1987), who suggest that depression and hopelessness in combination may be the important variable for understanding adolescent suicidal behavior. In their investigation of preadolescent youngsters, their results indicated that although hopelessness and depression together discriminated between attempters and nonattempters, when either one was entered into analyses first, the other no longer discriminated between the two groups. Based on these findings, Asarnow and colleagues have suggested that a subgroup of adolescents who are both depressed *and* hopeless may account for the frequently reported associations among depression, hopelessness, and suicide attempts. Nonetheless, other adolescents became suicidal when experiencing moderate levels of depression without significant feelings of hopelessness.

Dori and Overholser (1999), using the Hopelessness Scale for Children, found that adolescents who experienced higher levels of hopelessness during a depressive episode were more likely to have attempted suicide. Dori and Overholser (1999) suggested that hopelessness is a cognitive vulnerability that places an adolescent at risk for suicidal behavior during a depressive episode. Finally, Goldston, Daniel, Reboussin, Reboussin, Frazier, and Harris (2001) followed adolescents who had been hospitalized on a psychiatric inpatient unit up to 6 years following discharge. Among adolescents who had attempted suicide prior to the initial hospitalization, higher levels of hopelessness increased the risk for repeat suicide attempts.

Other Clinical Populations

Several investigations of adolescents in mixed settings and residential settings address hopelessness (Grossi & Violato, 1992; Kienhorst, deWilde, van den Bout, Diekstra, & Wolters, 1990; King, Raskin, Gdowski, Butkus, & Opiari, 1990). Here again, results are not entirely consistent. When they compared recent attempters with depressed nonattempters, Kienhorst and colleagues (Kienhorst *et al.*, 1990) found that attempters reported more hopelessness about their current situation and the future than their nonattempting counterparts. However, others failed to find these differences (Grossi & Violato, 1992; King *et al.*, 1990). Some inconsistencies may be understood based on the population under study (i.e., Grossi and Violato used a sample of adolescents in a residential facility who may have been more emotionally stabilized).

CLINICAL IMPLICATIONS

Researchers studying the relation between hopelessness and adolescent suicidality have collected data in a variety of clinical settings, such as ED, pediatric medical units, psychiatric inpatient programs, and residential treatment facilities. When analyzed in isolation, strong evidence exists for the importance of hopelessness in adolescent suicidality. However, when analyzed in the context of other psychosocial variables such as depression and family factors, results are more complicated. Although it seems that hopelessness plays an important role in the emotional presentation of suicidal adolescents, the extent to which hopelessness is important beyond that of depression remains unclear. Indeed, several studies have not demonstrated differences between suicide attempters and nonattempters when both groups are depressed (deWilde, *et al.*, 1993; Pinto & Whisman, 1996; Rotheram-Borus & Trautman, 1988). Some investigators assert that depression is the critical variable, others maintain that hopelessness is more important, and others propose that the two factors together should be the focus of research efforts.

It is central for clinicians to assess both depression and hopelessness. When treating the depressed suicide attempter, it may prove most useful to address hopelessness specifically at the outset of treatment, while treating the depression systematically over the longer course of psychotherapy. This treatment strategy may prove most efficacious given that hopelessness has been shown to be a predictor of treatment dropout among depressed, suicidal adolescents (Brent *et al.*, 1997).

ASSESSMENT OF HOPELESSNESS

The previous studies used several different measures to assess hopelessness in their samples: one designed for adults (Beck *et al.*, 1974) and one designed for children (Kazdin *et al.*, 1983, 1986). The Hopelessness Scale has been the most widely used instrument with adults; it has 20 true-false items describing negative future expectations and negative current attitudes. Beck *et al.* (1974) found three factors: one, labeled "loss of motivation," contained positively worded items (e.g., "I have great faith in the future"), while a second "affective" factor had mainly negatively worded items (e.g., "My future seems dark to me"), suggesting a lack of confidence in the future. A third factor, "future expectations," was similar to the second factor but had both negative and positive items, suggesting uncertainty about the future.

Kazdin and his colleagues adapted the adult scale for use with children (the Hopelessness Scale for Children-HSC; Kazdin *et al.*, 1986). In one study (Kazdin, French, Unis, Esveldt-Dawson, & Sherrick, 1983), a significant relationship between suicidal intent and the HSC was found among child psychiatric patients. In a factor analysis, Kazdin *et al.* (1986) found two factors, both of which reflected negative expectations about the future. Spirito, Williams, Stark, and Hart (1988) studied a sample of adolescent suicide attempters. Test-retest data (administered 10 weeks apart) were consistent with the moderate correlations reported by Kazdin *et al.* (1986) with a younger population over a somewhat shorter period of time. The suicide attempters answered the HSC differentially when presented with positively and negatively worded items. This led to two strong factors for attempters. Factor 1 comprised the negatively worded items of the scale indicating negative expectations about the future. Factor 2 comprised the positively worded items indicating some hope for change in the more distant future. These findings suggest the need to evaluate the two components of the scale separately in clinical samples of adolescents.

COPING

Results of research examining coping in suicidal adolescents generally reveal less effective coping in this population. However, the nature of the problem (i.e., failure to use coping strategies or use of ineffective strategies) is not clearly delineated at this time. This is partly the result of methodological differences between studies. Researchers evaluate the construct of coping from different theoretical perspectives, as well as utilize different measures of coping in studies. Although this makes it difficult to draw substantive conclusions, studies that employ global measures of coping, particularly cognitive coping, generally reveal that adolescent suicide attempters tend to use maladoptive and passive coping strategies.

ED Patients, Medical Inpatients, and Community Samples

Spirito, Overholser, & Stark (1989) examined differences in coping strategies reported by 76 adolescents hospitalized on a general pediatric unit following a suicide attempt and 186 adolescent community controls. Adolescents were asked to select a problem they encountered in the past month and complete the Kidcope (Spirito, Stark, & Williams, 1988), a checklist of 10 cognitive and coping strategies, with respect to the problem selected. Specifically, adolescents were asked to rate the frequency with which they used each strategy to cope with the problem, and how effective they believed the coping strategy was for them. In addition, adolescents were asked to respond to two additional questions regarding anxiety ("Did the situation make you nervous or anxious?") and depression ("Did the situation make you sad or depressed?"). The community controls were then further classified into a distressed ($n = 191$) or nondistressed ($n = 72$) group, as defined by their self-report of depression and/or anxiety in response to their selected personal problem. Results revealed that suicide attempters used wishful thinking more frequently than nondistressed controls, but less frequently than distressed controls.

Similar results were found by Rotheram-Borus, Trautman, Dopkins, and Shrout (1990), who compared coping strategies and a number of other cognitive variables reported by 77 adolescent minority female suicide attempters recruited from ED referrals, 39 psychiatrically disturbed nonsuicidal minority females recruited from outpatient clinic referrals, and 23 nondisturbed nonsuicidal minority female high school volunteers. Adolescents were asked to complete the Coping Style Questionnaire (Lazarus, 1981), which requires adolescents to describe the most stressful situation experienced in the previous month and then endorse coping statements from a checklist. Seven subscales were generated from these items including the following: focused on problems, blaming self, a combination of both avoidance and advice seeking, wishful thinking, minimizing threat, seeking support, and emotional coping. Results revealed that suicide attempters, relative to nondisturbed, nonsuicidal adolescents, were more focused on their problems and reported greater use of wishful thinking. No other differences were found across groups on coping style.

In a study by Lewinsohn, Rohde, and Seeley (1993) approximately 1700 adolescents randomly selected from nine high schools were asked to complete a coping questionnaire consisting of items from the Self-Control Scale (Rosenbaum, 1980), the Antidepressive Activity Questionnaire (Rippere, 1977; modified by Parker & Brown, 1979), and the Ways of Coping Questionnaire (Folkman & Lazarus, 1980). After controlling for depression severity, poor coping skills were more frequently reported by adolescents with a history of a suicide attempt compared to those without such a history.

Psychiatric Inpatients

A few studies have examined the use of active or adaptive coping strategies among suicide ideators and attempters in psychiatric hospitals. Results generally reveal active coping strategies to be less prominent in suicidal populations. Asarnow *et al.* (1987) examined coping strategies as one of four factors associated with depression and suicidal behavior in suicide attempters, suicide ideators, and nonsuicidal children and adolescents. Thirty psychiatrically hospitalized children and young adolescents completed the Coping Strategies Test, developed by the authors, which assessed children's responses to three stressful situations (disciplinary crisis at school, parental conflict, and death of mother). Responses were scored for interpersonal sensitivity, expectancies, number of solutions generated both before and after an obstacle is introduced, content of solutions (physical aggression, verbal aggression, running away, suicide, assertion, help seeking, active cognitive coping, avoidant cognitive coping), presence or absence of depressogenic statements, and presence or absence of adaptive planning. Results revealed that suicide ideators were significantly less likely to generate active cognitive coping strategies (e.g., self-comforting statements or instrumental problem solving) than nonsuicidal children. No other significant differences in coping strategies were found when suicide attempters or ideators were compared to nonsuicidal children.

A similar study was conducted by Wilson, Stelzer, Bergman, Kral, Inayatullah, and Elliott (1996) who compared adaptive coping strategies reported by 20 adolescent suicide attempters hospitalized on an adolescent inpatient psychiatry unit to 20 community controls. Adolescents were asked to identify the "most stressful event" that had ever taken place in their lives, generate a list of possible ways to cope with that event, provide an example of each coping strategy, and indicate which coping strategies they actually used to cope with the event. Raters then classified each coping strategy as either adaptive or maladaptive. Similar to the study conducted by Asarnow *et al.* (1987), there were no differences found between suicide attempters and controls regarding the number of adaptive strategies generated. However, attempters were shown to generate more maladaptive strategies than controls. Further, when analyses were restricted to strategies actually used, suicide attempters reported the use of fewer adaptive coping strategies in comparison to controls.

Other researchers have examined coping from the perspective of emotion-focused (e.g., efforts directed toward managing the negative emotional consequences of a situation) versus problem-focused (e.g., efforts directed toward the situation in an effort to change it directly) strategies. Results of most studies suggest that suicidal adolescents have a propensity to utilize emotion-focused coping more readily than problem-focused strategies. Puskar, Hoover, and Miewald (1992) compared coping methods used by 30 psychiatrically hospitalized adolescents exhibiting suicidal behavior (intent, plan, or attempt) and 16 psychiatrically hospitalized nonsuicidal adolescents. Although they failed to find differences between the suicidal and nonsuicidal inpatients in coping methods used, overall analyses conducted with the suicidal inpatients alone revealed that they used affective-oriented coping strategies significantly more than problem-oriented strategies. In contrast, the nonsuicidal inpatients used both types of coping strategies equally. The affect-oriented coping strategies most frequently used by suicidal inpatients included hope and resignation. The problem-oriented coping strategies least used included active change, goal setting, passive problem solving, and information seeking.

Wilson *et al.* (1996) failed to find a higher prevalence of emotion-focused coping strategies between 20 adolescent suicide attempters hospitalized on an adolescent inpatient psychiatry unit and 20 community controls, who were asked to indicate the strategies used in response to "the most stressful event" in their lives. However, when analyses were limited to maladaptive strategies used in response to the event, coping was more likely to be classified as emotion focused than problem focused.

Other Clinical Populations

Klimes-Dougan, Free, Ronsaville, Stilwell, Welsh, and Radke-Yarrow (1999) examined internalizing (e.g., emotion-focused) coping strategies as one of many predictors of suicidality in children and adolescents of depressed mothers. Specifically, 92 adolescents were administered an abbreviated version of the Self-Report Coping Scale (Causey & Dubow, 1992) to assess use of internalizing and externalizing strategies for coping with stress. The presence of suicidal ideation, plans, gestures, and attempts was assessed through individual items from structured diagnostic interviews. Results revealed that the use of internalizing coping strategies predicted lifetime report of suicide plans/attempts. In contrast, the use of externalizing coping strategies did not predict suicidality.

Rohde, Seeley, and Mace (1997) examined correlates of suicidal ideation and past suicide attempts in a sample of 555 adolescents detained in a juvenile detention facility. Differences in coping across gender and type of suicidal behavior were found. Adolescents completed a 15-item instrument designed to measure ineffective coping techniques and prosocial behavioral coping techniques (Rohde, Lewinsohn, Tilson, & Seeley, 1990). An inverse relationship was found between ineffective coping skills, and suicidal ideation and history of attempt, as well as an inverse relationship between behavioral coping skills and suicidal ideation in males. Coping skills were not correlated with suicidal ideation or attempts in females. Ineffective coping also emerged as a direct predictor of suicide attempts but not ideation in males. Males demonstrating higher levels of ineffective coping skills were almost twice as likely to make a suicide attempt. However, this relationship did not remain significant after controlling for social desirability.

Coping Efficacy

The effectiveness of chosen coping strategies (i.e., coping efficacy) has been identified as a predictor of suicidality in adolescents. Guiao and

Esparza (1995) examined the relationship between coping strategies and suicidality in 15 "troubled" Mexican-American adolescents recruited from community counseling centers and 35 "normal" Mexican-American adolescents voluntarily recruited from public high schools. Adolescents completed the Kidcope (Spirito, Stark *et al.*, 1988), in which they were asked to indicate a stressful event that occurred within the past month and then endorse the frequency and self-perceived efficacy of each coping strategy they used to deal with the identified situation. Suicidality was assessed via a two-item scale that assessed current suicide ideation and past suicide attempts. Poor coping efficacy emerged as a predictor of suicidality. A relationship was not found between frequency of coping behaviors and suicidality in adolescents.

CLINICAL IMPLICATIONS

Studies on coping strategies used by adolescent suicide attempters generally reveal that this group of adolescents may use less adaptive strategies. More important, it appears that attempters tend to use maladaptive and passive coping strategies, such as wishful thinking. When adaptive strategies are implemented by suicide attempters, they tend to be used to manage their emotional reactions rather than solve the problem that led to the suicidal ideation. In managing an adolescent suicide attempter, it is important to understand the extent to which the adolescent uses emotion-focused or problem-focused coping strategies and, further, if the adolescent perceives these strategies as helpful. Understanding the coping strategies employed by the adolescent will inform the treatment plan.

Assessment of Coping

Coping strategies should be evaluated in all adolescents who attempt suicide. Checklist or screening assessments of coping may be especially useful to clinicians because they are brief and easy to administer. The Kidcope (Spirito, Stark *et al.*, 1988) can be used to assess coping across a number of stressful situations and offers information regarding the frequency and perceived efficacy of a wide variety of cognitive and behavioral coping strategies. The Kidcope was designed to screen for a broad range of cognitive and behavioral strategies, but is sufficiently brief and thus can be used with relative ease in clinical practice. Specifically, the scale items assess 10 cognitive and behavioral coping strategies utilized by children and adolescents. Adolescents report the frequency and the perceived efficacy of each strategy in response to a stressor. There are several ways to conceptualize responses to the Kidcope. These include problem-focused versus emotion-focused strategies (Lazurus & Folkman, 1984), active versus passive, and approach versus avoidance. In most situations, the problem-focused, active, and approach strategies include cognitive restructuring, problem solving, and social support. The emotion-focused strategies include emotional regulation and social support, while the passive and avoidant strategies might include distraction, social withdrawal, wishful thinking, and resignation.

The brevity of the Kidcope presents some limitations in understanding the coping strategies employed by the adolescent. In such cases, more structured interviews might be appropriate. However, interviews increase the time needed for evaluation, which is a drawback. In some studies, administering a self-report screening measure and then interviewing the adolescents regarding their use of the two or three most frequently reported coping strategies has been one way to maximize both limited time and understanding of the coping strategies used.

A number of other scales are used to assess coping. The Self-Report Coping Survey (Causey & Dubow, 1992) is a 34-item scale that has two subscales (seeking social support and problem solving) labeled "Approach" and three subscales (distancing, internalizing, and externalizing) labeled "Avoidance." Distancing refers to avoiding thinking about the situation, internalizing refers to an anxious response or withdrawal, and externalizing reflects attempts to cope by diverting feelings toward others. The Adolescent Coping Orientation for Problem Experiences (A-COPE; Patterson & McCubbin, 1983) was based on interview data obtained from 10th through 12th grade students who were asked what they did to cope with stressors, what was the most difficult stressor encountered in their family, and what were other difficult life changes they had encountered. Items were subsequently factor-analyzed, revealing 12 categories of coping responses: ventilating feelings, seeking diversions, developing self-reliance and optimism, developing social support, solving family problems, avoiding problems, seeking spiritual support, investing in close friends, seeking professional support, engaging in a demanding activity, being humorous, and relaxing. Internal consistency is adequate, and concurrent validity has been demonstrated.

Finally, when coping is of primary interest, there is no substitute for an interview. Compared to self-report measures, interviewing children in depth about their coping strategies often enhances understanding of the nature of the coping process. Many interviews are derived from a theoretical model, for instance, monitoring/blunting (Miller, Sherman, Combs, & Kruus, 1992) and primary/secondary/relinquishing control strategies (Band, 1990), and thus assess only specific coping strategies. More general interviews do exist, and the approach used by Compas, Malcarne, and Fondacaro (1988) may be useful to clinicians. Compas *et al.* (1988) utilized an open-ended questionnaire format with older children and adolescents, ages 10 to 14. Participants were asked to identify a stressful everyday interpersonal event and a stressful academic event that had occurred within the past 3 months. For each stressor, children and adolescents generated a list of possible coping strategies and indicated which strategies they had actually used. Coping strategies are then classified by raters as either problem focused or emotion focused. Concurrent validity was demonstrated by a moderate relationship between coping and emotional/ behavioral problems. Comparisons can be made between the types of coping strategies generated and those actually employed to deal with stressors. This allows greater understanding of coping difficulties—that is, is the difficulty related to an inability to generate strategies or to an inability to choose the most appropriate strategy among a number of alternatives?

PROBLEM SOLVING

Based on a review of the literature, Spirito, Brown *et al.* (1989) concluded that suicide attempters displayed less adequate problem-solving abilities than either psychiatric or normal controls, and that this deficit was present among suicidal children, adolescents, and adults. It was unclear at that time whether this problem-solving deficit was state dependent or a more enduring personality characteristic. Since the time of the Spirito, Brown *et al.* (1989) review, additional studies determining the nature of the problem-solving deficits of adolescent suicide attempters have been relatively few. Recent research in this area has attempted to distinguish between the process and outcome of problem solving. Attitudes and skills that enable a person to find solutions to a problem constitute the process characteristics of problem solving. The quality of specific solutions are the outcomes (D'Zurilla & Maydeu-Olivares, 1995).

ED and Medical Patients

McLaughlin, Miller, and Warwick (1996) studied 60 adolescents hospitalized for taking deliberate drug overdoses, and compared them with a group of "at-risk" adolescents who were attending child psychiatric outpatient clinics but had no history of self-harm, and a second age and sex matched group drawn randomly from two local schools. They found that the attempters reported more problems with family, friends, and boyfriends/girlfriends compared to control groups. Further, analyses suggested that most (68%) of the adolescents who made an attempt expected that it would influence their problems, either because they would be dead, because they would get away from their problems for a time, or because it would make other people understand how badly they felt and provide help. Another 38% of the teens said that they were unable to think of anything else to do, indicating that their ability to generate solutions to problems had been exhausted. Thus, it seems that the overdose for the great majority of attempters in this sample can be seen as either a maladaptive way of trying to solve their problems or as a breakdown in the problem-solving process.

Psychiatric Inpatients

Several studies suggest that the relationship between traitlike problem-solving deficits and adolescent suicide attempters is not robust and that this relationship is more complicated and subtle than was first thought. Indeed, more recent research has implicated other aspects of the problem-solving process in adolescent suicidality. Fremouw, Callahan, and Kashden (1993) evaluated problem-solving deficits in 33 hospitalized suicidal adolescents and compared them with 21 adolescents hospitalized for other psychiatric problems, as well as 89 controls. Contrary to expectations, a common measure of problem solving, the Means-Ends Problem-Solving (MEPS; Platt, Spivack, & Bloom, 1975), did not distinguish between groups, though another measure, the Alternate Uses Test (AUT; Guilford, Christensen, Merrifield, & Wilson, 1978) did. Neither measure of problem solving was powerful in predicting suicide risk. Of further interest, negative life events did not interact with problem-solving deficits to predict suicide risk. In a related study, comparing the same groups as their previous study, Kashden, Fremouw, Callahan, and Franzen (1993) again did not find differences in the MEPS between groups. However, the more impulsive attempters reported fewer means to solve the problem relative to non-impulsive attempters. This finding led the authors to suggest that problem-solving training with adolescent suicide attempters might be more successful by addressing impulsivity as a component of training.

Wilson and colleagues (1996) examined 20 adolescents who had made suicide attempts and 20 nonpsychiatric control subjects on measures of problem solving, stress, and coping. This study, like Fremouw *et al.* (1993), used the MEPS and AUT. The suicidal group did not show deficits in the ability to generate solutions to standardized interpersonal problems or to their own most severe recent real-life stressor. However, they reported actually using fewer solutions than controls, were more likely to identify maladaptive behaviors as ways of coping, and perceived stressful events as less controllable than controls. These adolescents also had difficulty estimating their personal contributions to the onset of stressors. Rotheram-Borus, Trautman, Dopkins, and Shrout (1990) also administered the MEPS to 77 minority female adolescent suicide attempters, 39 nonsuicidal psychiatric patients, and 23 normal controls. The suicide attempters generated significantly fewer alternatives to problems and were more focused on problems. The results described using the MEPS are not consistent. These results may differ due to different MEPS stories used or different subpopulations studied (Wilson *et al.*, 1996).

Sadowski and Kelley (1993) compared 30 hospitalized adolescent suicide attempters, to 30 nonsuicidal psychiatrically disturbed hospitalized adolescents, and to 30 nonpsychiatrically disturbed nonattempting high school students, on the process of problem solving using the Social Problem-Solving Inventory (SPSI; D'Zurilla & Nezu, 1990). Adolescent suicide attempters had a more negative initial problem orientation and brought more maladaptive cognitive-emotional-behavioral response sets to problematic situations than did the other two groups. However, both suicide attempters and psychiatric controls had similar deficits in problem-solving skills (e.g., generation of alternatives, decision making, and solution implementation) compared with nonpsychiatric controls.

Curry, Miller, Waugh, and Anderson (1992) examined coping responses in 41 psychiatrically hospitalized adolescents. Based on a diagnostic interview, adolescents were classified as nonsuicidal ($n = 29$), suicide ideators ($n = 7$), or suicide attempters ($n = 5$). All adolescents completed the Health and Daily Living Form B (Moos, Cronkite, Billings, & Finney, 1983), which assesses for logical analysis, information seeking, problem solving, affective regulation, and emotional discharge coping. Results revealed a negative association between problem solving and suicide ratings; further, suicide attempters were significantly less likely to use problem-solving than suicide ideators or nonsuicidal adolescents. No other significant findings were reported.

Problem Irresolvability

Orbach, Mikulincer, Blumenson, Mester, and Stein (1999) developed the Subjective Experience of Problem Irresolvability (SEPI) to examine whether adolescents perceive that they are faced with solving irresolvable problems within the family. The SEPI was found to discriminate suicidal adolescents from nonsuicidal psychiatric and normal controls. Orbach *et al.* (1999) hypothesized that repeated experiences with irresolvable family problems results in an adolescent's perception that problems cannot be solved. Their data suggest that intervention might be more effective if it focuses on beliefs about problem solving rather than teaching problem-solving skills.

Research with College Students

Many of the studies that have examined problem solving and suicidality in the past decade have used college students and have focused on relations with suicidal ideation rather than suicide attempt status. It is unclear how these associations will parallel findings with younger teens who have attempted. Nevertheless, several studies are worth noting because they examine different facets of the problem-solving process.

Clum and his colleagues have examined the role of stress and confidence in problem solving. Yang and Clum (1994) studied a group of 101 Asian international students studying in the United States and conducted a path analysis including social support, stress, and problem-solving deficits as measured by the modified MEPS (Schotte & Clum, 1987). They found that problem-solving deficits, and the interaction of life stress and problem-solving deficits, were related to depressive symptoms, hopelessness, and suicidal ideation. They also examined problem-solving confidence and found that confidence directly predicted depressive symptoms and hopelessness, and indirectly predicted suicidal ideation. Clum and Febbraro (1994) assessed interpersonal problem-solving appraisal in a sample of 59 chronically suicidal college students. They found that problem-solving confidence was predictive of the severity of suicidal ideation. Further, stress mediated the relationship between perceived problem-solving skills and the level of suicidal ideation.

D'Zurilla, Chang, Nottingham, and Faccini (1998) examined the relations between problem-solving abilities, as measured by the SPSI-R, and suicide risk in college students. They found that a negative problem orientation was most highly related to hopelessness, depression, and suicide risk. Finally, Mraz, and Runco (1994) studied a sample of 81 undergraduates and assessed them on a number of problem-finding and solving tasks. They found that problem-generation scores, or participants' tendencies to identify many problems, were associated with levels of suicide ideation, even after controlling for levels of stress. The authors suggest that individuals considering suicide may perceive many problems but find few solutions.

ASSESSMENT OF PROBLEM SOLVING

The literature reviewed here suggests that most standard measures of problem solving, which primarily assess an adolescent's ability to solve a problem, do not discriminate suicidal from nonsuicidal adolescents. However, if a clinician suspects that an adolescent seems to have genuine difficulty with problem solving, then either the Means-Ends Problem Solving Procedure, Problem-Solving Inventory, or Social Problem-Solving Inventory may be administered for treatment planning.

The Means-End Problem-Solving Procedure (MEPS; Platt, Spivack, & Bloom, 1975) presents the adolescent with 10 stories, as well as desired outcomes for each story. The adolescent is asked to generate the middle of the story. The stories are then scored for the number of relevant means to the outcome that are generated. A poor score on the MEPS unfortunately does not allow for inference regarding where the difficulty in problem solving lies—for example, in problem orientation, comprehension, or generating solutions and consequences of these solutions (D'Zurilla et al., 1998). Therefore, modifications to the MEPS have been made. These modifications, such as those reported Schotte and Clum (1987), expand on the original MEPS procedure by having the person not only generate a list of potential solutions to a problem but also identify their own problems and evaluate the different solutions, such as by listing pros and cons for each solution (Yang & Clum, 1994).

The Problem-Solving Inventory (PSI; Heppner & Petersen, 1982) is a 32-item process measure that assesses problem-solving appraisal. Three factors have been identified on the scale: problem-solving confidence, approach-avoidance style, and personal control. The Social Problem-Solving Inventory (SPSI; D'Zurilla & Nezu, 1990) is probably the most comprehensive measure of problem solving. Based on the Social Problem-Solving model (D'Zurilla, 1986), this 70-item questionnaire measures both problem orientation and problem-solving skills. There are three subscales in the problem orientation factor, which assess cognition (beliefs, appraisal, attribution), emotion (distress, calm), and behavior (approach, avoidance). The problem-solving skills factor includes four subscales labeled problem definition and formulation, generation of alternative solutions, decision making, and solution implementation and verification. The items themselves reference real-life problem situations. This measure has been used with adolescent suicide attempters (e.g., Sadowski & Kelley, 1993). Recently, a 52-item revised SPSI was constructed based on factor analyses of the original scale (Maydeu-Olivares, & D'Zurilla, 1996). The scales included in the SPSI-R are positive problem orientation, negative problem orientation, rational problem solving, impulsivity/carelessness style, and avoidance style.

CLINICAL IMPLICATIONS

The research reviewed have casts doubt on the idea that adolescent suicide attempters have trait deficits in problem-solving abilities that are substantially worse than other teens, with or without psychiatric disorders. Instead, adolescent suicide attempters seem to perceive themselves as experiencing more stressors. Cognitive distortions regarding a problem and one's ability to solve problems may create a negative attitude toward solving problems. Because they perceive problems as difficult to control or resolve, these adolescents may generate ideas for solutions but may not actually employ them. Adolescent suicide attempters also appear to lack confidence in their ability to solve problems and are more likely to doubt the effectiveness of generated solutions, which may limit their implementation of these solutions. These findings suggest that cognitive distortions regarding problem-solving ability may be the most important factor to address with many adolescents.

Other types of cognitive distortion have been found in adolescent suicide attempters. For example, negative attributional styles have generally been found to be common in adolescent suicide attempters (Spirito, Overholser *et al.*, 1989). In addition, some researchers have found cognitive processing errors (e.g., overgeneralization, catastrophizing) to be evident in this population. Brent, Kolko, Allan, and Brown (1990) compared 42 affectively ill suicidal adolescent inpatients, the majority of whom had attempted suicide in the past, to 14 affectively ill nonsuicidal adolescent patients. The suicidal group reported higher levels of cognitive distortion on the Cognitive Negative Errors Questionnaire (Leitenberg, Yost, & Carroll-Wilson, 1986) than the depressed, nonsuicidal adolescents. Similarly, it may be that depression in adolescents who attempt suicide affects their cognitions regarding their ability to solve problems. It may be helpful to develop an individualized assessment approach that would clarify for a given teen whether skill deficits, lack of problem solving self-confidence, or extremely difficult environmental problems are more central. Clearly, teens will vary on these issues.

From the literature described here, future research is needed to better understand how an individual's problem orientation can vary over time and how negative attitudes and beliefs may interfere with effective implementation of solutions that teens are able to generate. Clinicians working with individual patients should also assess these issues. In the meantime, it may be possible to more directly target the negative thinking that leads teens to doubt either their ability to solve problems or the likely effectiveness of actually engaging in generated solutions. This type of approach may be more effective than a strict problem-solving skills training approach. D'Zurilla *et al.* (1998), based on their work with college students, suggest the following process leading up to suicidal behavior. Suicide attempters, when confronted with a problem that they believe threatens their well-being, blame themselves for the problem, doubt their ability to solve the problem, and view the problem as unsolvable. Given this mind-set, adolescent suicide attempters prefer to avoid or put off trying to solve the problem, recruit others to solve the problem, or wait for the problem to resolve itself. This formulation suggests that clinicians should always first assess the adolescent's perception of the solubility or irresolvability of the problem. When problems are perceived as irresolvable, therapists must practice working through multiple problem situations with adolescents so they can begin to more accurately gauge the solvability of problems. This instruction in turn will encourage adolescents to begin to solve easier problems on their own. Successes with problem solving will help adolescents build confidence, and with greater confidence, greater motivation to address more difficult problems may develop.

The type of problem-solving intervention might vary according to the level of suicidal ideation. For example, concentrating on a positive orientation to problem solving might be sufficient with adolescents whose suicidal ideation is relatively low following a suicide attempt. In more severe cases, a more intensive intervention might be necessary that focuses on both problem orientation and the specific steps of problem solving (D'Zurilla *et al.*, 1998).

Sadowski and Kelley (1993) found that suicide attempters exhibit more emotion dysregulation during problem solving than a comparison group. Therefore, one key in working with adolescent suicide attempters is to help them manage their affect when trying to solve problems. Another suggestion from the literature is that adolescent suicide attempters tend to use avoidant coping responses. These adolescents may avoid making decisions or attempt to solve problems until they are overwhelmed (Sadowski & Kelley, 1993). Thus, affect management strategies may be necessary before attempting to work on problem solving.

REFERENCES

Asarnow, J. R., Carlson, G. A., & Guthrie, D. (1987). Coping strategies, self-perceptions, hopelessness, and perceived family functioning in depressed and suicidal children. *Journal of Consulting and Clinical Psychology, 55*, 361–366.

Asarnow, J. R., & Guthrie, D. (1989). Suicidal behavior, depression, and hopelessness in child psychiatric inpatients. A replication and extension. *Journal of Clinical Child Psychology, 18*, 129–136.

Band, E. B. (1990). Children's coping with diabetes: Understanding the role of cognitive development. *Journal of Pediatric Psychology, 15*, 27–42.

Beck, A. T., Weissman, A., Lester, D., & Trexler, L. (1974). The measurement of pessimism: The Hopelessness Scale. *Journal of Consulting and Clinical Psychology, 62*, 861–865.

Boergers, J., Spirito, A., & Donaldson, D. (1998). Reasons for adolescent suicide attempts: Associations with psychological functioning. *Journal of the American Academy of Child and Adolescent Psychiatry, 37*, 1287–1293.

Brent, D., Holder, D., Kolko, D., Birmaher, B., Baugher, M., Roth, C., Iyengar, S., & Johnson, B. (1997). A clinical psychotherapy trial for adolescent depression comparing cognitive, family, and supportive therapy. *Archives of General Psychiatry, 54*, 877–885.

Brent, D., Kolko, D., Allan, M., & Brown, R. (1990). Suicidality in affectively disordered adolescent inpatients. *Journal of the American Academy of Child and Adolescent Psychiatry, 29*, 586–593.

Brown, L. K., Overholser, J., Spirito, A., & Fritz, G. K. (1991). The correlates of planning in adolescent suicide attempts. *Journal of the American Academy of Child and Adolescent Psychiatry, 30*, 95–99.

Causey, D. L., & Dubow, E. F. (1992). Development of a self-report coping measure for elementary school children. *Journal of Clinical Child Psychology, 21*, 47–59.

Clum, G., & Febbraro, G. (1994). Stress, social support, and problem-solving appraisal/skills: Prediction of suicide severity within a college sample. *Journal of Psychopathology and Behavioral Assessment, 16,* 69–83.

Compas, B. E., Malcarne, V. L., & Fondacaro, K. M. (1988). Coping with stressful events in older children and young adolescents. *Journal of Consulting and Clinical Psychology, 56,* 405–411.

Curry, J. F., Miller, Y., Waugh, S., & Anderson, W. B. (1992). Coping responses in depressed, socially maladjusted, and suicidal adolescents. *Psychological Reports, 71,* 80–82.

deWilde, E., Kienhorst, I., Diekstra, R., & Wolters, W. (1993). The specificity of psychological characteristics of adolescent suicide attempts. *Journal of the American Academy of Child and Adolescent Psychiatry, 32,* 51–59.

Dori, G., & Overhoser, J. (1999). Depression, hopelessness, and self-esteem: Accounting for suicidality in adolescent psychiatric inpatients. *Suicide and Life Threatening Behavior, 29,* 309–318.

D'Zurilla, T. (1986). *Problem-solving Therapy: A social cognitive approach to clinical intervention.* New York.

D'Zurilla, T., Chang, E., Nottingham, E., & Faccini, L. (1998). Social problem-solving deficits and hopelessness, depression, and suicidal risk in college students and psychiatric inpatients. *Journal of Clinical Psychology, 54,* 1091–1107.

D'Zurilla, T., & Mayden-Olivares, A. (1995). Conceptual and methodological issues in social problem-solving assessment. *Behavior Therapy, 26,* 409–432.

D'Zurilla, T., & Nezu, A. (1990). Development and preliminary evaluation of the social problem solving inventory. *Psychological Assessment, 2,* 156–163.

Folkman, S., & Lazarus, R. S. (1980). An analysis of coping in a middle-aged community sample. *Journal of Health and Social Behavior, 21,* 219–239.

Fremouw, W., Callahan, B., & Kashden, J. (1993). Adolescent suicidal risk: Psychological, problem-solving, and environmental factors. *Suicide and Life-Threatening Behavior, 23,* 46–54.

Goldston, D., Daniel, S., Reboussin, B., Reboussin, D., Frazier, P., & Harris, A. (2001). Cognitive risk factors and suicide attempts among formerly hospitalized adolescents: A prospective naturalistic study. *Journal of the American Academy of Child and Adolescent Psychiatry, 40,* 91–99.

Grossi, V., & Violato, C. (1992). Attempted suicide among adolescents: A stepwise discriminant analysis. *Canadian Journal of Behavioural Science, 24,* 410–413.

Guiao, I. Z., & Esparza, D. (1995). Suicidality correlates in Mexican American teens. *Issues in Mental Health Nursing, 16,* 461–479.

Guilford, J., Christensen, P., Merrifield, P., & Wilson, R. (1978). *Alternate uses: Manual of instructions and interpretations.* Orange, CA: Sheridan Psychological Services.

Heppner, P., & Petersen, C. (1982). The development of and implications of a personal problem solving inventory. *Journal of Counseling Psychology, 29,* 66–75.

Kashden, J., Fremouw, W., Callahan, T., & Franzen, M. (1993). Impulsivity in suicidal and nonsuicidal adolescents. *Journal of Abnormal Child Psychology, 21,* 339–352.

Kazdin, A. E., French, N. H., Unis, A. S., Esveldt-Dawson, K., & Sherrick, R. B. (1983). Hopelessness, depression and suicidal intent among psychiatrically disturbed children. *Journal of Consulting and Clinical Psychology, 51,* 504–510.

Kazdin, A. E., Rodgas, A., & Colbus, D. (1986). The Hopelessness Scale for Children: Psychometric characteristics and concurrent validity. *Journal of Consulting and Clinical Psychology, 54,* 241–245.

Kienhorst, W., deWilde, E., van den Bout, J., Diekstra, R., & Wolters, W. (1990). Characteristics of suicide attempters in a population-based sample of Dutch adolescents. *British Journal of Psychiatry, 156*, 243–248.

King, C. A., Raskin, A., Gdowski, C. L., Butkus, M., & Opipari, L. (1990). Psychosocial factors associated with urban adolescent female suicide attempts. *Journal of the American Academy of Child and Adolescent Psychiatry, 29*, 289–294.

Klimes-Dougan, B., Free, K., Ronsaville, D., Stilwell, J., Welsh, C. J., & Radke-Yarrow, M. (1999). Suicidal ideation and attempts: A longitudinal investigation of children of depressed and well mothers. *Journal of the American Academy of Child and Adolescent Psychiatry, 38*, 651–659.

Lazarus, R. S. (1981). The stress and coping paradigm. In C. Eisdoifer, C. Cohen, A. Kleinman, & P. Maxin (Eds.), *Models for Clinical Psychopathology* (pp. 177–214). Jamaica, NY: Spectrum Publications.

Lazarus, R., & Folkman, S. (1984). *Stress, appraisal, and coping.* New York: Springer.

Leitenberg, H., Yost, L., & Carroll-Wilson, M. (1986). Negative cognitive errors in children: Questionnaire development, normative data, and comparisons between children with and without self-reported symptoms of depression, low self-esteem, and evaluation anxiety. *Journal of Consulting and Clinical Psychology, 54*, 528–536.

Lewinsohn, P., Rohde, P., & Seeley, J. R. (1993). Psychosocial characteristics of adolescents with a history of suicide attempt. *Journal of the American Academy of Child and Adolescent Psychiatry, 32*, 60–68.

Marciano, P. L., & Kazdin, A. E. (1994). Self-esteem, depression, hopelessness, and suicidal intent among psychiatrically disturbed inpatient children. *Journal of Clinical Child Psychology, 23*, 151–160.

Maydeu-Olivares, A, & D'Zurilla, T. J. (1996). A factor-analytic study of the social problem-solving inventory: An integration of theory and data. *Cognitive Therapy and Research, 20*, 115–133.

McLaughlin, J., Miller, P., & Warwick, H. (1996). Deliberate self-harm in adolescents: Hopelessness, depression, problems and problem-solving. *Journal of Adolescence, 19*, 523–532.

Melges, F., & Bowlby, J. (1969). Types of hopelessness in psychopathological process. *Archives of General Psychiatry, 20*, 690–699.

Miller, S. M., Sherman, H. D., Combs, C., & Kruus, L. (1992). Patterns of coping with short-term medical and dental stressors: Nature, complications, and future directions. In A. M. LaGreca, L. J. Siegel, J. L. Wallander, & C. E. Walker (Eds.), *Stress and coping in child health* (pp. 157–190). New York: Guilford.

Mitchell, M. G., & Rosenthal, D. M. (1992). Suicidal adolescents: Family dynamics and the effects of lethality and hopelessness. *Journal of Youth and Adolescence, 21*, 23–33.

Moos, R., Cronkite, R., Billings, A., & Finney, J. (1983). *Health and daily living form manual.* Palo Alto, CA: Unpublished manuscript, Social Ecology Lab, Department of Psychiatry and Behavioral Sciences, Stanford University.

Morano, C. D., Cisler, R. A., & Lemerond, J. (1993). Risk factors for adolescent suicidal behavior: Loss, insufficient familial support, and hopelessness. *Adolescence, 28*, 851–865.

Mraz, W., & Runco, M. (1994). Suicide ideation and creative problem solving. *Suicide and Life-Threatening Behavior, 24*, 38–47.

Negron, R., Piacentini, J., Graae, F., Davies, M., & Shaffer, D. (1997). Microanalysis of adolescent suicide attempters and ideators during the acute suicidal episode. *Journal of the American Academy of Child and Adolescent Psychiatry, 36*, 1512–1519.

Orbach, I., Mikulincer, M., Blumenson, R., Mester, R., & Stein, D. (1999). The subjective experience of problem irresolvability and suicidal behavior: Dynamics and measurement. *Suicide and Life-Threatening Behavior, 29*, 150–164.

Parker, G. B., & Brown, L. B. (1979). Repertoires of response to potential precipitants to depression. *Australian and New Zealand Journal of Psychiatry, 13*, 327–333.

Patterson, J., & McCubbin, J. (1983). *ACOPE-Adolescent Coping Orientation for Problem Experiences*, University of Wisconsin, Madison (Unpublished manuscript).

Pinto, A., & Whisman, M. (1996). Negative affect and cognitive biases in suicidal and nonsuicidal hospitalized adolescents. *Journal of the American Academy of Child and Adolescent Psychiatry, 35*, 158–165.

Platt, J., Spivack, G., & Bloom, W. (1975). *Manual for the Means-End Problem Solving Procedure (MEPS): A measure of interpersonal problem-solving skills*. Philadelphia: Hahnemann Medical College and Hospital, Department of Mental Health Sciences.

Puskar, K., Hoover, C., & Miewald, C. (1992). Suicidal and nonsuicidal coping methods of adolescents. *Perspectives in Psychiatric Care, 28*, 15–20.

Rippere, V. (1977). Some cognitive dimensions of anti-depressive behavior. *Behavior Research and Therapy, 15*, 57–63.

Rohde, P., Lewinsohn, P. M., Tilson, M., & Seeley, J. R. (1990). Dimensionality of coping and its relationship to depression. *Journal of Personality and Social Psychology, 58*, 499–511.

Rohde, P., Seeley, J. R., & Mace, D. E. (1997). Correlates of suicidal behavior in a juvenile detention population. *Suicide and Life-Threatening Behavior, 27*, 164–175.

Rosenbaum, M. (1980). A schedule for assessing self-control behaviors: Preliminary findings. *Behavior Therapy, 11*, 109–121.

Rotheram-Borus, M. J., & Trautman, P. D. (1988). Hopelessness, depression and suicidal intent among adolescent suicide attempters. *Journal of the American Academy of Child and Adolescent Psychiatry, 127*, 700–704.

Rotheram-Borus, M. J., Trautman, P. D., Dopkins, S., & Shrout, P. (1990). Cognitive style and pleasant activities among female adolescent suicide attempters. *Journal of Consulting and Clinical Psychology, 58*, 554–561.

Sadowski, C., & Kelley, M. L. (1993). Social problem solving in suicidal adolescents. *Journal of Consulting and Clinical Psychology, 61*, 121–127.

Schotte, D., & Clum, G. (1987). Problem-solving studies in suicidal psychiatric patients. *Journal of Consulting and Clinical Psychology, 55*, 49–54.

Spirito, A., Brown, L., Overholser, J., & Fritz, G. (1989). Attempted suicide in adolescence: A review and critique of the literature. *Clinical Psychology Review, 9*, 335–363.

Spirito, A., Overholser, J., & Stark, L. J. (1989). Common problems and coping strategies II: Findings with adolescent suicide attempters. *Journal of Abnormal Child Psychology, 17*, 213–221.

Spirito, A., Stark, L., & Williams, C. (1988). Development of a brief checklist to assess coping in pediatric patients. *Journal of Pediatric Psychology, 13*, 555–574.

Spirito, A., Williams, C., Stark, L. J., & Hart, K. (1988). The Hopelessness Scale for Children: Psychometric properties and clinical utility with normal and emotionally disturbed adolescents. *Journal of Abnormal Child Psychology, 16*, 445–458.

Swedo, S., Rettew, D., Kuppenheimer, M., Lunn, D., Dolan, S., & Goldberger, E. (1991). Can adolescent suicide attempters be distinguished from at-risk adolescents? *Pediatrics, 88*, 620–629.

Wilson, K., Stelzer, J., Bergman, J., Kral, M., Inayatullah, M., & Elliot, C. (1996). Problem solving, stress, and coping in adolescent suicide attempts. *Suicide and Life-Threatening Behavior, 25*, 241–261.

Yang, B., & Clum, G. (1994). Life stress, social support, and problem-solving skills predictive of depressive symptoms, hopelessness, and suicide ideation in an Asian student population: A test of a model. *Suicide and Life-Threatening Behavior, 24*, 127–139.

CHAPTER 6

Behavioral Factors: Substance Use

Robyn Mehlenbeck, Anthony Spirito, Nancy Barnett, and James Overholser

RATES OF SUBSTANCE USE

In their review article, Spirito, Brown, Overholser, and Fritz (1989) found substance use to be an important risk factor associated with adolescent suicide attempts. Suicide attempters reported high rates of substance use, ranging from 23 to 42%. Overall, the researchers observed a strong relationship between substance abuse and attempted suicide, particularly lethal attempts (Spirito *et al.*, 1989). Only one study found that rates of substance use were not significantly higher in suicide attempters as compared to a group of nonsuicidal adolescents referred for psychiatric evaluation (Spirito, Stark, Fristad, Hart, & Owens-Stively, 1987). In his review of the literature, Crumley (1990) also found a significant association between suicidal behavior and substance use in adolescents. Crumley concluded that substance use is related to increased incidence, increased repetitiveness, increased seriousness of intent, and increased medical lethality of adolescent suicide attempts.

In the past decade, many studies have explored the relationship between substance abuse and suicide attempts. The large number of these studies underscores the importance of substance abuse as a risk factor for suicidal behavior. This review approaches the literature from three different perspectives. First, articles are examined that focus on substance use among suicide attempters in various clinical samples, including attempters in inpatient and outpatient settings and delinquent or homeless youth. A second approach examines suicide attempts in adolescent substance users. The third group of studies examines the relationship between substance abuse and suicide attempts in adolescent community samples. By reviewing this diverse range of literature, we hope to evaluate the role that substance use can play in suicidal behavior by adolescents.

SUBSTANCE USE AMONG PSYCHIATRIC INPATIENT SUICIDE ATTEMPTERS

A high rate of substance use has been seen in adolescents admitted to the hospital (either a general or psychiatric hospital) following a suicide attempt. Rates of alcohol use or other drug use range from 35% (Swedo *et al.*, 1991) to 42% (Hawton & Fagg, 1992). Swedo and colleagues (1991) examined 20 suicide attempters, a clinical comparison group of 14 adolescents with a known risk factor for a suicide attempt such as a suicidal ideation or depression, and 34 controls from a pediatric outpatient clinic. Results showed that 100% of attempters admitted to having tried alcohol compared to 94% of the clinical comparison group and 66% of the control group. Marijuana use was also fairly high in the attempter group (35%) and the clinical comparison group (57%) but not in the control group (10%). These results suggest that substance use may serve as a nonspecific risk factor for suicidal behavior.

The relationship between substance use and suicidal behavior may be influenced by the time of the substance consumption. One study found that at least 25% of patients presenting for a suicide attempt had been drinking alcohol in the 6 hours prior to the attempt (Hawton & Fagg, 1992). This figure was higher in males (38.7%) than in females (20.8%). In a sample of 422 adolescent suicide attempters, Kotila and Lonquist (1988) reported that 40% of females and 53% of males had consumed alcohol prior to the attempt. Alcohol use at the time of the attempt may play a critical role in the suicidal act. Many people behave in a less controlled and less inhibited manner when under the influence of alcohol.

It seems likely that substance use may influence suicidal behavior by its disinhibiting effects. The adolescent male will become more impulsive and irresponsible while under the influence of alcohol or marijuana. Suicidal behavior may be seen as part of a larger array of impulsive acts. Alcohol consumption may promote the depressed and suicidal adolescent to act on these urges.

A significant association has been found between the presence of an affective disorder and substance abuse in adolescent suicide attempters (Brent, Kolko, Allan, & Brown, 1990). Brent and colleagues (1990) evaluated 42 depressed and suicidal adolescents, compared to 14 nonsuicidal, depressed adolescents. The suicidal group included adolescents hospitalized because of suicidal ideation, suicide threats, or suicide attempts. Among the 28 suicide attempters, the lethality of suicidal intent was significantly correlated with substance abuse.

Overholser, Freiheit, and DiFilippo (1997) examined emotional distress and substance abuse in a sample of 115 adolescent suicide attempters. Results showed that suicidal intent was closely related to depression and hopelessness for all subjects. Furthermore, alcohol abuse by males was significantly related to depression and hopelessness but not suicidal intent. Alcohol use by females was not related to depression, hopelessness, or suicidal intent. Thus, among adolescent males, alcohol use may be indirectly related to suicidality via its relationship with depression and hopelessness.

Kelly, Lynch, Donovan, and Clark (in press) tested 482 adolescents, more than half of whom were receiving treatment at inpatient or residential settings. Major depression and alcohol use disorders increased the risk for a suicide attempt among both males and females. Among females, conduct disorder was also an independent predictor of suicide attempts. Kelly *et al.* (in press) found a statistical trend for alcohol use disorders, in combination with conduct disorders, to increase the risk for suicide attempts among females almost three-fold compared to those with only one of these conditions.

King and colleagues (1996) examined 73 adolescent psychiatric inpatients with major depression compared to 30 inpatient adolescents who met diagnostic criteria for both major depression and substance abuse. The level of suicidal ideation and behavior in the overall sample was high, with 82% of all subjects endorsing significant suicidal ideation, intent, or behavior within the 6 months prior to hospitalization. No differences were seen across groups in the presence or severity of suicidal ideation or the severity of prior suicide attempts. However, King and colleagues (1996) found that depressed females who abuse alcohol or other drugs tend to report depressive episodes that began earlier and last longer than depressed female adolescents who do not abuse alcohol or other drugs. Thus, substance abuse by adolescent females may reflect a failed attempt to regulate depressive tendencies or, alternatively, substance abuse may eventually result in depression. Also, depressed females who abused substances were likely to be diagnosed with a comorbid conduct disorder.

There may be few differences between adolescents who attempt suicide and those who report suicidal ideation. Brent, Kolko, and colleagues (1993) examined suicidal adolescents compared to a psychiatric, non-suicidal control group. The observed rates of substance abuse did not significantly differentiate suicide attempters (38%), ideators (30%), or non-suicidal (28%) adolescents. In contrast, Kosky, Silburn, and Zubrick (1990) found that 22% of child and adolescent suicide attempters had a history of alcohol or drug use whereas only 5% of suicidal ideators admitted to substance use. Thus, further research is needed to clarify the subtle but important differences between suicide attempters and ideators.

In a study of completed suicide, Brent and colleagues (1994) evaluated 63 adolescent suicide victims with a history of affective illness as compared to 23 adolescent community controls who reported a history of affective illness. Results showed that comorbid substance abuse was significantly higher in the suicide victims than the community controls, despite the common presence of a history of affective illness in both groups. Thus, the combination of substance abuse and depression is more likely to lead to lethal suicidal behavior than either factor alone. Brent and colleagues (1994) suggest that patients with early onset, chronic depression complicated by substance use are at high risk for lethal suicidal behavior.

SUBSTANCE USE IN OTHER CLINICAL SAMPLES

Several other studies have examined the relationship between substance use and suicide attempts in specific clinical samples. These samples include psychiatric outpatients, adolescent delinquents, runaway and homeless youth, and drug users. Each of these samples will be reviewed in an attempt to identify general patterns that can be observed across settings.

Outpatients

In a longitudinal study of 183 psychiatric outpatients, Kovacs, Goldstein, and Gatsonis (1993) found that children and adolescents who had a diagnosis of substance abuse or conduct disorder had no higher rate of suicide attempts than patients with other nonaffective disorder diagnoses. However, the highest rate of suicide attempts was seen in the adolescents with comorbid diagnoses of substance abuse and a depressive disorder (Kovacs et al., 1993). Thus, the combined presence of depression and substance abuse may place the adolescent at significantly elevated risk for suicidal behavior.

In a small study, Jones (1997) evaluated 15 African-American adolescent suicide attempters seen in an emergency department compared to a control group of 15 adolescents seen in the same emergency department for a minor illness. The suicide attempters reported higher levels of alcohol and drug use. Fombonne (1998) examined data from more than 6000 patients, 8 to 18 years old, who were seen in a child psychiatric service in London over a 20-year period from 1970 to 1990. During this time period, suicidal behavior increased significantly among adolescent males. Alcohol use was associated with a substantial increase in suicidal behavior. In a related study, Wannan and Fombonne (1998) found that substance abuse, depression, and adult-child relationship disturbance predicted suicidal behavior in both boys and girls. Thus, in several different outpatient settings, results tend to converge on the finding that depression and substance abuse combine in a lethal manner. Either depression or alcohol use may be related to a variety of adjustment issues during adolescence. However, the combined presence of depression and alcohol abuse reflects a serious problem that often reveals suicidal tendencies.

Delinquent Adolescents

Three studies have examined substance abuse and suicidal behavior in delinquent adolescents. Putnins (1995) examined 126 adolescent offenders in Australia (ages 12 to 18, with 87% falling between the ages of 14 to 17). Results showed that adolescents who had reported a history of deliberate self-injury and attempted suicide could be differentiated from adolescents who reported no suicidal behavior or ideation based on their frequency of alcohol use. Suicidal adolescents reported more frequent alcohol use. Marijuana use did not differ between the two groups, although other substances that are infrequently used by student samples, including hallucinogens and narcotics, were used at rates of two to six times higher in the suicide attempter group than those without suicidal behavior (Putnins, 1995).

In contrast to these findings, Kempton and Forehand (1992) did not find that substance abuse was related to suicide attempts in their study of 51 male juvenile delinquents, ages 11 to 18 years. Using a logistic regression analysis, the only significant variable differentiating attempters from nonattempters was race: suicide attempts were three times more common in white versus African-American youth. Substance abuse was not found to differentiate suicide attempters from nonattempters. However, statistical considerations, including the small number of attempters in the study ($n = 15$) and the high proportion of African Americans in the sample (70%), may account for the lack of findings.

Rohde, Seely, and Mace (1997) examined 60 juvenile delinquents (average age = 14.9 years old). Results revealed no differences in alcohol or drug use between attempters and nonattempters. Interestingly, there was a statistical trend for cannabis abuse but not alcohol abuse to be associated with lower rates of suicide attempts. It was suggested that cannabis use may function as a form of escapist coping behavior in delinquent adolescents. Although excessive reliance on alcohol use may also be a maladaptive coping behavior like marijuana use, alcohol use seems to be more highly related to suicidal behavior.

Delinquents seem to be quite different from adolescent psychiatric patients. Thus, alcohol abuse may reflect different issues, different needs, and different problems in delinquents compared to psychiatric patients. We cannot be sure that we are dealing with the same degree or type of emotional distress when we examine delinquent youth. Substance abuse by delinquent youth may reflect antisocial tendencies rather than suicide risk. Furthermore, studies on delinquent samples need to include measures of depression in order to examine the comorbid presence of depression and substance abuse.

Runaway and Homeless Adolescents

Runaway and homeless adolescents have received attention regarding suicidal behavior and substance use. In the past decade, five studies have looked at this relationship. In a study of 576 runaway adolescents (12 to 17 years old), Rotheram-Borus (1993) found that 37% had attempted suicide in the past, and 23% of the suicide attempters reported consuming alcohol and drugs prior to the attempt. Stiffman (1989) found that among a sample of 291 shelter adolescents (ages 12 to 18), 30% reported a previous suicide attempt. Those who had attempted suicide were three times more likely than nonattempters to have experienced problems with "heavy" alcohol use and two times more likely to report "regular" illicit drug use.

Yoder, Hoyt, and Whitback (1998) found similar results in their study of 297 homeless and runaway adolescents (ages 12 to 21). Homeless and runaway adolescents who had attempted suicide were significantly more likely to have a history of drug use than those who had not attempted suicide. In a large epidemiologic study, Gould and colleagues (1998) found that adolescents who had run away from home were nearly three times more likely to have engaged in suicidal behavior, even after controlling for psychiatric disorders.

Greene and Ringwalt (1996) evaluated 640 shelter adolescents (ages 12 to 17) and 600 street adolescents (ages 18 to 21) from across the United States. Results directly examined the relationship between suicide attempts and substance use. Shelter and street adolescents who had used substances (particularly sedatives, hallucinogens, and inhalants) were significantly more likely to have attempted suicide at some time in their lives compared to similar adolescents who had not used substances. Overall, for both shelter and street adolescents, substance use (i.e., marijuana, heroin, or analgesic use) increased the odds of a suicide attempt almost twofold. Of those who had attempted suicide, 28% of the shelter sample and 49% of the street sample admitted to alcohol or drug use in the two days before their most recent suicide attempt. Sedative use increased the odds of a suicide attempt by almost seven-fold in the shelter sample.

These findings show the potentially strong relationship between drug abuse and suicidal behavior. When working with runaway teens, it is important to evaluate the presence of substance abuse, family history of substance abuse, and lifetime presence of prior suicidal acts.

Community Clinics

Kipke, Montgomery, and MacKenzie (1993) surveyed a group of 1121 youth, ages 12 to 24, who were seen at a free primary care health clinic regarding adolescent health risk behaviors. The clinic population included 698 runaway, homeless youth in the area of the clinic and 423 nonhomeless but high-risk youth with little access to health care services. A history of attempted suicide was found to be associated with substance use in both the homeless and nonhomeless groups. In nonhomeless youth, alcohol and marijuana use increased the odds of a suicide almost twofold. The odds were slightly higher for users of other drugs, including stimulants and hallucinogens, and almost threefold for users of narcotics/analgesics and intravenous drugs.

SUICIDE ATTEMPTS AMONG ADOLESCENT SUBSTANCE ABUSERS

High rates of suicidal ideation and prior suicide attempts have been reported by adolescents who were receiving treatment for substance use or abuse. In one study of 298 adolescent patients (ages 13 to 19) who abused drugs (predominantly marijuana, hashish, and alcohol), 67% of the patients reported suicidal ideation, and 30% admitted to at least one prior suicide attempt (Berman & Schwartz, 1990). Adolescents who admitted to a prior suicide attempt were compared to nonattempters (matched for age and gender). Attempters reported significantly more depression and were more likely to report suicidal ideation during their drug treatment. Berman and Schwartz (1990) also found that both the wish to hurt oneself and actual suicide attempts increased significantly after the onset of drug use, with 78% of the suicide attempts occurring after the drug use began, and 40% of the suicide attempter sample reported using drugs within 8 hours of their suicide attempt. Thus, drug use is closely aligned with suicidal behavior. If an adolescent tries to cope with emotional distress through intoxication (or other recreational drug use), the situation is unlikely to improve and will often get worse. The risk of suicide is likely to increase. Furthermore, acute intoxication can impair judgment and increase impulsivity, creating additional risk factors for suicidal acts.

High rates of suicide attempts have been found in a group of adolescents receiving residential treatment for substance abuse. Deykin and Buka (1994) evaluated 300 adolescent drug abusers (ages 15 to 19) as part of their residential treatment for drug abuse. Suicidal ideation was common, with 40% of the males and 75% of the females reporting thoughts of suicide. Furthermore, previous suicide attempts were common, with 28% of males and 60% of females reporting at least one prior suicide attempt. Overall, the rates of suicidal ideation and attempts were quite high in this sample of adolescent drug users. These rates were five to seven times higher than the prevalence of suicidal ideation and attempts found in the general population.

SUBSTANCE USE AND SUICIDE ATTEMPTS IN COMMUNITY SAMPLES

The relationship between substance use and suicide attempts can also be explored through surveys of adolescents in community settings. These data are typically collected as part of a large survey, such as those conducted by the Centers for Disease Control with the Youth Risk Behavior Surveillance Survey (YRBS), examining a number of adolescent health risk behaviors. Thus, most of the data are cross-sectional and correlational. The majority of the data have been collected in school settings. For example, data from the 1993 YRBS national survey of more than 16,000 students from 155 schools revealed that alcohol use, binge drinking, and marijuana use significantly increased the risk for a planned suicide attempt, but not suicidal ideation (Simon & Crosby, 2000).

In a sample of 3764 high school students in South Carolina (Garrison, McKeown, Valois, & Vincent, 1993), 7.5% of the students reported having made a suicide attempt in the previous year. Although female gender was the most consistent predictor of suicide attempts, cigarette use, alcohol use, and illicit drug use were all significant predictors of suicide attempts. For suicide attempts requiring medical attention (seen in 1.5% of the sample), marijuana and alcohol use were at least twice as prevalent as was substance use in the nonattempter sample. Other drugs, such as intravenous drugs and cocaine, were three to six times as prevalent. Thus, even in community samples, suicide risk is increased by the presence of drug use.

Similar patterns have been found in high schools in Hawaii. Of 1779 native Hawaiian high school students, 4.3% reported a suicide attempt within the prior 6 months (Yuen *et al.*, 1996). Attempters endorsed twice the number of substance abuse symptoms as did nonattempters. A logistic regression analysis revealed that substance abuse symptoms were a significant predictor of suicide attempts, as were depressive symptoms and perceived family support.

In North Carolina, the YRBS survey was administered to 3064 high school students, with 4.5% reporting having made a suicide attempt in the past year (Felts, Chenier, & Barnes, 1992). Substance use was shown to correlate significantly with suicidal ideation and attempts, with cocaine use being most closely associated with a suicide attempt. This was followed by alcohol use, marijuana use, and needle drug use, all of which were significantly correlated with suicide attempts. Vannatta (1996) also studied the relationship between suicidal behavior and substance use in 3461 junior high and high school students. Overall rates of substance use in the 30 days prior to administering this survey were between 25% (over-the-counter drugs) and 41% (alcohol). Approximately 21% of the sample reported contemplating suicide in the prior 30 days, with 17% reporting an actual attempt. Alcohol use was a predictor of suicide attempt for males, while over-the-counter drug use was a significant predictor of a suicide attempt for females.

In examining rates of psychiatric comorbidity and suicide attempts in junior high and high school students, Wagner, Cole, and Schwaitzman (1996) surveyed 1050 adolescents in grades 7 through 12. Of the sample, 14% of the adolescents reported a prior suicide attempt. Youth who reported prior alcohol and other drug use were significantly more likely to have made a prior suicide attempt. The wording of the questions did not make it possible to determine whether current drug use was related to a prior suicide attempt or vice versa. Adolescents with comorbid self-reported depression and alcohol use were more likely to have made a suicide attempt than those with alcohol use or depression alone. Adolescents with comorbid depression and drug use were more likely to have attempted suicide than those reporting depression alone but not more likely than those reporting only drug use. A similar pattern was found for comorbid conduct problems and alcohol or drug use. Overall, the Wagner *et al.* (1996) findings indicate that comorbid substance use and depression or conduct problems increases the likelihood of high school students reporting a prior attempt. However, comorbidity did not increase the risk of a suicide attempt in students compared to those reporting drug use alone. These findings suggest that high school students who present with substance use, comorbid with depression or conduct problems, as well as students who present with drug use alone are more likely to report suicide attempts than students without comorbid disorders. Thus, when working in a school setting, professionals should evaluate suicide risk whenever working with a teen who has been abusing drugs or who displays the comorbid presence of depression and alcohol use.

Reifman and Windle (1995) examined the relationship between suicidal behavior and alcohol consumption longitudinally in students from two different high schools. There were 662 students in the larger school, and 283 students in the smaller school. In the smaller cohort, alcohol consumption at baseline predicted suicidal behavior at 6-month follow-up, even after statistically controlling for suicidal behavior at time one. In both samples, comorbid alcohol consumption and depression predicted suicidal behavior prospectively, again highlighting the increased risk for suicide attempt when comorbid depression and alcohol use are present. Further analyses revealed that compared to ideators, suicide attempters were more likely to report using substances to cope with stressors and to have a higher proportion of substance-using peers. Thus, motives for alcohol use should be investigated as part of a comprehensive evaluation, because they suggest potential areas of investigation in psychotherapy.

Several relevant studies have been conducted in Europe. As part of a larger survey study in the Netherlands, Garnefski, Diekstra, and detteus (1992) examined the relationship between adolescent suicide attempts and substance use. A total of 570 15- and 16-year old high school students were selected for this study; one group was made up of students with a history of previous suicide attempts (285 students), and a matched control group was composed of students with no history of suicide attempts (285 students). Results showed that both male and female suicide attempters reported spending significantly more money on drugs than nonattempters, and female attempters spent significantly more money on alcohol than female nonattempters. Similar findings were found in a population of 9393 Dutch adolescents (Kienhorst, deWilde, van den Bout, Diekstra, & Wolters, 1990). Adolescents who had attempted suicide (2.2% of the total sample) reported greater use of both soft and hard drugs, as well as alcohol, in the week prior to the survey. After suicidal thoughts, use of soft drugs was the most significant predictor of suicide attempts. These studies demonstrate that the relationship between substance use and suicidal behavior holds across cultures.

Gender Differences

Adcock, Nagy, and Simpson (1991) found gender differences in a sample of 3803 junior high and senior high school students regarding both rates of substance use and suicide attempts. Males reported significantly higher rates of alcohol use in the 30 days prior to the survey (54% versus 38% for females), although more females (19%) reported attempting suicide compared to males (12%). To examine high-risk behaviors by adolescents, Adcock and colleagues combined alcohol consumption with another high-risk behavior, sexual intercourse. Students reporting both high-risk behaviors were almost three times as likely to have attempted suicide than students who reported no alcohol consumption and no history of sexual intercourse. This finding was observed for both males and females. Thus, the relationship between alcohol use and suicide risk is complex. Alcohol use alone may not be a significant predictor of suicide. However, alcohol use combined with other problematic behaviors may reflect emotional distress, a chaotic lifestyle, or a lack of parental supervision, all capable of adding to the adolescent's burden, and potentially increasing the risk of suicide.

The relationships between alcohol use and suicide ideation and attempts were examined as part of the National Adolescent Student Health Survey that was administered to 11,400 8th and 10th graders in the United States (Windle, Miller-Tutzauer, & Domenico 1992). Although the results were split by gender and age, a consistent pattern was observed. In students who reported heavy alcohol consumption (greater than six drinking occasions per month), both 8th- and 10th-grade students reported more suicide attempts than those in the light consumption or abstaining groups. More important, in the heavy consumption group, 37% of 8th-grade females and 39% of 10th-grade females had attempted suicide. In the heavy consumption group, 28% of 8th-grade males and 22% of 10th-grade males had attempted suicide. When compared to abstainers, even those who endorsed light alcohol consumption (one to five times in the month) had a greatly increased incidence of suicide attempts (rates ranged from 11 to 22% versus 6 to 11% for abstainers). Overall, the rate of suicide attempts increased significantly with the increased level of alcohol use for both age groups and genders.

Other studies have found gender differences in the relationship between suicide attempts and substance use. Levy and Deykin (1989) examined 424 older adolescent students (ages 16 to 19) and found that 3.5% of the sample had attempted suicide. The odds of a suicide attempt were almost four times greater if substance use was also diagnosed. A small gender difference was also apparent, with substance-using males (11%) reporting significantly higher levels of suicide attempts than substance-using females (8.7%).

Kinkel, Bailey, and Josef (1989) surveyed 2690 junior high and high school students and found gender differences in rates of suicide attempts, as well as evidence for substance use as a significant risk factor. Females were twice as likely to report a previous suicide attempt than males. Females who reported high frequency of alcohol use (10 or more occasions over the prior month) were almost twice as likely to report a suicide attempt than those who reported a low frequency of alcohol use (14%

versus 8%). This finding was not found for males, although males who reported alcohol use were more likely to report a suicide attempt than those who did not report alcohol use. A similar pattern was noted for marijuana use, in that heavy-use females were more likely to report a suicide attempt than low-to-moderate-use females. Although the findings differ, these studies emphasize the importance of examining gender differences in relation to substance use and suicide attempts. It appears that heavy substance use, particularly for younger females, is an important risk factor for a suicide attempt, while in older adolescents it may put males at a slightly greater risk.

Ethnicity

Ethnic differences have been found when examining the relationship between suicide attempts and substance use. In a longitudinal study of 6010 6th through 8th grade males, Vega, Gil, Warheit, Apospori, and Zimmerman (1993) found that 8.2% of the total sample had reported suicide attempts in the past year. The rates of attempts ranged for different ethnic groups, from 6.7% of Caribbean blacks to 11.4% of Haitians, 8.5% Cuban Americans, and 9% other Hispanics (not Cuban Americans). Use of any recreational drug (with the exception of alcohol) was a clear and significant risk factor for suicide attempts across all ethnic groups. Psychoactive drug use was found to be an important predictor of suicide attempts among Hispanics, African-Americans and White non-Hispanics, even when preexisting suicidal ideation and previous attempts were statistically controlled. Both legal and illegal drug use significantly contributed to suicide attempts in the Other Hispanic sample.

SURVEYS IN GENERAL POPULATION SETTINGS

The relationship between psychopathology (including substance use disorders) and suicide attempts was examined as part of the Methods of the Epidemiology of Child and Adolescent Mental Disorders Study (MECA) (Gould et al., 1998). The MECA study targeted youth, ages 9 to 17, in Connecticut, Georgia, New York, and Puerto Rico (for further methodology, see Lahey, Flagg, & Bird, 1996). Substance abuse/dependence was one of only two factors (the other being separation anxiety) that differentiated suicide ideators from attempters. Suicide attempters reported significantly more symptoms of both substance abuse and separation anxiety. Substance abuse/dependence was independently associated with an increased risk of suicide attempt, over eight times that of youth who had not used substances. Similar to the study by Wagner *et al.* (1996), comorbidity (i.e., drug abuse plus either depression or conduct problems) was found in almost half of the attempters (47.6%) compared to 7.7% of the nonsuicidal youth.

Juon and Ensminger (1997) followed a community sample of African-American youth from first grade (original sample of 1242 youth) through adolescence (939 mothers/705 teenagers were located and participated) to young adulthood in order to examine prospectively the predictors of suicidal behavior. A total of 4.1% of the sample stated that they had attempted suicide, with 5.4% of females compared to 2.6% of males admitting to suicide attempts. Alcohol use was reported by 90% of the sample respondents during adolescence and, consequently, was not related to differential rates of suicidal behavior. Interestingly, self-rated drug use was not associated with suicidal behaviors during adolescence for either males or females, with the exception of cocaine and/or marijuana use for females. In young adulthood, drug use emerged as a significant risk factor for suicide attempts for both males and females. These findings suggest that among African-American youth, drug use experimentation during adolescence is common and is not associated with suicidal behavior. However, when substance use continues into young adulthood, it may result in abuse and can be accompanied by suicidal behavior.

Wunderlich, Bronisch, and Wittchen (1998) randomly sampled a group of 3021 young adults (ages 14–24) in Munich, Germany, to examine the relationship between suicide attempts and comorbid psychiatric disorders in adolescents and young adults. Findings indicated that the presence of any substance use disorder increased the chance of suicide attempt almost three-fold. Of the total sample, 4.6% met diagnostic criteria for illicit substance abuse/dependence, 18.8% met criteria for nicotine dependency, and 15.9% met criteria for alcohol abuse/dependency. Much higher rates were found for the suicide attempters: 20% met diagnostic criteria for illicit substance abuse/dependence, 51.7% met criteria for nicotine dependence, and 35% met criteria for alcohol abuse/dependence. Thus, suicide attempts were associated with higher rates of drug abuse and dependence.

A large survey study in Norway with more than 10,000 adolescents (Rossow & Wichstrom, 1994) examined the incidence of substance use and attempted suicide. Alcohol use was associated with an almost three-fold increase in attempted suicide in both boys and girls. Marijuana use was associated with a four-fold increase in attempted suicide in boys and girls and an almost three times higher risk in girls. Thus, the general pattern holds in several countries. Higher rates of substance use are seen in adolescents who have attempted suicide. Conversely, higher rates of suicide attempt are seen in adolescents who abuse substances, especially when other problems are also present.

SUBSTANCE USE AND SUICIDAL IDEATION IN COMMUNITY SAMPLES

Three studies have examined predictors of suicidal ideation, but not actual suicide attempts, in high school samples. In the first study, Kirkpatrick-Smith, Rich, Bonner, and Jans (1991–1992) found that substance use was an independent predictor of suicidal ideation in a sample of 790 adolescents. DeMan, Labreacher-Gauthier, and LeDuc (1993) conducted a survey study in a high school sample of 558 students in Quebec and found that drug and alcohol use were positively related to suicidal ideation. In a cross-cultural study of adolescents in France and Quebec, Choquet, Koves, and Poutignat (1993) reported similar findings regarding the relationship between suicidal ideation and substance use. Although they did not assess suicide attempts, their findings are notable in that 10% of the French adolescents and 15% of the Canadian adolescents endorsed significant suicidal ideation. The risk of significant suicidal ideation ranged from 1.5 (for regular tobacco use) to 4.9 (for illicit drug use) times greater if an adolescent endorsed substance use than if no substance use was present. Similar patterns were found in both countries for tobacco use, illicit drug use, and use of psychotropic medications. Alcohol use differentiated suicidal ideators from nonideators only in Canada which may be related to the acceptance of daily alcohol consumption in France. Thus, when we consider suicidal ideation to be an important precursor to suicidal acts, we find similar patterns of risk. Adolescent drug use serves as a risk factor for suicidal ideation.

SUBSTANCE USE AND COMPLETED SUICIDE IN ADOLESCENCE

In studies examining completed suicide in adolescence, substance use consistently emerges as a risk factor. Kotila (1992) performed a 5-year follow-up evaluation of 422 suicide attempters who had presented to an emergency department for medical treatment. Results showed that severe alcohol abuse and other illegal drug use at the time of the initial attempt was significantly more common in the adolescents who had completed suicide during the follow-up period (*n* = 13) as compared to the attempters who were still alive at the end of the follow up period (*n* = 349). Thus, alcohol and drug use may play an important role in eventual death by suicide, helping to differentiate adolescents who attempt suicide from those who will ultimately complete it.

Hawton, Fagg, Platt, and Hawkins (1993) examined risk of completed suicide in adolescents and young adults (up to age 24) who had made a previous suicide attempt. In their sample, 41 subjects had completed suicide (all with a previous unsuccessful attempt). An additional 21 deceased subjects were regarded as "possible suicide." Finally, 124 control subjects had a history of attempted suicide but had not completed suicide. Hawton *et al.* (1993) found that adolescents who had completed suicide were almost four times as likely to misuse substances as adolescents who had attempted suicide. However, only 29% of the suicide attempter control group misused substances. Consistent with other studies, substance use was a significant predictor of a suicide attempt and was an even greater predictor of suicide completion (56% of the completer group used substances). Thus, substance use seems to be a central risk factor that should be examined whenever evaluating teens for possible suicide risk.

Other studies of suicide completers also indicate that substance use or abuse plays a significant role in increasing suicide risk. A retrospective study of 58 adolescent and young adult suicide completers (Runeson, 1990) found that 47% met criteria for a substance use disorder. In addition, 20% of the subjects who did not meet criteria for any substance use disorder were intoxicated at the time of the suicide attempt. Acute intoxication can play a role in rash and impulsive acts by teenagers (as well as adults).

As part of the San Diego Suicide Study (Rich, Sherman, & Fowler, 1990), 14 adolescent suicide victims were identified. Fifty percent of these adolescents met criteria for substance use disorder, and four displayed comorbid depression. Shaffer, Gould, *et al.* (1996) conducted a psychologic autopsy study to examine the relationship between demographic information and psychiatric risk factors of 170 adolescents who committed suicide compared to a community control group matched for age, sex and race. They found that 35% of the sample who had committed suicide met criteria for a substance abuse disorder, with 42% of the males and

12% of the females meeting diagnostic criteria. Shaffer, Gould, *et al.* (1996) also reported that substance use significantly increased the risk of suicide for male adolescents by almost six-fold when compared to a control group, and substance use was present in two-thirds of the 18- to 19-year-old male suicide completers.

Brent, Perper, and colleagues (1993) found similar striking results in a smaller sample of 67 suicide completers compared to a community control sample of 67 demographically matched adolescents. Rates of substance abuse were 8.5 times higher in the suicide completer group compared with the matched control group. Substance abuse was the third highest risk factor for completed suicide, behind the diagnoses of major depression and bipolar disorder—mixed state. Brent, Perper, *et al.* (1993) also found that the comorbid diagnosis of substance abuse and a mood or anxiety disorder significantly increased the risk of completed suicide, increasing the odds of a completed suicide 17 times when compared with an adolescent with a substance abuse diagnosis alone. Lifetime rates of substance abuse (30.3% versus 10.6%) were significantly higher in suicide completers relative to controls.

Using a slightly different approach, Bukstein and colleagues (1993) examined a sample of adolescents who all had a lifetime history of substance use. Twenty-three suicide completers were compared to 12 matched community controls. At the time of their death, suicide completers were more likely to have active substance use, comorbid major depression, and family history of substance use and depression. Active substance use by adolescents increased risk of suicide above and beyond the risk of lifetime history of substance use.

CONCLUSIONS: ADOLESCENT SUICIDE ATTEMPTS AND SUBSTANCE USE

In summary, numerous recent studies have examined the relationship between suicide attempts and substance abuse in adolescents. The majority of the studies indicate that substance use is a high–risk factor for suicide attempts, particularly in school and community samples. Students who report substance use are at higher risk for suicide attempts than students who report no substance use. Females who use substances heavily may be at greatest risk for a suicide attempt. In examining adolescent runaway and shelter youth, findings consistently emphasized a strong relationship between substance use and suicide attempts. However, among juvenile delinquents the findings were mixed, and one study actually found lower rates of marijuana use in the attempter group.

One of the clearest findings to emerge was that comorbidity of substance use and affective (mood or anxiety) symptoms was highly predictive of suicide attempts in adolescence, posing a greater risk than either disorder alone. One study indicated that the odds of a completed suicide in an adolescent with comorbid diagnoses (substance use and mood/anxiety disorder) were 17 times that of an adolescent who only used substances (Brent, Perper *et al.*, 1993). Furthermore, there is a much higher risk of suicide completion when the adolescent has a history of substance use, even without comorbidity. Higher rates of substance use were found in suicide completers compared to adolescent suicide attempters. One study suggested that active, current substance use was a greater risk factor for attempted and completed suicide than lifetime substance use history.

Some differences in the relationship to suicide attempts emerged in the type of substances used. Almost all of the studies suggested that risk of attempted suicide was higher when adolescents reported using hard drugs or "illicit" substances. In comparison, findings on alcohol use and marijuana use were mixed. This may be due to the common tendency among adolescents to experiment with alcohol and marijuana, whereas the use of other drugs (e.g., cocaine) seems less common. Adolescent females seemed to be at particular risk for a suicide attempt when they reported a history of alcohol use.

Overall, the evidence suggests that when an adolescent presents with substance abuse, he or she is likely to be at higher risk for a suicide attempt than the general population. The reverse is also true in that when an adolescent presents with a suicide attempt, there is a higher risk of substance use history than seen in the general population. Finally, if an adolescent presents with comorbid symptoms of substance use and an affective disorder, the evidence is clear and consistent that the adolescent is at a very high risk for a suicide attempt. The clinical implications of these findings are discussed next.

CLINICAL IMPLICATIONS: ASSESSMENT OF ALCOHOL AND OTHER DRUG USE IN SUICIDE ATTEMPTERS

Given the high rates of substance use among adolescents who attempt suicide and the increased risk among this subgroup of adolescents, it is important to assess substance use among adolescent suicide attempters. When working with suicidal teens, it is important to evaluate the current and lifetime use of various drugs. This evaluation can be done in an informal manner by asking the adolescent about current recreational patterns and peer group drug use. Then, the interview can move more directly to a discussion of the teen's drug use, abuse, and potential dependence.

During adolescence, substance use and abuse are likely to be of recent origin. Research on suicidal behavior in adults has shown the serious negative consequences of long-term alcohol abuse. Adolescent experimentation may not be very important. However, it can become quite dangerous when continued reliance on drug use develops into a pattern of abuse or dependence. When alcohol abuse or dependence have been present for 10 years or longer, many problems accumulate. The adult with alcohol dependence is likely to report social, occupational, financial, and health problems that are secondary to his or her chronic alcohol consumption. However, because of the relatively short duration of alcohol abuse in most adolescents, there has not been sufficient time for these problems to accumulate. Hence, some of the short-term consequences of alcohol abuse may play a more pivotal role in adolescent suicide. The two most important problems related to adolescent substance abuse are interpersonal conflict that arises because of the substance abuse and the lowered inhibitions and poor judgment that occur during acute intoxication.

Adolescents may try using alcohol consumption as a maladaptive means of coping with life problems. When feeling alone, frustrated, or depressed, the adolescent may try using alcohol or drugs to suppress these negative emotions. However, such strategies rarely help to alter life problems or change adverse living conditions. Mental health professionals need to help adolescents understand the dangers of alcohol and drug use. More important, we need to help teens learn effective strategies for confronting and coping with difficult life situations.

MANAGEMENT AND TREATMENT OF ADOLESCENT SUICIDE ATTEMPTERS WITH COMORBID SUBSTANCE USE/ABUSE

Substance abuse is common in adolescents who attempt suicide as well as those who complete it. However, substance abuse is also common in many adolescents, especially adolescent psychiatric patients, runaway teens, and delinquent youth. Thus, substance abuse alone seems to be a non-specific risk factor for suicide. However, when substance abuse is combined with other risk factors, especially depression, the risk becomes stronger and more focused. Substance abuse and comorbid depression can become a potent and lethal combination. Adolescents who abuse substances during a depressive episode may be struggling with a variety of situational problems and limited coping skills. A comprehensive assessment and thorough treatment plan can help these troubled teens learn to make specific changes in their life situation, coping skills, and emotional pain.

When a suicidal adolescent also suffers from a substance abuse problem, the risk of self-injury is greatly increased. Clinicians need to evaluate and monitor the comorbid presence of depression and substance abuse. When both diagnoses are present, the adolescent is at a substantially elevated risk of serious self-injury. Treatment for both depression and substance abuse will be needed. Short-term hospitalization may help lower the risk of suicidal behavior until treatment has helped to reduce the psychiatric symptomatology.

Several mechanisms for the relationship between substance use and suicidal behavior have been proposed. Specifically, substance use may interfere with problem solving under stress, which in turn leads to suicidal ideation or behavior. When under stress, adolescents may use alcohol or other drugs as a misguided effort at coping, perhaps using drugs to suppress negative emotions. Alternatively, significant substance use may negatively affect peer relationships and social support resulting in suicidal ideation or behavior. When compared to adults, adolescents often have less tolerance for extreme mood states and limited judgment and behavioral self-control. Therefore, the effects of substances on behavior may have more dramatic effects on adolescents than adults and can lead to suicidal behavior (Bukstein, 1995). When adolescents learn to remain abstinent from recreational drugs, they will be forced to confront their feelings of emotional distress. If the adolescent is unprepared for the negative emotional reaction, the situation may get worse before it gets better. It is important to help adolecents develop effective coping strategies that can be used to manage difficult interpersonal situations and negative emotional states.

King, Naylor, Evens, and Shain (1993) noted that alcohol use and family dysfunction were related in their psychiatrically hospitalized sample and that these two factors predicted the severity of suicidal behavior. For girls with both alcohol use/abuse and family dysfunction, King *et al.* (1993) speculated that alcohol may have a disinhibiting effect that increases impulsive or angry responding, which when combined with the adolescent's view of his or her family as dysfunctional, may result in suicidal behavior. Thus, family therapy can be important when working with suicidal teens. Family therapy may help to change dysfunctional family interactions, can explore depressive patterns, and may be necessary in order for the entire family to confront substance use patterns.

ISSUES IN THE ASSESSMENT OF ADOLESCENT SUBSTANCE USE

Although it is important to thoroughly assess substance use and abuse among adolescents who attempt suicide, a number of issues need to be considered when questioning adolescents about alcohol and drug use. These issues are reviewed next.

Validity of Adolescent Self-Report

There is a possibility of inaccurate self-report with any type of assessment, but possibly more so when illicit behavior is being measured. The interviewer should keep in mind that situational factors may influence the adolescent's self-report. In some situations, the teen may be motivated to present a tough bravado, inflating his or her drug use patterns. However, in other situations, the teen may minimize or deny any history of drug use in order to avoid punishment. When a suicidal teen reports using alcohol or other drugs on a regular basis, the clinician should be advised to continue with a more detailed evaluation of drug use. This may include gathering information from secondary sources (e.g., parents, teachers, or probation officer) and possibly requesting urine screens to monitor drug use.

In any assessment situation, it is important to make sure that the conditions are conducive to accurate self-report. These include establishing rapport with the adolescent, being clear about how the information will be used and who will have access to it, and addressing any concerns the adolescent might have about the assessment. For a more detailed review of these issues, see Winters (in press) and Stinchfield (1997).

Parent Report of Adolescent Behavior

Interviewing parents about adolescent behavior is suggested when a general sense of adolescent behavior is needed, but parents are typically not good reporters of the *specifics* of adolescent drug use (Winters, in press). Nevertheless, including family members in the assessment may provide additional important information beyond the specific details of the drug use per se and may make parental engagement in treatment more smooth.

Assessment of Drugs and Alcohol Use

Important elements for measuring the use of alcohol and drugs are frequency and quantity of use and whether there is a preferred drug. The *pattern* of substance use is relevant. For example, one high-volume episode (e.g., severe intoxication) may reflect a greater problem than more frequent but relatively low-level use or vice versa. By the same token, one episode of use that leads to a serious consequence, or any use of some drugs (e.g., IV drug use), would warrant concern. However, simply measuring volume of use may not provide enough information to determine whether a problem exists. The consequences of the drug or alcohol use should be assessed as well.

Similarly, it is important to assess whether suicidal ideation or other problematic behaviors arise primarily when a substance has been used. Measures of substance use (e.g., quantity/frequency or lifetime use) may not identify associated risky behaviors such as indiscriminate sexual behavior or driving while intoxicated. Most measures described in this chapter address consequences of substance use, but not always concurrent behavior that could be a problem.

One caveat is that assessment of *typical* use of alcohol or drugs may lead to an underestimation of *heavy* use. An adolescent's pattern of alcohol use may be characterized by days of heavy episodic drinking interspersed with days of lower levels of drinking. If the adolescent is asked, "How much do you drink on a typical day?" he or she might respond by *averaging* the amount he or she drinks or by reporting the *most common* pattern, both which could result in an underestimation of a more problematic pattern of episodic heavy drinking. Thus, it is important to ask specific questions designed to evaluate occasional patterns of heavy use. Also, the use and abuse of various drugs will be influenced by their cost and availability. Drug use by peers and family members can play important roles.

Other Considerations

The assessment of alcohol and drug use by family members should be considered. Greene and Ringwalt (1996) found that adolescents who reported a family history of substance use were twice as likely to attempt suicide than those without familial substance use. A history of drug use by parents or siblings may put an adolescent at greater risk. Therefore, the clinical assessment might include family history of addiction. Brief measures can be used when time is critical. For example, the short form of the Michigan Alcoholism Screening Test (SMAST; Selzer, Vinokur, & van Rooijen, 1976) is a 13-item self-report measure designed to detect alcohol problems in adults and is appropriate for parents of suicide attempters. The scores on the SMAST have been shown to be highly correlated with an alcoholism diagnosis. Scoring is the sum total of each positively scored item. Each positive item is scored a 1. Scores of 3 to 4 indicate possible alcoholism, and a score of 5 or greater indicates alcoholism.

Random urine testing might also be used for checking the accuracy of adolescent report but is limited in that with the exception of marijuana, biochemical tests only detect relatively recent use. However, biochemical testing also affects the therapist-adolescent relationship. The adolescent is likely to feel resentful of the therapist who requires random urine tests and may feel that the therapist does not trust the adolescent's self-report of drug use. Some of these concerns may be minimized by establishing a general policy for drug testing, so the adolescent does not feel "picked on" by the therapist. Also, it is helpful if a colleague is in charge of the drug testing so that the testing can be removed from the therapy environment.

CHOOSING AN INSTRUMENT: BRIEF SCREEN OR INTERVIEW?

Table 1 presents measures of adolescent substance use and abuse. These measures can be categorized into the more brief and less intense screening measures, which tend to be self-administered, and the more intensive

TABLE 1 Screening Instruments

	Source	Description	Items	Notes
Adolescent Alcohol Involvement Scale (AAIS)	Mayer and Filstead, 1979	Self-administered. Measures characteristics of drinking experience including type and frequency, reasons, effects of drinking and perceptions.	14	
Adolescent Drinking Index (ADI)	Harrel and Wirtz, 1989	Self-administered. Measures alcohol involvement and related factors.	24	Four major domains: psychological symptoms, physical symptoms, social symptoms, and loss of control.
Adolescent Drug Involvement Scale (ADIS)	Moberg and Hahn, 1991	Adaptation of the Adolescent Alcohol Involvement Scale (AAIS). Assesses level of use of drugs other than alcohol. Includes items of recency of drug use, reasons for use, consequences of use, and adolescent and other's appraisal of the drug use.	12	
Personal Experience Screening Questionnaire (PESQ)	Winters, 1992	Self-administered. Drug and alcohol use and problems in related areas as well as psychosocial factors.	40	Has a problem severity scale and measures tendency to distort. Norms available on normal, offender and drug-abusing populations.
Problem Oriented Screening Instrument for Teenagers (POSIT)	Rahdert, 1991	Self-administered. Drug and alcohol use and problems and potential service needs in 10 related areas.	139	Scoring systems are available that provide cutoff scores for low, medium, and high risk for each of the 10 problem areas.
Rutgers Alcohol Problem Index (RAPI)	White and Labouvie, 1989	Self-administered/self-report of alcohol-related problems.	23	
Substance Abuse Subtle Screening Inventory (SASSI)	Miller, 1990	Self-administered. Drug and alcohol use and problems in related areas.	81	

in-depth comprehensive or diagnostic-type interviews (see Table 2), which are less structured and interviewer driven (Winters & Stinchfield, 1995). Screening tools should be used when information about the adolescent is limited, when time is limited, or when it is not known whether a more comprehensive assessment is warranted. A more comprehensive interview is most appropriate when trying to determine the presence or absence of a disorder or when trying to identify which type of treatment is appropriate. Typically, the more comprehensive assessments indicate the severity of the drug or alcohol use and address other areas of psychosocial functioning, including personal and family relationships, education or work performance, and medical or legal problems. Some of these instruments provide diagnostic information, whereas scaled instruments provide scale scores that can be compared to age norms to determine severity. Diagnostic interviews that are based on DSM diagnostic criteria may not be appropriate for use on adolescents due to substantial differences between adolescents and adults in the display and development of substance abuse diagnostic symptoms and due to the underrepresentation of adolescents in diagnostic studies (Deas, Riggs, Langenbucher, Goldman, & Brown, 2000).

The selected assessment tool must meet the needs of the tester and be appropriate for use with the adolescent patient. Therefore, the presenting problem, the setting, and the information sought by the clinician will determine what tools to consider. All of the following instruments have been developed for use with adolescents and have adequate to very good psychometric properties. It should be noted that the background and training of the assessor must be appropriate for the measure selected. Some instruments require training in administration. For other summaries of assessment issues and instruments, see Allen and Columbus (1995), Center for Substance Abuse Treatment (1999), Farrow, Smith, and Hurst (1993), and Leccesse and Waldron (1994).

WHAT QUESTIONS SHOULD DEFINITELY BE ASKED?

Whether or not a standardized measure is used, clinicians should be sure to ask basic questions about substance use. Clinicians should ask about the quantity and frequency of drinking and other drug use, the reasons for drug use (e.g., to relax) and whether or not the teen dirinks alone. In addition, the negative consequences of drinking should be investigated,

TABLE 2   Interviews

	Source	Description	Items[a]	Notes
Adolescent Diagnostic Interview (ADI)	Winters and Henly, 1993a	Generates DSM-IV diagnosis and assesses substance involvement and level of functioning in related problem areas.		Also screens for other mental health disorders.
Adolescent Drug Abuse (ADAD)	Friedmand and Utada, 1989	Structured, generates DSM-IV dx, assesses nine problem areas as well.	150	Modeled after the Addiction Severity Index, a measure of drug abuse for adults (McLellan et al., 1980). Need for additional treatment in each of the problem areas is rated by the interviewer. Some training required. A computerized version is available.
Adolescent Problem Severity Index (APSI)	Metzger, Kushner, and McLellan, 1991	Structured/semistructured. Assesses drug use patterns, drug and alcohol-related problems and psychosocial risk factors	Varies depending on responses	Computer software for scoring is available.
Comprehensive Addiction Severity Index—Adolescent (CASI)	Meyers, 1991	Assesses drug use patterns, drug and alcohol-related problems, and psychosocial risk factors.	Varies depending on responses	Includes urine drug screen results as part of the assessment.
Customary Drinking and Drug Use Record (CDDR)	Brown et al., 1998	Domains of substance use, negative consequences, withdrawal, and psychological/behavioral dependence.	Varies depending on responses	Does not incorporate questions of other psychosocial risk areas.

Measure	Reference	Number of items	Description	Notes
Diagnostic Interview Schedule for Children (DISC)	Shaffer, Fisher, et al., 1996		Generates DSM-IV diagnosis and assesses related psychosocial problem areas. Drug involvement, comorbidity.	Four subscales on alcohol abuse; seven subscales on alcohol dependence. Number of items vary by extent of alcohol problem.
Minnesota Multiphasic Personality Inventory—Adolescent (MMPI-A)	Weed, Butcher, and Williams, 1994	Full MMPI: 550; subscales: 13 (ACK) and 36 (PRO)	Self-administered. Two scales measure alcohol/drug problem acknowledgment (ACK) and alcohol/drug problem proneness (PRO).	
Personal Experience Inventory (PEI)	Winters and Henly, 1993b	276	Self-administered screen. Drug and alcohol use and problems in related areas. Divided into sections of 1 chemical involvement, and 2 psychosocial risk factors.	Other problems also assessed by PEI including suicide potential and other mental health symptoms. The PEI and the PESQ (above) are part of a multitool assessment system called the Minnesota Chemical Dependency Adolescent Assessment Package (MCDAAP).
Teen Addiction Severity Index (T-ASI)	Kaminer, Bukstein, and Tarter, 1991	133	Semistructured. Assesses drug use patterns, drug and alcohol-related problems. Has seven subscales of other areas	Severity ratings are generated from the interviewer and the adolescent. Some training is needed.

[a] Number of items is not presented for all measures in this section. Most interviews are semistructured and therefore vary in length depending on the adolescent's response.

for example, forgetting one's behaviors while drinking, mood changes, and broken rules one wouldn't normally consider violating. Finally, whether or not friends or adults have told the adolescent that he or she has a problem with drinking should also be investigated. Perhaps the most efficient way to investigate these most essential questions would be to administer a recently developed brief screen for adolescents developed by Knight, Shrier, Bravender, Farrell, Vander Bitt, and Shaffer (1999).

REFERENCES

Adcock, A. G., Nagy, S., & Simpson, J. A. (1991). Selected risk factors in adolescent suicide attempts. *Adolescence, 26*, 817–828.

Allen, J. P., & Columbus, M. (Eds.). (1995). *Assessing alcohol problems: A guide for clinicians and researchers.* Bethesda, MD: National Institute on Alcohol Abuse and Alcoholism.

Berman, A., & Schwartz, R. H. (1990). Suicide attempts among adolescent drug users. *American Journal of Diseases of Children, 144*, 310–314.

Brent, D. A., Kolko, D. J., Allan, M. J., & Brown, R. V. (1990). Suicidality in affectively disordered adolescent inpatients. *Journal of the American Academy of Child Adolescent Psychiatry, 29*, 586–593.

Brent, D. A., Kolko, D. J., Wartella, M. E., Boylan, M. B., Moritz, G., Baugher, M., & Zelenak, J. (1993). Adolescent psychiatric inpatients' risk of suicide attempt at 6-month follow up. *Journal of the Academy of Child and Adolescent Psychiatry, 21*, 95–105.

Brent, D., Perper, J., Moritz, G., Allman, C., Friend, A., Roth, C., Schwers, J., Barach, L., & Baugher, M. (1993). Psychiatric risk factors for adolescent suicide: A case control study. *Journal of the American Academy of Child and Adolescent Psychiatry, 32*, 521–529.

Brent, D. A., Perper, J. A., Moritz, G., Baugher, M., Schweers, J., & Roth, C. (1994). Suicide in affectively ill adolescents: A case-control study. *Journal of Affective Disorders, 31*(3), 193–202.

Brown, S. A., Myers, M. G., Lippke, L., Tapert, S. F., Stewart, D. G., & Vik, P. W. (1998). Psychometric evaluation of the customary drinking and drug use record (CDDR): A measure of adolescent alcohol and drug involvement. *Journal of Studies on Alcohol, 59*, 427–438.

Bukstein, O. G. (1995). *Adolescent substance abuse: Assessment, prevention, and treatment.* New York: Wiley.

Bukstein, O. G., Brent, D. A., Perper, J. A., Mortiz, G., Schweers, J., Roth, C., & Balach, L. (1993). Risk factors for completed suicide among adolescents with a lifetime history of substance abuse: a case-control study. *Acta Psychiatrica Scandinavica, 88*, 403–408.

Center for Substance Abuse Treatment. (1999). *Screening and assessing adolescents for substance use disorders.* U.S. Department of Health and Human Services. Pub. No. 99–3344.

Choquet, M., Koves, V., & Poutignat, N. (1993). Suicidal thoughts among adolescents: an intercultural approach. *Adolescence, 28*, 649–659.

Crumley, F. E. (1990). Substance abuse and adolescent suicidal behavior. *Journal of the American Medical Association, 263*.

Deas, D., Riggs, P., Langenbucher, J., Goldman, M., & Brown, S. (2000). Adolescents are not adults: Developmental considerations in alcohol users. *Alcoholism: Clinical & Experimental Research, 24*, 232–237.

DeMan, A., Labrecher-Gauthier, L., & LeDuc, C. (1993). Parent-child relationships and suicidal ideation in French-Canadian adolescents. *Journal of Genetic Psychology, 154*, 17–23.

Deykin, E., & Buka, S. (1994). Suicidal ideation and attempts among chemically dependent adolescents. *American Journal of Public Health, 84*, 634–639.

Farrow, J. A., Smith, W. R., & Hurst, M. D. (1993). *Adolescent drug and alcohol assessment instruments in current use: A critical comparison.* Division of Alcohol and Substance Use. WA.

Felts, W. M., Chenier, T., & Barnes, R. (1992). Drug use and suicide ideation and behavior among North Carolina public school students. *American Journal of Public Health, 82*, 870–872.

Fombonne, E. (1998). Suicidal behaviors in vulnerable adolescents. *British Journal of Psychiatry, 173*, 154–159.

Friedman, A. S., & Utada, A. (1989). A method for diagnosing and planning the treatment of adolescent drug abusers. Adolescent drug abuse diagnosis instrument. *Journal of Drug Education, 19*, 285–312.

Garnefski, N., Diekstra, R. F. W., & deHeus, P. (1992). A population-based survey of the characteristics of high school students with and without a history of suicidal behavior. *Acta Psychiatrica Scandinavia, 86*, 189–196.

Garrison, C. Z., McKeown, R. E., Valois, R. F., & Vincent, M. L. (1993). Aggression, substance use and suicidal behaviors in high school students. *American Journal of Public Health, 83*, 179–184.

Gould, M. S., King, R., Greenwald, S., Fisher, P., Schwab-Stone, M., Kramer, R., Flisher, A. J., Goodman, S., Canino, G., & Shaffer, D. (1998). Psychopathology associated with suicidal ideation and attempts among children and adolescents. *Journal of American Academy of Child and Adolescent Psychiatry, 37*, 915–923.

Greene, J. M., & Ringwalt, C. L. (1996). Youth and Familial Substance Use's Association with Suicide Attempts among Runaway and Homeless Youth. *Substance Use & Misuse, 31*, 1041–1058.

Harrell, A., & Wirtz, P. M. (1989). Screening for adolescent problem drinking: Validation of a multidimensional instrument for case identification. *Psychological Assessment, 1*, 61–63.

Hawton, K., & Fagg, J. (1992). Deliberate self-poisoning and self-injury in adolescents: A study of characteristics and trends in Oxford, 1976–1989. *British Journal of Psychiatry, 161*, 816–823.

Hawton, K., Fagg, J., Platt, S., & Hawkins, M. (1993). Factors associated with suicide after parasuicide in young people. *British Medical Journal, 306*, 1641–1644.

Jones, R. (1997). The role of drugs and alcohol in urban minority adolescent suicide attempts. *Death Studies, 21*, 189–202.

Juon, H. S., & Ensminger, M. S. (1997). Childhood, adolescent, and young adult predictors of suicidal behaviors: A prospective study of African-Americans. *Journal of Child Psychology and Psychiatry, 38*, 553–563.

Kaminer, Y., Bukstein, O., & Tarter, R. E. (1991). The Teen-Addiction Severity Index: Rationale and reliability. *International Journal of Addictions, 26*, 219–226.

Kelly, T., Lynch, K., Donovan, J., & Clark, D. (in press). Alcohol use disorders and risk factor interactions for adolescent suicidal ideation and attempts. *Suicide and Life Threatening Behavior.*

Kempton, T., & Forehand, R. (1992). Case histories and shorter communications. *Behavior Research and Therapy, 30*, 537–541.

Kienhorst, C. W., deWilde, E. J., van den Bout, J., Diekstra, R. F., & Wolters, W. H. (1990). Characteristics of suicide attempts in a population-based sample of Dutch adolescents. *British Journal of Psychiatry, 156*, 243–248.

King, C., Hill, E., Naylor, M., Evens, T., & Shain, B. (1993). Alcohol consumption in relation to other predictors of suicidality among adolescent inpatient girls. *Journal of the American Academy of Child and Adolescent Psychiatry, 32*, 82–88.

King, C. A., Ghaziuddin, N., McGovern, L., Brand, E., Hill, E., & Naylor, M. (1996). Predictors of comorbid alcohol and substance abuse in depressed adolescents. *Journal of the American Academy of Child and Adolescent Psychiatry, 35*, 743–751.

Kinkel, R. J., Bailey, C. W., & Josef, N. C. (1989). Correlates of suicide attempts: Alienation, drugs, and social background. *Journal of Alcohol and Drug Education, 34*, 85–96.

Kipke, M., Montgomery, S., & MacKenzie, R. (1993). Substance use among youth seen at a community-based health clinic. *Journal of Adolescent Health, 14*, 289–299.

Kirkpatrick-Smith, J., Rich, A. R., Bonner, R., & Jans, F. (1991–1992). Psychological vulnerability and substance abuse as predictors of suicide ideation among adolescents. *Omega: Journal of Death and Dying, 24*, 21–23.

Knight, J., Shrier, L., Bravender, T., Farrell, M., Vander Bitt, J., & Shaffer, H. (1999). A new brief screen for adolescent substance abuse. *Archives of Pediatric and Adolescent Medicine, 153*, 591–596.

Kosky, R., Silburn, S., & Zubrick, S. R. (1990). Are children and adolescents who have suicidal thoughts different from those who attempt suicide? *Journal of Nervous and Mental Disease, 178*, 38–43.

Kotila, L. (1992). The outcome of attempted suicide in adolescence. *Journal of Adolescent Health, 13*, 415–417.

Kotila, L., & Lonquist, J. (1988). Adolescent suicide attempts: Sex differences predicting suicide. *Acta Psychiatrica Scandinavica, 77*, 264–270.

Kovacs, M., Goldston, D., & Gatsonis, C. (1993). Suicidal behaviors and childhood-onset depressive disorders: A longitudinal investigation. *Journal of the American Academy of Child Adolescent Psychiatry, 32*, 8–20.

Lahey, B. B., Flagg, E. W., & Bird, H. R. (1996). The NIMH Methods for Epidemiology of Child and Adolescent Mental Disorders (MECA) Study: Background and methodology. *Journal of the American Academy of Child and Adolescent Psychiatry, 35*, 855–864.

Leccesse, M., & Waldron, H. B. (1994). Assessing adolescent substance use: A critique of current measurement instruments. *Journal of Substance Abuse Treatment, 11*, 553–563.

Levy, J. C., & Deykin, E. Y. (1989). Suicidality, depression, and substance abuse in adolescence. *American Journal of Psychiatry, 146*, 1462–1467.

Mayer, J., & Filstead, W. J. (1979). The Adolescent Alcohol Involvement Scale: An instrument for measuring adolescent use and misuse of alcohol. *Journal of Alcohol Studies, 4*, 291–300.

McClellan, A. T., Luborsky, L., Woody, G. E., & O'Brien, C. P. (1980). An improved diagnostic evaluation instrument for substance abuse patients: The Addiction Severity Index. *Journal of Nervous and Mental Disease, 168(1),* 26–33.

Metzger, D., Kushner, H., & McLellan, A. T. (1991). *Adolescent Problem Severity Index.* Philadelphia: University of Pennsylvania.

Meyers, K. (1991). *Comprehensive Addiction Severity Index for Adolescents.* Philadelphia, PA: University of Pennsylvania.

Miller, G. (1990). *The Substance Abuse Subtle Screening Inventory-Adolescent Version.* Bloomington, IN: SASSI Institute.

Moberg, D. P., & Hahn, L. (1991). The adolescent drug involvement scale. *Journal of Adolescent Chemical Dependency, 2,* 75–88.

Overholser, J. C., Freiheit, S. R., & DiFilippo, J. M. (1997). Emotional distress and substance abuse as risk factors for suicide attempts. *Canadian Journal of Psychiatry, 42,* 402–408.

Putnins, A. L. (1995). Recent drug use and suicidal behavior among young offenders. *Drug and Alcohol Review, 14,* 151–158.

Rahdert, E. E. (1991). *The Adolescent Assessment/Referral System Manual.* Rockville, MD: U.S. Department of Health and Human Services, ADAMHA, National Institute on Drug Abuse, DHHS Pub. No. (ADM) 91–1735.

Reifman, A., & Windle, M. (1995). Adolescent suicidal behaviors as a function of depression, hopelessness, and alcohol use and social support: A longitudinal investigation. *American Journal of Community Psychology, 23,* 329–343.

Rich, A. R., Sherman, M., & Fowler, R. C. (1990). San Diego Suicide Study: The adolescents. *Adolescence, 25,* 855–865.

Rohde, P., Seely, J., & Mace, D. (1997). Correlates of suicidal behavior in a juvenile detention population. *Suicide and Life-Threatening Behavior, 27,* 164–175.

Rossow, I., & Wichstrom, L. (1994). Parasuicide and the use of intoxicants among Norwegian adolescents. *Suicide and Life-Threatening Behavior, 24,* 174–183.

Rotheram-Borus, M. J. (1993). Suicidal behavior and risk factors among runaway youths. *American Journal of Psychiatry, 150,* 103–107.

Runeson, B. (1990). Psychoactive substance use disorder in youth suicide. *Alcohol and Alcoholism, 25,* 561–568.

Selzer, M., Vinokur, A., & van Rooijen, L. (1976). A self-administered Short Michigan Alcoholism Screening Test (SMAST). *Journal of Studies on Alcohol, 36,* 117–126.

Shaffer, D., Fisher, P., Dulcan, M., Davies, M., Piacentini, J., Schwab-Stone, M., Lahey, B., Bourdon, K., Jensen, P., Bird, H., Canino, G., & Regier, D. (1996). The NIMH Diagnostic Interview Schedule for Children (DISC 2.3): Description, acceptability, prevalences, and performance in the MECA study. *Journal of the American Academy of Child and Adolescent Psychiatry, 35,* 865–877.

Shaffer, D., Gould, M. S., Fisher, P., Trautman, P., Moreau, D., Klienman, M., & Flory, M. (1996). Psychiatric diagnosis in child and adolescent suicide. *Archives of General Psychiatry, 53,* 339–348.

Simon, T., & Crosby, A. (2000). Suicide planning among high school students who report attempting suicide. *Suicide and Life-Threatening Behavior, 30,* 213–221.

Spirito, A., Brown, L., Overholser, J., & Fritz, G. (1989). Attempted suicide in adolescence: A review and critique of the literature. *Clinical Psychology Review, 9,* 335–363.

Spirito, A., Stark, C., Fristad, M., Hart, R., & Owens-Stively, J. (1987). Adolescent suicide attempters hospitalized in a pediatric unit. *Journal of Pediatric Psychology, 12,* 171–189.

Stiffman, A. R. (1989). Suicide attempts in runaway youth. *Suicide and Life-Threatening Behavior, 19,* 147–159.

Stinchfield, R. D. (1997). Reliability of adolescent self-reported pretreatment alcohol and other drug use. *Substance Use and Misuse, 32,* 63–76.

Swedo, S., Rettew, D., Kuppenheimer, M., Lum, D., Dolan, S., & Goldberger, E. (1991). Can adolescent suicide attempters be distinguished from at risk adolescents? *Pediatrics, 88,* 620–629.

Vanetta, R. A. (1996). Risk factors related to suicidal behavior among male and female adolescents. *Journal of Youth and Adolescence, 25,* 149–160.

Vega, W. A., Gil, A., Warheit, G., Apospori, E., & Zimmerman, R. (1993). The relationship of drug use to suicide ideation and attempts among African-American, Hispanic and white non-Hispanic male adolescents. *Suicide and Life-Threatening Behavior, 23,* 110–119.

Wagner, B. M., Cole, R. E., & Schwartzman, P. (1996). Comorbidity of symptoms among junior and senior high school suicide attempters. *Suicide and Life-Threatening Behavior, 26,* 300–307.

Weed, N. C., Butcher, J. N., & Williams, C. L. (1994). Development of MMPI-A Alcohol/Drug Problem Scales. *Journal of Studies on Alcohol, 55,* 304.

White, H., & Labouvie, E. (1989). Towards the assessment of adolescent problem drinking. *Journal of Studies in Alcohol, 50,* 30–37.

Windle, M., Miller-Tutzauer, C., & Domenico, D. (1992). Alcohol use, suicidal behavior and risky activities among adolescents. *Journal of Research on Adolescence, 2,* 317–330.

Winters, K. (in press). Assessing adolescent substance use problems and other areas of functioning: State of the art. In P. M. Monti, S. M. Colby, & T. A. O'Leary (Eds.) *Adolescents, alcohol and substance abuse: Reaching teens through brief interventions.* New York: The Guilford Press.

Winters, K. C. (1992). Development of an adolescent alcohol and other drug abuse screening scale: Personal Experience Screening Questionnaire. *Addictive Behaviors, 17,* 479–490.

Winters, K. C., & Henly, G. A. (1993a). *The Adolescent Diagnostic Interview Schedule and User's Manual.* Los Angeles: Western Psychological Services.

Winters, K. C., & Henly, G. A. (1993b). *Personal experience inventory and manual.* Los Angeles: Western Psychological Services.

Winters, K. C., Latimer, W. W., & Stinchfield, R. D. (1999). DSM-IV criteria for adolescent alcohol and cannabis use disorders. *Journal of Studies on Alcohol, 60,* 337–344.

Winters, K. C., & Stinchfield, R. D. (1995). Current issues and future needs in the assessment of adolescent drug abuse. In E. Rahdert & D. Czechowicz (Eds.). *Adolescent drug abuse: Clinical assessment and therapeutic interventions (NIDA Research Monograph, 156)* (pp. 146–171). Rockville, MD: U.S. Department of Health and Human Services.

Wunderlich, W., Bronisch, T., & Wittchen, H. U. (1998). Comorbidity patterns in adolescents and young adults with suicide attempts. *European Archives of Psychiatry and Clinical Neuroscience, 248,* 87–95.

Yoder, K. A., Hoyt, D. R., & Whitbeck, L. B. (1998). Suicidal behavior among homeless and runaway adolescents. *Journal of Youth and Adolescence, 27*, 753–771.

Yuen, N., Andrade, N., Nahulu, L., Makini, G., McDermott, J. F., Danko, G., Johnson, R., & Waldron, J. (1996). The rate and characteristics of suicide attempters in the native Hawaiian adolescent population. *Suicide and Life-Threatening Behavior, 26*, 27–36.

CHAPTER 7

Behavioral Factors: Impulsive and Aggressive Behavior

C. Esposito, A. Spirito, and J. Overholser

Mood state and cognitions tend to be the focus of most clinical evaluations of adolescent suicide attempters. However, behavior disturbance is also very common in this group of adolescents. Substance use has previously been discussed. This chapter focuses on impulsive and aggressive behavior among suicide attempters, which commonly co-occur in the same individual.

IMPULSIVE BEHAVIOR

Impulsivity is a construct that has received a moderate amount of attention in the adolescent suicide literature. Most research conducted within the past 10 years generally reveals a relationship between impulsivity and suicidality. Kingsbury, Hawton, Steinhardt, and James (1999) examined impulsivity as one of many psychological factors associated with overdoses in adolescents. Thirty-three medically hospitalized adolescent suicide attempters (ages 12 to 18, mean age 16.1 years), 30 nonsuicidal psychiatrically hospitalized adolescents (mean age 15.8 years), and 30 secondary school and further education students (mean age 15.9 years) completed the Plutchik Impulsivity Scale (Plutchik & van Praag, 1989) on two occasions, 6 weeks apart. The first interview in the overdose group was completed following an overdose. Results revealed the overdose group to have higher impulsivity scores than the psychiatric control group at Time 1 but not at Time 2, although there was a trend in the same direction. Further, when depression was controlled and analyses were repeated, attempters exhibited significantly higher impulsivity scores than the psychiatric controls at Time 2 but not at Time 1. These results suggest that impulsivity often accompanies suicidal behavior but may not be a stable personality characteristic of adolescents who attempt suicide impulsively. Nonetheless, because impulsivity was also independent, at least to a certain extent, of depression, Kingsbury *et al.* (1999) have suggested that impulsivity should be assessed in adolescent suicide attempters and addressed in some portion of the adolescent's treatment.

Pfeffer, Hurt, Peskin, and Siefker (1995) conducted a longitudinal study to examine the role of impulsivity in child and adolescent suicide attempts. Sixty-nine psychiatrically hospitalized patients and 42 nonpatients completed baseline assessments (ages 4 to 14) and were followed-up 6 to 8 years later (ages 10 to 21). Based on results from the Spectrum of Suicidal Behavior Scale (Pfeffer, 1986), children and adolescents were grouped as suicide attempters, suicide ideators, nonsuicidal patients, and nonsuicidal nonpatients. Impulse control was measured via the Impulse Control Scale of the Child Suicide Potential Scales (Pfeffer, 1986). Results revealed that nonpatients, compared to all patient groups, had significantly greater impulse control at initial assessment. Further, in examining the relationship between baseline data and follow-up, patients were dichotomized into a "good" outcome group if they did not have a history of suicidality previous to study entry and did not make a suicide attempt during the study, a "poor" outcome group if they made a suicide attempt during the duration of the study, and an "improved" outcome group if they exhibited suicidal ideation or behavior previous to study entry but demonstrated no suicidality during the course of the study. When differences between these groups were analyzed at follow-up, results indicated that children and adolescents with a good course had significantly better impulse control than children and adolescents with an improved or poor course. Thus, impulse control may be an important variable in preventing the risk of suicidal behavior. However, these findings also imply that impulse control may be a rather stable trait, difficult to cultivate in adolescents as a potential means of curtailing suicidal tendencies.

Using a cross-sectional study design, Lehnert, Overholser, and Spirito (1994) examined differences in anger and impulsivity in 104 medically hospitalized adolescent suicide attempters and 323 high school students (mean age 15). Impulsivity was measured using the Impulse Control Scale from the Offer Self-Image Questionnaire (OSIQ; Offer, Ostrov & Howard, 1982). Results revealed that suicide attempters had significantly lower scores on the Impulse Control Scale when compared to community controls. These results indicate greater impulsivity among adolescent suicide attempters in comparison to community controls, although many of the items on the OSIQ tap anger more than impulsivity.

Kashden, Fremouw, Callahan, and Franzen (1993) conducted a study to examine the link between cognitive impulsivity and suicidality in adolescents. Specifically, 23 adolescents psychiatrically hospitalized for suicidal ideation or attempts (ages 13 to 17), 20 psychiatrically hospitalized nonsuicidal adolescents (ages 14 to 17), and 20 high school students (ages 14 to 17) completed the delay and vigilance tasks of the Gordon Diagnostic System, a laboratory measure that consists of three tasks designed to measure cognitive impulsivity and sustained attention. Results revealed suicide attempters to have significantly higher commission errors than the psychiatric and community control groups, suggesting greater impulsivity in the suicidal group. This difference remained when the effects of both hopelessness and depression were covaried. No differences were found across groups in measures of sustained attention. Thus, suicidal behavior in some adolescents may be characterized by a tendency to act without forethought, perhaps rushing to conclusions or behaving inappropriately in a hurried manner.

Most of the studies reviewed here suggest a direct relationship between impulsivity and suicidality in adolescents. However, the same results have not necessarily emerged when impulsivity is included as one of many predictors of suicidality in multivariate analyses, possibly reflecting an indirect relationship between impulsivity and suicidality. Beautrais, Joyce, and Mulder (1999) examined personality traits and cognitive styles linked to suicidal behavior, one of which was impulsivity. They compared 129 adolescents and young adults (ages 13 to 24) medically hospitalized for serious suicide attempts to 153 young adults (ages 18 to 24) selected randomly from electoral rolls. Impulsivity was measured via the Barratt Impulsivity Scale (Barratt, 1965). Scores on this scale were divided into quartiles to provide a measure of low to high impulsivity. As expected, results revealed that the risk of serious suicide attempt was significantly related to impulsiveness, with those scoring in the top quartile having a six-fold higher rate of suicide attempts than those in the lowest quartile. However, when impulsivity was included in a multivariate analysis with measures of hopelessness, neuroticism, external locus of control, self-esteem, and extroversion, impulsivity was not found to be related to serious suicide risk. The authors conclude that this nonsignificant finding was largely explained by substantial correlations between impulsivity and other personality/cognitive measures, such as external locus of control. Thus, measures of impulsivity may be related to suicide risk, but impulsivity is also related to many other problematic behaviors that also can be involved in suicidal acts.

Researchers have also examined the relationship between impulsivity and suicidality as a function of subgroup differences. Wetzler, Asnis, Hyman, Virtue, Zimmerman, and Rathus (1996) examined the link between impulsivity and suicidality in 225 depressed adolescent outpatients (ages 12 to 20 years). The majority of these adolescents were diagnosed with adjustment disorder, major depressive disorder, or dysthymia. Adolescents were categorized into one of four groups for analyses: suicide attempters who required medical treatment, suicide attempters who did not require medical treatment, suicide ideators with no history of attempts, and nonsuicidal patients. Using the Plutchik Impulsivity Scale (Plutchik & van Praag, 1989), the only difference that emerged was between suicide ideators and nonsuicidal outpatients. Suicide ideators had significantly higher impulsivity scores than the nonsuicidal outpatients, but there was no link between suicide attempts and impulsivity in this depressed population. These findings suggest that the depressed adolescents who made suicide attempts did not do so impulsively. Brown, Overholser, Spirito, and Fritz (1991) categorized adolescent suicide attempters as impulsive versus nonimpulsive based on their degree of reported premeditation prior to the attempt. In line with results reported by Wetzler *et al.* (1996), the nonimpulsive attempters were found to be significantly more depressed and hopeless than the impulsive group.

A few studies have also been conducted to determine whether differences in impulsivity emerge between adolescents who make one suicide attempt in comparison to repeat attempters. Hawton, Kingsbury, Steinhardt, James, and Fagg (1999) examined impulsivity as one of many psychological factors linked to repetition of suicide attempts in 45 adolescents (ages 12 to 18) admitted to a general hospital after self-poisoning. Adolescents completed the Plutchik Impulsivity Scale (Plutchik & van

Praag, 1989). Results failed to reveal a significant difference in impulsivity between nonrepeaters and repeaters. Similar results were found by Stein, Apter, Ratzoni, Har-Even, and Avidan (1998) who examined the association between measures of negative affect, one of which was impulsivity, and multiple suicide attempts in 32 adolescents medically hospitalized for a first suicide attempt, 19 adolescents medically hospitalized for a repeat attempt, 109 nonsuicidal psychiatrically hospitalized adolescents, and 85 randomly selected community controls (ages 12 to 18). Impulsivity was measured via interviewer ratings in the context of administration of the Suicide Potential Scale (SPS; Pfeffer, 1986). Adolescents with a single suicide attempt did not differ in level of impulsivity from those with multiple suicide attempts. The adolescents with a single suicide attempt, adolescents with multiple suicide attempts, and nonsuicidal psychiatric controls demonstrated significantly less impulse control than community controls. These results suggest that adolescents who made multiple suicide attempts were no more impulsive than first-time attempters or even other psychiatric patients. Rather, other factors beyond impulsivity accounted for repeat suicide attempts.

Gender differences in the relationship between impulsivity and suicidality have been the focus of two investigations, one that includes a juvenile delinquent sample and the other a medically hospitalized population. Rohde, Seeley, and Mace (1997) examined impulsivity as one of many correlates of suicidal ideation and past suicide attempts in a sample of 555 adolescents (mean age = 15 years) detained in a juvenile detention facility. Impulsivity was measured through 19 items from the impulsivity dimension of the Schedule for Normal and Abnormal Personality (Clark, 1992). There was a positive relationship between impulsivity and suicidal ideation in males and females, as well as a positive relationship between impulsivity and suicide attempts in females, but not in males. Further, impulsivity was more strongly associated with suicidal ideation than attempts in males, but not females. When impulsivity was entered into a multiple logistic regression analysis along with 15 other variables, it did not emerge as a predictor of suicidal ideation in males. However, when multivariate analyses were limited to females, impulsivity did emerge as one predictor of suicidal ideation along with younger age and depression. Females who reported higher levels of impulsivity were three times as likely to report suicidal ideation. When predicting suicide attempts in multivariate analyses, impulsivity, major life events, and no biological parent in the home emerged as predictors for females. In fact, females with higher levels of impulsivity were four times more likely to have made a suicide attempt. The same relationship did not hold for males. In males, ineffective coping doubled the likelihood of having made a suicide attempt, but impulsivity did not increase the odds of an attempt.

Horesh, Gothelf, Ofek, Weizman, and Apter (1999) examined the relationship between impulsivity, violence, aggression, and suicidality in 118 medically hospitalized adolescents. Sixteen adolescents made multiple serious suicide attempts, 33 made nonserious suicide attempts, 16 had suicidal ideation only, and 40 exhibited no suicidality. Suicidality was assessed by the K-SADS (Chambers *et al.*, 1985) as well as the Suicide Potential Scale (SPS; Pfeffer, 1986). Impulsivity was measured using the Plutchik Impulsivity Scale (Plutchik & Van Praag, 1989). Results revealed that impulsivity was significantly and positively correlated with suicidality on both measures of suicidality in males, and, further, that this relationship remained significant even after partialling out violence, aggressive feelings, and self-aggression. In females, impulsivity was only significantly and positively correlated with suicidality measured via the K-SADS, and no relationship remained when aggression was partialled out. The findings of the Rohde *et al.* (1997) and Horesh *et al.* (1999) studies are inconsistent but do suggest differential relationships between impulsivity and suicidal behavior based on gender.

Finally, one study was conducted to closely investigate the impact of impulsivity on different types of suicidal behavior. McKeown, Garrison, Cuffe, Waller, Jackson, and Addy (1998) conducted a longitudinal study examining incidence and predictors of suicidal behaviors, one of which was impulsivity, in 247 children and adolescents recruited from six public middle and high schools. Approximately 29% of the sample was less than 12 years old, 38% were 13, 29% were 14, and 5% were older than 15 years of age. Participants completed assessment instruments, approximately 1 year apart. Adolescents were categorized into one of four groups based on results of the K-SADS: a serious suicide attempt, a plan for committing suicide or preparations made for a suicidal gesture, moderate suicidal ideation, and mild or no suicidal ideation or behavior. Impulsivity was measured using one item from the K-SADS, in which severity of impulsivity was rated on a 6-point scale, based on responses to a question about acting before thinking about consequences. Logistic regression analyses revealed that impulsivity increased the odds of an adolescent reporting suicide plans almost twofold. There was no relationship to suicidal ideation or attempts at follow-up. Furthermore, impulsivity remained a significant predictor of a suicide plan when included in a final multivariate model along with female gender, undesirable life events, family cohesion, and prior suicidal behavior. According to the authors, this finding raises the possibility that suicidal acts may be considered impulsive due to lack of forethought about consequences, but not necessarily method.

AGGRESSIVE BEHAVIOR

Impulsive and aggressive behavior often co-occur, which can make it difficult to determine which behavior plays the more important role in suicidal behavior. For example, in the Horesh *et al.* (1999) cross-sectional study examining impulsivity in 118 medically hospitalized adolescents, aggression was also assessed. The relationship between impulsivity and suicidality remained significant after controlling for degree of violence. However, this relationship was no longer significant when aggressive feelings and aggressive conduct were partialled out of the analyses. Thus, in some adolescents, aggressive tendencies may play a stronger role than impulsivity in suicide risk.

As described in Chapter 4, anger is a common mood state among adolescents who attempt suicide. Aggressive behavior often accompanies this angry affect. A few studies have reported on aggressive behavior, rather than relying only on the self-report of anger, in clinical samples of adolescent suicide attempters. Aggressive behavior has been found to be strongly related to suicide attempts among female psychiatric patients (Pfeffer, Newcorn, Kaplan, Mizruchi, & Plutchik, 1988) and associated with conduct disorder diagnoses among both male and female adolescents (e.g., Brent *et al.*, 1993). Consequently, one way to estimate the degree of aggressive behavior among adolescent suicide attempters is to examine studies that document the rates of psychiatric disorders in this population, specifically conduct disorder. For example, Feldman and Wilson (1997) studied suicidal adolescents with and without a conduct disorder diagnosis and found that suicide attempters diagnosed with conduct disorder were characterized by a tendency to exhibit aggressive behavior more than suicidal adolescents without this diagnosis.

Simon and Crosby (2000) reported on data collected from the 1993 national school-based Youth Risk Behavior Survey including more than 16,000 students. The adolescents who reported unplanned, impulsive suicide attempts (*n* = 251) were more likely to report a history of fighting, being injured in a fight, and weapon carrying. Vannatta (1996), in a survey of more than 3000 7th- through 12th-grade students, found that frequency of aggressive and violent behaviors increased with level of suicidality (from no suicidality to suicide attempt) in this student sample. These behaviors included trouble with police, physical fighting, and property damage. Garrison, McKeown, Valois, and Vincent (1993), in a survey of more than 3000 high school students, also found that aggressive behavior, such as fighting and carrying weapons, was strongly associated with all forms of suicidal behavior, including suicide attempts, even after controlling for substance use.

Studies with clinical populations have not consistently found a relationship between aggressive and suicidal behavior. Brent *et al.* (1993) compared inpatient suicide attempters to never-suicidal psychiatric controls. The attempter group had a higher number of borderline symptoms compared to controls but did not differ on lifetime history of aggression, assaultive behavior, or tendency toward impulsive aggression. Gould *et al.* (1998), using data collected from more than 1000 children who participated in the Methods of the Epidemiology of Child and Adolescent Mental Disorders (MECA) study, did not find an independent contribution of disruptive behavior disorder to suicide attempts. Aggressiveness, however, was a significant predictor of suicidal ideation, even after controlling for the presence of a psychiatric disorder. Gould *et al.* (1998) concluded that the relationship found between disruptive behavior disorder and suicidal behavior in previous studies may have been mediated by substance abuse. Similarly, Renaud, Brent, Birmaher, Chiappetta, and Bridge (1999) found that adolescents diagnosed with disruptive behavior disorders are at risk for completed suicide when they have comorbid substance abuse, as well as a past history of a suicide attempt and parents with a history of substance abuse or a mood disorder.

ASSESSMENT OF IMPULSIVE AND AGGRESSIVE BEHAVIOR

The assessment of impulsive and aggressive behavior is an important component of any thorough evaluation of an adolescent who attempts suicide. Impulsivity has both cognitive and behavioral components. Impulsive children often respond quickly and make mistakes across a wide variety of tasks. This tendency to respond quickly without thinking may be due to biologically based differences in "cognitive tempo" (Barratt & Patton, 1983). Such a cognitive style may place an adolescent who attempts suicide at higher risk for future suicidality. Information about cognitive style has traditionally been gathered using measures such as the Matching Familiar Figures Test (MFFT; Kogan, Rosman, Day, Albert, & Phillips, 1964). For most clinicians, administering measures such as the MFFT is impractical and not likely to provide clinically useful information.

Behavioral impulsivity may be considered a form of behavioral disinhibition, which in turn results in diminished behavioral control. Tasks have been designed to assess behavioral impulsivity in laboratory studies but these are not useful for clinicians. Instead, to best assess for impulsivity, the suicide attempt itself should be classified as impulsive or planned. Once this has been decided, it may be useful to determine whether the adolescent reports a history of other impulsive behaviors. For example, does the adolescent show signs of impatience, have a difficult time waiting, consider multiple options before making a decision, act without thinking, become easily bored, or switch activities often? The adolescent's ability to delay gratification might be assessed by asking questions about past behaviors, such as whether birthday or holiday money is spent immediately or a portion set aside to be saved. Relatively brief assessment instruments can be administered to further assess impulsivity. The Plutchik Impulsivity Scale (Plutchik & van Praag, 1989) contains 15 items tapping impulsivity, such as the ability to plan one's actions. Pfeffer's (1986) Impulse Control subscale on the Child Suicide Potential Scale includes items such as frustration tolerance, as well as ability to delay action, plan future events, tolerate deprivation, and tolerate restlessness when restricted from typical activities.

When assessing anger, clinicians should not only ask questions pertaining to mood state, as described in Chapter 4, but also aggressive behavior. The Jesness Inventory (Jesness, 1996) is a self-report measure that contains 11 personality subscales, including one labeled "Manifest Aggression." Items on this scale tap fighting, being easily provoked to anger, out-of-control behavior, and angry outbursts. Pfeffer's (1986) subscale entitled "Spectrum of Assaultive Behavior" on the Child Suicide Potential Scales includes the following five classes of aggressive behavior: assaultive ideation, assaultive threats, mild assaultive actions, serious assaultive actions, and homicide. Assaultive ideation refers to thoughts about wanting to hurt or kill someone. Assaultive threats include statements about wanting to hurt or kill someone as well as actions such as threatening someone with a knife. Mild assaultive actions refers to mild injuries inflicted on a victim such as hitting, kicking, or throwing something at someone. Serious assaultive action refers to infliction of significant injuries requiring medical care. These actions include pushing someone down violently, causing injury, cutting someone with a knife, setting fires, and sexually violent acts such as molestation or rape. Homicide is the final category included on Pfeffer's scale.

Finally, it is useful to obtain ratings of aggressive behaviors from significant adults in the adolescent's environment. The parent and teacher reports described in Chapter 4 under the assessment of depression, such as the Behavior Assessment Scale for Children and the Child Behavior Checklist, also contain subscales that assess aggressive behavior. These measures may provide useful information for clinicians regarding the degree of aggressive behavior demonstrated by suicidal adolescents.

CLINICAL IMPLICATIONS

Impulsivity and aggressiveness should be routinely assessed when planning a disposition following an adolescent's suicide attempt. However, there have been a variety of problems in the objective assessment of impulsivity and aggressiveness. A range of measures have been used, often relying on self-report from the adolescent. Unfortunately, it may be difficult for many adolescents to rate these tendencies objectively. Some investigators have used full scales, distinct subscales, and single items in their efforts to measure impulsivity and aggressiveness. Impulsivity has been examined as a cognitive process (Kashden *et al.*, 1993), a behavioral style, a personality trait (Beautrais *et al.*, 1999; Rohde *et al.*, 1997), or an aspect of the suicidal behavior itself (Brown *et al.*, 1988). Furthermore, because of the wide range of measures that have been used in the different studies, it becomes much harder to identify consistent patterns of findings across studies.

The two constructs may be intertwined. Aggressive behavior may be linked to underlying levels of poor impulse control. However, both impulsivity and aggressiveness may be nonspecific risk factors for suicidal behavior. For example, several studies have found that adolescent psychiatric patients report higher levels of impulsivity than nonpatient controls (Lehnert *et al.*, 1994; Pfeffer *et al.*, 1995), but impulsivity has not been found to serve as an essential risk factor due to its overlap with other predictors of suicide (Beautrais *et al.*, 1999). Hence, both impulsivity and aggressiveness may reflect some degree of psychopathology in the adolescent and may increase the risk of deviant behavior, but these factors may not be clear indicators of suicide risk. Research suggests that depressed adolescents often display serious suicidal tendencies that are not impulsive in nature (Beautrais *et al.*, 1999; Brown *et al.*, 1988).

Psychotherapy may be used to cultivate impulse control in adolescents. Cognitive strategies to address impulsive behavior are indicated prior to discharge and should be routinely included in short-term treatment protocols for impulsive and aggressive adolescents (see Chapter 14). Impulsivity may be best characterized as a tendency to act without thinking instead of a stable personality trait. Hence, an impulsive act can occur in many settings and often reflects a poor choice that has been selected from a limited range of alternatives. The adolescent may benefit from strategies designed to reduce impulsive tendencies by learning to stop when confronted with a major problem and seek to identify a wide range of possible options. A simple series of steps can help adolescents learn to plan a range of options and anticipate various outcomes when attempting to solve difficult situational or interpersonal problems (see Chapter 14). Also, the impulsive adolescent may need to learn to tolerate discomfort with painful emotions or aversive situations before reacting.

REFERENCES

Barratt, E. S. (1965). Factor analysis of some psychometric measures of impulsiveness and anxiety. *Psychological Reports, 16*, 544–547.

Barratt, E. S., & Patton, J. H. (1983). Impulsivity: Cognitive, behavioral, and psychophysiological correlates. In M. Zuckerman (Ed.), *The biological bases of sensation seeking, impulsivity, and anxiety* (pp.77–116). Hillsdale, NJ: Erlbaum.

Beautrais, A. L., Joyce, P. R., & Mulder, R. T. (1999). Personality traits and cognitive styles as risk factors for serious suicide attempts among young people. *Suicide and Life Threatening Behavior, 29*, 37–47.

Brent, D., Johnson, B., Bartle, S., Bridge, J., Rather, C., Matta, J., Connolly, J., & Constantine, D. (1993). Personality disorder, tendency to impulsive violence, and suicidal behavior in adolescents. *Journal of the American Academy of Child and Adolescent Psychiatry, 32*, 69–75.

Brown, L. K., Overholser, J., Spirito, A., & Fritz, G. K. (1991). The correlates of planning in adolescent suicide attempts. *Journal of the American Academy of Child and Adolescent Psychiatry, 30*, 95–99.

Chambers, W. J., Puig-Antich, J., Hirsch, M., Paez, P., Ambrosini, P., Tabrizi, A., & Davies, M. (1985). The assessment of affective disorders in children and adolescents by semi-structured interview: Test-retest reliability of the Schedule for Affective Disorders and Schizophrenia for School-aged Children, Present Episode Version. *Archives of General Psychiatry, 42*, 696–702.

Clark, L. A. (1992). *Manual for the Schedule for Normal and Abnormal Personality* (SNAP). Minneapolis: University of Minnesota Press.

Feldman, M., & Wilson, A. (1997). Adolescent suicidality in urban minorities and its relationship to conduct disorders, depression, and separation anxiety. *Journal of the American Academy of Child and Adolescent Psychiatry, 36,* 75–84.

Garrison, C., McKeown, R., Valois, R., & Vincent, M. (1993). Aggression, substance use, and suicidal behaviors in high school students. *American Journal of Public Health, 83,* 179–184.

Gould, M., King, R., Greenwald, S., Fisher, P., Schwab-Stone, M., Kramer, R., Flisher, A., Goodman, S., Canino, G., & Shaffer, D. (1998). Psychopathology associated with suicidal ideation and attempts among children and adolescents. *Journal of the American Academy of Child and Adolescent Psychiatry, 37,* 915–923.

Hawton, K., Kingsbury, S., Steinhardt, K., James, A., & Fagg, J. (1999). Repetition of deliberate self-harm by adolescents: The role of psychological factors. *Journal of Adolescence, 22,* 169–178.

Horesh, N., Gothelf, D., Ofek, H., Weizman, T., & Apter, A. (1999). Impulsivity as a correlate of suicidal behavior in adolescent psychiatric inpatients. *Crisis, 20,* 8–14.

Jesness, C. (1996). *The Jesness Inventory.* North Tonawanda, New York: MHS.

Kashden, J., Fremouw, W., Callahan, T., & Franzen, M. (1993). Impulsivity in suicidal and non-suicidal adolescents. *Journal of Abnormal Psychology, 21,* 339–352.

Kingsbury, S., Hawton, K., Steinhardt, K., & James, A. (1999). Do adolescents who take overdose have specific psychological characteristics? A comparative study with psychiatric and community controls. *Journal of the American Academy of Child and Adolescent Psychiatry, 38,* 1125–1131.

Kogan, J., Rosman, B., Day, D., Albert, J., & Phillips, W. (1964). Information processing in the child: Significance of analytic and reflective attitudes. *Psychological Monographs, 78* (No 1, Whole #578).

Lehnert, K. L., Overholser, J. C., & Spirito, A. (1994). Internalized and externalized anger in adolescent suicide attempters. *Journal of Adolescent Research, 9,* 105–119.

McKeown, R. E., Garrison, C. Z., Cuffe, S. P., Waller, J. L., Jackson, K. L., & Addy, C. L. (1998). Incidence and predictors of suicidal behaviors in a longitudinal sample of young adolescents. *Journal of the American Academy of Child and Adolescent Psychiatry, 37,* 612–619.

Offer, D., Ostrov, E., & Howard, K. (1982). *The Offer Self-Image Questionnaire for Adolescents: A manual.* Chicago: Michael Reese Hospital.

Pfeffer, C. R. (1986). *The suicidal child.* New York: Guilford Press.

Pfeffer, C. R., Hurt, S. W., Peskin, J. R., & Siefker, C. A. (1995). Suicidal children grow up: Ego functions associated with suicide attempts. *Journal of the American Academy of Child and Adolescent Psychiatry, 34,* 1318–1325.

Pfeffer, C., Newcorn, J., Kaplan, G., Mizruchi, M., & Plutchik, R. (1988). Suicidal behavior in adolescent psychiatric inpatients. *Journal of the American Academy of Child and Adolescent Psychiatry, 27,* 357–361.

Plutchik, R., & van Praag, H. M. (1989). The measurement of suicidality, aggressivity, and impulsivity. *Clinical Neuropharmacology* (Vol. 9, Supp 4). New York: Raven Press.

Renaud, J., Brent, D., Birmaher, B., Chiapetta, L., & Bridge, J. (1999). Suicide in adolescents with disruptive disorder. *Journal of the American Academy of Child and Adolescent Psychiatry, 38,* 846–851.

Rohde, P., Seeley, J. R., & Mace, D. E. (1997). Correlates of suicidal behavior in a juvenile detention population. *Suicide and Life Threatening Behavior, 27,* 164–175.

Simon, T., & Crosby, A. (2000). Suicide planning among high school students who report attempting suicide. *Suicide and Life Threatening Behavior, 30*, 213–221.

Stein, D., Apter, A., Ratzoni, G., Har-Even, D., & Avidan, G. (1998). Association between multiple suicide attempts and negative affects in adolescents. *Journal of the American Academy of Child and Adolescent Psychiatry, 37*, 488–494.

Vannatta, R. (1996). Risk factors related to suicidal behavior among male and female adolescents. *Journal of Youth and Adolescence, 25*, 149–160.

Wetzler, S., Asnis, G. M., Hyman, R., Virtue, C., Zimmerman, J., & Rathus, J. H. (1996). Characteristics of suicidality among adolescents. *Suicide and Life Threatening Behavior, 26*, 37–45.

CHAPTER 8

Social Factors:
Family Functioning

Jamie Hollenbeck, Jennifer Dyl, and Anthony Spirito

Family issues play a central role in many adolescent suicide attempts. Prolonged and progressive family disruptions, inadequate family relationships, and ineffective parent-child relationships may result in adolescent suicidal behavior (Kurtz & Derevensky, 1993). Multigenerational familial difficulties, such as isolation, abandonment, long-lasting feuds, emotional cutoffs, violence, and abuse, may also result in an adolescent's suicidal behavior (Gutstein, 1991). Family influences on the suicidal behavior of adolescents have therefore been investigated from multiple conceptual bases including familial psychopathology, such as a family history of suicidal behavior, family composition, family histories of abuse, and family conflict. Adaptive factors including perceived support, communication, and problem solving have also been studied. Findings from studies in these areas of family functioning conducted in the past decade are summarized in this discussion.

FAMILIAL SUICIDAL BEHAVIOR AND PSYCHOPATHOLOGY

Prior to 1990, there was considerable evidence for a high frequency of psychiatric illness within the families of adolescent suicide attempters. For example, a 1982 emergency department study (Garfinkel, Froese, & Hood, 1982) evaluated children and adolescents who had attempted suicide compared to youth with medical problems. Results showed that 50% of the suicide attempters reported having a family history of psychiatric disorders compared with 16% in the control group. More recent studies have confirmed earlier findings that parental psychiatric disorders and family history of suicidal behavior are risk factors for attempted suicide among adolescents. For example, Laederach, Fischer, Bowen, and Ladame (1999) examined 148 Swiss adolescents hospitalized after a suicide attempt and found that approximately 20% reported having a family member who had attempted suicide. Stiffman (1989) compared runaways with and without prior suicide attempts and found the attempter group had higher rates of family suicidal behavior, antisocial behavior, and general psychopathology.

Brent, Kolko, Allan, and Brown (1990) examined affectively disordered adolescents and young adults (aged 13 to 29 years) hospitalized in a psychiatric inpatient program. These patients completed measures of cognitive distortion, social skills, and familial-environmental stress. The suicidal patients demonstrated a greater likelihood of exposure to familial suicidality within the 12 months prior to hospitalization as compared to nonsuicidal, affectively disturbed patients. Additionally, the degree of suicidal intent of the attempter group was related to family conflict and to a family history of suicidal behavior. In a later report, Brent, Kolko, *et al.* (1993) examined just the adolescent participants in their data set, comparing 13 suicide attempters with 21 youths who had no history of suicide attempt. No differences were found between suicidal and nonsuicidal groups in terms of family history of suicidal behavior. However, the small number of patients reduced the statistical power needed for detecting differences between the groups. Overall, these studies with clinical samples do suggest that the families of adolescent suicide attempters often have higher rates of psychopathology and suicidal behavior than adolescent psychiatric patients without suicidal behavior.

Several studies examining family psychopathology in community samples have yielded positive findings. Sorenson and Rutter (1991) found that a maternal history of suicide attempts raised the probability of an adolescent suicide attempt by nearly seven-fold. Grossman, Milligan, and Deyo (1991) studied a large sample of adolescents on a Navaho reservation, 971 who had attempted suicide compared to 5666 adolescents with no history of suicide attempts. A family history of attempted or completed suicide was more common in the attempters, even after controlling for adolescent mental health. In another study, Bridge, Brent, Johnson, and Connolly (1997) examined familial aggregation of psychiatric disorders and suicide attempts in a community sample of 58 adolescents. The adolescents were recruited and assessed for DSM-III Axis I disorders and suicide attempts using family study and family history methodology. The rate of suicide attempts was significantly greater among relatives of adolescent suicide attempters when compared to relatives of participants with no lifetime history of psychiatric disorder (62.5% versus 2.9%). Other psychiatric problems, including a higher rate of Axis I disorders (100% versus 46.0%) and conduct disorders (50.0% versus 5.8%), were also more prevalent among the relatives of participants who attempted suicide versus relatives of participants with no history of a psychiatric disorder. Using a community sample, Fergusson and Lynskey (1995) found substance abuse and antisocial behavior to be more common in the families of 29 adolescents with a history of suicide attempts compared to 925 adolescents without a history of suicide attempts. Thus, these studies suggest that psychopathology and a family history of suicidal behavior are both found more frequently in the families of adolescent suicide attempters compared to controls.

One community study did not find differences between attempters and controls. Lewinsohn, Rohde, and Seeley (1993, 1994) compared a community sample of adolescents at baseline and follow-up. At baseline, 121 students reported a prior suicide attempt, and at follow-up 26 adolescents reported a suicide attempt in the prior year. For both samples, there was no difference between attempters and more than 1400 nonattempters on suicidal behavior of a family member in a prior year. de Wilde, Kienhorst, Diekstra, and Wolters (1992) compared high school students with a history of suicide attempts to adolescents with and without self-reported depressed mood. The suicide attempters and depressed adolescents did not differ in their rates of family mental health problems in the prior year, but both groups had higher rates than the nondepressed youths. Thus, suicidal behavior may indeed be higher in the families of adolescents who attempt suicide compared to both controls and adolescents with other psychiatric disorders. However, family psychopathology may not be specific to adolescent suicidal behavior but rather common in adolescents with psychiatric disorders.

Several studies have examined family history of psychopathology in relation to completed suicides. Brent and colleagues (1994) compared 67 suicide victims with 67 living controls that were matched on demographic factors. Both groups were assessed on several familial variables including family constellation, familial stressors, and familial psychopathology. When compared to the control group, first-degree relatives of adolescent suicide completers were more likely to have been diagnosed with a psychiatric disorder—including any affective disorder, alcohol abuse, or drug abuse—and to have a history of a suicide attempt. Other difficulties, such as parental legal trouble and parental unemployment, were also more common among the completers than controls. In a related study, Brent, Perper, *et al.* (1993) found that parental depression increased the risk of an adolescent's suicide, even after controlling for the adolescent's depression.

The risk of suicide attempts in first- and second-degree relatives of adolescent suicide completers does not appear to be explained by the presence of psychiatric disorders within the family (e.g., Brent, Bridges, Johnson, & Connolly, 1996). Gould, Fisher, Parides, Flory, and Shaffer (1996) found in a case-control study of adolescent suicide that the suicide victims were more likely than controls to have had a mother with a history of mood disorder symptoms, a father with a history of legal troubles, and a family history of suicidal behavior. In the Gould *et al.* (1996) study, a father's history of trouble with the police and a family history of suicidal behavior significantly increased the risk of suicide beyond the risk attributed to the adolescent's psychopathology. Thus, among adolescents who complete suicide, a significant degree of dysfunction in their families is evident. Brent *et al.* (1994) speculated that parental psychopathology may increase the risk for an adolescent's suicide by decreasing parental support to the adolescent or increasing the amount of conflict at home. Therefore, clinical work with suicidal adolescents is likely to benefit from a family focus during both assessment and treatment.

CLINICAL IMPLICATIONS: FAMILY HISTORY OF SUICIDAL BEHAVIOR AND PSYCHOPATHOLOGY

A family history of suicidal behavior and psychopathology is common in adolescent suicide attempters. It is important to investigate psychopathology and suicidal behavior in the biological parents of adolescents who attempt suicide. Whenever possible, information should be collected regarding the psychiatric history of first-degree relatives. It is particularly important to inquire about depression, bipolar disorder, substance abuse, suicide attempts, and completed suicide. Understanding the family psychiatric history helps the clinician to better evaluate possible biological risk factors. More important, identification of the parent's emotional disturbance and referral for treatment may be an essential component in the successful treatment of the adolescent.

FAMILY COMPOSITION: EFFECTS OF DIVORCE AND SEPARATION

Divorce and separation within families of suicide attempters have been cited as potential background risk factors for adolescent suicide attempts. Presumably, these structural changes in the family result in a lack of familial support for the adolescent. However, the literature within the past decade has been equivocal on the effects of divorce on adolescent suicidal behavior.

Two studies conducted at medical centers yielded conflicting findings. Adams, Overholser, and Lehnert (1994) found higher rates of divorce and separation among inpatient suicide attempters compared to ideators and high school students, but not compared to nonsuicidal psychiatric patients. However, a similar study drawing a sample of suicide attempters from a general medical center found no difference between attempters and ideators on the likelihood of coming from an intact family. However, attempters and ideators came from intact families less often than nonsuicidal adolescents (Paluszny, Davenport, & Kim, 1991).

King, Raskin, Gdowski, Butkus, and Opipari (1990) found that psychiatrically hospitalized adolescent suicide attempters were less likely to be living with their mothers as compared to nonattempters. Other studies of inpatient psychiatric samples have found no difference in rates of marital separation and divorce among clinical populations including suicide attempters. Borst and Noam (1989) did not find differences in the rates of marital separation and divorce between suicide attempters and nonsuicidal psychiatric inpatients. Similarly, Kovacs, Goldston, and Gatsonis (1993) found no difference in rates of marital separation or divorce between inpatient ideators, attempters, and nonsuicidal adolescents. At follow-up, living in an intact family did not predict either suicidal ideation or attempt.

Studies with community samples have also yielded conflicting results. de Wilde *et al.* (1992) studied life events during three time periods, including childhood (up to 12 years of age), adolescence, and the year prior to the attempt in a community sample. The researchers compared 48 adolescent suicide attempters to 66 depressed and 43 nondepressed adolescents on their responses to a semistructured interview and several self-report questionnaires. During childhood, suicide attempters experienced more parental separation and unemployment of family members compared to depressed and nondepressed adolescents. Also, during adolescence, the attempters experienced more parental separation and divorce as well as changes in their living situation and caregiver. During the year prior to the attempt, the attempters also experienced more changes in their living situations and caretakers than the depressed and nondepressed adolescents.

Rubenstein, Halton, Kasten, Rubin, and Stechler (1998) examined parental marital status as a mediating variable of previously identified stress and protective factors and as a factor directly associated with adolescent suicidal behavior. A total of 272 10th- and 11th-grade students (14% reported suicidal behavior) completed a measure of depression and the Family Adaptability and Cohesion Scales (Olson, Portner, & Lavee, 1985). Remarriage most dramatically increased the risk of suicidality, as did parental separation and divorce. Vanatta (1996), in a study of high school students, also found that not living with both parents increased the risk for suicidal behavior.

Several studies with community samples have not found differences in parental marital status between suicide attempters and nonsuicidal adolescents. Fergusson and Lynskey (1995) compared 29 suicide attempters to 925 adolescents with no history of a suicide attempt and found no differences in the number of changes of parental figures. Similarly, Grossman *et al.* (1991) compared 971 youths on a Navaho reservation who attempted suicide to 5666 reservation youths with no history of suicidal behavior. Initial findings revealed a difference between groups on parental separation. However, these results did not hold after statistical analyses controlled for the presence of substance use, child maltreatment, and use of mental health service.

Two studies have examined the marital status of parents of adolescents who committed suicide. In their study of adolescent suicide victims, Brent and colleagues (1994) found that suicide completers were less likely to be living with both biological parents and more likely to have residential instability when compared to the control group. The biological parents of these adolescents were also more likely than matched living controls to have had residential instability. However, when family history of psychopathology was considered at the same time, family constellation was not related to suicide. Gould *et al.* (1996), in a case-control psychological autopsy study of adolescent suicide, found that the suicide victims were more likely to come from nonintact families of origin.

In conclusion, the role of parental divorce and separation in adolescent suicidal behavior is not clear. Whether clinical or community samples are studied or whether adolescents who attempt or complete suicide are the focus of investigation, the results have conflicted across studies. Thus, parental divorce and separation do not appear to be a specific risk factor for adolescent suicide attempts.

CLINICAL IMPLICATIONS

When evaluating any adolescent, including one who has made a suicide attempt, the clinician must determine the parents' marital status and evaluate the role of family composition and disruption on the adolescent's suicidal behavior. The treatment plan must address the role of parental separation in the adolescent's self-destructive behavior. This may include individual work regarding the adolescent's emotional response to parental separation and ongoing conflict that results in stress and behavior disturbance. Family sessions need to address any conflict between parents and how it affects their ability to consistently manage their adolescent's behavior.

PHYSICAL AND SEXUAL ABUSE

In the past decade, a number of investigations have examined the role of physical and sexual abuse on adolescent suicidal behavior. Studies with clinical populations have been inconsistent. Silverman, Reinherz, and Giaconia (1996) conducted a longitudinal study comparing adults who reported being abused prior to the age of 18 to those not reporting abuse. As adults, the abused participants reported more psychiatric symptoms, suicidal ideation, and suicide attempts than their nonabused counterparts. Shaunessey, Cohen, Plummer, and Berman (1993) studied psychiatrically hospitalized adolescent attempters and ideators. Adolescents reporting a history of abuse in any form had higher rates of suicide attempts than those without an abuse history. Two other studies of adolescent psychiatric patients also found that suicide attempts were related to a history of sexual abuse (Lipschitz, Winegar, Nicolaou, Hartnick, Wolfson, & Southwick, 1999) or a history of physical or sexual abuse (Grilo, Sanislow, Fehon, Martino, & McGlashan, 1999).

Other studies have not found differences in abuse when adolescent suicide attempters are compared to other clinical samples. deWilde and colleagues (1992) found higher rates of childhood sexual abuse among adolescent suicide attempters compared to community controls but not when compared to depressed adolescents. Brent, Kolko, *et al.* (1993) followed 134 adolescents for 6 months after discharge from a psychiatric unit. Thirteen of the adolescents attempted suicide, but the attempters did not differ from the adolescents who had not attempted suicide on their history of physical or sexual abuse. Finally, in a study of completed suicide, Brent *et al.* (1994) compared 67 suicide completers with a matched sample of community controls. The completers had a higher rate of physical, but not sexual, abuse in the year prior to their suicide. These findings indicate that abuse is commonly reported by psychiatric patients but does not appear specifically related to suicide attempts or completed suicide. Abuse seems likely to increase the risk of psychiatric symptomatology in general.

Similar conflicting findings have been found in the rates of suicidal behavior among other clinical samples of abused adolescents. DeBellis, Lefter, Trickert, and Putnam (1994) compared sexually abused girls to a matched community sample of nonabused girls. The abused group reported significantly higher rates of suicidal ideation and attempts. However, Brand, King, Olson, Ghaziuddin, and Naylor (1996) compared psychiatrically hospitalized, depressed adolescents with a history of sexual abuse to depressed inpatients without a history of sexual abuse. There was no difference between the two groups on suicidal ideation or behavior.

Other studies have examined the relation of suicidal behavior to abuse in runaway youth or youth being treated for substance abuse. Deykin and Buka (1994) compared 109 suicide attempters in a drug and alcohol treatment program to 191 adolescents in the same program with no history of suicide attempts. The male attempters reported a significantly greater history of physical and sexual abuse than the males without a suicide attempt history. Edwall, Hoffman, and Harrison (1989) compared 47 girls in an inpatient substance treatment program who reported a history of sexual abuse to 234 girls without a history of sexual abuse. The girls with a history of sexual abuse reported a higher rate of past suicide attempts. In a similar study with a larger sample from a substance abuse program, Harrison and Hoffman (1989) found that adolescents with a history of sexual abuse had higher rates of suicide attempts in the past year than those without a history of abuse. Molnar, Shade, Kral, Booth, and Watters (1998) examined abuse and suicide attempts in a large sample of street youth. Sexual and physical abuse before leaving home were independent predictors of suicide attempts. A history of abuse increases the odds of attempting suicide two to four-fold. Thus, unlike the findings in the psychiatric sample, sexual and physical abuse are consistently related to suicide attempts in street youth and substance-abusing youth.

Studies that have used community samples have also consistently found higher rates of abuse in adolescents who report a history of suicide attempts. Grossman *et al.* (1991) found that adolescent suicide attempters reported significantly more physical and sexual abuse, even after statistically controlling for mental health services and substance use. Hernandez, Lodico, and DiClemente (1993) studied more than 5500 high school students, including many African-American and Native American teens. Sexual and physical abuse was significantly associated with suicide attempts after controlling for race. Riggs, Alario, and McHorney (1990) compared 72 high school students who attempted suicide to 528 students with no prior attempt and found higher rates of physical and sexual abuse in the suicide attempter group. Wagner, Cole, and Schwartzman (1995) evaluated 147 suicide attempters from rural schools as compared to 261 high school students who reported depressed mood or suicidal ideation. The suicide attempter group reported their parents physically hurt them more often than did the comparison group. Similarly, in a large sample of high school students, an adolescent with a history of sexual abuse was 12 times more likely to make a noninjurious suicide attempt and 47 times more likely to make an injurious suicide attempt than an adolescent without a sexual abuse history (Bensley, Van Eenwyk, Spieker, & Schoder, 1999). A history of physical abuse placed the adolescent at a five times higher likelihood for a noninjurious attempt and 12 times higher likelihood for an injurious suicide attempt.

CLINICAL IMPLICATIONS

The literature provides fairly consistent support for the notion that sexual and physical abuse is common in adolescents who attempt suicide. However, in psychiatric samples, particularly psychiatrically hospitalized adolescents, a history of abuse does not appear more frequent than that found in other nonsuicidal clinical groups. Nonetheless, clinicians should inquire about abuse history when evaluating and treating adolescents who have attempted suicide. Asking adolescents about abuse requires clinical skill. Incidents of abuse not previously reported must be reported, and the reporting process will affect the therapist's relationship with the adolescent. For many adolescent suicide attempters, their abuse history may be a significant trigger for suicidal behavior. Consequently, addressing the psychological sequelae of abuse, although initially quite difficult and upsetting, may reduce the incidence of future suicidal behavior by reducing the potential for an adolescent's abuse history to trigger emotional distress.

FAMILY CONFLICT

Family conflict includes a continuum of behaviors from verbal disagreements between family members to domestic violence. Research conducted in the 1970s and 1980s found family conflict to be prominent in the families of adolescents who attempt suicide (see Spirito, Brown, Overholser, & Fritz, 1989). Studies in the past decade have had similar findings.

A study in Northern Ireland examined the psychiatric assessments of 124 adolescents hospitalized as a result of attempted suicide (Davies & Cunningham, 1999). Among the most frequently recorded stressors included family conflict and family illness. Several other studies have documented more disturbed family functioning in the families of adolescent suicide attempters compared to nonsuicidal psychiatric patients (e.g., Brent *et al.*, 1990). King and colleagues (1990) found that psychiatrically hospitalized suicide attempters reported more family adjustment problems and poorer relationships with maternal figures than nonsuicidal hospitalized adolescents. Kosky, Silburn, and Zubrick (1990) compared 258 suicide ideators to 82 suicide attempters. Suicide attempters reported chronic family discord, including hostility, quarreling, scapegoating, and verbal abuse at higher rates than suicide ideators and nonclinical controls. Paluszny *et al.* (1991) found that suicide attempters hospitalized on a pediatric unit reported more family problems than nonsuicidal adolescent pediatric clinic patients, but not more than suicide ideators. However, both attempters and ideators reported more chaotic families than the control adolescents. In a prospective study of adolescent patients, King, Segal, Kaminski, Naylor, Ghaziuddin, and Radpour (1995) found that family dysfunction predicted suicide attempts during the 6-month follow-up after discharge from an inpatient psychiatric facility. In a study of adolescents who completed suicide, Brent and colleagues (1994) found that adolescents who die by suicide were more likely than controls to have conflict with their parents over their lifetime compared to controls.

Other studies have examined more specific dimensions of family functioning. Adams *et al.* (1994) studied family system and parent-adolescent dyadic relationships as related to suicidal ideation and suicide attempts. The Family Assessment Measure (Skinner, Steinhauer, & Santabarbara, 1983) was administered to adolescent psychiatric inpatients who had attempted suicide ($n = 35$), adolescent inpatients who had not attempted suicide ($n = 29$), high school students with suicidal ideation ($n = 33$), and high school students without suicidal ideation ($n = 37$). Both hospitalized attempters and nonhospitalized ideators perceived their family functioning as dysfunctional and viewed the mother-adolescent relationships as conflicted. This perception of family dysfunction among the ideators and attempters was not evident in the nonsuicidal adolescents, in either the clinical or high school control group. Furthermore, the nonsuicidal high school students and nonsuicidal inpatients did not differ in their perceptions of family functioning.

Mitchell and Rosenthal (1992) compared suicidal adolescents, including ideators and attempters, to nonsuicidal patient groups on several aspects of family functioning. The degree of overprotection and enmeshment was comparable across the two groups, but suicidal families had higher levels of conflict avoidance and a tendency to deny difficulties. de Wilde *et al.* (1992), using an adapted version of the Family Environment Scale (Moos & Moos, 1981), did not find differences between suicide attempters and depressed adolescents. However, both clinical groups reported less cohesion and more conflict than normal controls. Campbell, Milling, Laughlin, and Bush (1993) examined the perceptions of preadolescent psychiatric inpatients (ages 7 through 11) and their parents utilizing a structured interview and the Family Environment Scale. Both parents and suicidal preadolescents reported family conflict, family disorganization, and a lack of family achievement orientation. Preadolescents also described their families as less cohesive and less emotionally expressive.

Several studies of high school students have reported findings similar to those with clinical samples. Bjarnason and Thorlindsson (1994) examined a variety of predictors of adolescent suicide attempts in a sample that included all 9th and 10th graders in Iceland. Results demonstrated a negative correlation between attempted suicide and living with both parents, parents knowing their children's whereabouts on weekends, and time spent with parents. Serious parental conflict was positively correlated with suicide attempts. In South Australia, Martin, Rozanes, Pearce, and Allison (1995) examined the relationship between adolescents' perceptions of family relationships, suicidal thoughts, and suicide attempts using the

Family Assessment Device (Epstein, Baldwin, & Bishop, 1983). The participants ($n = 352$) were 10th- and 11th-grade high school students. Overall family dysfunction was associated with suicidal ideation, self-injurious behavior, suicide attempts, and severe depression. The subscales most strongly associated with suicide attempts were family roles (i.e., the degree to which there are established patterns of behavior among family members) and affective responsiveness (i.e., sharing of appropriate emotions among family members). However, further analyses indicated that family dysfunction influences adolescent suicidal behaviors via indirect pathways, including depression. Thus, family problems may underlie feelings of depression, and the emotional turmoil pushes the adolescent toward suicidal behavior.

Finally, family conflict has also been investigated in completed suicide during adolescence. Brent, Perper, *et al.* (1993) found that the parents of adolescents who had completed suicide reported greater parent-adolescent conflict than community controls. However, this finding became nonsignificant after statistically controlling for the psychiatric disorders of the adolescents.

CLINICAL IMPLICATIONS: FAMILY CONFLICT

The studies reviewed here lend support to the hypothesis that adolescent suicide attempters have more conflicted family and parent-child relationships when compared to community samples. Many, but not all, studies also indicate that a high level of conflict seen in the families of suicide attempters is more common than that found in the families of psychiatric comparison groups. Therefore, family conflict and parent-child relationships should be assessed thoroughly because these areas may play an important role in suicide risk. Family conflict may need to be a central focus of therapy for suicidal adolescents, even when the primary treatment modality is individual therapy.

PERCEIVED FAMILY SUPPORT

Perceived lack of family support has been associated with increased rates of suicidal ideation and attempts (Dubow, Kausch, Blum, Reed, & Bush, 1989). Several recent studies have also found this to be true. For example, Rubenstein and colleagues (1998) found that family cohesiveness served as a protective factor against suicidal behavior for nonintact families.

Swedo, Rettew, Kuppenheimer, Lum, Dolan, and Goldberger (1991) compared 21 adolescent suicide attempters, 15 at-risk adolescents, and 34 controls on a number of individual and family characteristics. A 1-hour structured interview was used to gather information about family constellation, family relationships, psychiatric history, sexual and physical abuse, and substance use. Strained relationships between adolescents and their parents differentiated attempters and controls. The families of adolescent suicide attempters were not perceived as providing sufficient emotional support by their adolescents compared to controls. Similarly, Kienhorst, de Wilde, Diekstra, and Wolters (1992) found that adolescent suicide attempters reported less parental support than depressed adolescents. Another study compared physically abused adolescents who did and did not attempt suicide (Kaplan, Pelcovitz, Salzinger, Mandell, & Weiner, 1997). Findings suggested that the attempters were more likely to perceive their families as lacking cohesiveness and maternal support.

Morano, Cisler, and Lemerond (1993) examined the relationship between hopelessness, loss, and social and family support for adolescents admitted to a psychiatric inpatient facility. The researchers matched 20 adolescent suicide attempters and 20 nonattempters for gender and depression scores. The best predictors of suicidal behavior were the loss of a significant other and limited family support. As compared to the nonattempters, the attempters reported similar levels of satisfaction with social support but significantly less family support. Additionally, the adolescents who experienced the loss of a significant other and perceived less family support were highly likely to be suicide attempters.

Berit, Ekeberg, Wichstrom, and Haldorsen (2000) compared 91 adolescents hospitalized following a suicide attempt to a community sample of nonattempters. The adolescents were asked whether they turned to parents in three stressful situations (trouble with police, feeling low, and future plans for education). The control group was three times more likely to turn to their parents for support in these situations than the suicide attempters.

Lack of parental support and family cohesiveness have also been studied in community samples. The findings are less consistent than those observed with clinical samples. As part of a larger study, Windle and Windle (1997) administered the Perceived Social Support from Family measure (PSS-Fa; Procidano & Heller, 1983) to 975 10th- and 11th-grade students. Adolescents with a prior suicide attempt reported lower levels of perceived family support than nonattempters. Lewinsohn *et al.* (1994) followed high school students for 1 year and found that lower family support at baseline was associated with suicide attempts at follow-up. This relation held even after controlling for depression, but not prior suicide attempts. One study did not find such a relationship. Garrison, Jackson, Addy, McKeown, and Waller (1991) found that family adaptability, but not family cohesion, was negatively related to suicide attempts, but this relationship was not significant after controlling for depression.

There is reasonably consistent support for the notion that an adolescent's perception of family support is negatively associated with suicidal behavior. For clinicians, it is important to determine whether this lack of perceived support is a problem with the parents not being available or the adolescents not seeking help when parents could be helpful.

FAMILY COMMUNICATION AND PROBLEM SOLVING

Many clinicians have described the families of adolescent suicide attempters as characterized by poor problem-solving skills and a pattern of indirect communication. However, the research has been less convincing. In a study previously described, both suicide attempters and suicide ideators rated their families as demonstrating poor adaptation to change and poor problem solving (Adams *et al.*, 1994). King *et al.* (1990) found that adolescent suicide attempters were less likely to confide in parents or guardians than were nonsuicidal psychiatrically hospitalized adolescents. Martin and colleagues (1995), in a study of Australian high school students, found that the problem-solving and communication subscales of the Family Assessment Device (Epstein *et al.*, 1983) were most strongly associated with plans for a suicide attempt.

Similar findings have been reported in studies of completed suicide. Gould *et al.* (1996), in their study of adolescent suicide victims, found that the suicide victims had significantly less frequent and less satisfying communication with their parents. In addition, for adolescents older than 16 years, poor communication with fathers increased the risk for suicide beyond that contributed by the adolescent's psychopathology.

Despite the positive findings revealed here, Wagner (1997), in his review of the literature, concluded that there is only modest evidence to support poor family communication and problem solving as a specific risk factor for suicidal behavior. When specific problems are found, the designs of most studies make it impossible to determine whether these problem-solving and communication deficits existed prior to the suicide attempt or resulted from the suicide attempt.

CLINICAL IMPLICATIONS

Given the importance of family communication and problem solving in the functioning of healthy families, clinicians will need to assess problem-solving and communication skills in the families of suicide attempters. Communication among family members is believed by many clinicians to be a prerequisite to improving family functioning because communication needs to be established before any other family work, such as problem solving, can be accomplished. Therapy goals for the families of suicide attempters may include enhancing family communication and problem solving while reducing power struggles within the home (Adams *et al.*, 1994).

ASSESSMENT OF FAMILY FUNCTIONING

Family therapy models dictate the range and focus of clinical assessment measures that are available. For clinicians, the self-report family assessment measure is a valuable tool that may serve several purposes, including (1) proffering one source of information during the evaluation and diagnostic phase of treatment, (2) serving as an empirical and conceptual aide used to guide the course of treatment, and (3) a serving as vehicle for comparing pre- and post-treatment family functioning.

There are a number of family assessment measures, varying in format, length, underlying theoretical constructs, intended recipient(s), and psychometric properties. In determining which measure will be the most useful, clinicians may wish to consider benefits and drawbacks of the available measures. A brief description of six commonly used structured, self-report family assessment measures follows.

Mcmaster Family Assessment Device

The FAD-III (Epstein, Baldwin, & Bishop, 1983) operationalizes the McMaster Model of Family Functioning describing organizational and transactional patterns found to distinguish healthy from unhealthy families. The FAD-III, composed of 60 items, may be completed by all family members over the age of 12. Participants rate their degree of agreement/disagreement with each item on a scale from 1 to 4. There are seven subscales.

The problem solving subscale focuses on the family's ability to solve problems together (i.e., "we usually act on our decisions regarding problems"; "we confront problems involving feelings"). The communication subscale focuses on the degree to which exchanges of information among family members are clear and direct (i.e., "people come right out and say things instead of hinting at them"; "we don't talk to each other when we are angry"). The roles subscale focuses on the degree to which there are established patterns of behavior for family members, such as provision of resources, nurturance and support (i.e., "we discuss who is to do household jobs"; "we have trouble meeting our bills"). The affective responsiveness subscale focuses on the extent to which individual family members are able to experience appropriate affect toward one another (i.e., "we express tenderness"; "some of us just don't respond emotionally"). The affective involvement subscale focuses on the degree to which family members value and express interest in others' activities, with the healthiest families displaying an intermediate level of involvement (i.e., "if someone is in trouble, the others become too involved"; "we are too self-centered"). The behavior control subscale focuses on the way in which families react to emergency situations, as well as focusing on patterns of control (flexible, rigid, laissez-faire, and chaotic) (i.e., "we don't know what to do when an emergency comes up"; "there are rules about dangerous situations"). The general functioning subscale includes items drawn from the other six subscales and assesses the overall health/pathology of the family.

The FAD-III utility in discriminating differences between individual family members' perceptions of functioning has been observed. It has also been found to effectively distinguish clinical from nonclinical samples (Sawyer, Sarris, Baghurst, & Cross, 1988), including distinguishing families with suicidal members (Woods & Waasenaar, 1989). Kabacoff, Miller, Bishop, and Epstein (1990) investigated psychometric properties of the FAD-III by comparing psychiatric, nonclinical, and medical populations. Internal scale reliabilities and factorial reliabilities were found to be favorable and the proposed factor structure was supported.

Family Assessment Measure

The FAM-III (Skinner, Steinhauer, & Santabarbara, 1983), based on Skinner's process model of family functioning, rests on the premise that adaptive family functioning and organization is related to specific areas including role performance, communication, affect expression, and values and norms. The FAM-III assesses three levels of family functioning: (1) the whole family system (general scale, 50 items), (2) various dyadic relationships (dyadic scale, 42 items), and (3) individual family functioning (self-rating scale, 42 items). Both the general scale and the dyadic scale include seven subscales: (1) task accomplishment, (2) role performance, (3) communication, (4) affective expression, (5) affective involvement, (6) control, and (7) values/norms. Respondents rate items on a 4-point Likert scale, ranging from "strongly agree" to "strongly disagree." The FAM-III also includes social desirability and response style scales. Brief, 14-item FAMS are also available for each scale. The FAM-III takes 20 to 30 minutes to administer. The FAM-III has been shown to effectively discriminate between normal and problem families (Bernstein, Svingen, & Garfinkel, 1990; Skinner et al., 1983).

Psychometric properties of the FAM-III have been evaluated in a variety of clinical and nonclinical settings. Reliability has been reported as favorable, with strong explanatory and predictive utility (Skinner, Steinhauer, & Sitarenios, 2000). Interrcorrelations among the subscales range from .55 to .79, with some suggesting that a general factor of family adjustment may underlie the subscales (Skinner, 1987). The FAM-III has demonstrated adequate reliability for overall scores and for subscale scores.

Parent–Adolescent Communication Scale

The PACS (Barnes & Olson, 1982) was developed in response to observations that family communication is particularly important during the adolescent years. The PACS is a 20-item self-report questionnaire, optimally completed by parent-adolescent pairs, a format that enables assessment of family members' perceptions of one another. There are two forms of the scale, including (1) parent forms and (2) child forms (the adolescent may complete one form for each parent). Parents may also rate their own and their spouse's abilities as parents. Responses are rated on a 5-point Likert scale.

The PACS includes two subscales: (1) openness in parent-adolescent communication and (2) problems in parent-adolescent Communication. The openness scale includes items such as "It is easy for me to express all my true feelings to my (mother/father/child), and "My (mother/father/child) is always a good listener." The problems scale includes items such as "My (mother/father/child) has a tendency to say things to me which would be better left unsaid" and "I don't think I can tell my (mother/father/child) how I really feel about some things."

Barnes and Olson (1982) recommend that the PACS be used to supplement initial clinical assessments, to help define treatment goals, and to provide pre- and post-treatment data comparisons in order to determine treatment effectiveness. Strong positive correlations between adolescents' and parents' perceptions of communication and effective family functioning have been reported (Jackson, Bijstra, Oostro, & Bosma, 1998; Marett, Sprenkle, & Lewis, 1992). Strong positive correlations have also been found between effective parent-adolescent communication as assessed by the PACS and adaptive adolescent functioning (Amerikaner, Monks, Wolfe, & Thomas, 1994).

Studies have found strong inverse relationships between effective parent-adolescent communication and degree of psychopathology, including self-harming behaviors (e.g., Tulloch, Blizzard, & Pinkus, 1997). Adequate validity and reliability have been reported on the PACS (Barnes & Olson, 1982, 1985).

Family Environment Scale

The FES (Moos & Moos, 1986) is based on a conceptual framework that focuses on person-environment interactions and the impacts of these transactions on family adaptation. It is a 90-item true/false self-report questionnaire, which examines 11 characteristics of the family environment. All family members may complete the FES. There are three forms of the FES: (1) *The Real Form* (Form-R), which assesses respondents' perceptions of their actual family environments, (2) the *Ideal Form* (Form I), which assesses respondents' conceptions of their ideal family environment, and (3) the *Expectations Form* (Form E), which assesses respondents' expectations about changes in family events.

The FES includes 11 subscales, which are clustered into three groups: (1) the relationship group, (2) the personal growth group, and (3) the system maintenance group. The relationships group consists of three subscales: cohesion (degree of family mutual support), expressiveness (degree of encouragement of open self-expression), and conflict (degree of family anger and conflict). The personal growth group includes five scales measuring the degree to which the family values the following: independence, achievement orientation, intellectual-cultural orientation, active-recreational orientation, and moral-religious values. The system maintenance group includes two scales assessing the degree to which the family emphasizes organization (such as structuring family activities) and control (such as focusing on rules and authority).

In addition to computing a score for each individual, individual family members' scores may also be averaged to determine an overall family score (Moos & Moos, 1986). The FES has been found to distinguish clinical from nonclinical populations (Reichertz & Frankel, 1990). The FES has also been found to be an effective measure as a pre- and post-test measure of the effectiveness of family treatment (Aktan, Kumpfer, & Turner, 1996). Internal consistency for the individual scales averages .75, and test–retest reliability averages .80 at one year (Moos & Moos, 1986).

Family Adaptability and Cohesions Scale-III

The FACES-III (Olson, Portner, & Lavee, 1985) is based on the Circumplex Model of Marital and Family Systems (Olson, Portner, & Bell, 1982). The model proposes two curvilinear dimensions of family functioning (1) cohesion and (2) adaptability. The cohesion dimension focuses on the degree of warmth and emotional closeness family members experience. The adaptability dimension focuses on the ability of the family to change in response to situational and developmental stress (Olson *et al.*, 1982). The adaptability dimension has been likened to concepts of parental control and permissiveness–restrictiveness (Henggeler, Burr-Harris, Bourduin, & McCallum, 1991). According to the model, family health is thought to be associated with balanced (moderate) scores on the cohesion and adaptability dimensions of the measure, while dysfunctional family patterns are believed to be associated with *either* high or low scores on both dimensions.

The 20-item FACES III may be taken twice—once for perceived and once for ideal descriptions of the family. The perceived-ideal discrepancy is considered to be an indirect measure of family satisfaction. Participants rate items on a 5-point Likert scale ranging from 1 "almost never" to 5 "almost always." The norms available include mean scores for three populations of families: (1) adults (2) families with adolescents, and (3) young couples.

On the FACES-III, a "distance from center score," or the numerical value of the respondents' score (irrespective of sign), difference between the respondent's cohesion/adaptability raw score and the cohesion adaptability mean score reported for the normative sample may be computed.

Families may then be identified as either balanced, midrange, or extreme. Balanced families fall into the central area of both dimensions and represent the optimal family type. These families are viewed as being free to change levels of cohesion and adaptability to meet their needs. Midrange families are characterized by midrange levels on one dimension and extreme (high or low) on the other dimension. Extreme families are those exhibiting extremely high or low levels on both the cohesion and adaptability dimensions.

Research studies comparing clinical versus nonclinical samples across various disorders on the FACES-III, as well as those correlating FACES-III scores with measures of adaptive functioning, have been mixed in terms of which model is supported (Barnes & Olson, 1985; Henggeler *et al.*, 1991), with some findings supportive of a linear model and others supporting a curvilinear model. Given these inconsistent findings, the clinician may need to determine for himself or herself whether to conceptualize optimal family functioning as linear or curvilinear with respect to the dimensions of adaptability and cohesion or may decide to use the FACES-III in a purely descriptive manner.

The FACES-III has been found to have favorable reliability and validity (Olson, 1986). Norms have been established in samples of adults, adolescents, and several types of problem families. The two subscales have been found to be statistically unique entities that do not correlate with one another; adequate reliability has been reported. The internal alpha coefficients of the cohesion and adaptability scales are .87 and .80, and the test retest reliabilities are .83 and .80 (Olson *et al.*, 1982).

Structural Family Interaction Scale-Revised

The SFIS-R (Perosa, Hanson, & Perosa, 1981) is based on Minuchin's (1974) contention that an optimal balance between family enmeshment and disengagement is associated with healthy adolescent development. The SFIS-R, designed to be completed by parent-adolescent pairs, contains 83 items representing family interactions, on which respondents rate items on a 4-point Likert scale ranging from 1 (very false) to 4 (very true). Items of the SFIS-R are broken into eight subscales. Three of the subscales assess system-wide family dynamics and five assess intergenerational boundaries.

On the SFIS-R, the three subscales assessing system-wide family dynamics include (1) enmeshment/disengagement (17 items, measuring the degree of support, responsiveness, involvement, and sense of differentiation family members experience), (2) flexibility/rigidity (9 items, measuring the degree to which the family is able to change in response to either situational stress or increases in autonomy demands of adolescence, and (3) family conflict/avoidance (8 items, measuring the degree to which family members avoid or express differences). Across these three subscales, high scores represent a greater degree of enmeshment, flexibility, and avoidance of conflict, respectively.

The five SFIS-R subscales assessing intergenerational boundaries include (1) the parental-coalition/cross-generational triad (11 items, measuring the degree to which boundaries between parents form rigid patterns of communication as a way of avoiding marital conflicts through triangulation, detouring, and/or parent-child coalitions), (2) mother-child cohesion/estrangement (9 items) and (3) father-child cohesion/estrangement (10 items, each measuring the degree to which the mother or father provide nurturance, promoting feelings of parent-child closeness); (4) overprotection/autonomy (9 items, measuring the degree to which one or both parents encourage the child to think for himself or herself as opposed to being overinvolved/overprotective); and (5) spouse conflict resolved/unresolved (40 items, measuring the degree to which conflicts between spouses are effectively resolved). Across these five subscales, higher scores reflect greater use of parent-child coalitions, as well as a greater degree of cohesion, overprotectiveness, and resolution of parental differences, respectively.

The development of the original SFIS was based on data comparing normative families to problem families, which led to a revision with 13 primary scales and 10 secondary scales. Perosa *et al.* (1981) reported that interscale correlations fall within patterns predicted by the theory. Adequate internal consistency has been reported. The SFIS-R has been widely used in clinical settings including as an aid in discriminating suicidal from nonsuicidal families (Mitchell & Rosenthal, 1992).

CONCLUSIONS

The family system is clearly an important consideration for clinical work with adolescent suicide attempters. Understanding the adolescent's family can be crucial in assessment, crisis intervention, and treatment. Many principles from traditional schools of family therapy are beneficial when working with adolescent suicide attempters. However, some considerations warrant highlighting when working with these adolescents and their families. This section contains some general guidelines, which in some cases are derived from the literature that has been summarized and in other cases are based on clinical experience.

During the initial family contact, it is imperative to establish clear guidelines for the progression of treatment. Issues such as confidentiality, boundaries, family involvement, and specific treatment goals should be reviewed. In addition, psychoeducation for the family members can be beneficial in alleviating some of the anxiety the family is experiencing. Educating families about suicide risk is mandatory. This should include the following types of information:

- Suicide it the third leading cause of death for adolescents.
- The most frequent method of attempting suicide is by drug overdose. The fact that a suicide attempt is by overdose by no means minimizes the importance of the suicide attempt and should be dealt with in a serious manner by both family and professionals.
- The "last straw" events that lead teenagers to attempt suicide are very common, such as family conflict, a breakup with a boyfriend or girlfriend, legal problems, or school difficulties. The underlying motives for a suicide attempt include wanting to die, expressing anger, getting relief from a terrible state of mind, escaping a difficult situation, or being disappointed by a trusted person.
- A previous suicide attempt increases an adolescent's chances of eventually completing suicide. Other risk factors include a family history of suicide, a problem with alcohol or other drug abuse, and access to firearms.
- Adolescents who complete suicide often talk about it or give warning signals prior to the act. These signals may include written or verbal statements about death or the desire to end one's life; giving away personal possessions; abrupt changes in mood or behavior, such as ending long-term friendships; and signs of depression such as a change in eating and sleeping, apathy, statements about feeling hopeless, and looking very sad. These signs don't always mean that a teenager is thinking of suicide, but they should alert others to talk with the teenager about what is on his or her mind.
- If at all concerned, parents should not be afraid to ask a teenager if he or she is thinking about suicide; talking about suicide doesn't make teenagers do it! Showing concern and asking questions

calmly is the first step when dealing with a suicidal adolescent. Asking teenagers how they feel and if they have thoughts of ending their life keeps open lines of communication and sets the stage for professional intervention. If the teen has a specific plan to act on a suicidal impulse, the risk is greater and there is a need for immediate intervention.

The parental relationship is an important consideration when working with attempters. While the research is not conclusive, parental divorce or separation may serve as a distal stimulus for suicide attempts in some adolescents. Parental remarriage may be an equally important stressor that needs to be addressed when an adolescent has a history of suicidal behavior. As a starting point, the therapist should emphasize to the parents, stepparents, and other significant adults in the adolescent's environment that it is important to put aside differences in the ensuing weeks to ensure the adolescent is safe. Long-standing family and marital issues can be addressed once the situation has stabilized.

Research supports a relationship between family conflict and adolescent suicidal behavior. Consequently, it is important to assess and assist families with conflict resolution. Developing skills for effective communication is paramount. The goal of improved communication can be particularly helpful in addressing the frequent adolescent perception that their parents are not supportive. Improving family communication may alleviate the feelings of emotional isolation while rebuilding trust between the parents and adolescent. Parents need guidance in ways to be supportive without being intrusive. Communication about daily activities and limits is necessary before a family's problem-solving abilities can be improved and more satisfying family relationships established.

Support from extended family can be beneficial to the adolescent and the parents of the adolescent suicide attempter. Grandparents or aunts and uncles can provide daily emotional support, respite, information during sessions, or even transportation to appointments. The possibility of extended family involvement will likely be related to the characteristics of the individual family, including their cultural background. Given each family's unique characteristics, it is important to assess the families' current level of extended family support along with their desire or comfort level for reaching out to other family members. Some therapists directly involve extended family members in the adolescent's treatment. Including extended family may be beneficial in addressing multigenerational familial difficulties such as isolation, abandonment, long-lasting feuds, emotional cutoffs, violence, and abuse (Gutstein, 1991), which in turn may reduce the adolescent's suicidal behavior.

Although some families welcome support from their extended family, others may experience guilt or shame associated with their circumstances. Parental feelings of shame and anger or blame may be best initially processed in the absence of the adolescent, as these intense feelings could initially be damaging to the adolescent. However, the adolescent will likely have experienced emotional sequelae related to their parents' feelings and will likely need to address these perceptions and feelings in sessions that include the adolescent and the parents.

Parental psychopathology is another indicator that a collateral session should be considered. As summarized previously, several studies have shown a relationship between parental psychopathology and adolescent suicide attempts. Although not addressed in the literature, the stress of having a suicidal child is likely to exacerbate the parent's symptoms. Consequently, parental psychiatric symptomatology is an important area for consideration, both for assessment and treatment. The impact of parental psychopathology on the adolescent is pervasive but is often difficult to address during the adolescent's treatment. In such cases, referrals for family members are appropriate because their symptoms will not be sufficiently addressed within the family therapy format. Coordination of the parent and adolescent's treatment is important, but often difficult to implement.

As with most treatments, maximizing family strengths can be key to guiding a family out of a crisis. Families may have strengths in a variety of areas, such as conflict resolution, communication, parental relationships, or extended family support. Highlighting these areas can be healing and normalizing for the family and set the stage for the difficult work of addressing dysfunctional aspects of the family system.

REFERENCES

Adams, D. M., Overholser, J. C., & Lehnert, M. A. (1994). Perceived family functioning and adolescent suicidal behavior. *Journal of the Academy of Child and Adolescent Psychiatry, 33*, 498–507.

Aktan, G. B., Kumpfer, K. L., & Turner, C. W. (1996). Effectiveness of a family skills training program for substance use prevention with inner city African-American families. *Substance Use and Misuse, 31*, 157–175.

Amerikaner, M., Monks, G., Wolfe, P., & Thomas, S. (1994). Family interaction and individual psychological health. *Journal of Counseling and Development, 72,* 614–620.

Barnes, H. L., & Olson, D. H. (1982). Parent-adolescent communication scale. In D. H. Olson (Ed.), *Family inventories: Inventories used in a national survey of families across the family life cycle* (pp. 33–48). St. Paul: MN: Family Social Science. University of Minnesota.

Barnes, H. L., & Olson, D. H. (1985). Parent-adolescent communication and the Circumplex model. *Child Development, 56,* 438–447.

Bensley, L., Van Eenwyk, J., Spieker, S., & Schoder, J. (1999). Self-reported abuse history and adolescent problem behaviors: I Antisocial and suicidal behaviors. *Journal of Adolescent Health, 24,* 163–172.

Berit, G., Ekeberg, O., Wichstrom, L., & Haldorsen, T. (2000). Young suicide attempters: A comparison between a clinical and epidemiological sample. *Journal of the American Academy of Child and Adolescent Psychiatry, 39,* 868–875.

Bernstein, G. A., Svingen, P. H., & Garfinkel, B. D. (1990). School phobia: Patterns of family functioning. *Journal of the American Academy of Child and Adolescent Psychiatry, 29,* 24–30.

Bjarnason, T., & Thorlindsson, T. (1994). Manifest predictors of past suicide attempts in a population of Icelandic adolescents. *Suicide and Life-Threatening Behavior, 24,* 350–358.

Borst, R., & Noam, G. G. (1989). Suicidality and psychopathology in hospitalized children and adolescents. *Acta Paedapsychiatrica,* 165–175.

Brand, E. F., King, C. A., Olson, E., Ghaziuddin, N., & Naylor, O. (1996). I. Depressed adolescents with a history of sexual abuse: In diagnostic comorbidity and suicidality. *Journal of the American Academy of Child and Adolescent Psychiatry, 35,* 34–41.

Brent, D. A., Kolko, D. J., Allan, M. J., & Brown, R. V. (1990). Suicidality in affectively disordered adolescent inpatients. *Journal of the American Academy of Child and Adolescent Psychiatry, 29(4),* 586–593.

Brent, D., Kolko, D., Wartella, M., Boylan, M., Moritz, G., Baugher, M., & Zelenak, J. (1993). Adolescent psychiatric inpatients' risk of suicide attempt at 6-month follow-up. *Journal of the American Academy of Child and Adolescent Psychiatry, 32,* 95–105.

Brent, D., Perper, J., Morritz, G., Baugher, M., Roth, C., Barach, L., & Schwears, J. (1993). Stressful life events, psychopathology, and adolescent suicide: A case control study. *Journal of the American Academy of Child and Adolescent Psychiatry, 32,* 521–529.

Brent, D. A., Perper, J. A., Mortiz, G., Liotus, L., Schweers, J., Balach, L., & Roth, C. (1994). Familial risk factors for adolescent suicide: A case-control study. *Acta Psychiatrica Scandinavica, 89,* 52–58.

Brent, D. A., Bridge, J., Johnson, B. A., & Connolly, J. (1996). Suicidal behavior runs in families. *Archives of General Psychiatry, 53,* 1145–1152.

Bridge, J. A., Brent, D. A., Johnson, B. A., & Connolly, J. (1997). Familial aggregation of psychiatric disorders in a community sample of adolescents. *Journal of the Academy of Child Adolescent Psychiatry, 36(5),* 628–636.

Campbell, N. B., Milling, L., Laughlin, M. D., & Bush, E. (1993). The psychosocial climate of families with suicidal pre-adolescent children. *American Journal of Orthopsychiatry, 63,* 142–145.

Davies, M., & Cunningham, G. (1999). Adolescent parasuicide in the Foyle area. *Irish Journal of Psychological Medicine, 16(1),* 9–12.

DeBellis, M. D., Lefter, L., Trickert, P. K., & Putman, F. W. (1994). Urinary catecholamine secretion in sexually abused girls. *Journal of the American Academy of Child and Adolescent Psychiatry, 33,* 320–327.

deWilde, E. J., Kienhorst, C. W. M., Diekstra, R. F. W., & Wolters, W. H. G. (1992). The relationship between adolescent suicidal behavior and life events in childhood and adolescence. *American Journal of Psychiatry, 149(1),* 45–51.

Deykin, E. Y., & Buka, S. L. (1994). Suicidal ideation and attempts among chemically dependent adolescents. *American Journal of Public Health, 84,* 634–639.

Dubow, E. F., Kausch, D. F., Blum, M. C., Reed, J., & Bush, E. (1989). Correlates of suicidal ideation and attempts in a community sample of junior and high school students. *Journal of Clinical Child Psychology, 18 (2),* 158–166.

Edwall, G. E., Hoffman, N. G., & Harrison, P. A. (1989). Psychological correlates of sexual abuse in adolescent girls in chemical dependency treatment. *Adolescence, 24,* 279–288.

Epstein, N. B., Baldwin, L., & Bishop, D. S. (1983). The McMaster Family Assessment Device. *Journal of Marital and Family Therapy, 9,* 171–180.

Fergusson, D. M., & Lynskey, M. T. (1995). Childhood circumstances, adolescent adjustment, and suicide attempts in a New Zealand birth cohort. *Journal of the American Academy of Child and Adolescent Psychiatry, 34,* 612–622.

Garfinkel, P. E., Froese, A., & Hood, J. (1982). Suicide attempts in children and adolescents. *American Journal of Psychiatry, 139,* 1257–1261.

Garrison, C., Jackson, K., Addy, C., McKeown, R., & Waller, J. (1991). Suicidal behavior in young adolescents. *American Journal of Epidemiology, 133,* 1005–1014.

Gould, M., Fisher, P., Parides, M., Flory, M., & Shaffer, D. (1996). Psychosocial risk factors in child and adolescent completed suicide. *Archives of General Psychiatry, 53,* 1155–1162.

Grilo, C., Sanislow, C., Fehon, D., Martino, S., & McGlashan, T. (1999). Psychological and behavioral functioning in adolescent psychiatric inpatients who report histories of childhood abuse. *American Journal of Psychiatry, 156,* 538–543.

Grossman, D. C., Milligan, C., & Deyo, R. A. (1991). Risk factors for suicide attempts among Navajo adolescents. *American Journal of Public Health, 81,* 870–874.

Gutstein, S. E. (1991). Adolescent Suicide: The loss of reconciliation. In F. Walsh & M. McGoldrick (Eds.), *Living beyond loss: Death in the family* (pp. 241–259). New York: W. W. Norton.

Harrison, P. A., & Hoffman, N. G. (1989). Sexual abuse correlates: Similarities between male and female adolescents in chemical dependency treatment. *Journal of Adolescent Research, 4,* 385–399.

Henggeler, S. W., Burr-Harris, A. W., Bourdin, C. M., & McCallum, G. (1991). Use of the family adaptability and cohesion evaluation scales in child clinical research. *Journal of Abnormal Child Psychology, 19,* 53–63.

Hernandez, J. T., Lodico, M., & DiClemente, R. J. (1993). The effects of child abuse and race on risk-taking in male adolescents. *Journal of the National Medical Association, 85,* 593–597.

Jackson, S., Bijstra, J., Oostra, L., & Bosma, H. (1998). Adolescents' perceptions of communication with parents relative to specific aspects of relationships with parents and personal development. *Journal of Adloescence, 21,* 305–322.

Kabacoff, R. I., Miller, I. W., Bishop, D. S., & Epstein, N. B. (1990). A psychometric study of the McMaster Family Assessment Device in psychiatric, medical, and non-clinical samples. *Journal of Family Psychology, 3,* 431–439.

Kaplan, S. J., Pelcovitz, D., Salzinger, S., Mandell, F., & Weiner, M. (1997). Adolescent physical abuse and suicide attempts. *Journal of the American Academy of Child and Adolescent Psychiatry, 28,* 912–917.

Kienhorst, C., deWilde, E., Diekstra, R., & Wolters, W. (1992). Differences between adolescent suicide attempters and depressed adolescents. *Acta Psychiatrica Scandinavica, 85,* 222–228.

King, C., Raskin, A., Gdowski, C., Butkus, M., & Opipari, L. (1990). Psychosocial factors associated with urban adolescent female suicide attempts. *Journal of the American Academy of Child and Adolescent Psychiatry, 29,* 289–294.

King, C., Segal, H., Kaminski, K., Naylor, M., Ghaziuddin, N., & Radpour, L. (1995). A prospective study of adolescent suicidal behavior. *Suicide and Life-Threatening Behavior, 25,* 327–338.

Kosky, R., Silburn, S., & Zubrick, S. (1990). Are children and adolescents who have suicidal thoughts different from those who attempt suicide? *Journal of Nervous and Mental Disease, 178,* 38–43.

Kovacs, M., Goldston, D., & Gatsonis, C. (1993). Suicidal behaviors and childhood-onset depressive disorders: A longitudinal investigation. *Journal of the American Academy of Child and Adolescent Psychiatry, 32,* 8–20.

Kurtz, L., & Derevensky, J. L. (1993). Stress and coping in adolescents: The effects of family configuration and environment on suicidality. *Canadian Journal of School Psychology, 9,* 204–216.

Laerderach, J., Fischer, W., Bowen, P., & Ladame, F. (1999). Common risk factors in adolescent suicide attempters revisited. *Crisis, 20,* 15–22.

Lewinsohn, P. M., Rohde, P., & Seeley, J. R. (1993). Psychosocial characteristics of adolescents with a history of suicide attempt. *Journal of the American Academy of Child and Adolescent Psychiatry, 32,* 60–68.

Lewinsohn, P. M., Rohde, P., & Seeley, J. R. (1994). Psychosocial risk factors for future adolescent suicide attempts. *Journal of Consulting and Clinical Psychology, 62,* 297–305.

Lipschitz, P., Winegar, R., Nicolaou, A., Hartnick, E., Wolfson, M., & Southwick, S. (1999). Perceived abuse and neglect as risk factors for suicidal behavior in adolescent inpatients. *Journal of Nervous and Mental Disease, 187,* 32–39.

Marret, K. M., Sprenkle, D. H., & Lewis, R. A. (1992). Family members' perceptions of family boundaries and their relationship to family problems. *Family Therapy, 19,* 233–242.

Martin, G., Rozanes, P., Pearce, C., & Allison, S. (1995). Adolescent suicide, depression and family dysfunction. *Acta Psychiatrica Scandinavica, 92,* 336–344.

Minuchin, S. (1974). *Families and family therapy.* Cambridge, MA: Harvard University Press.

Mitchell, M., & Rosenthal, D. (1992). Suicidal adolescents: Family dynamics and the effects of lethality and helplessness. *Journal of Youth and Adolescence, 21,* 23–33.

Molnar, B., Shade, S., Kral, A., Booth, R., & Watters, J. (1998). Suicidal behavior and sexual/physical abuse among street youth. *Child Abuse and Neglect, 22,* 213–222.

Moos, R. H., & Moos, B. S. (1981). *Family Environment Scale Manual.* Palo Alto, CA: Consulting Psychologist Press.

Moos, R. H., & Moos, B. S. (1986). *Family Environment Scale Manual* (2nd ed.). Palo Alto, CA: Consulting Psychologist Press.

Morano, C. D., Cisler, R. A., & Lemerond, J. (1993). Risk factors for adolescent suicidal behavior: Loss, insufficient familial support, and hopelessness. *Adolescence, 28(112),* 851–865.

Olson, D. H., Portner, J., & Bell, R. (1982). Family adaptibility and cohesion evaluation scales. In D. H. Olson, H. L. McCubbin, H. Barnes, A. Larsen, M. Muxen, & M. Wilson (Eds.), *Family Inventories*. St. Paul: Minnesota Press.

Olson, D. H., Portner, J., & Lavee, Y. (1985). *FACES III*. St. Paul, MN: Family Social Science, University of Minnesota.

Paluszny, M., Davenport, C., & Kim, W. (1991). Suicide attempts and ideation: Adolescents evaluated on a pediatric ward. *Adolescence, 26,* 209–215.

Perosa, L., Hanson, J., & Perosa, S. (1981). Development of the Structural Family Interaction Scale. *Family Therapy, 8,* 77–90.

Procidano, M., & Heller, K. (1983). Measures of perceived social support from friends and family: Three validational studies. *American Journal of Community Psychology, 11,* 1–24.

Reichertz, D., & Frankel, H. (1990). Family environments and problematic adolescents: Toward an empirically based typology. *Community Alternatives—International Journal of Family Care, 2,* 51–74.

Riggs, S., Alario, A. J., & McHorney, C. (1990). Health risk behavior and attempted suicide in adolescents who report prior maltreatment. *Journal of Pediatrics, 116,* 815–821.

Rubenstein, J. L., Halton, A., Kasten, L., Rubin, C., & Stechler, G. (1998). Suicidal behavior in adolescents: Stress and protection in different family contexts. *American Journal of Orthopsychiatry, 68,* 274–284.

Sawyer, M. G., Sarris, A., Baghurst, P. A., & Cross, D. G. (1988). Family Assessment Device: Reports from mothers, father, and adolescents in community and clinical families. *Journal of Marital and Family Therapy, 14,* 287–296.

Shaunessey, K., Cohen, J., Plummer, B., & Berman, A. (1993). Suicidality in hospitalized adolescents: Relationship to prior abuse. *American Journal of Orthopsychiatry, 63,* 113–119.

Silverman, A. B., Reinherz, H. Z., & Giaconia, R. M. (1996). The long-term sequelae of child and adolescent abuse: A longitudinal community study. *Child Abuse & Neglect, 20(8),* 709–723.

Skinner, H. A. (1987). Self-report instruments for family assessment. In T. Jacob (Ed.), *Family Interaction and Psychopathology*. New York: Plenum Press.

Skinner, H. A., Steinhauer, P. D., & Santabarbara, J. (1983). The family assessment measure. *Canadian Journal of Community Mental Health, 2,* 91–105.

Skinner, H. A., Steinhauer, P. D., & Sitarenios, G. (2000). Family Assessment Measure (FAM) and process model of family functioning. *Journal of Family Therapy, 22,* 190–210.

Sorenson, S. B., & Rutter, C. M. (1991). Transgenerational patterns of suicide attempt. *Journal of Consulting and Clinical Psychology, 59,* 861–866.

Stiffman, A. (1989). Suicide attempts in runaway youths. *Suicide and Life-Threatening Behavior, 19,* 147–159.

Swedo, S. E., Rettew, D. C., Kuppenheimer, M., Lum, D., Dolan, S., & Goldberger, E. (1991). Can adolescent suicide attempters be distinguished from at-risk adolescents? *Pediatrics, 88(3),* 620–629.

Tulloch, A. L., Blizzard, L., & Pinkus, Z. (1997). Adolescent-parent communication and self-harm. *Journal of Adolescent Health, 21,* 267–275.

Vanatta, R. (1996). Risk factors related to suicidal behavior among male and female adolescents. *Journal of Youth and Adolescence, 25,* 149–160.

Wagner, B. (1997). Family risk factors for child and adolescent suicidal behavior. *Psychological Bulletin, 121,* 246–298.

Wagner, B. M., Cole, R. E., & Schwartzman, P. (1995). Psychosocial correlates of suicide attempts among junior and senior high school youth. *Suicide and Life-Threatening Behavior, 25,* 358–372.

Windle, R., & Windle, M. (1997). An investigation of adolescents' substance use behaviors, depressed affect, and suicidal behaviors. *Journal of Child Psychology and Psychiatry, 38,* 921–929.

Woods, N., & Waasenaar, D. R. (1989). Family characteristics of Indian parasuicide patients: A controlled study. *South African Journal of Psychiatry, 19,* 172–174.

CHAPTER 9

Social Factors:
Peer Relationships

Mitchell J. Prinstein

Interpersonal factors, and specifically difficulties in peer functioning, have frequently been cited as precipitants to adolescents' suicidal behavior. Hawton and colleagues (1996) reported that 36.7% of suicide attempters under the age of 16 years list friendship difficulties as a main precipitant to their suicidal behavior; 10% of young teens report that social isolation directly led to a suicide attempt, and 11% attempted suicide following a conflict with a boyfriend or girlfriend. In a study of substance-using suicidal teens, social isolation from peers was reported as a suicide precipitant by 30% of attempters (Berman & Schwartz, 1990). Spirito, Overholser, and Stark (1989) reported that 27% of adolescent suicide attempters cite boyfriend/girlfriend difficulties as a primary precipitant to suicidal behavior, with an additional 10% listing a friendship problem as the main precipitant. Ireland, Davies and Cunningham (1999) reported that peer stressors led to 36% of suicide attempts, with victimization from peers as the most common of these precipitants (22%). Given the developmental significance of peer relationships during adolescence, the link between peer difficulties and severe emotional distress, including suicidal ideation and behavior, is not surprising.

Yet, despite results suggesting that peer relationship difficulties cause some adolescents to engage in self-harmful behavior, few studies have examined peer functioning as a factor that may predict future suicidality or differentiate suicidal from nonsuicidal teens. This is especially surprising given that past investigations have consistently associated peer functioning with suicide-related domains of adjustment and psychological symptoms. For instance, numerous investigations have revealed that peer rejection, poor friendship quality, and deviant peer affiliation are prospectively associated with future symptoms of depression, anxiety, conduct disorder, academic achievement, and numerous health-risk behaviors, including substance use and risky sexual behavior (e.g., Coie, Lochman, Terry, & Hyman, 1992; Dishion, Patterson, Stoolmiller, & Skinner, 1991; Panak & Garber, 1992; Parker & Asher, 1987).

Investigations designed specifically to examine linkages between peer functioning and adolescent suicidality are rare, however in a review of extant literature conducted one decade ago, Spirito, Brown, Overholser, and Fritz (1989) concluded that peer relationships and social competence may be significant predictors of adolescent suicidal ideation and suicidal behavior, particularly among clinical samples of teens. Several early psychiatric reports reviewed by Spirito and colleagues (1989) suggested that suicidal adolescents were highly likely to report peer problems (e.g., friendship difficulties, social isolation from peers) during clinical interviews (e.g., Khan, 1987; Kosky, Silburn, & Zubrick, 1986; Rohn, Sarles, Kenny, Reynolds, & Heald, 1977; Tishler, McKenry, & Morgan, 1981) or on problem checklists (Topol & Reznikoff, 1982), sometimes more frequently than by nonsuicidal hospitalized controls (e.g., Topol & Reznikoff, 1982). Suicide reattempters also reported significantly less frequent peer contact as compared to adolescents with a history of a single suicide attempt (Stanley & Barter, 1970).

Although still a grossly neglected area of research, several additional investigations on peer functioning and suicidality have emerged in the past 10 years. Unfortunately, few of these studies have utilized current theoretical models or standard methodological practices from the peer relations literature. However, these investigations do begin to offer some support for future research in the area of peer functioning and suicidality.

PEER FUNCTIONING

The broad and growing literature on adolescent peer functioning has identified a number of specific constructs that each offer a unique perspective on adolescents' experiences with peers and uniquely predict clinically relevant outcomes, including internalizing and externalizing symptoms, academic functioning, and health-risk behaviors. Thus, clinicians and researchers interested in examining adolescent peer functioning should recognize the many components of peer relations that may be relevant predictors of adolescents' psychological symptoms, including suicidality. Hartup's (1996) review of these diverse peer relations constructs (adapted here) suggests that three questions may be used as a useful heuristic for investigators reviewing the literature on peer relationships and psychological adjustment, and for clinicians interested in screening adolescents' peer functioning.

A central question reflected in research on peer relations and for clinicians to begin an assessment of adolescent peer functioning pertains to adolescents' overall reputation among their classmates: "Is the teen liked by peers?" Investigators have sought to answer this question by examining a number of related constructs. For instance, peer sociometric status indicates the extent to which children and adolescents are predominantly liked by peers (i.e., popular), disliked (i.e., rejected), both liked and disliked (i.e., controversial), or neither liked nor disliked by peers (i.e., rarely nominated; neglected). Adolescents' overall reputations are also reflected in the extent to which peers consider them to exhibit a variety of social behaviors, such as prosocial behavior, aggression, or withdrawn behavior. Teens' affiliation with reputation-based peer crowds (e.g., the "jocks," "burnouts," "brains") and adolescents' own perceptions of their social acceptance among peers also broadly fit within this larger class of constructs regarding adolescents' reputation among peers, as do consequences of low peer status, such as peer victimization.

Adolescents' specific relationships with individual peers is also an important domain of peer functioning that is distinct from overall peer reputations. In other words, clinicians might ask, "Does the teen have friends?" As noted by Hartup (1996), even adolescents with low social reputations may participate in rewarding, reciprocal friendships with peers, and this can independently predict or buffer psychological distress above and beyond the effects of peer status. Research has demonstrated that not only are the number of adolescents' friendships relevant to adjustment, but the quality of these relationships (e.g., conflict, emotional support, intimacy, trust, etc.) is an important contributor to psychological development (Hartup, 1996). A related issue regarding friendships is the extent to which teens are relationally aggressive or victimized within their friendships, suggesting that some adolescents may use their relationship as a weapon when engaged in conflict (e.g., by withdrawing friendship support in retaliation or making continued companionship contingent on relationship demands) (Crick & Bigbee, 1998). Inquiries as to whether a teen has friends might also include adolescents' relationships with boyfriends or girlfriends. Adolescents' satisfaction with their dating status and the quality of their romantic relationships are clinically relevant, particularly if adolescents report aggression or victimization between romantic partners or significant distress caused by the recent breakup of a romantic relationship.

After determining whether an adolescent is liked by peers, and whether she or he has friends, further questioning should include an assessment of the characteristics of adolescents' friends; in other words, "What are the teen's friends like?" Given the powerful social influence that peers exert on adolescents' behavior, the psychological adjustment and personal characteristics of individual peers becomes an important factor affecting adolescents' choice of friends and the effects of these friendships on subsequent behavior and adjustment. Indeed, the strongest predictor of teens' engagement in health-risk behaviors (e.g., substance use, sexual behavior, illegal behavior) is typically the extent to which teens' friends engage in these behaviors (e.g., Dishion *et al.*, 1991). Indeed, research has demonstrated that affiliation with peers experiencing internalizing symptoms may be predictive of adolescents' own internalizing symptoms as well (Hogue & Steinberg, 1995).

Perhaps most important when examining adolescent peer functioning is a comprehensive perspective on all three of these broad constructs of peer functioning (i.e., peer reputations, friendships, and peer influence). Clinicians and researchers hoping to best understand adolescents' social experiences might consider that weaknesses in one area of peer functioning (e.g., peer rejection) may be buffered by relative strengths in another social domain (e.g., social support from a close friend). Similarly, a consideration of multiple peer relations constructs may reveal more toxic combinations of social influences, such as adolescents' high levels of friendship quality (e.g., companionship and esteem support) paired with deviant peer group affiliation, which may exacerbate negative influences on adolescent behavior. Thus, recent research on the role of peer functioning in adolescent psychological adjustment has benefited from more complex models that consider peer experiences holistically and how these experiences may interact as contributors to psychopathology or resilience. Case conceptualizations might similarly consider the multiple, interacting influences of adolescents' peer experiences on psychopathology and suicidality.

PEER FUNCTIONING AND SUICIDAL BEHAVIOR

Efforts to examine associations between domains of peer functioning and adolescent suicidality have been limited. Historically, the search for interpersonal correlates of adolescent suicide began with an exclusive focus on family functioning and the quality of social interactions with parents (see Wagner, 1997, for a review). Indeed, numerous domains of family interaction were found to be significantly associated with suicide, such as parent-child conflict, parenting style and discipline, perceived social support from parents, family communication, problem solving, cohesion, and global family dysfunction (Wagner, 1997). Once this important link between adolescent suicidality and family interpersonal experiences was revealed, investigators began to examine parallel domains of peer interpersonal functioning, with an initial focus on adolescents' social support from friends as a potential correlate of suicidal ideation and behavior. The review that follows presents these findings on peer support and suicidality initially. Next, investigations that have examined friendship quality more broadly are reviewed, followed by investigations that have utilized broad screening measures of overall peer dysfunction. Lastly, recent investigations that examine multiple peer factors as predictors of adolescent suicidality are presented, as well as a model that may be helpful for future research in this area and for clinical conceptualizations of peer functioning and suicidality.

Perceived Social Support from Friends

Efforts to establish a link between peer functioning and suicidality have most commonly examined adolescents' perceived social support from peers. These investigations follow a recent trend in the suicide literature to better differentiate the source of social support associated with suicidal ideation and behavior; therefore, these investigations often examine peer social support in comparison to perceived support from family members (Rudd, 1993). However, these studies have generally yielded mixed results, likely due to varied methodologies and important differences in the constructs assessed. For example, in a sample of Swedish and Turkish teens, Eskin (1995) examined perceived social support from friends and family among other predictors of suicidality. The results provided partial support for a linkage between peer support and suicidality. Social support from the family, but not from friends, differentiated past suicide attempters from nonattempters. However, when examining current suicide risk, perceived social support from friends, the number of adolescents' friends, and family support were all significant predictors of suicide risk, even after controlling for prior suicide attempts and past psychiatric history. Thus, social support from peers and from the family were each relevant to an adolescent's suicidality.

In contrast, Yuen and colleagues (1996) examined the association between peer and family social support in a sample of approximately 1800 Hawaiian high school teens. Adolescents' prior suicidality in the past 6 months was assessed using one item from a life events checklist (i.e., "tried to commit suicide"). Adolescents who reported that they had attempted suicide had significantly lower levels of family social support as compared to nonattempters; however, no significant difference emerged for levels of peer social support.

Reifman and Windle (1995) conducted one of the few longitudinal studies of peer support and suicidality. In two high school samples, peer support was included in a model to predict suicidal thoughts, suicidal communication, and suicidal attempts 6 months later. Additional predictors included prior suicidality, depression, gender, alcohol consumption, hopelessness, and family support. When controlling for all other predictors, no significant direct effect between peer support and suicidality was revealed. A single, perhaps spurious, association was revealed when examining the buffering effects of peer support. Results suggested that social support from peers moderated the association between depression and later suicidal behavior, such that highly depressed teens who perceive high levels of peer support were less likely to exhibit later suicidal behavior. However, this interaction effect also suggested that high peer support was associated with greater risk of suicidal behavior among nondepressed teens (Reifman & Windle, 1995). Without information on the characteristics of adolescents' friends, it is difficult to determine whether social support might promote healthy adjustment or encourage symptomatic behavior among teens.

Lewinsohn, Rohde, and Seeley (1994) also report longitudinal findings on peer support and suicidality in a large normative sample. In this often-cited study, more than 1500 high school teens completed a battery of composite measures assessing numerous psychosocial factors at two time points approximately 1 year apart. However, peer support in this investigation was operationalized as a combination of items from Harter's (1988) social competence self-concept scale, the UCLA Loneliness Scale (Russell, Peplau, & Cutrona, 1980), and the social competence index from broad behavior problem checklists (e.g., YRS; Achenbach & Edelbrock, 1987), and these results may be better interpreted as a hybrid measurement of perceived social competence and peer-related distress. In logistic regressions, Lewinsohn *et al.* (1994) revealed a significant association between peer support and a history of a past suicide attempt, and also a significant association between peer support and the likelihood of a future attempt. However, this latter, prospective association was mediated by depression symptoms. These findings suggest that lack of peer support leads to increased depression, which in turn may lead to suicidal behavior.

In an effort to better explicate the role of social support from peers and parents as predictors of suicidal ideation, Harter, Marold, and Whitesell (1992) proposed and tested a self-development model among middle school teens, ages 12 to 15. Social support from parents and peers were included in this model as mediators between specific domains of self-competence/adequacy and a depression composite (including depressed affect, hopelessness, and low self-worth) that was subsequently linked to suicidal ideation. Results from this study supported a two pathway model, in which specific areas of perceived incompetence (i.e., physical appearance, athletic ability, peer likability) were associated with the depression composite and subsequently suicidal ideation via peer support, whereas self-competence in the areas of behavioral conduct and scholastic competence were associated with the depression composite and suicidal ideation via parent social support. Results also supported a direct link between suicidal ideation and parent support, but not peer support. Thus, the results from this investigation suggest that peer support may be an important factor in predicting depression and suicide for adolescents experiencing specific deficits in perceived self-competence.

Friendship Quality

In addition to perceived social support from peers, several recent investigations have examined the number and quality of adolescent friendships as predictors of suicidal ideation and behavior. Again, mixed support is provided for the role of peer functioning in adolescent suicidality. Rubenstein, Heeren, Housman, Rubin, and Stechler (1989) examined friendship quality in a normative sample of high school-aged adolescents. Using a measure previously developed by the authors of the study (Rubenstein & Rubin, 1986), six domains of friendship quality were assessed, including (a) social comfort/satisfaction, (b) amount of time with friends, (c) emotional support and intimacy, (d) family support for peer relationships, (e) loyalty and trust, and (f) ambivalence and conflict. Analyses in this study were conducted to identify variables that discriminated between teens who reported extremely high (top 90%) or extremely low (bottom 10%) suicidal ideation. After controlling for shared variability among friendship predictors, significant findings suggested that high levels of suicidal ideation were associated with high levels of ambivalence and conflict in friendships, low levels of social comfort and satisfaction, and low levels of parental support for peer relationships. When a total friendship composite was compared to family cohesion as predictors of suicidal ideation, only family cohesion effectively identified teens with high or low levels of suicidal ideation.

Cole, Protinsky, and Cross (1992) also compared high school teens with extremely high (top 5%) and extremely low (bottom 55%) suicide risk scores, using norms from Beck's Hopelessness Scale (Beck, Weissman, Lester, & Trexler, 1974) and an item assessing suicidal ideation within the past year. Friendship quality was assessed using a combination of items on the Offer Self-Image Questionnaire (Offer, Ostrov, & Howard, 1982) and additional items designed to measure perceptions of interpersonal relationships (Youniss & Smollar, 1985). In univariate and multivariate analyses, teens at a high rate for suicide reported significantly greater difficulties with peer relationships as compared to teens at low risk for suicide.

Using a well-known instrument for the assessment of friendship relationship quality (Inventory of Parent and Peer Attachment; Armsden & Greenberg, 1987), DiFilippo and Overholser (2000) examined attachments with mother, father, and close friends as concurrent predictors of depression and suicidal ideation severity in a sample of 59 psychiatric inpatients. The results provided preliminary support for the unique variability in depression and suicide explained by friendship quality. After controlling for attachment to mother and father, low levels of close friend attachment significantly predicted higher depression symptoms and suicidal ideation, particularly among girls. When controlling for depression, however, attachment to parents and peers were no longer significantly associated with suicidal ideation. This pattern of results suggests a mediational model, in which peer and parent relationship quality are each independent, significant predictors of depression, which in turn is associated with greater levels of suicidal ideation.

Windle's (1994) investigation of friendship quality and suicidal ideation is the only known study to offer longitudinal data in this area. Adapting a set of friendship quality items by Youniss and Smollar (1985), Windle (1994) examined four friendship predictors, including reciprocity of relations, overt hostility, covert hostility, and self-disclosure among 10th- and 12th-grade students over a 1-year interval. Significant concurrent correlations suggested that greater levels of covert hostility and lower levels of reciprocity in close, same-gender friendships were associated with greater levels of depressive symptoms and suicidal ideation. In prospective analyses, however, none of the four friendship variables were significant predictors of changes in depressive symptoms or suicidal ideation over time.

Additional Indicators of Peer Functioning

In addition to perceived social support from peers and friendship quality, several investigations have examined associations between peer functioning and suicidality using broad indicators of social competence, peer contact, or peer-related distress. As in the research reviewed earlier, these findings have continued to suggest that peer functioning is significantly associated with suicidal ideation. However, the extent to which peer variables are significant predictors after controlling for depression, or as compared to family predictors, is still unknown. Bjarnason and Thorlindsson (1994) included a broad measure of peer contact in their study of more than 7000 9th and 10th graders. Items on socializing with peers and a recent breakup with a romantic partner were included in a logistic regression model to classify suicidal from nonsuicidal teens. Social contact was a significant predictor in this model, suggesting that increased social contact was related to a lower likelihood of suicidal behavior.

Shagle and Barber (1995) examined suicidal ideation in a normative sample combining 5th-, 8th-, and 10th-grade students. Four items pertaining to companionship with friends or romantic partners were combined as a measure of "peer involvement," and concurrent analyses revealed no associations between this measure and suicidal ideation. Kandel, Raveis, and Davies (1991) also assessed overall contact with peers and romantic partners, using a similar set of three items among over 590 9th- and 11th-grade high school students. No significant associations were observed between peer contact and suicidal ideation. Kandel *et al.* (1991) reported a trend for boys with high levels of suicidal ideation to be less likely to date, as compared to boys with low suicidality. Similarly, Dubow, Kausch, Blum, Reed, and Bush (1989) examined "peer activities" as a subset of items from the Health and Daily-Living Youth Form (Moos, Cronkite, Billings, & Finney, 1986), as well as a brief measurement of suicidal ideation and suicidal behavior. In a large sample of more than 1300 normative children between grades 7 through 12, no significant associations were revealed between peer activities and suicidality.

Adams, Overholser, and Spirito (1994) included peer-related stressors (i.e., feeling pressured by peers, emotional problems with a friend) within an inventory of life stressors to differentiate suicide-attempting psychiatric inpatients from same-aged high-school control adolescents. Suicidal teens reported greater levels of peer-related distress as compared to controls. In addition, within the group of suicide attempters, higher levels of peer-related distress were significantly associated with higher levels of suicidal ideation severity.

In a study of 70 clinically referred adolescents between the ages of 13 and 18 who recently made a suicide attempt, Ritter (1990) examined social competence as a potential factor that differentiated high- and low-risk attempters. High-risk suicidal teens were defined as adolescents who stated a desire to die or whose recent suicidal behavior was of high lethality or required emergency medical treatment. Low-risk attempters denied a desire to die and exhibited suicidal behavior of low lethality. The Youth Self-Report Social Competence Scale was used as an index of peer functioning, which includes three items regarding the number of an adolescent's friends, the frequency of peer contact, and the adolescent's perceptions of his or her ability to relate to peers. Significant differences on this measure suggested that high-risk suicidal girls were significantly more socially competent than low-risk suicidal girls; no significant differences were observed for boys.

EXAMINING MULTIPLE DOMAINS OF PEER FUNCTIONING

Recent research has begun to examine the relative associations and interactions between multiple domains of peer functioning on adolescent suicidality. Rigby and Slee (1999) reported significant associations between both peer victimization and peer support with suicidal ideation in two samples of Australian teens (n's > 800). Using self-report data on overt peer victimization, significant correlations suggested that high levels of victimization were associated with more severe suicidal ideation. Similarly, low levels of best-friend social support were associated with more severe suicidal ideation. When considered together, both peer support and peer victimization were independently associated with suicidal ideation, cumulatively accounting for about 7% of the variance in suicidal ideation for boys and 17% for girls. Integrating these two domains of peer functioning, these investigators also examined a mediational model in which peer victimization may be related to lower levels of best-friend support, and subsequently, suicidal ideation. A moderator model was also examined by testing interaction terms between peer victimization and social support. Partial support for the mediational hypothesis was revealed; best-friend support was a partial mediator for boys and for girls; however, the association between peer victimization and suicidal ideation remained significant. No significant effects were observed for peer support as a moderator. Rigby and Slee (1999) also provided the first known data on adolescent suicidality and peer functioning using peer nomination data. Overall, these results were consistent with self-reported data; for both genders, teens nominated as targets of peer victimization also reported high levels of suicidal ideation.

Our own work also has looked at multiple areas of peer functioning and adolescent suicidality (Prinstein, Boergers, Spirito, Little, & Grapentine, 2000). In a sample of 96 suicidal psychiatric inpatients, Prinstein *et al.* (2000) used multiple self-report measures to derive four factors of peer functioning, including adolescents' close friendship support, perceived peer acceptance, perceived peer rejection, and deviant peer affiliation. Peer functioning variables and a measure of global family dysfunction were included in a conceptual model of adolescent suicidal ideation severity that also considered the mediating role of psychological symptoms from a structured diagnostic assessment (e.g., depressive symptoms, generalized anxiety symptoms, externalizing symptoms, and substance abuse/dependence symptoms). Results from structural equation modeling revealed several significant paths between adolescents' peer functioning and suicidal ideation severity. First, after controlling for other significant associations, direct pathways between low levels of close friendship support and high levels of perceived peer rejection were significantly associated with more severe suicidal ideation. Significant indirect pathways also suggested that perceived peer rejection and peer acceptance were associated with suicidal ideation via depression, and deviant peer affiliation was associated with suicidal ideation via substance use symptoms. Effect sizes for these results suggested that peer functioning was a stronger predictor of suicidal ideation as compared to family dysfunction, and the entire risk factor model accounted for 32% of variance in adolescent suicidal ideation.

Our recent work has also examined characteristics of adolescents' closest friends as correlates to adolescent suicidal ideation and suicidal behavior (Prinstein, Boergers, & Spirito, 2001). In a sample of 527 high school teens, adolescents were asked to list their closest friends, and also the number of these friends who expressed suicidal ideation or engaged in suicidal behavior. Adolescents also completed a portion of Harter's (1988) self-perception scale to yield an assessment of perceived social acceptance. Results indicated significant associations between the proportion of adolescents' suicidal friends and their own suicidal ideation and frequency of suicidal behavior. Integrating domains of peer functioning, adolescents' perceived social acceptance was examined as a potential moderator of the association between adolescents' and their friends' suicidality. Results revealed a marginal effect, suggesting that adolescents with high levels of perceived social acceptance were partially buffered from the deleterious effects of suicidal friends on their own suicidality. Lastly, when combining adolescents' affiliation with suicidal friends, perceived social acceptance, and two additional risk factors (i.e., family dysfunction and depression) as predictors of suicidal behavior in a cumulative four-factor risk model, findings supported the combined impact of interpersonal variables on suicidal behavior. Each these four risk factors contributed to the rate of suicidal behavior among normative adolescents, such that 3.5% of adolescents with zero risk factors reported a suicide attempt, 15.5% of adolescents with one risk factor reported a suicide attempt, 21.2% of adolescents with two risk factors had attempted suicide, and 52.6% of teens with three or more risk factors had attempted suicide.

We have also compared cognitive-interpersonal models of suicidality between normative and clinically referred samples to examine differences in peer correlates of suicidality across a range of symptom severity (Prinstein, Boergers, Spirito, & Little, 2000). Using samples of 51 psychiatric inpatients and 51 high school teens matched on gender, grade, ethnicity, and age, adolescents reported the frequency of their overt and relational victimization from peers and completed measures of dysphoric interpersonal schema, loneliness, depressive symptoms, and suicidal ideation. A four-step mediational model was conceptualized in which victimization experiences contribute to maladaptive interpersonal schema; this schema is associated with loneliness; and symptoms of loneliness are associated with concurrent depression and subsequently suicidal ideation. Results from structural equation modeling supported this model for psychiatric inpatients, but only for relational victimization. In other words, dysphoric schema mediated the association between relational victimization and loneliness, loneliness mediated the association between schema and depression, and depression mediated the association between loneliness and suicidal ideation. Among the high school adolescents, who on average reported significantly lower levels of suicidal ideation, unmediated associations between overt and relational victimization and suicidal ideation were revealed for girls, suggesting these forms of victimization were direct predictors of concurrent suicidality. Overall, these results offer additional evidence for the potential role of peer experiences in adolescent suicidality and suggest that adolescents' stressful peer experiences may lead to suicidal ideation due to their effect on distorted cognitions and ultimately interpersonal distress.

SUMMARY AND FUTURE DIRECTIONS: A PROPOSED MODEL

The abundance of research findings suggesting that adolescents' peer experiences are important predictors of psychological adjustment, coupled with preliminary findings linking peer experiences specifically to suicidal ideation and behavior, suggests that adolescent peer functioning deserves further attention in empirical work to better identify risk factors for adolescent suicide. However, these investigations have yielded mixed results as to whether adolescents' peer experiences are independent, direct predictors of suicidality or only antecedents of suicide-related domains of psychosocial functioning (e.g., depression or loneliness). Contributing to this ambiguity, few studies have examined constructs that reflect current conceptual work in peer functioning (e.g., sociometric status, reciprocated friendships, etc.) or used established methodologies developed within the peer relations literature. Additionally, few prospective investigations have been conducted, and it remains difficult to disentangle the directional influence of peer difficulties on subsequent suicidality from the reciprocal impact of suicidal ideation on an adolescent's ability to develop and maintain adaptive relationships with peers. Thus, it is premature to conclude that peer functioning is either a direct or indirect predictor of suicidality, and future work is sorely needed to elucidate these preliminary findings.

Future research may be best guided by a consideration of the multiple mechanisms that may link peer functioning and adolescent suicide. Such an approach would recognize the multifinality of peer functioning as a broad construct that leads to a variety of psychological outcomes and also the equifinality of adolescent suicidal behavior as an outcome that can be predicted by a host of divergent predictors. Figure 1 provides a heuristic model to illustrate at least four potential pathways in which peer functioning, specifically peer rejection, may lead to adolescent suicidality. In this model, suicidal behavior is conceptualized as a reaction to a stressor or precipitant, and various psychosocial factors are considered as potential moderators that may increase or diminish the likelihood that distressed adolescents will respond to a stressor with self-harmful or suicidal behavior. Peer rejection is considered both a direct predictor and an early risk factor that may alter the subsequent development of adaptive social functioning and adolescents' ability to sufficiently cope with stressors. Thus, negative peer experiences may lead to developmental vulnerabilities that leave some adolescents insufficiently equipped to deal with life stressors that can be successfully negotiated by other teens.

Each of the pathways between peer rejection and suicidality depicted in Figure 1 are derived from prior findings in the peer relations and suicide literature. Rather than orthogonal trajectories or a model for potential subtypes of suicidal adolescents, it is hypothesized that these pathways are likely to be coexisting, multiple processes that may jointly occur within an individual adolescent. Thus, peer rejection may produce multiple risks for adolescent suicide, and each of these pathways may contribute to and correlate with one another over time.

The first pathway depicted in Figure 1 provides an example of peer functioning as a direct predictor of suicidality. Peer rejected children and adolescents experience greater levels of peer victimization (Olweus, 1991; Perry, Kusel, & Perry, 1988). As an interpersonal stressor, peer

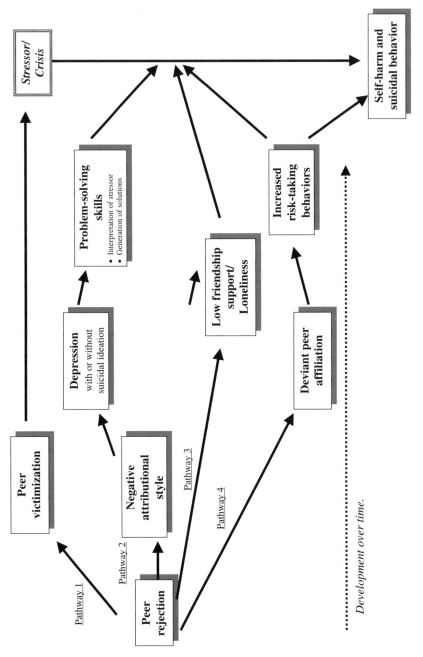

FIGURE 1   Potential pathways between peer functioning and suicidality.

victimization may be a direct precipitant to suicidal behavior (Hawton et al., 1996; Rigby & Slee, 1999). Prior work on suicide precipitants has also suggested that adolescents' recent breakup with a romantic partner can also act as an important precipitant (Hawton et al., 1996), suggesting another direct pathway between interpersonal experiences and suicidality. Peer experiences may also indirectly contribute to cognitive, social, and emotional vulnerabilities that leave distressed adolescents susceptible to self-harm behavior. For instance, the second illustrated pathway posits that adolescents who are rejected by peers may be more likely to develop negative attributional styles, placing these teens at risk for depressive symptoms (Quiggle, Garber, Panak, & Dodge, 1992). Depressed adolescents are more prone towards misinterpretation of social cues and have limited problem-solving ability for dealing with interpersonal stressors. Thus, peer rejection may not only increase the likelihood of interpersonal stressors for teens, but combinations of negative peer experiences and depressogenic cognitions may also impair an adolescent's ability to interpret and respond to interpersonal stressors adaptively.

Because peer-rejected adolescents also experience difficulties forming and maintaining friendships, these adolescents may also have diminished access to social support from peers and may experience heightened levels of loneliness (Burgess, Ladd, Kochenderfer, Lambert, & Birch, 1999). This third pathway, therefore, suggests that rejected adolescents may experience greater levels of social isolation and peer-related distress; each of these domains have been significantly associated with suicidal ideation and behavior in past work (Lewinsohn et al., 1994; Prinstein et al., 2000a). Peer support may also act as a resilience factor when adolescents are confronted with an interpersonal stressor, thus adolescents with low levels of peer support are ill-equipped to effectively deal with these stressors.

Lastly, the link between peer rejection and later deviant peer affiliation (Dishion et al., 1991) offers a fourth potential pathway to suicidal behavior. Adolescents who affiliate with deviant peers are more likely to engage in risk-taking behaviors (Dishion et al., 1991; La Greca, Prinstein, & Fetter, 2001), including increased self-harm and suicidal behaviors. In addition, deviant peers' increased impulsivity may hinder teens' ability to effectively cope with stressors and increase teens' cognitive access to risky and impulsive solutions for managing emotional distress. This is often noted as an explanation for the engagement in suicidal behavior by teens without prior history of suicidal ideation.

Overall, the hypotheses briefly described here illustrate multiple mechanisms by which peer experiences may contribute to the development of suicidal ideation and behavior. The co-occurrence of these pathways within individual adolescents suggests that a single predisposing characteristic, such as peer rejection, may potentiate an increased number of stressors and influence the development of multiple competencies that could be utilized by distressed adolescents. Investigations that pursue explanations for a link between this important domain of adolescent functioning and suicidality will importantly contribute to an understanding of the interpersonal nature of adolescent suicide.

CLINICAL IMPLICATIONS

Assessment of Peer Functioning

This brief review suggests that clinicians may wish to comprehensively assess adolescents' peer functioning to help determine risk for suicidality and should consider the multiple constructs of peer functioning when doing so. For instance, clinicians may include all three questions listed previously during an initial interview to assess whether adolescents are liked by peers, have friends, and what their friends are like. Related questions would include an assessment of adolescents' peer crowd affiliation: whether teens report that they belong to the deviant crowd (e.g., "burnouts"), athletic crowd (e.g., "jocks"), or academically oriented crowd (e.g., "brains"), for example. Similarly, do adolescents report that they are victimized by peers (i.e., teased, picked on, hit, pushed) or even by friends (i.e., left out of activities, made the subject of rumors and gossip, threatened that their friendship may be in jeopardy)? In terms of friendships, it is important to ask adolescents whether they have friends and to ensure that they can identify specific relationships; it is wise to ask adolescents if they can name specific individuals that they would consider close friends. Adolescents may be asked to characterize their relationships with their close friends, including their assessments of the frequency of conflict, companionship, and their perceptions of support from peers. Also, teens may be asked to report the kinds of activities they engage in with their friends, as well as the perceived frequency of their friends' risk behaviors. Teens are typically less reluctant to report their friends' risk behaviors, than their own behavior. Information on friends can offer helpful insight into the types of activities that teens may be exposed to routinely.

Of course, a number of established measures with sound psychometric properties exist to examine peer functioning, although only some of these instruments have been used clinically and few are relevant to peer experiences in adolescence specifically. A full review of assessment procedures for peer functioning is provided by Bierman and Welsh (1997) and La Greca and Prinstein (1999). Because adolescents, as compared to younger children, are less frequently monitored by parents and spend less time interacting with individual teachers, many measures relevant to adolescent peer functioning rely on teens' own report or peer report. For instance, an assessment of peer status (i.e., whether a teen is liked by peers) typically includes ratings and nominations from a sample of adolescents' peers. However, this approach is difficult to utilize with clinically referred teens due to confidentiality and practical constraints. Zakriski and colleagues offer more detail on this issue and some potential solutions (Zakriski & Prinstein, 2001; Zakriski, Seifer, Sheldrick, Prinstein, Dickstein, & Sameroff, 1999). Alternatively, several measures of *perceived* peer status are available; assessment of perceptions eliminates the need for peer report and may be more relevant to adolescents' internalizing symptoms (Panak & Garber, 1992). For example, Harter's (1988) Self Perception Profile for Adolescents includes subscales of self-concept in social acceptance and friendship domains. Teens' reports on these scales can be compared to norms provided by Harter (1988).

Several self-report instruments are available to examine adolescent friendship quality (see review by Furman, 1996). For instance, the Network of Relationships Inventory (Furman & Buhrmester, 1992) examines a range of friendship qualities (e.g., companionship, conflict, esteem support, reliable alliance) for adolescents' relationships with their best friends and boyfriends or girlfriends. A variety of similar measures exist (see Bierman & Welsh, 1997; Furman, 1996; La Greca & Prinstein, 1999).

A formal assessment of friends' characteristics and potential peer influence has not been developed for clinical use, although strategies used by investigators could be adapted easily into assessment practice (see Dishion et al., 1991; Fergusson & Horwood, 1996; Prinstein et al., 2001). For this assessment, adolescents and parents may be asked to indicate the total number of adolescents' close friends, followed by the number of these friends (or an estimation: "none," "few," "most," "all") who engage in a variety of risk behaviors. Research reports have supported the reliability and validity of this assessment (e.g., Dishion et al., 1991).

Treatment Implications

Although research has yielded only preliminary findings, there is some evidence to suggest that suicidal adolescents are likely to report peer stressors, low perceptions of support from peers, poor friendship quality, and affiliation with deviant or suicidal friends. These studies, and related studies on adolescents with peer difficulties, also suggest that these adolescents may be likely to experience significant distress related to their peer experiences and may be prone towards misinterpretation of social experiences and demonstrate poor problem-solving abilities when faced with a peer dilemma or stressor (Quiggle *et al.*, 1992; Sadowski & Kelly, 1993). Teens at risk for suicide may experience multiple peer difficulties and several psychological consequences as a result of peer rejection, as depicted in Figure 1. These are important considerations when working with teens who may be suicidal. Cognitive interventions, for instance, may challenge a teen's interpretations of negative peer experiences and help develop appropriate and adaptive strategies for addressing these stressors. Behavioral interventions may focus on social skills and friendship skills training to help teens initiate and maintain more supportive relationships with peers. Interpersonal therapy for depressed adolescents might also address these goals.

Overall, the consideration of adolescents' peer relationships as predictors of suicidality continues to be a relatively unexplored area of research. These preliminary findings and adolescents' own reports on the importance of peer stressors as precipitants of suicidal behavior suggest that further exploration of peer factors may be fruitful for both developmental psychopathology research and for clinical practice with teens at risk.

REFERENCES

Achenbach, T. M., & Edelbrock, C. S. (1987). *Manual for the youth self-report and profile.* Burlington, VT: University of Vermont, Department of Psychiatry.

Adams, D. M., Overholser, J. C., & Spirito, A. (1994). Stressful life events associated with adolescent suicide attempts. *Canadian Journal of Psychiatry, 39,* 43–48.

Armsden, G. C., & Greenberg, M. T. (1987). The inventory of parent and peer attachment: Individual differences and their relationship to psychological well-being in adolescence. *Journal of Youth and Adolescence, 16,* 427–454.

Beck, A. T., Weissman, A., Lester, D., & Trexler, L. (1974). The measurement of pessimism: The hopelessness scale. *Journal of Consulting and Clinical Psychology, 42,* 861–865.

Berman, A. L., & Schwartz, R. H. (1990). Suicide attempts among adolescent drug users. *AJDC, 144,* 310–314.

Bierman, K. L., & Welsh, J. A. (1997). Social relationship deficits. In E. J. Mash & L. G. Terdal (Eds.), *Assessment of childhood disorders* (3rd ed.). New York: Guilford.

Bjarnason, T., & Thorlindsson, T. (1994). Manifest predictors of past suicide attempts in a population of Icelandic adolescents. *Suicide and Life-Threatening Behavior, 24*, 350–358.

Burgess, K. B., Ladd, G. W., Kochenderfer, B. J., Lambert, S. F., & Birch, S. H. (1999). Loneliness during early childhood: The role of interpersonal behaviors and relationships. In K. J. Rotenberg & S. Hymel (Eds.), *Loneliness in childhood and adolescence.* New York: Cambridge University Press.

Coie, J. D., Lochman, J. E., Terry, R., & Hyman, C. (1992). Predicting early adolescent disorder from childhood aggression and peer rejection. *Journal of Consulting and Clinical Psychology, 60*, 783–792.

Cole, D. E., Protinsky, H. O., & Cross, L. H. (1992). An empirical investigation of adolescent suicidal ideation. *Adolescence, 27*, 813–818.

Crick, N. R., & Bigbee, M. A. (1998). Relational and overt forms of peer victimization: A multiinformant approach. *Journal of Consulting and Clinical Psychology, 66*, 337–347.

Davies, M., & Cunningham, G. (1999). Adolescent parasuicide in the Foyle area. *Irish Journal of Psychiatric Medicine, 16*, 9–12.

DiFilippo, J. M., & Overholser, J. C. (2000). Suicidal ideation in adolescent psychiatric inpatients as associated with depression and attachment relationships. *Journal of Clinical Child Psychology, 29*, 155–166.

Dishion, T. J., Patterson, G. R., Stoolmiller, M., & Skinner, M. L. (1991). Family, school, and behavioral antecedents to early adolescent involvement with antisocial peers. *Developmental Psychology, 27*, 172–180.

Dubow, E. F., Kausch, D. F., Blum, M. C., Reed, J., & Bush, E. (1989). Correlates of suicidal ideation and attempts in a community sample of junior high and high school students. *Journal of Clinical Child Psychology, 18*, 158–166.

Eskin, M. (1995). Suicidal behavior as related to social support and assertiveness among Swedish and Turkish high school students: A cross-cultural investigation. *Journal of Clinical Psychology, 51*, 158–172.

Fergusson, D. M., & Horwood, L. J. (1996). The role of adolescent peer affiliations in the continuity between childhood behavioral adjustment and juvenile offending. *Journal of Abnormal Child Psychology, 24*, 205–221.

Furman, W. (1996). The measurement of friendship perceptions: Conceptual and methodological issues. In W. M. Bukowski, A. F. Newcomb, & W. W. Hartup (Eds.), *The company they keep* (pp. 41–65). New York: Cambridge University Press.

Furman, W., & Buhrmester, D. (1992). Age and sex differences in perceptions of networks of personal relationships. *Child Development, 63*, 103–115.

Harter, S. (1988). *Manual for the Self-Perception Profile for Adolescents*, University of Denver.

Harter, S., Marold, D. B., & Whitesell, N. R. (1992). Model of psychosocial risk factors leading to suicidal ideation in young adolescents. *Development and Psychopathology, 4*, 167–188.

Hartup, W. W. (1996). The company they keep: Friendships and their developmental significance. *Child Development, 67*, 1–13.

Hawton, K., Fagg, J., & Simkin, S. (1996). Deliberate self-poisoning and self-injury in children and adolescents under 16 years of age in Oxford, 1976–1993. *British Journal of Psychiatry, 169*, 202–208.

Hogue, A., & Steinberg, L. (1995). Homophily of internalized distress in adolescent peer groups. *Developmental Psychology, 31*, 897–906.

Kandel, D. B., Raveis, V. H., & Davies, M. (1991). Suicidal ideation in adolescence: Depression, substance use, and other risk factors. *Journal of Youth and Adolescence, 20*, 289–309.

Khan, A. U. (1987). Heterogeneity of suicidal adolescents. *Journal of the American Academy of Child and Adolescent Psychiatry, 26*, 92–96.

Kosky, R., Silburn, S., & Zubrick, S. (1986). Symptomatic depression and suicide ideation: A comparative study with 628 children. *Journal of Nervous and Mental Disease, 178*, 38–43.

La Greca, A. M., & Prinstein, M. J. (1999). Peer group. In W. K. Silverman & T. H. Ollendick (Eds.), *Developmental issues in the clinical treatment of children and adolescents*. New York: Wiley.

La Greca, A. M., Prinstein, M. J., & Fetter, M. D. (2001). Adolescent peer crowd affiliation: Linkages with health-risk behaviors and close friendships. *Journal of Pediatric Psychology, 26*, 131–143.

Lewinsohn, P. M., Rohde, P., & Seeley, J. R. (1994). Psychosocial risk factors for future adolescent suicide attempts. *Journal of Consulting and Clinical Psychology, 62*, 297–305.

Moos, R. H., Cronkite, R. C., Billings, Aaa. G., & Finney, J. W. (1986). *Health and daily living form manual*. Palo Alto, CA: Stanford University Medical Center, Social Ecology Laboratory.

Morano, C., Cisler, R., & Lemerond, J. (1993). Risk factors for adolescent suicidal behavior: Loss, insufficient familial support, and hopelessness. *Adolescence, 28*, 851–865.

Offer, D., Ostrov, E., & Howard, K. I. (1982). *A manual for the OSIQ for adolescents* (3rd ed.). Chicago: Michael Reese Hospital and Medical Center.

Olweus, D. (1991). Bully/victim problems among school children: Basic facts and effects of a school based intervention program. In B. J. Peplar & K. H. Rubin (Eds.), *The development and treatment of childhood aggression* (pp. 411–448). Hillsdale, NJ: Erlbaum.

Panak, W. F., & Garber, J. (1992). Role of aggression, rejection, and attributions in the prediction of depression in children. *Development and Psychopathology, 4*, 145–165.

Parker, J. G., & Asher, S. R. (1987). Peer relations and later personal adjustment: Are low-accepted children at risk? *Psychological Bulletin, 102*, 357–389.

Perry, D. G., Kusel, S. J., & Perry, S. C. (1988). Victims of peer aggression. *Developmental Psychology, 24*, 807–814.

Prinstein, M. J., Boergers, J., & Spirito, A. (2001). Adolescents' and their friends' health-risk behavior: Factors that alter or add to peer influence. *Journal of Pediatric Psychology, 26*, 287–298.

Prinstein, M. J., Boergers, J., Spirito, A., & Little, T. D. (2000). Cognitive models of peer victimization, interpersonal schema and suicidality in adolescent non-clinical and inpatient samples. In M. K. Nock & M. J. Prinstein (Co-Chairs), *Cognitive risk factors and treatment approaches for suicidal adolescents*. Association for Advancement of Behavior Therapy, New Orleans, LA.

Prinstein, M. J., Boergers, J., Spirito, A., Little, T. D., & Grapentine, W. L. (2000). Peer functioning, family dysfunction, and psychological symptoms in a risk factor model for adolescent inpatients' suicidal ideation severity. *Journal of Clinical Child Psychology, 29*, 392–405.

Quiggle, N. L., Garber, J., Panak, W. F., & Dodge, K. A. (1992). Social information processing in aggressive and depressed children. *Child Development, 63,* 1305–1320.

Reifman, A., & Windle, M. (1995). Adolescent suicidal behaviors as a function of depression, hopelessness, alcohol use, and social support: A longitudinal investigation. *American Journal of Community Psychology, 23,* 329–354.

Rigby, K., & Slee, P. (1999). Suicidal ideation among adolescent school children, involvement in bully-victim problems, and perceived social support. *Suicide and Life-Threatening Behavior, 29,* 119–130.

Ritter, D. R. (1990). Adolescent suicide: Social competence and problem behavior of youth at high risk and low risk for suicide. *School Psychology Review, 19,* 83–95.

Rohn, R. D., Sarles, R. M., Kenny, T. J., Reynolds, B. J., & Heald, F. P. (1977). Adolescents who attempt suicide. *The Journal of Pediatrics, 90,* 626–638.

Rubenstein, J. L., Heeren, T., Housman, D., Rubin, C., & Stechler, G. (1989). Suicidal behavior in "normal" adolescents: Risk and protective factors. *American Journal of Orthopsychiatry, 59*(1), 59–71.

Rubenstein, J. L., & Rubin, C. (1986). *The adolescent friendship inventory.* Unpublished manuscript.

Rudd, M. D. (1993). Social support and suicide. *Psychological Reports, 72,* 201–202.

Russell, D., Peplau, L. A., & Cutrona, C. E. (1980). The Revised UCLA-Loneliness Scale: Concurrent and discriminant validity evidence. *Journal of Personality and Social Psychology, 39,* 472–480.

Sadowski, C., & Kelly, M. L. (1993). Social problem solving in suicidal adolescents. *Journal of Consulting and Clinical Psychology, 61,* 121–127.

Shagle, S. C., & Barber, B. K. (1995). A social-ecological analysis of adolescent suicidal ideation. *American Journal of Orthopsychiatry, 65,* 114–124.

Spirito, A., Brown, L., Overholser, J., & Fritz, G. (1989). Attempted suicide in adolescence: Current findings and implications for future research and clinical practice. *Clinical Psychology Review, 9,* 335–363.

Spirito, A., Overholser, J., & Stark, L. J. (1989). Common problems and coping strategies II: Findings with adolescent suicide attempters. *Journal of Abnormal Child Psychology, 17,* 213–221.

Stanley, J. E., & Barter, J. T. (1970). Adolescent suicidal behavior. *American Journal of Orthopsychiatry, 40,* 87–96.

Tishler, C. L., McKenry, P. C., & Morgan, K. C. (1981). Adolescent suicide attempts: Some significant factors. *Suicide and Life-Threatening Behavior, 11,* 86–92.

Topol, P., & Reznikoff, M. (1982). Perceived peer and family relationships, hopelessness, and locus of control as factors in adolescent suicide attempts. *Suicide and Life-Threatening Behavior, 11,* 86–92.

Wagner, B. M. (1997). Family risk factors for child and adolescent suicidal behavior. *Psychological Bulletin, 121,* 246–298.

Windle, M. (1994). A study of friendship characteristics and problem behaviors among middle adolescents. *Child Development, 65,* 1764–1777.

Youniss, J., & Smollar, J. (1985). *Adolescent relations with mothers, fathers, and friends.* Chicago; University of Chicago Press.

Yuen, M., Andrade, N., Nahulu, L., Makini, G., McDermott, J. F., Danko, G., Johnson, R., & Waldron, J. (1996). The rate and characteristics of suicide attempters in the Native Hawaiian adolescent population. *Suicide and Life-Threatening Behavior, 26,* 27–36.

Zakriski, A. L., & Prinstein, M. J. (2001). Sociometric status of child inpatients in clinical and normative peer groups: Is peer status in a clinical setting a useful measure of adjustment? *Applied Developmental Psychology, 22,* 1–17.

Zakriski, A. L., Seifer, R., Sheldrick, R. C., Prinstein, M. J., Dickstein, S., & Sameroff, A. J. (1999). Child-focused versus school-focused sociometrics: A challenge for the applied researcher. *Journal of Applied Developmental Psychology, 20,* 481–499.

CHAPTER 10

Social Factors: Isolation and Loneliness versus Social Activity

Sylvia M. Valeri, PhD

More than 30 years ago, Barter, Swaback, and Todd (1968) found that poor social functioning was associated with repeat suicide attempts among adolescents. Similarly, Wenz (1979) reported that social alienation was a key feature leading to suicidal acts among teenagers. Today, across studies of adolescent mental health, there is a general consensus that social experiences, broadly construed, are related to adolescents' overall well-being and level of impairment. More specifically, impaired social functioning in adolescence, including social isolation, alienation, and feelings of loneliness, has been associated with increased suicidal ideation and suicide attempts. In contrast, positive social experiences may be useful in ameliorating the negative behaviors and mood states that are related to adolescent suicide attempts. Social skills and increased social activities, for instance, may offer opportunities to connect with peers, decrease isolation and feelings of loneliness, and perhaps buffer adolescents from stressful events that may lead to suicidal thoughts and suicidal behavior. In addition, increased social activities may have a direct effect on an adolescent's mood and self-worth.

In this chapter we focus on these various aspects of social functioning that are not specifically related to family relationships (Chapter 8) or peer relationships (Chapter 9). First, negative social functioning features are discussed, including social withdrawal and isolation, alienation, and feelings of loneliness. Although these features may represent somewhat overlapping constructs (i.e., the difference between feeling alienated and feeling lonely might be a matter of semantics), research in each area is presented separately since these features of social functioning are typically measured in different ways. Second, we present research findings on adolescents' involvement in social activities, an aspect of social functioning that may buffer the teen against increased or continued suicidal ideation and suicide attempts. Following the literature review, we present various strategies to assess social factors that are related to adolescent suicidal behavior. Finally, we discuss clinical implications that can guide clinicians in their work with suicidal teens.

SOCIAL WITHDRAWAL AND ISOLATION

Social withdrawal is one aspect of disturbed social functioning that has been identified as a predictor of suicidality among adolescents. Spirito, Overholser, and Stark (1989), for example, examined the coping strategies reported by 76 adolescents hospitalized on a general pediatric unit following a suicide attempt. The coping strategies of the suicide attempters were compared to those of 186 adolescent community controls. The community controls were further divided into a distressed or nondistressed group, as defined by their self-report of depression or anxiety in response to selected personal problems. As a part of the investigation, all adolescents were asked to select a problem that they encountered in the previous month and, using the Kidcope (Spirito, Stark, & Williams, 1988), describe the cognitive and behavioral coping strategies that they used to deal with the problem. The adolescent suicide attempters used social withdrawal more frequently than both the distressed and nondistressed controls to cope with different problems (e.g., problems with friends, school, parents, and boyfriends/girlfriends). Groholt, Ekeberg, Wichstrom, and Haldorsen (2000) reported parallel findings. This study found that both inpatient and community samples of adolescents with past histories of suicide attempts often chose not to seek support from others when presented with both neutral and stressful situations.

In a subsequent investigation, Spirito, Francis, Overholser, and Frank (1996) also found a high prevalence of social withdrawal in adolescent suicide attempters who were psychiatrically hospitalized, but this finding was not specific to suicide attempters. In this study, differences in the use of coping strategies were examined among five groups of adolescents: 40 suicide attempters admitted to a general hospital, 108 psychiatrically hospitalized suicide attempters, 32 psychiatrically hospitalized suicide ideators, 22 nonsuicidal psychiatric inpatients, and 56 non-suicidal high school controls. All adolescents completed the Kidcope (Spirito *et al.*, 1988) in response to a scenario depicting a conflict with their parents and indicated how often they thought they would use each of the 10 coping strategies (e.g., distraction, problem solving). Results revealed that the psychiatrically hospitalized adolescents (suicide attempters, ideators, and nonsuicidal inpatients) all scored significantly higher on social with-drawal than the general hospitalized suicide attempters and controls. No differences were found between the five groups on the total number of coping strategies used, positive coping strategies, or negative coping strategies.

In addition, Hawton, Fagg, and Simkin (1996) examined the extent of social isolation in children and adolescents ages 8 to 15 who had attempted suicide. Youth in the study had been taken to a medical hospital for deliberate self-harm and subsequently, many were referred to an emergency psychiatric service that included a structured psychosocial assessment. For 212 of the 750 participants, clinicians completed check-lists indicating problems that preceded the suicidal behavior. Findings from these lists of problems indicated that social isolation was the fifth most frequently reported problem/condition by the children and teenagers. Problems with family, friends, boyfriend/girlfriend, and school-work were the top four reported problems that preceded the self-harm behavior.

Finally, Negron, Piacentini, Graae, Davies, and Shaffer (1997) examined psychological and behavioral contingencies that characterized and differ-entiated adolescent suicide attempters and ideators. Thirty-five ideators and 32 attempters being treated in a suicide disorders clinic were included in the study. All participants were administered semistructured question-naires that were used to assess the emotional, cognitive, and behavioral status of the adolescents before, during, and after the suicidal episode. Information from these questionnaires indicated that, compared to ideators, adolescent suicide attempters were more often isolated and did not tell anyone what they were thinking during the period of suicidal ideation. Rohn, Sarles, Kenny, Reynolds, and Heald (1977) reported similar findings. In this investigation, 50% of a sample of 65 adolescent suicide attempters seen in an emergency room described themselves as "loners" or as being socially isolated before their suicide attempt. This finding was especially true for the male attempters.

LONELINESS

Loneliness is another social functioning dimension that has been linked to suicidal behaviors in youth. With respect to adolescent suicide attempts, three cross-sectional investigations have examined the role of loneliness. First, Rossow and Wichstrom (1994) studied the relationship between loneliness and suicide attempts in a sample of approximately 11,000 Norwegian adolescents ranging in age from 12 to 19. Data for the investigation were drawn from self-administered questionnaires as part of an epidemiological survey of Norwegian youth. Included in the questionnaires was a shortened version of the UCLA Loneliness Scale (Russell, Peplau, & Cutrona, 1980). Study findings indicated that the proportion of attempted suicide was higher among adolescents with high scores on the loneliness scale.

Second, a subsample of adolescents from the Rossow and Wichstrom (1994) investigation was included in an investigation that also involved medically hospitalized suicide attempters (Groholt et al., 2000). The investigators compared the adolescents that were hospitalized for a suicide attempt to two subsets from the community sample described previously—adolescents with a history of a self-reported suicide attempt and those without a history of self-reported suicide attempt. Similar to the previous investigation, the shortened version of the UCLA Loneliness Scale was used to assess whether loneliness might differentiate the three groups of comparison. Loneliness was a significant risk factor for suicide attempts among the community sample with a history of suicidal behavior, but not for the hospitalized adolescents. Moreover, both groups with past suicide attempts reported that they typically did not seek support from others.

A third study that examined the relationship between suicide attempts and loneliness focused on substance-abusing adolescents and a matched adolescent control group (Berman & Schwartz, 1990). The substance abusing teenagers ($n = 298$) were recruited from outpatient treatment facilities, and the nondrug control group ($n = 105$) was drawn from consecutive outpatient visits to a private pediatric practice. All participants completed questionnaires assessing suicidal behavior and a range of other psychosocial variables during their outpatient appointments. Data collected from these surveys indicated that substance-abusing adolescents who attempted suicide were more likely to report chronic loneliness in childhood compared to drug-using nonattempters and the non-drug-using control teenagers.

In addition to suicide attempts, other investigations examining the role of self-reported loneliness have looked at its relationship to suicidal ideation. Roberts, Roberts, and Chen (1998) studied this relationship in a community sample of middle school students (grades six through eight). The students ranged in age from 10 to 17 and the findings were based on self-administered questionnaires completed during school. Loneliness was measured using an 8-item scale developed for research with adolescents (Roberts, Lewinsohn, & Seeley, 1993). The analyses indicated that adolescents reporting a greater degree of loneliness were almost twice as likely to manifest suicidal thinking (Roberts *et al.*, 1998).

Similarly, in a sample of college students (mean age 19.4), Clum and colleagues (1997) compared students with a high degree of suicidal ideation to students with low degree of suicidal ideation on various measures, including loneliness. Feelings of loneliness were measured by the Revised UCLA Loneliness Scale (Russell *et al.*, 1980). Self-reported loneliness related to more frequent suicidal ideation even after controlling for depressive symptoms, age, and education level. This relationship was consistent across analyses that focused on females and males separately and on the sample as whole.

ALIENATION

Alienation, a subjective feeling similar to loneliness, has also been associated with adolescent suicidal behavior. As measured by the Minnesota Multiphasic Personality Inventory for Adolescents (MMPI-A, Butcher *et al.*, 1992), alienation refers to a general feeling of being misunderstood and unloved by others. In addition, adolescents with high scores on the alienation content scale tend to feel considerable emotional distance from others and believe they are getting a "bum rap" or "raw deal" in life. Kopper, Osman, Osman, and Hoffman (1998) used the MMPI-A to assess which scales or subscales, including the alienation content scale, might be associated with suicidal risk. Suicidal risk was measured by the Suicide

Probability Scale (Cull & Gill, 1982) and subjects included 143 adolescent inpatients. It is unclear how many participants had a history of suicidal behavior. The findings indicated that for boys, alienation scores consistently contributed to the prediction of suicide probability. More specifically, boys' alienation scores predicted suicide probability over and above depression scores, psychopathic deviate scores, and hypomania scores on the MMPI-A. These results highlight the role of alienation as a risk factor for suicidal behavior in adolescent males.

In a study with an outpatient adolescent sample, similar findings emerged. De Man, Leduc, and Labreche-Gauthier (1993) found that stronger feelings of alienation (as measured by a 9-item Anomy Scale; McClosky & Schaar, 1965) were positively correlated with suicidal ideation. However, in multiple regression analyses, adolescent's alienation scores were not found to be significant predictors of suicidal ideation. Because analyses were not conducted separately for boys and girls, it is unclear whether results would be different for adolescent males and females as in the Kopper *et al.* study (1998) described earlier.

SOCIAL ACTIVITY AND SOCIAL SKILLS

In their review of empirical work on the friendships of disturbed adolescents, LaGaipa and Wood (1981) reported that many emotionally disturbed youth have few friends, are withdrawn, and thus are lonely. Other studies indicate that engaging in pleasant activities protects against feelings of depression (e.g., Clarke, Lewinsohn, & Hops, 1990). Therefore, examining adolescent activities, both social activities and solitary activities, may be an important step in identifying protective factors in youth that have attempted suicide. Yet the study of daily activities in suicidal youth has received minimal attention. Kotila and Longvist (1988), in a sample of 422 hospitalized adolescent attempters, reported that females were more likely to be in school and engage in regular daily activities compared to males. Males, on the other hand, had a higher rate of unemployment that was frequently linked to deviant behavior compared to females. Similarly, Nakamura, McLeod, and McDermott (1994), through a retrospective chart review, evaluated the temporal patterns of suicidal behavior of approximately 300 adolescent suicide attempters. Findings indicated that suicide attempts most often occurred weekdays after school in the afternoon or evening. The authors noted that these are times that adolescents are likely to be home, alone, and to have free time.

Mazza and Eggert (in press) examined the activities of adolescents at risk for suicide in greater detail. The investigators examined the typical weekday and weekend activity profiles of four groups of teens: (1) those at suicide risk and high-risk for school dropout, (2) suicide-risk-typical students, (3) those with nonsuicide-risk but at high-risk for school dropout, and (4) nonsuicide-risk-typical students. Findings showed that, in general, adolescents who were at suicide risk were more likely to engage in solitary activities compared to their nonsuicidal peers. This finding was consistent for both males and females. In contrast to the finding on solitary activities (e.g., watching TV alone), the suicide-risk adolescents who were also at high-risk for school dropout showed significantly higher levels of social activity compared to the typical students. Thus, the authors argue that youth at risk for both suicide and school dropout frequently may be overlooked or missed regarding suicide-risk because they may be perceived as socially active and connected with friends.

At the same time, it is important to keep in mind that adolescents with a history of suicidality may not have the requisite social skills to engage in activities with others. For example, Brent, Kolko, Allan, & Brown (1990) examined the social skills of 42 suicidal and 14 nonsuicidal affectively disturbed youth in a psychiatric inpatient unit. The study participants ranged in age from 13 to 19 and were administered a comprehensive battery to assess psychosocial factors that might differentiate suicidal and nonsuicidal adolescents. Included in the battery was the Adolescent Assertion Expression Scale (Connor, Twentyman, & Dann, 1979). Data from this measure indicated that the suicidal youth were more submissive and less assertive than the nonsuicidal teens. Thus, whereas adolescents would likely benefit from increased social interactions, these findings suggest that social skills training may be an important first step in facilitating the development of interpersonal relationships.

ASSESSMENT

There are several different approaches by which clinicians can assess the areas of social functioning related to adolescent suicidal behavior. To begin with, standardized measures can be used to examine aspects of social functioning. The Kidcope (Spirito *et al.*, 1988), for example, can be used to assess how adolescents cope with stressful situations. In particular, it can be used to assess whether adolescents use social withdrawal as a way to cope with stressful events, a strategy associated with suicide attempts. In addition, the UCLA Loneliness Scale (Russell *et al.*, 1980) is a frequently used measure in research to examine the degree of loneliness experienced by teens. Sample items include "There are people I can talk to," "I feel left out," and "There are people I feel close to."

If a structured measure is not available, questions that assess feelings of loneliness, isolation, and social activity are likely to provide useful information. Examples of opening questions that may lead to further discussion of these content areas are as follows:

Loneliness and Isolation

- Do you often feel alone? Do you prefer to be alone?
- Do you feel disconnected from others?
- Do you feel as if no one understands you?
- How often are you by yourself or not interacting with others? What may lead you to be by yourself?

Social Activity

- How do you spend your time? Are you involved in any school organizations? Do you have a job outside of your home? What activities do you participate in after school?
- Are you usually alone or with others when engaging in different activities?
- When was the last time that you went to a ball game, party, or a movie with peers or family?
- Do you ever feel bored?
- What is a typical day like for you?

The research on social activities suggests that clinicians should carefully explore how adolescents spend their time after school, in the evenings, and on the weekends. Adolescents spending a substantial amount of time alone and/or engaged in solitary activities will likely benefit from participation in after-school programs, sports, or other social activities. One questionnaire that can be used to more formally assess social activities is the Social Adjustment Inventory for Children and Adolescents (SAICA; John, Gammon, Prusoff, & Warner, 1987). The SAICA is a semi-structured interview that is administered to children and/or parents by trained assessors. Spare time activities is one of the four areas measured and the subscale of the SAICA that may prove especially useful in assessing an adolescent's social activities.

Similarly, informal interviews or standardized measures can be used to gauge an adolescent's feelings of alienation. More specifically, questions that address whether a teen feels understood, cared for, loved, or cheated in life can provide useful information about his or her degree of alienation. Some items from the MMPI-A (Butcher *et al.*, 1992) that assess social alienation include (1) "I am sure that I get a raw deal from life," (2) "No one seems to understand me," (3) "If people had not had it in for me I would have been much more successful," (4) "I wish I could be as happy as others seem to be," (5) "Even when I am with people I feel lonely most of the time," and (6) "I do many things which I regret afterwards." More "true" responses to such items indicate a greater sense of alienation.

To assess the social skills of adolescents, clinicians can role-play with their clients meeting or interacting with peers. Role-playing may highlight deficits in being assertive or indicate whether the adolescent has a tendency to be submissive—both characteristics found in adolescents with a history of suicidal behavior. If an adolescent has difficulty engaging in role plays, vignettes or hypothetical situations can be used to gauge assertiveness. That is, after describing the hypothetical situations, clinicians can then ask whether the adolescent is likely to respond one way (e.g., "I will speak up when treated unfairly") versus another (e.g., "I'm unlikely to say anything with treated unfairly"). In general, clinicians can keep an eye out for aspects of interactions associated with good social skills, including appropriate eye contact and physical distance, proper salutations, and appropriate voice tone (e.g., not yelling, not too quiet). An adolescent's ability to share, refrain from interrupting, respond to praise with praise, and express dissent in clear and appropriate ways are also facets of skilled social interactions that should be evaluated.

In addition, self- and parent-report questionnaires can be used to assess children's social skills. For example, the Teenage Inventory of Social Skills (TISS; Inderbitzen & Foster, 1992) is a self-report measure with separate versions for boys and girls. Sample items include "I ask other guys to go places with me," "I push girls I do not like," and "I tell guys how I really feel about things." As mentioned earlier, in the Brent *et al.* study (1990), the Adolescent Assertion Expression Scale (Connor *et al.*, 1979) was used to measure other dimensions of social interactions, specifically assertiveness and submissiveness.

CLINICAL IMPLICATIONS

Taken together, the findings from the studies reviewed here consistently indicate that social withdrawal and isolation are common among suicidal disturbed adolescents. Thus, it would be wise for clinicians to engage the aid of family, peers, and school staff in closely monitoring adolescents following a suicide attempt so as to prevent opportunities wherein the adolescent may engage in self-harm behaviors. In addition, clinicians should carefully assess the amount of time that suicide attempters spend alone and have nothing to do, especially during weekday afternoons. Given the tendency to isolate and not engage in activities, interventions geared at increasing involvement with others and developing hobbies or other skills might be beneficial. The involvement of families and school staff may be needed to help increase social interactions among adolescents who have attempted suicide and need direction in pursuing social activities.

Considering the results of Brent *et al.* (1990), social skills training may be a necessary first step in helping these adolescents develop the prerequisite tools needed to engage with others and participate in social activities successfully. Yet even if adolescents seem engaged in social activities and well connected with peers, results from Mazza and Eggert (in press) suggest that using only outwardly visible criteria to identify suicidal risk (i.e., is a teenager interacting with friends) is not an effective strategy. This is supported by the finding that youth at risk for both suicide and school dropout engaged in more social activities than typical students (Mazza & Eggert, in press). Consequently, direct inquiries about suicidal ideation and behaviors are needed to supplement observable indicators (e.g., involvement with peers) that can sometimes indicate poor functioning.

A sense of self-efficacy may be another key component that can facilitate the development of interpersonal relationships in adolescent suicide attempters. Given the frequent presence of depressive symptoms (including poor self-worth and self-efficacy) in suicidal adolescents, clinical work with this population may benefit from a clearer understanding of the extent to which inadequate social skills and low self-efficacy interfere with the development of supportive interpersonal relationships. Poor social skills and a disturbed sense of self-efficacy may be also linked to the tendency to isolate in adolescents with suicidal behavior.

Based on the extant literature, it is unclear whether social withdrawal occurs when first confronted with stressful events or results only after other coping strategies have been unsuccessful. Thus, it would be useful to assess adolescents' repertoire of coping strategies and effectiveness in using them successfully. It may be the case that disturbed adolescents consider social withdrawal and isolation (or even suicide) their only or best option when faced with stressors. If this were the case, clinicians would be wise to focus efforts on building adaptive coping responses so as to curb the adolescent's tendency to isolate and engage in harmful behaviors.

Consistent with the research on social withdrawal and isolation, adolescent suicide attempters and ideators are also more likely to report feelings of loneliness compared to comparison groups. That is, prior to suicide attempts or during periods of suicidal ideation, disturbed adolescents report being physically alone, as well as feelings of loneliness. This finding further highlights the potential benefits of increasing social activities and developing emotional connections with others when treating adolescents with a history of suicidal behavior. At the same time, clinicians may also want to assess the degree to which reported feelings of loneliness are influenced by cognitive distortions associated with depressive symptomatology. It may be that depressed and suicidal teens are distorting the degree to which others are involved in their lives and are willing to offer support, which in turn may lead to more feelings of loneliness.

Moreover, while there is a paucity of research linking feelings of alienation and suicidality, feelings of alienation may be related to increased suicidal ideation in adolescents, or at least adolescent males. Findings from Kopper et al. (1998) suggest that clinicians should closely monitor boys who report emotional distance from others, believe they are being treated unfairly, and feel no one cares about, understands, likes, or is kind to them (Butcher et al., 1992). Boys who may not get along well with others, feel others are out to get them, do not believe they have as much fun as other adolescents, and have difficulty self-disclosing should also be followed closely (Butcher et al., 1992).

REFERENCES

Barter, J. T., Swaback, D. O., & Todd, D. (1968). Adolescent suicide attempts: A follow-up study of hospitalized patients. *Archives of General Psychiatry, 19,* 523–527.

Berman, A. L., & Schwartz, R. H. (1990). Suicide attempts among adolescent drug users. *American Journal of Disease of Children, 144,* 310–314.

Brent, D. A., Kolko, D. J., Allan, M. J., & Brown, R. V. (1990). Suicidality in affectively disordered adolescent inpatients. *Journal of the American Academy of Child and Adolescent Psychiatry, 29,* 586–593.

Butcher, J. N., Williams, C. L., Graham, J. R., Archer, R. P., Tellegen, A., Ben-Porath, Y. S., & Kaemmer, B. (1992). *Manual for administration, scoring, and interpretation of the Minnesota Multiphasic Personality Inventory for Adolescents: MMPI-A*. Minneapolis, MN: University of Minneapolis Press.

Clarke, G. N., Lewinsohn, P. M., & Hops, H. (1990). *Leader's manual for adolescent groups: Adolescent coping with depression course*. Eugene, Oregon: Castalia.

Clum, G. A., Canfield, D., Arsdel, M. V., Yang, B., Febbraro, G., & Wright, J. (1997). An expanded etiological model for suicide behavior in adolescents: Evidence for its specificity relative to depression. *Journal of Psychopathology and Behavioral Assessment, 19*, 207–222.

Connor, J. M., Twentyman, C. T., & Dann, L. N. (1979). *A self-report measure of assertiveness in young adolescents*. Paper presented at the annual meeting of the American Association for Behavior Therapy, San Francisco, CA.

Cull, J. G., & Gill, W. S. (1982). *Suicide Probability Scale*. Los Angeles, CA: Western Psychological Services.

De Man, A. F., Leduc, C. P., & Labreche-Gauthier, L. (1993). Correlates of suicidal ideation in French-Canadian adolescents: personal variables, stress, and social support. *Adolescence, 28*, 819–830.

Groholt, B., Ekberg, E., Wichstrom, L., & Haldorsen, T. (2000). Young suicide attempters: A comparison between a clinical and an epidemiological sample. *Journal of the American Academy of Child and Adolescent Psychiatry, 39*, 868–875.

Hawton, K., Fagg, J., & Simkin, S. (1996). Deliberate self-poisoning and self-injury in children and adolescents under 16 years of age in Oxford, 1976–1993. *British Journal of Psychiatry, 169*, 202–208.

Inderbitzen, H. M., & Foster, S. L. (1992). The teenage inventory of social skills: Development, reliability, and validity. *Psychological Assessment, 4*, 451–459.

John, K., Gammon, G. D., Prusoff, B. A., & Warner, V. (1987). The Social Adjustment Inventory for Children and Adolescents (SAICA): Testing of a new semistructured interview. *Journal of the American Academy of Child and Adolescent Psychiatry, 26*, 898–911.

Kopper, B. A., Osman, A., Osman, J. R., & Hoffman, J. (1998). Clinical utility of the MMPI-A content scales and Harris-Lingoes subscales in the assessment of suicidal risk factors in psychiatric adolescents. *Journal of Clinical Psychology, 54*, 191–200.

Kotila, L., & Longvist, J. (1988). Adolescent suicide attempts: Sex differences predicting suicide. *Acta Psychiatrica Scandinavica, 77*, 264–270.

LaGaipa, J. J., & Wood, H. D. (1981). Friendship in disturbed adolescents. In S. Duck & R. Gilmour (Eds.), *Personal relationships in disorder* (pp. 169–189). London: Academic Press.

Mazza, J. J., & Eggert, L. L. (in press). Activity profiles among suicidal and non-suicidal high-risk and typical adolescents. *Suicide and Life-Threatening Behavior*.

McClosky, H., & Schaar, J. H. (1965). Psychological dimensions of anomy. *American Sociological Review, 30*, 14–40.

Nakamura, J. W., McLeod, C. R., & McDermott, J. F. (1994). Temporal variation in adolescent suicide attempts. *Suicide and Life-Threatening Behavior, 24*, 343–349.

Negron, R., Piacentini, J., Graae, F., Davies, M., & Shaffer, D. (1997). Microanalysis of adolescent suicide attempters and ideators during the acute suicidal episode. *Journal of the American Academy of Child and Adolescent Psychiatry, 36*, 1512–1519.

Roberts, R. E., Lewinsohn, P. M., & Seeley, J. R. (1993). A brief measure of loneliness suitable for use with adolescents. *Psychological Reports, 72,* 1379–1391.

Roberts, R. E., Roberts, C. R., & Chen, Y. R. (1998). Suicidal thinking among adolescents with a history of attempted suicide. *Journal of the American Academy of Child and Adolescent Psychiatry, 37,* 1294–1300.

Rohn, R. D., Sarles, R. M., Kenny, T. J., Reynolds, B. J., & Heald, F. P. (1977). Adolescents who attempt suicide. *The Journal of Pediatrics, 90,* 626–638.

Rossow, I., & Wichstrom, L. (1994). Parasuicide and use of intoxicants among Norwegian adolescents. *Suicide and Life-Threatening Behaviors, 24,* 174–183.

Russell, D., Peplau, L. A., & Cutrona, C. E. (1980). The Revised UCLA Loneliness Scale: Concurrent and discriminant validity evidence. *Journal of Personality and Social Psychology, 39,* 472–480.

Spirito, A., Francis, G., Overholser, J., & Frank, N. (1996). Coping, depression, and adolescent suicide attempts. *Journal of Clinical Child Psychology, 25,* 147–155.

Spirito, A., Overholser, J., & Stark, L. J. (1989). Common problems and coping strategies II: Findings with adolescent suicide attempters. *Journal of Abnormal Child Psychology, 17,* 213–221.

Spirito, A., Stark, L. J., & Williams, C. (1988). Development of a brief coping checklist for use with pediatric populations. *Journal of Pediatric Psychology, 13,* 389–407.

Wenz, F. (1979). Sociological correlates of alienation among adolescent suicide attempts. *Adolescence, 14,* 19–30.

CHAPTER 11

High-Risk Populations

Julia M. DiFilippo, Cristianne Esposito, James Overholser, and Anthony Spirito

Identifying high-risk groups for suicidal behavior is an important way to tailor prevention and intervention efforts. Preventive efforts can be applied to the groups as a whole to help reduce the onset of suicidal behavior, and high-risk populations can be screened to identify those adolescents in need of intervention. This chapter reviews six high-risk groups for adolescent suicidal behavior: (1) gay, lesbian, and bisexual youth; (2) homeless, runaway, and delinquent youth; (3) incarcerated youth; (4) youth exposed to suicidal behavior; (5) multiple attempters; and (6) adolescents with self-mutilative behavior. The chapter addresses specific implications for the assessment and treatment of the various high-risk groups.

GAY, LESBIAN, AND BISEXUAL YOUTH

In the past decade, increased attention has focused on suicide risk among gay, lesbian, and bisexual (GLB) youth. As part of the Secretary's Task Force on Youth Suicide published by the U.S. Department of Health and

Human Services, Gibson (1989) reviewed the existing scientific literature and estimated that GLB youth are two to three times more likely to attempt suicide relative to their peers. In addition, Gibson (1989) stated that GLB adolescents "may comprise up to thirty percent of completed youth suicides annually" (p. 3–110). Although the remark was not based on scientific research and likely represents a gross overestimate (Muehrer, 1995), Gibson's (1989) article raised awareness of the importance of assessing sexual orientation within the context of suicide.

Rates of adolescent suicide attempts appear to be higher among gay, lesbian, and bisexual youth than among heterosexual youth. Remafedi, French, Story, Resnick, and Blum (1998) cite eight peer-reviewed studies that found attempted suicide rates ranging from 20 to 42%. However, in their own statewide survey of high school students, Remafedi *et al.* (1998) reported the following rates of suicide attempts: 28.1% of bisexual/homosexual males, 20.5% of bisexual/homosexual females compared to 14.5% of heterosexual females and 4.2% of heterosexual males. The ratio of male-to-female suicide attempts is reversed in gay, lesbian, and bisexual youth compared to heterosexual youth: rates are higher among gay and bisexual males than among lesbians. Bagley and Tremblay (2000) reviewed the recent literature and concluded that GLB youth have a rate of suicidal behavior two to eight times greater than heterosexual youth. Even larger differences have been found for suicide attempts requiring medical treatment.

Research with Samples from Social, Recreational, and Support Groups

The majority of subsequent research has examined suicidal behavior among adolescents recruited from GLB social, recreational, and support groups. Although the studies have not included control groups, the prevalence of suicide attempts among these GLB youths is significantly higher than estimates of 8 to 12% in general high school populations (e.g., Garland & Zigler, 1993; Smith & Crawford, 1986). For example, in one study, 39% of 197 adolescents attending GLB social and recreational groups in an urban setting reported suicidal ideation within a week of research participation, and 42% endorsed having made at least one suicide attempt in their lifetime (Hershberger, Pilkington, & D'Augelli, 1996, 1997). Findings from other studies using similar convenience samples yield comparable prevalence rates for suicidal behavior (Hammelman, 1993; Hershberger & D'Augelli, 1995; Proctor & Groze, 1994; Remafedi, 1987; Remafedi, Farrow, & Deisher, 1991). Over 50% of suicide attempts among a sample of gay and bisexual male adolescents were rated as having "moderate to high" potential lethality and "moderate to low" likelihood of rescue (Remafedi *et al.*, 1991).

However, there has been controversy around the relationship between sexual orientation and suicidal behavior. With regard to completed suicide, information about sexual orientation is not included on death certificates, and there are no known psychological autopsy studies within the past decade that include questions related to sexual orientation. In addition, several researchers raise significant concerns about the representativeness of previous research with convenience samples. For example, Hartstein (1996) noted that previous studies have not used adequate methods of assessing sexual orientation, not included matched heterosexual control subjects, and sampled only the segment of the GLB population who have already self-identified and "come out." Indeed, information obtained from youth at settings such as support groups, crisis centers, and runaway shelters may reflect high levels of distress and may not be representative of the general GLB population (Muehrer, 1995).

Research with School-Based Samples

Three recent school-based studies have been conducted in order to over-come the limitations of previous research using samples obtained from social, recreational, and support groups. All three investigations (i.e., Faulkner & Cranston, 1998; Garofalo, Wolf, Kessel, Palfrey, & DuRant, 1998; Remafedi *et al.*, 1998) involve large random samples of high school students, include at least one item related to sexual orientation, and examine a wide array of health risk behaviors. In one study (Faulkner & Cranston, 1998), high school students who reported exclusively same-sex contact were more likely to have seriously contemplated suicide within the previous year (10% versus 3%), attempted suicide within the previous year (i.e., 12% versus 2%), and made a suicide attempt requiring medical attention (8% versus 1%), relative to peers who endorsed exclusively heterosexual contact. Another recent study (Garofalo *et al.*, 1998) com-pared high school students self-identified as gay, lesbian, or bisexual with peers either self-identified as heterosexual or unsure. Garofalo and colleagues (1998) reported significantly elevated rates of suicide attempts in the previous year among GLB students, relative to non-GLB peers (35% versus 10%).

Remafedi and colleagues (1998) examined gender differences in the prevalence of suicidal behavior among homosexual/bisexual versus heterosexual high school students. Interestingly, GLB males and females had similarly high rates of reported suicidal behavior but only GLB males differed significantly from their heterosexual male counterparts (Remafedi *et al.*, 1998). In other words, there was no significant difference in the rates of suicidal ideation, attempts, or intent for the two female groups. In contrast, GLB males had significantly higher rates of suicide ideation (31% versus 20%), attempts (28% versus 4%), and intent (15% versus 4%) compared with heterosexual males (Remafedi *et al.*, 1998). Thus, there appears to be a significant interaction between gender and sexual orientation in regard to suicide risk.

Reasons for Suicidal Behavior among GLB Youth

Suicidal behavior is best understood within the context of understanding a number of important developmental and interpersonal challenges that GLB youth experience in contemporary society. Indeed, the process of exploring sexual orientation and "coming out" is a central developmental task for GLB youth that often creates unique internal and interpersonal stresses. "Coming out" for adolescents can be conceptualized along four dimensions: (1) recognizing oneself as gay, lesbian, or bisexual, (2) exploring sexual orientation through gathering information and contact with the GLB community, (3) disclosing one's sexual orientation to others, and (4) becoming comfortable with and accepting one's sexual orientation (Rotheram-Borus & Fernandez, 1995).

Unlike heterosexual peers, GLB adolescents experience thoughts, feelings, and attractions that run counter to the dominant cultural values, resulting in a sense of "otherness" and isolation, anxiety, and depression (D'Augelli, 1996). Particularly during the initial recognition of homoerotic feelings, GLB youth are unlikely to have access to GLB role models who could help guide them through their coming-out process (Rotheram-Borus & Fernandez, 1995). Unresolved conflict and lack of interpersonal support may precipitate shame, avoidance, and denial (Carrion & Lock, 1997). Further exploration of sexual orientation takes place through same-gender sexual activity, participation in GLB organizations, or gravitation to geographical areas identified as having large GLB populations (Rotheram-Borus & Fernandez, 1995).

Disclosure to heterosexual peers and family members is often delayed due to well-justified fears of disapproval, discrimination, and violence (Savin-Williams, 1994). According to a recent large-scale school-based study (Faulkner & Cranston, 1998), high school students with exclusively same-gender sexual experience reported significantly greater exposure to violence than peers with exclusively heterosexual experience. For example, students with same-gender experience reported significantly more frequent incidents of being threatened or injured with a weapon at school, having property stolen or deliberately damaged at school, and not wanting to go to school because of concerns about personal safety, relative to controls (Faulkner & Cranston, 1998). Other studies have found that 70 to 80% of GLB students report a history of verbal or physical abuse at school related to their sexual orientation (Pilkington & D'Augelli, 1995; Remafedi, 1987). Only a small number of GLB youth describe their family's response as supportive following the disclosure of their sexual orientation (D'Augelli, 1996). Indeed, approximately one-third of GLB youth report having been insulted by a family member, and 10% acknowledge having been physically assaulted by a family member due to their coming out (Pilkington & D'Augelli, 1995).

Given the aforementioned negative responses to disclosure, it is not surprising that GLB youth are at elevated risk for a variety of academic problems, runaway behavior, substance abuse, prostitution, and emotional disorders (Savin-Williams, 1994). Nearly 30% of homosexual or bisexual male adolescents in one study dropped out of high school, most often due to verbal and physical abuse from peers (Remafedi, 1987). Of the students who remained in school, the majority reported frequent truancy or deterioration in academic performance. GLB youth cite the following primary emotional concerns: stress related to sexual identity; disruption of peer and family relationships; isolation; distress caused by discrimination, harassment, or violence; anxiety related to sexual health; and AIDS (D'Augelli, 1996).

Several researchers have examined factors surrounding suicidal behavior among GLB adolescents. For example, suicide attempts are frequently linked with sexual milestones, such as recognition of homoerotic feelings or disclosure of sexual orientation to significant others (Remafedi et al., 1991; Savin-Williams, 1994). Suicidal behavior is often associated with family conflict (44%) or other interpersonal turmoil related to sexual orientation (33%) (Remafedi et al., 1991). Remafedi et al. (1998) summarized risk factors for attempted suicide in gay and bisexual males, including self-identification as gay at a younger age, substance use, female gender role, interpersonal conflict regarding sexual orientation, and nondisclosure of sexual orientation to others. These youth also experience unique psychosocial stressors, such as acts of victimization, which may precipitate suicidal behavior.

Comparisons between GLB suicide attempters and nonattempters reveal that attempters recognized and disclosed their sexual orientation at an earlier age, had more same-gender sexual partners, and were more involved in GLB social activities (Hershberger *et al.*, 1996, 1997). In addition, suicide attempters had lost more friends and experienced more victimization due to their sexual orientation relative to nonattempters (Hershberger *et al.*, 1996, 1997). Compared with gay and lesbian adolescents, youth who self-identified as bisexual were five times more likely to have a history of multiple suicide attempts (Hershberger *et al.*, 1997).

Clinical Implications

Findings from previous research involving suicidal behavior among GLB youth provide notable implications for assessment and treatment. GLB adolescent males are at elevated risk for suicidal behavior, particularly if they recognize their orientation early, experience violence, use substances to cope with problems related to sexual orientation, and are rejected by family members (Hammelman, 1993). Therefore, it is important that psychologists and other clinicians establish a constructive and trusting therapeutic relationship with the adolescent, facilitate discussion of feelings around significant stressors, empower the adolescent with appropriate role models and support systems, and work with schools and families to reduce violence and improve tolerance and support.

Sexual orientation is a commonly neglected area of inquiry by clinicians working with adolescents. The studies described here, however, underlie the importance of assessing sexual orientation as part of the management of adolescent suicide attempters. D'Augelli (1996) has outlined the key areas for suicide assessment of lesbian, gay, and bisexual youth. These include information about developmental milestones related to sexual orientation and gender identity. Sexual activity history including age of onset, age of partners, and coercive experiences help the clinician to understand the nature of these sexual experiences in relation to suicidality. It is also important to assess to whom the adolescent has disclosed his or her sexual orientation, both family and peers, including whether such disclosure has led to greater sexual isolation or victimization. Fears about disclosure should also be assessed, including fears of victimization based on sexual orientation. Finally, the adolescent's exposure to other lesbian, gay, and bisexual youth who have attempted suicide should be examined.

One recent study (Safren & Heimberg, 1999) highlighted the importance of appreciating the impact of psychosocial stressors on the development of depression, hopelessness, and suicidal behavior among GLB adolescents. Fifty-six GLB participants in after-school recreational programs for sexual minorities were compared with 48 heterosexual participants in after-school programs for job training and recreation. As expected based on previous research, GLB youth had significantly higher levels of depression, hopelessness, and suicidal behavior relative to heterosexual controls. However, after accounting for psychosocial variables (e.g., stressors or social supports), the significant group differences in depression, hopelessness, and current suicidality were no longer evident (Safren & Heimberg, 1999). Two major implications of these results are that (1) the elevated risk of emotional difficulties and suicidal behavior among GLB youth appears to be secondary to stressors within the context of contemporary society, and (2) emotional difficulties and elevated suicide risk among GLB youth may be reduced through appropriate psychosocial and therapeutic interventions.

HOMELESS, RUNAWAY, AND DELINQUENT YOUTH

Homeless, runaway, and delinquent youth report very high rates of attempted suicide. Reported rates vary somewhat, likely due to whether the youth are assessed at shelters, in the street, or in treatment programs. Approximately 30% of youth reported a history of attempted suicide in a study conducted at a homeless shelter in Missouri (Stiffman, 1989) compared to 37% in homeless shelters in New York City (Rotheram-Borus, 1993). When street youth are included in surveys, the rates of attempted suicide are usually higher—for example, 42% in Toronto (Smart & Walsh, 1993) and 40% in Los Angeles (Unger, Kipke, Simon, Montgomery, & Johnson, 1997). Among youth in treatment programs, the rates tend to be even higher. For example, Smart and Ogborne (1994) reported that 53% of homeless adolescents in a substance abuse program reported attempting suicide compared to 30% of housed youth in the same program.

Between 25% and 40% of attempters acknowledge having made their most recent attempt within the month prior to entering the shelter (Rotheram-Borus, 1993; Stiffman, 1989). In a study of 291 adolescents using runaway shelters in St. Louis, the majority of suicide attempters made their first attempt between the ages of 12 and 15 and reported more than one suicide attempt (Stiffman, 1989). The most common precipitants to the suicide attempts involved trouble at home or school, and approximately 90% of attempts were impulsive (i.e., planned either only one day prior to the attempt or on the same day as the attempt) (Stiffman, 1989). Nearly half of the attempters never received any professional help following their attempt. The runaway adolescents continued to exhibit high risk for suicide, as one in every three attempters considered a suicide plan within 1 week prior to participation in the research (Stiffman, 1989).

Another study involving 576 predominantly African-American and Hispanic runaway adolescents in the New York City area found similar statistics for suicide attempts (Rotheram-Borus, 1993). In addition, 54% percent of runaway adolescents reported current depressive symptoms, and 37% had significant conduct problems, including school dropout (44%), truancy (52%), school expulsion (22%), arrests (14%), destruction of property (10%), and gang membership (8%) (Rotheram-Borus, 1993). Thus, it is clear that runaway adolescents are at increased risk for depression, behavioral problems, and suicide.

Yoder (1999) examined psychosocial variables that distinguish suicide attempters, ideators, and nonsuicidal youth in a sample of 527 homeless and runaway adolescents in the Midwest. Relative to suicide ideators and nonsuicidal youth, adolescents with at least one prior suicide attempt were more likely to have experienced physical or sexual abuse by an adult caregiver or experienced sexual victimization on the streets, to have a family history of emotional difficulties, and to have a friend who attempted suicide (Yoder, 1999). The accumulation of these psychosocial risk factors, along with depression and low self-esteem, significantly increased the probability of adolescent suicidal behavior (Yoder, 1999). Runaways with a suicide attempt history were significantly more likely to be suicidal and depressed at the time of their interview (Rotheram-Borus, 1993).

Delinquent youth and those with significant behavioral difficulties and oppositional behavior have also been shown to be at high risk for suicidal behavior. In a report based on a psychological autopsy of adolescent suicides, Gould, Fisher, Parides, Flory, and Shaffer (1996) identified psychosocial factors that contributed to suicide risk beyond the presence of psychiatric illnesses (i.e., behavioral, substance, and mood disorders). Compared with community controls, adolescents who completed suicide were more likely to have had a recent disciplinary crisis (e.g., suspension from school or appearance in juvenile court) or failed a grade in school (Gould et al., 1996). Adolescents who were neither working nor in school were at a significantly elevated risk for suicide, even after taking into account those individuals living in residential facilities or psychiatric hospitals (Gould et al., 1996). Reckless and runaway behaviors were significant predictors of suicide risk for adolescent boys, even after controlling for the presence of psychiatric illnesses.

A psychological autopsy of 53 adolescent suicide completers in Finland (Marttunen, Aron, Henriksson, & Lonnqvist, 1994) examined additional family and peer stressors. No community control group was included in the study. Consistent with Shaffer et al. (1996), antisocial behavior was reported in nearly half of the 44 male adolescent suicide completers and one-third of the nine females. Recurrent problems with truancy, running away, and stealing; physical violence toward another person; and legal difficulties were found to be common among the suicide completers, with each antisocial behavior noted in 25 to 43% of the cases (Marttunen et al., 1994). Male suicide completers with a history of antisocial behavior were identified as having had more significant psychosocial stressors, relative to those without a history of antisocial behavior. For example, separation from parents for at least 1 year, parental divorce, parental alcohol abuse, and domestic violence were more common among males with antisocial behavior compared with males without antisocial behavior. All violent male suicide completers had been separated from their parents, and 88% had lost their father before age 12 (Marttunen et al., 1994). Furthermore, male suicide completers with antisocial behavior were less likely to attend school and were more likely to have had arguments with romantic partners relative to males without antisocial behavior. Although there was no significant difference in the prevalence of depressive disorders among males with antisocial behavior versus those without, male suicide completers with antisocial behavior were more likely to have a history of alcohol problems, previous suicide attempts, and frequent psychiatric contacts (Marttunen et al., 1994).

Clinical Implications

The high rate of attempted suicide among homeless, runaway, and delinquent youth underscores the importance of addressing suicidality and the overall mental health needs of this high-risk population. Because a history of suicide attempts puts these adolescents at risk for future suicide attempts, intervention with this group may be even more critical than the overall population of runaway and homeless adolescents. Given that a low percentage of delinquent and runaway adolescents at risk for suicide come to the immediate attention of mental health professionals, it especially is important that there be increased training for other responsible adults (e.g., staff working with adjudicated youths, runaway service intake workers) in regard to adolescent suicide risk. The impulsivity and recency of many suicide attempts among the delinquent and runaway population also underscores the necessity to develop screening measures and systematic triage programs in settings not often equipped with professionals with extensive mental health training.

In one recent study, Thompson and Eggert (1999) examined the validity of a self-report questionnaire, the Suicide Risk Screen (SRS), to identify suicidal adolescents among potential high school dropouts. The SRS items were embedded in a longer student questionnaire and were composed of three sets of empirically based risk factors, including suicidal behaviors, depression, and alcohol/drug involvement. Based on performance on the SRS, potential high school dropouts were categorized into varying levels of suicide-risk groups (Thompson & Eggert, 1999). The SRS categorization was strongly associated with other measures of suicide risk (e.g., a general suicide ideation measure, clinician ratings). Similarly, the SRS was highly correlated in expected directions with related risk factors (e.g., anger/aggression, anxiety, family distress) and protective factors (e.g., coping strategies, personal control, social supports) (Thompson & Eggert, 1999). As anticipated, the SRS evidenced high sensitivity but low specificity (as the ethical cost of a false negative is much greater than that of a false positive). The SRS or other validated suicide risk questionnaires may serve as useful adjuncts to clinical judgment for persons working with runaways and dropouts.

Findings from studies involving suicide risk among runaway adolescents highlight the need for more effective triage programs in shelters and outreach programs serving the homeless population. One such triage model (Rotheram-Borus & Bradley, 1991) was designed to provide thorough suicide risk assessment without requiring extensive mental health training. Upon admission to the runaway agency, youth participated in a two-stage interview screening procedure with paraprofessionals. First, a preliminary 10-minute interview assessed the presence or absence of eight factors associated with adolescent suicide risk (e.g., past suicidal behavior, depression, behavioral problems, alcohol/drug abuse). Contingent upon information from the first interview, youth considered to be at more imminent risk for suicide (e.g., five or more risk factors, a suicide attempt within the past month, current suicidal ideation) participated in a second interview (Rotheram-Borus & Bradley, 1991). Staff training through vignettes and videotaped sessions, detailed written agency suicide protocols, and strong collaboration between the runaway agency and nearby mental health centers were found to be effective components of the triage program. Over a 2-year period, the number of suicide attempts decreased in the runaway centers, and there was a high agreement between paraprofessionals' and psychiatrists' evaluations of adolescent suicide risk (Rotheram-Borus & Bradley, 1991).

INCARCERATED ADOLESCENTS

Current research generally reveals incarcerated adolescents to be at high risk for engaging in suicidal behavior. In a study conducted by Morris, Harrison, Knox, Tromanhauser, Marquis, & Watts (1995), 1801 incarcerated adolescents across 39 facilities in the United States were administered a modified version of the Centers for Disease Control Youth Risk Behavior Surveillance System (YRBS). As part of this survey, adolescents were asked to indicate the frequency with which they engaged in suicidal behavior within the past year. Approximately 22% of incarcerated adolescents reported that they seriously considered suicide, 20% made a suicide plan, 16% made at least one attempt, and 8% were injured due to a suicide attempt. Compared to data reported in 1991 from high school students who completed the YRBS, rates of suicidal ideation and planning were comparable across populations. However, rates of suicide attempts (15.5% versus 7%) and injury resulting from attempts (8.2% versus 2%) were found to be higher in the incarcerated population. Further, when these rates were examined as a function of gender and race, pronounced differences emerged. Specifically, 35% of incarcerated females reported making a suicide attempt within the past year in comparison to only 11% of high school females. Of those adolescents who made an attempt, 20% of incarcerated females sustained injury, whereas injury only occurred in 2% of high school females. For males, those incarcerated reported twice as many suicide attempts and resulting injuries than high school males. Racial differences also emerged between populations. Caucasian youths reported the highest suicide rates followed by Native

American Indian/Alaskan Native youth and "other" in the incarcerated population, whereas Hispanic followed by Caucasian and African-American youth reported the highest suicide rates in the high school population.

A number of smaller and more recent community studies have also been conducted to examine the prevalence of suicidality within incarcerated populations. Reported rates of current suicidal ideation in incarcerated adolescents range from 14.2% (Rohde, Seeley, & Mace, 1997) to 51% (Esposito & Clum, 1999), with lifetime rates of suicidal ideation reported to be as high as 72% (Uchida, 1995). Lifetime history of reported suicide attempts range from 19.4% (Rohde, Seeley, & Mace, 1997) to 61% (Alessi, McManus, Brickman, & Grapentine, 1984) in incarcerated adolescent populations. Demographically, most studies reflect a higher prevalence of suicide attempts and suicidal ideation in incarcerated adolescents who are female (Morris *et al.*, 1995), Caucasian (Kempton & Forehand, 1992; Morris *et al.*, 1995) or Native American (Morris *et al.*, 1995), and younger in age (Rohde *et al.*, 1997b).

Rohde, Seeley, and Mace (1997) examined suicidal behavior among 555 adolescents (457 male, 97 female) placed in juvenile detention centers while awaiting trial or treatment placement. Over one-third of these adolescents reported having thought about committing suicide over their lifetime, and approximately 14% expressed suicidal ideation within 1 week of participation in the study (Rohde, Seeley, & Mace, 1997). Furthermore, nearly one-fifth of the adolescents reported a history of at least one suicide attempt.

Notable gender differences emerged in Rohde, Seeley, and Mace's (1997) study involving suicidal behavior among adolescents in juvenile detention centers. First of all, the lifetime prevalence of suicidal behavior was higher for females than males. Approximately 50% of females reported a lifetime history of suicidal ideation, and 40% stated that they had made a past suicide attempt (Rohde, Seeley, & Mace, 1997). However, among adolescents with a past suicide attempt, males were more likely than females to report chronic and current suicidal ideation (Rohde, Seeley, & Mace, 1997). In addition, the correlates of suicidal behavior differed on the basis of gender. For example, suicidal behavior in males was associated with depression and diminished interpersonal ties, whereas suicidal behavior in females was related to impulsivity and affective instability (Rohde, Seeley, & Mace, 1997).

Within incarcerated adolescent populations, correlates of suicide attempts most often examined are psychopathology, substance use, family factors, and various psychosocial deficits/stressors. Current (Harris & Lennings, 1993; Rohde, Mace, & Seeley, 1997; Rohde, Seeley, & Mace, 1997) and lifetime suicidal ideation (Rohde, Mace, & Seeley, 1997) have been found to be significantly associated with a history of suicide attempts. In a study conducted by Rohde, Mace, and Seeley (1997), a current diagnosis of dysthymia, as well as lifetime diagnoses of major depressive disorder, dysthymia, and anxiety disorders were also linked with a history of suicide attempts. Rates of suicide attempts were approximately twice as high for adolescents with these internalizing disorders. Further, gender was found to moderate the association between suicide attempts and disruptive behavior disorders. Suicide attempts were associated with the absence of oppositional defiant and conduct disorder in females and the presence of these disorders in males. Interestingly, substance use disorders were not associated with a history of suicidal behavior in their study. However, psychotic features/disorders resulting from substance use, such as hallucinations induced by methamphetamine and methamphetamine-induced residual and late onset psychotic disorder, have been linked to suicide attempts in incarcerated adolescents (Uchida, 1995).

Other researchers have focused investigations on symptoms of psychopathology associated with a history of suicidality as opposed to psychiatric diagnoses. A number of studies have shown high scores on measures of depressive symptoms (Cole, 1989; Harris & Lennings, 1993; Rohde, Mace, & Seeley, 1997; Rhode, Seeley, & Mace, 1997) and borderline symptoms (Rohde, Mace, & Seeley, 1997; Rhode, Seeley, & Mace, 1997) to be linked to a history of suicide attempts in incarcerated adolescents. The number of conduct symptoms reported by incarcerated adolescents has not been shown to predict a history of suicide attempts (Kempton & Forehand, 1992).

Mixed results have been reported in studies examining the association between substance use and suicidality in incarcerated adolescents. Some researchers have found a high frequency of hallucinogen, sedatives/hypnotic, narcotic, stimulant, inhalant, and alcohol use in the month prior to incarceration to be associated with a history of suicide attempts (Putnins, 1995). Similarly, illicit drug use, injected drug use (Morris *et al.*, 1995), and general substance use (Rohde, Seeley, & Mace, 1997) have been linked to a history of suicide attempts. In contrast, a few studies have failed to find a relationship between substance use and a history of suicide attempts (Harris & Lennings, 1993; Kempton & Forehand, 1992). Specifically, cannabis use has not been linked to a history of suicide attempts in incarcerated adolescent populations (Putnins, 1995; Rohde, Mace, & Seeley, 1997).

Studies examining family factors associated with suicidality have revealed poor parental supervision, no biological parent in the home (Rohde, Seeley, and Mace, 1997), a paternal affectionless control bonding style (high overprotective behavior paired with low care by parent) (McGarvey, Kryzhanovskaya, Koopman, Waite, & Canterbury, 1999), and a history of parental alcohol problems (Uchida, 1995) to be correlated with a history of suicide attempts in incarcerated adolescent populations. Interestingly, family disharmony has not been linked to suicide attempts in this population (Harris & Lennings, 1993).

Other correlates of suicide attempts in incarcerated adolescents include anger, impulsivity, suicide by a friend, major life events, loneliness, poor coping skills (Rohde, Seeley, & Mace, 1997), low survival and coping beliefs (Cole, 1989), low social desirability (Cole, 1989; Rhode, Seeley, & Mace, 1997), gang membership, a history of sexually transmitted diseases (Morris *et al.*, 1995), and a history of childhood abuse (Morris *et al.*, 1995; Uchida, 1995). Results of studies examining the link between hopelessness and suicide attempts are mixed (Cole, 1989; Kempton & Forehand, 1992).

In addition to studies conducted with general incarcerated adolescent populations, a few investigations have examined factors linked to suicidality in subgroups of this population. One study was conducted to examine correlates of suicidal ideation in a sample of juvenile offenders prior to sentencing. Battle, Battle, and Tolley (1993) examined data collected from 263 juvenile offenders (227 males and 34 females, ages 11 to 18) referred for a psychological evaluation at juvenile court to determine whether they were psychologically and intellectually competent to be sentenced at a correctional institution or whether they must be tried as adults. Approximately 26% ($n = 68$) of these adolescents expressed a wish to be dead and 12% ($n = 31$) wished to kill themselves. Adolescents who were physically abused by someone in their home or who abused alcohol were three times more likely to verbalize a wish for their own death. Adolescents who used marijuana or experienced an increase in unhappiness in the previous year were about twice as likely to express a wish for their own death. Alternatively, adolescents who listed their mothers as a helper during times of crisis were about two times less likely to experience a wish to be dead. When examining risk factors for the wish to kill oneself, adolescents who reported a history of sexual abuse by an adult were about nine times more likely to express this wish than those without such a history, those who abused alcohol were seven times more likely, those who abused cocaine were five times more likely, and those reporting a great level of unhappiness were twice as likely to report a wish to kill oneself. Alternatively, those who listed their mother or grandmother as one of the three most important persons or listed their mother as a helper in times of crisis were four times less likely to experience a wish to kill oneself.

Alessi and colleagues (1984) examined the relationship between psychiatric disorders and suicidality in 71 (40 males, 31 females) serious juvenile offenders incarcerated in a detention facility (ages 14 through 18). Offenders were chosen for this study if they met two or more of the following criteria: adjudication for violent felonies, adjudication for multiple (three or more) nonviolent felonies, multiple placements in the training school system, or assaultive in-program behavior. Sixty-eight percent ($n = 52$) of the sample demonstrated a suicidal tendency and 61% ($n = 41$) made a suicide attempt within the previous year. Adolescents were divided into four diagnostic groupings: thought disorders (including schizophrenia and schizoptypal and paranoid personality disorders), major affective disorders, borderline personality disorders, and other psychiatric disorders. Adolescents with major affective disorder or borderline personality disorder had a significantly higher suicidal tendency and made more suicide attempts than those within the other two diagnostic groupings combined (thought disorders or others). Further, the seriousness and medical lethality of attempts in those diagnosed with either of these two disorders was also greater.

Biggam and Power (1999) conducted a study to examine differences in psychological distress between suicidal, bullied, and protected prisoners. Twenty-five inmates placed under suicidal supervision after exhibiting parasuicidal behavior in main circulation, 25 inmates placed on protection due to the nature of their crime or because they had been victimized while in main circulation, 25 victims of bullying who were still in main prison circulation, and 25 comparison inmates in routine circulation and regarded as reasonably well adjusted to prison life (ages 16 to 21) were included in the study. All inmates were males and each completed measures of anxiety, depression, mood state, hopelessness, and problem solving. Results revealed the suicidal group to have significantly higher depression scores than all three comparison groups, as well as higher anxiety, depression, and problem-solving deficits than control group. A comparison of mood states revealed suicidal inmates to have higher scores in tension-anxiety and depression-dejection mood states than inmates in the protected and control groups. Further, suicidal inmates also demonstrated higher scores in anger-hostility, fatigue, and confusion-bewilderment, and lower scores in vigor mood states than the control group.

Evans, Albers, Macari, and Mason (1996) examined differences in suicidality and abuse histories among gang and nongang involved incarcerated youth. In total, 395 adolescents (334 males and 61 females, ages 12 to 18) completed self-report measures assessing presence of suicidal ideation within the previous month, suicide attempts within the previous year, and lifetime prevalence of sexual and physical abuse. Approximately 58% ($n = 194$) of males and 45% ($n = 29$) of females reported gang involvement. Thirty percent ($n = 113$) of adolescents indicated suicidal ideation (28.9% of males and 35.5% of females) within the previous month and 24% ($n = 97$) of the sample indicated one or more suicide attempts within the previous year (22.5% of males and 35.5% of females). Approximately 51% ($n = 202$) of adolescents indicated a history of physical abuse (46.8% of males and 75.4% of females), and 19.2% ($n = 76$) reported a history of sexual abuse (9.9% of males and 71.7% of females). Correlations computed between suicidal ideation and attempts for the whole sample were all moderately significant ($r = .45$ to .59). Analyses conducted to examine differences between gang and nongang members in suicidality revealed nongang members to report significantly more suicidal ideation but not suicide attempts than gang-involved adolescents. However, when analyses were conducted by gender, results revealed male nongang members to report significantly higher levels of suicidal ideation and suicide attempts than gang members but there were no differences found in suicidality across gang involvement in females. When levels of suicidal ideation and attempts were compared across gender, no significant differences were noted in reported levels of suicidal ideation; however, females did report significantly more suicide attempts than males. The same relationship was found to be true among gang members, with female gang members reporting significantly more suicide attempts but not suicidal ideation than male gang members. However, no differences in suicidality were found across male and female nongang members. Finally, analyses examining the impact of abuse and gang membership on suicidality revealed gang members with a history of sexual abuse to have significantly higher levels of suicidal ideation and attempts, but differences were not found in those reporting physical abuse. When the same analyses were conducted separately by gender, the only significant difference that emerged was that females who reported a history of sexual abuse were more likely to have attempted suicide.

Clinical Implications

The literature suggests that incarcerated adolescent populations are at higher risk for suicidal behavior than general high school populations. Correlates of suicidal behavior in incarcerated adolescents include histories of depression, anxiety, disruptive behavior, substance use, and borderline features. In addition, incarcerated adolescents with histories of suicide attempts tend to have unfavorable family environments, numerous psychosocial deficits, and significant life stressors. Interestingly, these correlates are similar to those found in studies examining suicidality in nonincarcerated populations (Beautrais, Joyce, & Mulder, 1996; Fergusson & Lynskey, 1995; Lewinsohn, Rohde, & Seeley, 1994; Summerville, Kaslow, Abbate, & Cronan, 1994). Although the risk factors for suicidality may be similar across both incarcerated and nonincarcerated populations, those in custody may experience these factors with greater frequency or severity, thus leading to greater suicide risk. Alternatively, there may be correlates specific to incarcerated populations not yet examined that increase suicide risk relative to nonincarcerated populations.

Previous research reflects the strong need for the development of suicide prevention and support services for incarcerated adolescents that would likely entail a comprehensive psychiatric and psychological assessment of all incarcerated adolescents upon intake into the detention facility followed by appropriate medication management and psychotherapy. Treatment of psychiatric disorders in this population is imperative if future suicide attempts are to be prevented. Further, given the high levels of sexual abuse experienced by this population and its relationship to suicidal behavior (especially in females), therapy and support services should be provided to address issues related to abuse. Incarcerated adolescents also might benefit from group therapy designed to teach problem solving, anger management, and adaptive coping skills to help remediate psychosocial deficits and improve decision-making skills when faced with life stressors. With such services in place, the juvenile justice system may decrease suicide risk in incarcerated adolescent populations.

ADOLESCENTS EXPOSED TO SUICIDAL BEHAVIOR

Another high-risk group for suicidal behavior is adolescents exposed to peer or family suicidal behavior. The majority of relevant research to date can be divided into two categories: (1) anecdotal reports of clusters of suicidal behavior following exposure in neighborhoods, schools, or psychiatric facilities, and (2) cross-sectional and longitudinal studies of the psychiatric sequelae of exposure to peer or family suicidal behavior.

Time-space clustering analysis indicates that suicide outbreaks occur primarily among adolescents and young adults, as opposed to other age groups (Gould, Wallenstein, Kleinman, O'Carroll, & Mercy, 1990). Several highly publicized suicide clusters have raised concerns about the role of imitation in elevating risk for adolescent suicidal behavior. For example, one anecdotal report (Davies & Wilkes, 1993) reviewed the social context surrounding five adolescent suicides by hanging that occurred over a 7-month period in a small city in rural Canada. The interpersonal relationships between the suicide completers ranged from being very close to remote. Four of the five adolescents were male and had a significant history of substance abuse, and all adolescents had a history of academic, behavioral, social, and family problems (Davies & Wilkes, 1993).

Another anecdotal report (Brent, Kerr, Goldstein, Bozigar, Wartella, & Allan, 1989) described an outbreak of suicidal behavior in a high school of 1496 students in an urban, working-class neighborhood. Six weeks prior to the outbreak in school, a 21-year-old male ex-student committed suicide via gunshot wound. The high school suicide outbreak began when two students made suicide attempts, one made a suicidal gesture, and two students committed suicide (one by firearms, the other by hanging) within a 7-day period. Within 18 days of the first suicidal behavior in the high school, seven students attempted suicide and 23 evidenced serious suicidal ideation (Brent, Kerr, *et al.*, 1989). The majority of students involved in the suicide cluster were friends or acquaintances of the 21-year-old suicide completer and had at least one psychiatric disorder that preceded the suicidal crisis. Students with a current major depressive disorder and those with a history of depression or suicidal behavior were the most likely to become suicidal during the outbreak (Brent, Kerr, *et al.*, 1989).

Suicidal contagion also has been reported in adolescent inpatient psychiatric facilities (Taiminen, Kallio-Soukainen, Nokso-Koivisto, Kaljonen, & Helenius, 1998). Taiminen and colleagues (1998) reported 64 acts of deliberate self-harm behavior on an inpatient facility in Finland over the course of a 12-month period, the majority of which appeared to have been influenced by contagion. All of the adolescents were females, mostly with a diagnosis of depression and borderline personality disorder. Suicidal imitation was more likely when the adolescents believed that the behavior would strengthen group cohesion and when the hospital unit was overcrowded (Taiminen et al., 1998).

Another line of research involves cross-sectional and longitudinal studies of adolescents who have been exposed to peer or family suicidal behavior. In a series of papers, Brent and his colleagues examined the psychiatric sequelae of exposure to suicide among friends and acquaintances of adolescent suicide victims. For example, one study (Brent et al., 1992) assessed the presence of psychiatric disorders and suicidal behavior among 58 friends and acquaintances of adolescent suicide victims as compared to 58 demographically matched unexposed controls. At the 6-month follow-up, adolescents exposed to suicide had higher rates of new onset major depressive disorder relative to controls but there was no difference in suicidal behavior between groups (Brent et al., 1992).

Subsequent research with larger samples has found no significant differences in the rates of suicide attempts between adolescents exposed to adolescent suicide and unexposed controls upon 3-month (Brent et al., 1993b), 6-month (Brent, Perper, Moritz, Liotus, Schweers, & Canobbio, 1994), and 3-year (Brent, Moritz, Bridge, Perper, & Canobbio, 1996b) follow-up. Suicidal ideation was more common among the exposed group but was nearly entirely explained by an increase of depression (Brent et al., 1993b). Furthermore, significant depressive and post-traumatic stress symptoms were evident up to three years after exposure to suicide (Brent et al., 1996b). Researchers hypothesized that adolescents within the social network of suicide completers may be inhibited from acting on suicidal ideation due to their firsthand knowledge about the consequences of suicide on significant others (Brent et al., 1993b; 1996b).

However, it is important to note that evidence from a recent study (Ho, Leung, Hung, Lee, & Tang, 2000) is not consistent with the findings of Brent and colleagues. Ho et al. (2000) found that peers of suicide completers demonstrated an elevated risk of suicidal ideation, plans, and acts relative to controls. In addition, the presence of psychiatric disorders did not entirely explain the increased risk of suicidal behaviors (Ho et al., 2000). Thus, further research is needed to reconcile findings regarding suicide risk among peers of suicide completers.

Relative to research on the peers of adolescents who completed suicide, there has been much less emphasis on the mental health and suicide risk among peers of suicide attempters. Only two known studies (i.e., Hazell & Lewin, 1993; Ho et al., 2000) had suicide risk among peers of suicide attempters as a central focus of investigation. Nevertheless, there is preliminary evidence that the peers of suicide attempters have elevated risk of psychopathology and suicidal behavior, even relative to the peers of suicide completers. Compared to nonexposed controls, peers of suicide attempters have been shown to have significantly higher rates of suicidal ideation (40% versus 14%) and suicide attempts (21% versus 5%; Ho *et al.*, 2000). Furthermore, peers of suicide attempters appear to be more deviant than peers of suicide completers, even prior to their exposure to the suicidal behavior (Hazell & Lewin, 1993).

Recent studies have examined the emotional functioning and suicide risk among adolescents who have experienced the suicidal death of a parent or sibling. Relative to unexposed controls, siblings of suicide completers demonstrate higher levels of depressive symptoms (including suicidal ideation) 6 months after the incident (Brent *et al.*, 1993c), but there are no significant differences between groups at 3-year follow-up (Brent *et al.*, 1996b). Another longitudinal study compared psychological functioning of youth who experienced the death of a parent due to suicide versus other causes (except homicide) up to 2 years after the loss (Cerel, Fristad, Weller, & Weller, 1999). Cerel and colleagues (1999) found no significant differences in depression or suicidal behavior among the two groups but the suicide-bereaved youth showed more global symptoms of psychopathology and behavioral dysregulation relative to controls.

In contrast, psychological autopsy studies of adolescent suicide completers (e.g., Brent, Bridge, Johnson, & Connolly, 1996; Gould *et al.*, 1996) and research involving individuals who have attempted suicide (e.g., Sorenson & Rutter, 1991) have found strong evidence for elevated suicide risk within families. Indeed, in one community study, a maternal history of suicide attempts raised the probability of suicide attempts by nearly a factor of seven (Sorenson & Rutter, 1991). Furthermore, the risk of suicide attempts in first- and second-degree relatives of adolescent suicide completers does not appear to be explained by the presence of psychiatric disorders within the family (Brent, Bridge, *et al.*, 1996).

Clinical Implications

Research on adolescents exposed to peer suicidal behavior provides several noteworthy implications for assessment and treatment. First, although anecdotal reports indicate that suicide imitation can occur (e.g., Brent *et al.*, 1989), the results of cross-sectional and longitudinal studies suggest that imitative suicide attempts occur infrequently among close friends and acquaintances of suicide completers. Nevertheless, adolescents exposed to suicidal behavior appear to be at increased risk for depression and other forms of psychopathology for extended periods of time. Many adolescents experience prolonged depression that is mislabeled as normal bereavement (Brent et al., 1992). In addition, preliminary evidence that the peers of suicide attempters may have elevated rates of psychopathology (even relative to the peers of suicide completers) supports the need for improving services for this subpopulation (Ho et al., 2000).

The majority of postvention techniques after adolescent suicide (e.g., Hazell, 1991) are brief, intensive efforts designed to prevent imitative suicidal behavior but do not address the adolescents' long-term needs for treatment of debilitating depression, anxiety, and conduct disturbance that may put them at risk for suicidal ideation or behavior in the long run (Brent et al., 1993c). Thus, it is important for clinicians involved in brief, postvention interventions to identify those adolescents who might benefit from longer-term psychotherapy and take steps to ensure that this high-risk subgroup receives adequate follow-up treatment.

MULTIPLE SUICIDE ATTEMPTERS

There is a small but significant group of adolescents who attempt suicide on multiple occasions. Prior attempts have been reported in approximately 20 to 30% of suicide attempters seen in a general hospital following a suicide attempt (Hawton & Fagg, 1992). Similarly, repeat attempts in the months following a suicide attempt have been reported as high as 2% at 1 month and 9% at 3 months following discharge from a general hospital and 23% at 1 month and 14% at 3 months after discharge from a psychiatric hospital (Spirito et al., 1992).

In one study (Gispert, Davis, Marsh, & Wheeler, 1987), multiple attempters at the index attempt had poorer school performance, more serious suicide intent, more anger and dysphoria, and a greater number of lifetime stressful events than first-time attempters. More recently, Hawton, Kingsbury, Steinhardt, James, and Fagg (1999) examined a population of suicide attempters seen in a general hospital. First-time attempters were compared to attempters who reported a prior attempt or who made a repeat attempt within the year following the index attempt. The multiple attempters had higher scores on measures of depression, hopelessness, trait anger, and lower scores on self-esteem and problem solving than first-time attempters. However, after controlling for depression, these differences were no longer found. The authors also assessed for the presence of major depressive disorder and found multiple attempters to have higher rates of this diagnosis than first-time attempters. It is important to note that these results do not necessarily indicate that depression is the sole contributing variable to repeated self-harm but rather that the study's relatively small sample size may have limited its ability to detect differences between groups.

Goldston and colleagues (1996), as well as Larsson and Ivarsson (1998), report similar findings to Hawton *et al.* (1999). Depressed mood differentiated repeat attempters from first-time attempters in both studies. Rates of major depression were higher in individuals who had reattempted suicide on one or multiple occasions compared to the first-time attempters (Goldston *et al.*, 1996). However, there was no difference in depressed mood among first-time attempters compared with patients with no history of attempts. This finding did not seem to be related to the age or gender of participants, method of assessment, or absolute level of depressed mood. Thus, multiple suicide attempts may be related to severe depression, whereas a single suicide attempt may be related to other mood states, as well as cognitive and behavioral factors. Finally, Lewinsohn, Rohde, and Seeley (1996) identified 73 adolescents among a community sample who had made one suicide attempt and 48 with two or more attempts. Multiple attempters were perceived as less interpersonally attached, had more functional impairment due to medical illness, and reported more hypomanic type behavior and more fluctuations in mood than first-time attempters.

Stein, Apter, Ratzoni, Har-Even, and Avidan (1998) compared psychiatrically hospitalized adolescents who were either first-time suicide attempters, multiple suicide attempters, or nonsuicidal to community controls. Both suicidal groups had higher levels of negative emotions than both nonsuicidal and community controls. Multiple attempters had higher levels of anxiety and depression than first-time attempters with a trend toward higher levels of aggression. Vajda and Steinbeck (2000) examined factors related to repeat suicide attempts in adolescents seen in an emergency department following a suicide attempt. At 1-year follow-up, alcohol and drug abuse, nonaffective psychotic disorders, and chronic medical conditions predicted repeat suicide. There was a trend for a history of sexual abuse to also be related to a repeat attempt.

Clinical Implications

Joiner, Rudd, Rouleau, and Wagner (2000) found in a sample of suicidal psychiatric inpatients that multiple suicide attempters experienced more intense but not longer suicidal crises than first-time attempters. Joiner and colleagues (2000) suggested that a previous suicide attempt affects the nature and intensity of suicidal experiences, which requires that clinicians pay attention to attempt status in managing suicide attempters. Multiple attempters appear to be a high-risk group experiencing more chronic life stressors and more severe psychological symptomatology (Larsson & Ivarsson, 1998). Rudd, Joiner, and Rajab (1996) found in a sample of young adults that repeat suicide attempters had a distinct pattern of symptoms compared to first-time attempters. Rudd *et al.* (1996) have suggested that, for multiple attempters, the subsequent attempts are more easily triggered by a range of interpersonal and external events. Depression appears to be particularly problematic among repeat attempters. Thus, it is particularly important to thoroughly assess depression in this group of attempters and to make sure that an adequate treatment plan, both pharmacologic and psychologic, is in place for the majority of repeat attempters.

ADOLESCENTS WITH SELF-MUTILATIVE BEHAVIOR

A subgroup of adolescent suicide attempters also reports engaging in self-injurious or self-mutilative behaviors (SMB). Methods of SMB are consistently of low lethality, with physical damage ranging from superficial to moderate. Skin cutting has been found to be the most common form of SMB followed by skin burning and self-hitting (Favazza & Conterio, 1989). Unlike suicide attempts, SMB is typically a highly repetitive act. In a review of case reports, Pattisan and Kahan (1983) found that 63% of subjects had multiple episodes of self-harm, ranging from 2 to more than 100 episodes, with an average of 21 per patient.

Depressed mood and heightened anxiety have been described as a precursor to self-harm among adult and adolescent mutilators (Rosenthal, Rinzler, Walsh, & Klausner, 1972; Ross & McKay, 1979; Winchel & Stanley, 1991). Relief and escape from emotional upset are commonly provided as reasons for self-harm, thereby strengthening and increasing the likelihood of future SMB. Increased incidence of substance abuse is also noted among adolescent self-mutilators, possibly related to a generally impulsive pattern of responding, consistent with the typically impulsive SMB actions (Walsh & Rosen, 1988).

Zlotnick, Donaldson, Spirito, and Pearlstein (1997) compared psychiatrically hospitalized adolescent suicide ideators and suicide attempters on

SMB. Suicide attempters reported a greater number of different types of SMB in the prior year than ideators. Walsh and Rosen (1988) found that a history of sexual and physical abuse, family alcohol abuse, and family violence during childhood were associated with the presence of SMB in adolescence. Guertin, Lloyd, Spirito, Donaldson, and Boergers (in press) compared 100 adolescent suicide attempters seen in a general hospital following a suicide attempt who reported SMB to those attempters without a history of SMB. The prevalence rate of SMB reported in this sample of suicide attempters (55%) was greater than that found in the general adolescent population (1.2%; Suyemoto, 1998) yet less than has been reported in a sample of inpatient adolescents suicide ideators (80%) and inpatient adolescent suicide attempters (87%; Zlotnick *et al.*, 1997). Carving on the skin and picking at a wound were the most commonly reported SMB, occurring in about one-third of the sample. The SMB group was significantly more likely to be diagnosed with oppositional defiant disorder, major depression, and dysthymia and had higher scores on measures of hopelessness, loneliness, anger, risk taking, reckless behavior, and alcohol use than the non-SMB group. Loneliness increased the odds of SMB about five-fold. In order to engage in the SMB, individuals typically isolate themselves from others. It may be that by the time an individual who self-mutilates proceeds to a suicide attempt, the feelings of loneliness have escalated due to the SMB and as a result are significantly greater than the feelings of loneliness commonly associated with suicide attempters without a history of SMB. These findings suggest that adolescents with SMB who attempt suicide are associated with a greater range of cognitive-affective and behavioral symptomatology than adolescents who attempt suicide but do not have a history of SMB.

Clinical Implications

Given the high base rate of SMB in adolescent suicide attempters (Guertin *et al.*, in press), adolescent suicide attempters should be routinely screened for SMB. Clinicians should directly treat the underlying disorder associated with suicidality and SMB (e.g., major depression) and assess its effect on SMB. Alternatively, one might address these symptoms (i.e., suicidal behavior and SMB directly). Dialectical behavior therapy (DBT; Linehan, 1993), which views acts of self-mutilation as maladaptive attempts at problem solving, has been found to be effective in reducing SMB in adult samples. The goals of DBT treatment include interpersonal effectiveness, emotional regulation, improved coping with negative affect, and increased problem-solving abilities. Clinicians might consider DBT with adolescent suicide attempters who self-mutilate, or at least incorporate some of the skills-training components of DBT into their treatment approaches. Recent efforts at adapting DBT for adolescents have been reported and appear promising (Miller, Rathus, Linehan, & Leigh, 1997).

The Functional Assessment of Self-Mutilation (FASM) is a self-report measure of self-mutilative behavior (Lloyd, Kelley, and Hope, 1997) that clinicians may find useful. Patients are asked to respond to whether they had purposefully engaged in the SMB behaviors in the past year, such as cutting or carving on the skin, burning the skin (i.e., with a cigarette, match, or other hot object), biting oneself (e.g., mouth or lip), and picking at areas of the body to the point of drawing blood. A principal components analysis of these self-mutilative behaviors yielded two factors labeled "major" and "minor" self-mutilation (Lloyd *et al.*, 1997). Items included in the major self-mutilation factor were cutting/carving, burning, tattooing, scraping the skin to draw blood, and erasing the skin to draw blood. The minor SMB behaviors included hitting oneself, pulling out one's hair, picking at a wound, inserting objects under the skin or nails, biting oneself, and picking areas of the body to the point of drawing blood.

CONCLUSION

Certain high-risk adolescents, such as those from the groups described in this chapter, warrant particular attention from clinicians due to increased risk of suicidal behavior. Clinicians working with adolescent suicide attempters therefore should be sure to inquire whether the adolescent falls into one of these groups. The risk for continued suicidal behavior may be elevated, and monitoring of suicidality is particularly important among these adolescents.

REFERENCES

Alessi, N. E., McManus, M., Brickman, A., & Grapentine, L. (1984). Suicidal behavior among serious juvenile offenders. *American Journal of Psychiatry*, *141*, 286–287.

Bagley, C., & Tremblay, P. (2000). Elevated rates of suicidal behavior in gay, lesbian, and bisexual youth. *Crisis*, *21*, 111–117.

Battle, A. O., Battle, M. V., & Tolley, E. A. (1993). Potential for suicide and aggresion in delinquents at juvenile court in southern city. *Suicide and Life Threatening Behavior, 23,* 230–244.

Beautrais, A. L., Joyce, P. R., & Mulder, R. T. (1996). Risk factors for serious suicide attempts among youths aged 13 through 24 years. *Journal of the American Academy of Child and Adolescent Psychiatry, 35,* 1174–1182.

Biggam, F. H., & Power, K. G. (1999). A comparison of the problem-solving abilities and psychological distress of suicidal, bullied, and protected prisoners. *Criminal Justice and Behavior, 26,* 196–216.

Brent, D. A., Bridge, J., Johnson, B. A., & Connolly, J. (1996). Suicidal behavior runs in families: A controlled family study of adolescent suicide victims. *Archives of General Psychiatry, 53,* 1145–1152.

Brent, D. A., Kerr, M. M., Goldstein, C., Bozigar, J., Wartella, M., & Allan, M. J. (1989). An outbreak of suicide and suicidal behavior in a high school. *Journal of the American Academy of Child and Adolescent Psychiatry, 28,* 918–924.

Brent, D. A., Mortiz, G., Bridge, J., Perper, J., & Canobbio, R. (1996a). The impact of adolescent suicide on siblings and parents: A longitudinal follow-up. *Suicide and Life-Threatening Behavior, 26,* 253–259.

Brent, D. A., Moritz, G., Bridge, J., Perper, J., & Canobbio, R. (1996b). Long-term impact of exposure to suicide: A three-year controlled follow-up. *Journal of the American Academy of Child and Adolescent Psychiatry, 35,* 646–653.

Brent, D. A., Perper, J. A., Moritz, G., Allman, C., Friend, A., Schweers, J., Roth, C., Balach, L., & Harrington, K. (1992). Psychiatric effects of exposure to suicide among the friends and acquaintances of adolescent suicide victims. *Journal of the American Academy of Child and Adolescent Psychiatry, 31,* 629–640.

Brent, D. A., Perper, J. A., Moritz, G., Allman, C., Liotus, L., Schweers, J., Roth, C., Balach, L., & Canobbio, R. (1993a). Bereavement or depression? The impact of the loss of a friend to suicide. *Journal of the American Academy of Child and Adolescent Psychiatry, 32,* 1189–1197.

Brent, D. A., Perper, J. A., Moritz, G., Allman, C., Schweers, J., Roth, C., Balach, L., Canobbio, R., & Liotus, L. (1993b). Psychiatric sequelae to the loss of an adolescent peer to suicide. *Journal of the American Academy of Child and Adolescent Psychiatry, 32,* 509–517.

Brent, D. A., Perper, J. A., Moritz, G., Liotus, L., Schweers, J., & Canobbio, R. (1994). Major depression or uncomplicated bereavement? A follow-up of youth exposed to suicide. *Journal of the American Academy of Child and Adolescent Psychiatry, 33,* 231–239.

Brent, D. A., Perper, J. A., Moritz, G., Liotus, L., Schweers, J., Roth, C., Balach, L., & Allman, C. (1993c). Psychiatric impact of the loss of an adolescent sibling to suicide. *Journal of Affective Disorders, 28,* 249–256.

Carrion, V., & Lock, J. (1997). The coming out process: Developmental stages for sexual minority youth. *Clinical Child Psychology and Psychiatry, 2,* 369–377.

Cerel, J., Fristad, M. A., Weller, E. B., & Weller, R. A. (1999). Suicide-bereaved children and adolescents: A controlled longitudinal examination. *Journal of the American Academy of Child and Adolescent Psychiatry, 38,* 672–679.

Cole, D. A. (1989). Psychopathology of adolescent suicide: Hopelessness, coping beliefs, and depression. *Journal of Abnormal Psychology, 98,* 248–255.

D'Augelli, A. R. (1996). Lesbian, gay, and bisexual development during adolescence and young adulthood. In R. P. Cabaj & T. S. Stein (Eds.), *Textbook of homosexuality and mental health* (pp. 267–288). Washington, DC: American Psychiatric Press.

Davies, D., & Wilkes, C. R. (1993). Cluster suicide in rural western Canada. *Canadian Journal of Psychiatry, 38,* 515–519.

Esposito, C. L., & Clum, G. A. (1999). Specificity of depressive symptoms and suicidality in a juvenile delinquent population. *Journal of Psychopatology and Behavioral Assesment, 21,* 171–182.

Evans, W., Albers, E., Macari, D., & Mason, A. (1996). Suicide ideation, attempts and abuse among incarcerated gang and nongang delinquents. *Child and Adolescent Social Work Journal, 13,* 115–126.

Faulkner, A. H., & Cranston, K. (1998). Correlates of same-sex sexual behavior in a random sample of Massachusetts high school students. *American Journal of Public Health, 88,* 262–266.

Favazza, A. R., & Conterio, K. (1989). Female habitual self-mutilators. *Acta Psychiatrica Scandinavica, 29,* 252–269.

Fergusson, M., & Lynskey, M. T. (1995). Childhood circumstances, adolescent adjustment, and suicide attempts in New Zealand Birth Cohort. *Journal of the American Academy of Child and Adolescent Psychiatry, 34,* 612–622.

Garland, A. F., & Zigler, E. (1993). Adolescent suicide prevention: Current research and social policy implications. *American Psychologist, 48,* 169–182.

Garofalo, R., Wolf, R. C., Kessel, S., Palfrey, S. J., & DuRant, R. H. (1998). The association between health risk behaviors and sexual orientation among a school—based sample of adolescents. *Pediatrics, 101,* 895–902.

Gibson, P. (1989). Gay male and lesbian youth suicide, *Report of the secretary's task force on youth suicide, Vol. 3 (DHHS Publication ADM 89–1623)* (pp. 110–142). Washington, DC: U.S. Government Printing Office.

Gispert, M., Davis, M., Marsh, L., & Wheeler, R. (1987). Predictive factors in repeated suicide attempts by adolescents. *Hospital and Community Psychiatry, 38,* 390–393.

Goldston, D., Daniel, S., Reboussin, D., Keeley, A., Ievers, C., & Brunstetter, R. (1996). First-time suicide attempters, repeat attempters, and previous attempters on an adolescent inpatient unit. *Journal of the American Academy of Child and Adolescent Psychiatry, 35,* 631–639.

Gould, M. S., Fisher, P., Parides, M., Flory, M., & Shaffer, D. (1996). Psychosocial risk factors of child and adolescent completed suicide. *Archives of General Psychiatry, 53,* 155–1162.

Gould, M. S., Wallenstein, S., Kleinman, M. H., O'Carroll, P., & Mercy, J. (1990). Suicide clusters: An examination of age-specific effects. *American Journal of Public Health, 80,* 211–212.

Guertin, T., Lloyd, E., Spirito, A., Donaldson, D., & Boergers, J. (in press). Self-mutilative behavior among adolescents who attempt suicide by overdose. *Journal of the American Academy of Child and Adolescent Psychiatry.*

Hammelman, T. L. (1993). Gay and lesbian youth: Contributing factors to serious attempts or considerations of suicide. *Journal of Gay and Lesbian Psychotherapy, 2,* 77–89.

Harris, T. E., & Lennings, C. J. (1993). Suicide and adolescence. *International Journal of Offender Therapy and Comparative Criminology, 37,* 263–270.

Hartstein, N. B. (1996). Suicide risk in lesbian, gay, and bisexual youth. In R. P. Cabaj & T. S. Stein (Eds.), *Textbook of homosexuality and mental health* (pp. 819–837). Washington, DC: American Psychiatric Press.

Hawton, K., & Fagg, J. (1992). Deliberate self-poisoning and self-injury in adolescents— A study of characteristics and trends in Oxford, 1976–1989. *British Journal of Psychiatry, 161,* 816–823.

Hawton, K., Kingsbury, S., Steinhardt, K., James, A., & Fagg, J. (1999). Repetition of deliberate self-harm by adolescents: The role of psychological factors. *Journal of Adolescence, 22,* 369–378.

Hazell, P. (1991). Postvention after teenage suicide: An Australian experience. *Journal of Adolescence, 14,* 335–342.

Hazell, P., & Lewin, T. (1993). Friends of adolescent suicide attempters and completers. *Journal of the American Academy of Child and Adolescent Psychiatry, 32,* 76–81.

Hershberger, S. L., & D'Augelli, A. R. (1995). The impact of victimization on the mental health and suicidality of lesbian, gay, and bisexual youth. *Developmental Psychology, 31,* 65–74.

Hershberger, S. L., Pilkington, N. W., & D'Augelli, A. R. (1996). Categorization of lesbian, gay, and bisexual suicide attempters. In C. J. Alexander (Ed.), *Gay and lesbian mental health: A sourcebook for practitioners* (pp. 39–59). New York: Harrington Park Press/ Haworth Press.

Hershberger, S. L., Pilkington, N. W., & D'Augelli, A. R. (1997). Predictors of suicide attempts among gay, lesbian, and bisexual youth. *Journal of Adolescent Research, 12,* 477–497.

Ho, T., Leung, P. W., Hung, S., Lee, C., & Tang, C. (2000). Mental health of peers of suicide completers. *Journal of Child Psychology and Psychiatry and Allied Disciplines, 41,* 301–308.

Joiner, T., Rudd, M. D., Rouleau, M., & Wagner, K. (2000). Parameters of suicide crises vary as a function of previous suicide attempts in youth inpatients. *Journal of the American Academy of Child and Adolescent Psychiatry, 39,* 876–880.

Kempton, T., & Forehand, R. (1992). Case histories and shorter communications: Suicide attempts among juvenile delinquents: the contribution of mental health factors. *Behavior Research and Therapy, 30,* 537–541.

Kotila, L., & Lonnqvist, J. (1987). Adolescents who make suicide attempts repeatedly. *Acta Psychiatrica Scandinavica, 76,* 386–393.

Larsson, B., & Ivarsson, T. (1998). Clinical characteristics of adolescent psychiatric inpatients who have attempted suicide. *Europeant Child and Adolescent Psychiatry, 7,* 201–208.

Lewinsohn, P., Rohde, P., & Seeley, J. (1996). Adolescent suicidal ideators and attempters: Prevalence, risk factors, and clinical implications. *Clinical Psychology: Science and Practice, 3,* 25–46.

Lewinsohn, P. M., Rohde, P., & Seeley, J. R. (1994). Psychosocial risk factors for future adolescent suicide attempts. *Journal of Consulting and Clinical Psychology, 62,* 297–305.

Linehan, M. (1993). *Cognitive behavioral treatment of borderline personality disorder.* New York: Guilford Press.

Lloyd, E. E., Kelley, M. L., & Hope, T. (1997). Self-mutilation in a community sample of adolescents: Descriptive characteristics and provisional prevalence rates. New Orleans, LA: Poster presented at the Society for Behavioral Medicine.

Marttunen, M. J., Aron, H. M., Henricksson, M. M., & Lonnqvist, J. K. (1994). Antisocial behaviour in adolescent suicide. *Acta Psychiatrica Scandinavica, 89*, 167–173.

McGarvey, E., Kryzhanovskaya, L. A., Koopman, C., Waite, D., & Canterbury, R. J. (1999). Incarcerated adolescents' distress and suicidality in relation to parental bonding styles. *Crisis, 20*, 64–69.

Miller, A., Rathus, J., Linehan, M., & Leigh, E. (1997). Dialectical behavior therapy adapted for suicidal adolescents. *Journal of Practical Psychiatry in Behavioral Health, 3*, 78–86.

Morris, R. E., Harrison, E. A., Knox, G. W., Tromanhauser, E., Marquis, D. K., & Watts, L. L. (1995). Health risk behavioral survey from 39 juvenile correctional facilities in the United States. *Journal of Adolescent Health, 17*, 334–344.

Muehrer, P. (1995). Suicide and sexual orientation: A critical summary of recent research and directions for future research. *Suicide and Life-Threatening Behavior, 25 (suppl)*, 72–81.

Pattison, E. M., & Kahan, J. (1983). The deliberate self-harm syndrome. *American Journal of Psychiatry, 140*, 867–872.

Pilkington, N. W., & D'Augelli, A. R. (1995). Victimization of lesbian, gay, and bisexual youth in community settings. *Journal of Community Psychology, 23*, 34–56.

Proctor, C. D., & Groze, V. K. (1994). Risk factors for suicide among gay, lesbian, and bisexual youth. *Social Work, 39*, 504–513.

Putnins, A. L. (1995). Recent drug use and suicidal behavior among young offenders. *Drug and Alcohol Review, 14*, 151–158.

Remafedi, G. (1987). Adolescent homosexuality: Psychosocial and medical implications. *Pediatrics, 79*, 331–337.

Remafedi, G., Farrow, J. A., & Deisher, R. W. (1991). Risk factors for attempted suicide in gay and bisexual youth. *Pediatrics, 87*, 869–875.

Remafedi, G., French, S., Story, M., Resnick, M., & Blum, R. (1998). The relationship between suicide risk and sexual orientation: Results of a population-based study. *American Journal of Public Health, 88*, 57–60.

Renaud, J., Brent, D. A., Birmaher, B., Chiappetta, L., & Bridge, J. (1999). Suicide in adolescents with disruptive disorders. *Journal of the American Academy of Child and Adolescent Psychiatry, 38*, 846–851.

Rohde, P., Mace, D. E., & Seeley, J. R. (1997). The association of psychiatric disorders with suicide attempts in a juvenile delinquent sample. *Criminal Behavior and Mental Health, 7*, 187–200.

Rohde, P., Seeley, J. R., & Mace, D. E. (1997). Correlates of suicidal behavior in a juvenile detention population. *Suicide and Life-Threatening Behavior, 27*, 164–175.

Rosenthal, R. J., Rinzler, C., Walsh, R., & Klausner, E. (1972). Wrist-cutting syndrome: The meaning of a gesture. *American Journal of Psychiatry, 128*, 1363–1368.

Ross, R. R., & McKay, H. B. (1979). *Self-Mutilation*. Lexington, MA: Heath.

Rotheram-Borus, M. J. (1993). Suicidal behavior and risk factors among runaway youths. *American Journal of Psychiatry, 150*, 103–107.

Rotheram-Borus, M. J., & Bradley, J. (1991). Triage model for suicidal runaways. *American Journal of Orthopsychiatry, 61*, 122–127.

Rotheram-Borus, M. J., & Fernandez, M. I. (1995). Sexual orientation and developmental challenges experienced by gay and lesbian youths. *Suicide and Life-Threatening Behavior, 25 (suppl.)*, 26–34.

Rudd, M. D., Joiner, T., & Rajab, H. (1996). Relationships among suicide ideators, attempters, and multiple attempters in a young adult sample. *Journal of Abnormal Psychology, 105,* 541–550.

Safren, S. A., & Heimberg, R. G. (1999). Depression, hopelessness, suicidality, and related factors in sexual minority and heterosexual adolescents. *Journal of Consulting and Clinical Psychology, 67,* 859–866.

Savin-Williams, R. C. (1994). Verbal and physical abuse as stressors in the lives of lesbian, gay male, and bisexual youths: Associations with school problems, running away, substance abuse, prostitution, and suicide. *Journal of Consulting and Clinical Psychology, 62,* 261–269.

Shaffer, D., Gould, M., Fisher, P., Trautman, P., Moreau, D., Kleinman, M., & Flory, M. (1996). Psychiatric diagnosis in child and adolescent suicide. *Archives of General Psychiatry, 53,* 339–348.

Smart, R., & Ogborne, A. (1994). Street youth in substance abuse treatment: Characteristics and treatment compliance. *Adolescence, 29,* 733–745.

Smart, R., & Walsh, G. (1993). Predictors of depression in street youth. *Adolescence, 28,* 41–53.

Smith, K., & Crawford, S. (1986). Suicidal behavior among "normal" high school students. *Suicide and Life-Threatening Behavior, 16,* 313–325.

Sorenson, S. B., & Rutter, C. M. (1991). Transgenerational patterns of suicide attempt. *Journal of Consulting and Clinical Psychology, 59,* 861–866.

Spirito, A., Plummer, B., Gispert, M., Levy, S., Kurkjian, J., Lewander, W., Hagberg, S., & DeVost, C. (1992). Adolescent suicide attempts: Outcomes at follow-up. *American Journal of Orthopsychiatry, 62,* 464–468.

Stein, D., Apter, A., Ratzoni, G., Har-Even, D., & Avidan, G. (1998). Association between multiple suicide attempts and negative affect in adolescents. *Journal of the American Academy of Child and Adolescent Psychiatry, 37,* 488–494.

Stiffman, A. R. (1989). Suicide attempts in runaway youths. *Suicide and Life-Threatening Behavior, 19,* 147–159.

Summerville, M. B., Kaslow, N. J., Abbate, M. F., & Cronan, S. (1994). Psychopathology, family functioning, and cognitive style in urban adolescents with suicide attempts. *Journal of Abnormal Child Psychology, 22,* 221–235.

Suyemoto, K. L. (1998). The functions of self-mutilation. *Clinical Psychology Review, 18,* 531–554.

Taiminen, T. J., Kallio-Soukainen, K., Nokso-Koivisto, H., Kaljonen, A., & Helenius, H. (1998). Contagion of deliberate self-harm among adolescent inpatients. *Journal of the American Academy of Child and Adolescent Psychiatry, 37,* 211–217.

Thompson, E. A., & Eggert, L. L. (1999). Using the Suicide Risk Screen to identify suicidal adolescents among potential high school dropouts. *Journal of the American Academy of Child and Adolescent Psychiatry, 38,* 1506–1514.

Uchida, C. (1995). Drug abuse and psychosocial background among juvenile delinquents: Correlation between self-destructive behaviors and traumatic experiences. *International Medical Journal, 2,* 34–37.

Unger, J., Kipke, M., Simon, T., Montgomery, S., & Johnson, C. (1977). Homeless youths and young adults in Lost Angeles: Prevalence of mental health problems and the relationship between mental health and substance abuse disorders. *American Journal of Community Psychology, 25,* 371–394.

Vajda, J., & Steinbeck, K. (2000). Factors associated with repeat suicide atempts among adolescents. *Australian and New Zealand Journal of Psychiatry, 34*, 437–445.

Walsh, B. W., & Rosen, P. M. (1988). *Self-mutilation: Theory, research, and treatment.* New York: Guilford Press.

Winchel, R. M., & Stanley, M. (1991). Self-injurious behavior: A review of the behavior and biology of self-mutilation. *American Journal of Psychiatry, 148*, 306–317.

Yoder, K. A. (1999). Comparing suicide attempters, suicide ideators, and nonsuicidal homeless and runaway adolescents. *Suicide and Life-Threatening Behavior, 29*, 25–36.

Zlotnick, C., Donaldson, D., Spirito, A., & Pearlstein, T. (1997). Affect regulation and suicide attempts in adolescent inpatients. *Journal of the American Academy of Child and Adolescent Psychiatry, 36*, 793–798.

CHAPTER 12

The Outcome of Suicide Attempts among Adolescents

Julie Boergers, and Anthony Spirito

Although a great deal of research has been conducted on suicidal behavior, less is known about the consequences of suicide attempts. Adolescent suicide attempters are at heightened risk for continued psychological and behavioral dysfunction, repeat suicide attempts, and completed suicide. In fact, approximately 30% of adolescents who commit suicide have a history of a prior attempt (Shaffer, Garland, Gould, Fisher, & Trautman, 1988). Therefore, it is important to understand the post-attempt course in adolescents in order to guide treatment and secondary prevention efforts.

Several different approaches are used to investigate outcomes among suicide attempters. Retrospective studies compare the characteristics of first-time suicide attempters with repeat attempters or conduct "psychological autopsies" of individuals who have completed suicide. Although retrospective studies yield important information, they are not follow-up studies per se and will not be reviewed in this chapter.

One type of follow-up study involves a review of official registries or records. Reviews of national health registries, for example, are commonly conducted in Finland and Sweden. In other countries, such as Great

Evaluating and Treating Adolescent Suicide Attempters

Britain, hospital readmission rates for suicide attempts are often examined. These types of studies may provide good estimates of rates of reattempt and rates of completed suicide, because researchers are able to examine an entire region of a country. However, national registries are limited in the descriptive information they can provide. In addition, reviews of hospital readmission rates may underestimate actual reattempt rates, because many adolescents do not seek medical attention for a suicide attempt. Examination of British hospital readmission data for adolescent suicide attempters has yielded estimates of repeat attempts ranging from 6 to 9% within 1 year of the initial attempt (Goldacre & Hawton, 1985; Hawton, Fagg, & Simikins, 1996; Sellar, Hawton, & Goldacre, 1990).

Studies that report findings on combined adolescent-adult populations are not reviewed here, because there may be significant age-related differences between adolescent and adult suicidal behavior. Finally, because the research literature suggests that there are significant differences between suicide ideators and suicide attempters, studies that combine adolescent suicide attempters and suicide ideators without examining for group differences will not be reviewed in this chapter.

This chapter reviews findings from follow-up studies of adolescent suicide attempters, focusing on post-attempt psychiatric course, repeat suicide attempts, completed suicide, and treatment engagement. We primarily review prospective follow-up studies of adolescents who have made a suicide attempt. Because this literature is relatively small, we cite articles published before 1990.

PSYCHOSOCIAL FUNCTIONING AT FOLLOW-UP

Many follow-up studies have attempted to make gross estimates of the overall adjustment of adolescents following a suicide attempt. Some studies have relied on the adolescents' own reports of their functioning. For example, Hawton, O'Grady, Osborn, and Cole (1982) interviewed 50 adolescents 1 month following their attempt; half described their overall adjustment as improved, whereas 40% reported no change. Angle, O'Brien, and McIntire (1983) constructed an overall index of adaptation, which took into account school, work, and interpersonal functioning. Twenty-four adolescent suicide attempters were contacted by phone 9 years later, and all described higher levels of life satisfaction and better interpersonal functioning. Functional adaptation at follow-up was not related to number of repeat attempts.

Granboulan, Rabain, and Basquin (1995) studied 127 adolescents who had attempted suicide and were contacted approximately 11 years later. They obtained information on psychosocial adjustment from a wide range of sources, including the patients themselves, their parents, and their physicians. Ratings of psychosocial adjustment incorporated questions about occupational status, social and family relationships, and any residual emotional difficulties. Based on these ratings, Granboulan and colleagues concluded that 39% of the 127 adolescents in their sample had improved, 22% seemed to be unchanged, and 33% presented with lower levels of functioning 11 years after the initial adolescent suicide attempt. Similarly, McIntire, Angle, Wikoff, and Schlicht (1977) used clinician ratings of adjustment and found that only 23% of 26 adolescents demonstrated improvements in functional adaptation by the time of the follow-up interview (6 to 24 months following discharge from a psychiatric hospital). Those adolescents whose living environment improved after their initial hospitalization were more likely to demonstrate improvements in overall adjustment.

Using a more objective measure of adjustment (the Child Behavior Checklist), Cohen-Sandler, Berman, and King (1982) found that 60% of 20 psychiatrically hospitalized suicidal children and adolescents (age 5 to 14 years) demonstrated behavioral and social functioning that was within normal limits at 18-month follow-up. There is some suggestion that psychosocial functioning at followup is related to receiving psychological intervention. Pillay and Wassenaar (1995) studied 40 adolescent suicide attempters. Those who had received no treatment by the time of the 6-month follow-up showed no spontaneous remission in the hopelessness they demonstrated at baseline. However, patients who received treatment improved significantly with respect to hopelessness.

Specific markers of adjustment have also been examined, including school functioning, social relationships, family functioning, behavior, and psychopathology. Regarding school functioning, Spirito and colleagues (1992) found that only 67.9% of suicide attempters seen in a general hospital and 72.8% of suicide attempters seen in a psychiatric hospital sample were attending school regularly when contacted at 3-month follow-up.

Poor family functioning is a correlate of adolescent suicide attempts, and, in fact, family difficulties persist at follow-up for many of these adolescents. Hawton and colleagues (1982) found that while improvement was likely in the areas of peer and romantic relationship difficulties, family problems and psychiatric problems were unlikely to have improved at 1 month post-attempt. Barter, Swaback, and Todd (1968) found that while

84% of nonattempter controls were living at home, only 42% of suicide attempters were living at home with their parents at the time of follow-up (mean = 21 months). In a study comparing psychiatrically hospitalized suicide attempters with psychiatric controls, suicide attempters were more likely to be placed outside the home after discharge (Cohen-Sandler et al., 1982). As they enter young adulthood, suicide attempters have been found to marry less frequently and divorce more often than controls with no history of suicide attempt (Otto, 1972).

Continued risky or conduct disordered behavior has also been observed among adolescent suicide attempters. In a 3-month follow-up, Spirito et al. (1992) found that 23% of adolescent suicide attempters were involved in physical fighting, and 14% had run away. Otto (1972) followed a large sample of adolescent suicide attempters in Sweden 10 to 15 years after their attempt and compared them to age-matched controls using government records. Suicide attempters had greater rates of conduct-disordered behavior, illness-related absences from work, and disability pensions. It is noteworthy that approximately one-third of the male suicide attempters in this sample had been arrested more than once in the 10 to 15 years following their suicide attempt (Otto, 1972). Similarly, in a 5-year follow-up of 552 French adolescents, contact with the criminal justice system was more frequent among suicide attempters than in a comparison group. In a 7-year follow-up study of British adolescent suicide attempters, 29% of 41 participants contacted had been convicted of a crime (Kerfoot & McHugh, 1992).

Adolescent suicide attempters are at increased risk for alcohol and substance abuse during the months and years following their suicide attempt. In the Spirito et al. (1992) study described earlier, 17% of attempters presenting to a general hospital and 14% of attempters presenting to a psychiatric hospital reported using alcohol at least once a week. Higher rates of alcohol use (Laurent, Foussard, David, Boucharlat, & Bost, 1998) and abuse (Otto, 1972) have been found in studies that follow adolescent suicide attempters and compare them to individuals without a history of suicide attempt. In Kerfoot and McHugh's sample (1992) described earlier, 37% reported substance abuse during the years following their adolescent suicide attempt. Mehr, Zeltzer, and Robinson (1982) found that adolescent suicide attempters were more likely to report a drug overdose within 8 years following their attempt than were adolescents who were followed after a hospitalization for injury or illness.

Adolescent suicide attempters are also at an increased risk for accidents, injuries, and death by other causes. This is likely related to the increased incidence of conduct disorder, substance abuse, and personality disorder among these adolescents. For example, Granboulan *et al.* (1995) found that in addition to those suicide attempters who later died by suicide within the 11-year follow-up period of the study (4%), another 7% of their sample died of "unnatural or violent causes," such as homicide, substance abuse, or motor vehicle crashes. Mehr *et al.* (1982) reported that five of the seven adolescent suicide attempters within 8 years following their attempt had been in a motor vehicle crash. In a short-term (3-month) follow-up, Spirito *et al.* (1992) found that about 10% of a general hospital sample and 15% of psychiatrically hospitalized adolescent suicide attempters had been in a motor vehicle crash. In addition, about 15% of the general hospital sample and almost one-third of the psychiatric hospital sample had received an injury that required emergency department care in the 3-month follow-up period.

Few studies have investigated whether suicide attempters demonstrate a higher incidence of maladjustment than other psychiatric patients. Cohen-Sandler and colleagues (1982) conducted a follow-up study comparing child and adolescent suicide attempters with depressed and psychiatric controls 18 months after hospitalization. They found that suicide attempters were highly likely to experience stress after their discharge, including school changes (74%), change in parental marital status (21%), and change in parental financial status (32%). However, their overall level of stressful life events after discharge did not differ significantly from the two psychiatric comparison groups. In general, there were no differences between the groups on parental ratings of internalizing and externalizing behavior at follow-up. In fact, the suicide attempters showed better social involvement than the depressed adolescents, who tended to be socially withdrawn during the follow-up (Cohen-Sandler *et al.*, 1982). Similarly, Stanley and Barter (1970) compared adolescent suicide attempters with psychiatrically hospitalized adolescents who had not made an attempt and found no significant difference in peer relationships, school performance, or living arrangements. However, the patients with repeat suicide attempts did demonstrate poorer academic performance and fewer peer relationships than the control group.

REPEAT SUICIDE ATTEMPTS

A significant percentage of adolescent suicide attempters will make a repeat attempt at some point in their lifetime. There is considerable variability in estimates of reattempts, and this variability appears to be associated with both the length of the follow-up period and the type of study.

Prospective studies of patients who are recontacted directly at follow-up yielded higher rates of repeat attempts. Most follow-up studies with suicidal adolescents have been conducted over relatively short periods of time due to difficulty recontacting participants. In general, higher repetition rates are found in studies with longer follow-up periods, despite the loss of participants to attrition. Among participants who are recontacted, rates of repeat attempts range from 10% within 3 months following the index attempt (Hawton et al., 1982; Spirito et al., 1992), 15% at 6 months (Brent et al., 1993), 12 to 20% at 1 year (Hawton et al., 1982; Hawton, Kingsbury, Steinhardt, James, & Fagg, 1999; Kienhorst, deWilde, Diekstra, & Wolters, 1991; White, 1974), and from 20 to 50% at 2- to 3-year follow-up (Cohen-Sandler et al., 1982; McIntire et al., 1977; Stanley & Barter, 1970). Because patients (and high-risk patients in particular) become much more difficult to contact as the follow-up period lengthens, the suicide attempt rates in some of studies may be underestimates.

Higher reattempt rates have typically been found among those adolescents who have been psychiatrically hospitalized, and lower rates have been found among adolescents who present to a general hospital. For example, Spirito and colleagues (1992) found that 9% of a general hospital sample had made a repeat attempt at 3-month follow-up, whereas 13.6% of the psychiatric hospital sample had made a repeat attempt. This may be related to severity of psychopathology; suicide attempters who are psychiatrically hospitalized are likely to have made a more serious attempt and to have more serious psychological difficulties.

There has been an effort to identify factors that can predict those adolescents who will make repeat attempts. A major risk factor that has emerged in the literature is the number of past suicide attempts. Survival analyses with adult suicide attempters demonstrate that with each attempt, there is a 32% increase in relative risk for reattempt (Leon, Friedman, Sweeney, Brown, & Mann, 1990). A similar pattern is observed with adolescents. For example, in a large, nonpatient sample of high school students, Lewinsohn, Rohde, and Seeley (1994) found that adolescents with a history of suicide attempt were 8.1 times more likely to make a suicide attempt than those with no prior history of attempt. Pfeffer and colleagues (1993) found that when compared to nonpatient controls, psychiatrically hospitalized preadolescent suicide attempters were six times more likely to attempt suicide during a 6- to 8-year follow-up. Similarly,

Goldston, Daniel, Reboussin, Reboussin, Frazier, and Kelley (1999) followed 180 psychiatrically hospitalized adolescents, approximately 40% of whom had made a prior suicide attempt. The number of prior attempts was the strongest predictor of a post-hospitalization attempt. Goldston and colleagues (1999) posit that after adolescents have made a suicide attempt, they cross a certain behavioral threshold, which then places them at increased risk for engaging in similar behavior, especially in response to internal or external cues similar to those present at the time of the initial attempt.

Other predictors of repeat attempts at follow-up include demographic factors, psychiatric disturbance at baseline, and lethality of the initial attempt. Older teens are more likely than younger teens to make repeat attempts (e.g., Cohen-Sandler et al., 1982; Goldacre & Hawton, 1985), and among older teens (ages 16 to 20), a higher percentage of males reattempt than females (Goldacre & Hawton, 1985). Affective disorders (Brent et al., 1993; Goldston et al., 1999; Pfeffer, Klerman, Hurt, Kakumen, Peskin, & Siefker, 1993) and chronic difficulties such as conduct problems and behavior problems (Hawton et al., 1982) or anxiety (Goldston et al., 1999) are similarly associated with reattempt. Greater lethality of a suicide attempt has generally been linked to repeat attempts (Cohen-Sandler et al., 1982; Hawton et al., 1982; McIntire et al., 1977; Otto, 1972; Pfeffer, Klerman, Hurt, Lesser, Peskin, & Siefker, 1991). However, Brent and colleagues (1993) found no evidence that the lethality of an attempt was predictive of a repeat attempt in a 6-month follow-up study, suggesting that all suicide attempts should be taken seriously.

Social factors and psychological characteristics may also contribute to repeat attempts. For example, environmental stress, parent-child discord (Cohen-Sandler et al., 1982; McIntire et al., 1977), death of a relative, and family financial problems (Brent et al., 1993) during the follow-up period have been implicated in repeat attempts. Adolescents who make a repeat attempt at follow-up have poorer social adjustment (Pfeffer et al., 1993; Stanley & Barter, 1970), poorer academic performance (Stanley & Barter, 1970), and are less likely to be living with a parent (Cohen-Sandler et al., 1982) than those who do not make repeat suicide attempts. Kienhorst and colleagues (1991) found that predictors of repeat attempts at 1 year included absence of father from the home, hopelessness, pessimism, weight gain, fatigue, history of suicidal ideation, and consideration of suicide as a potential option in the future. In a 1-year follow-up study, Hawton and colleagues (1999) found that adolescents who made a repeat attempt (*n* = 9) were characterized by poorer problem-solving skills at baseline (fewer and less effective solutions to hypothetical problems) than those who did not reattempt ($n = 36$). However, after controlling for depression, these group differences were reduced to nonsignificance.

The first several months following a suicide attempt appear to be the period of highest risk for adolescents. Goldacre and Hawton (1985) examined British hospital admission data on who made a repeat attempt within a year of the index attempt and found that 69% of boys and 41% of girls did so during the first 3 months. In a sample of 50 adolescents, Hawton et al. (1982) found that five of the seven repeat attempts occurred within the first 3 months following the initial attempt. Because both of these studies utilized a review of hospital readmission data, it is unlikely that they are artificially inflated by increased enrollment rates in the early period following the attempt. A prospective study of psychiatrically hospitalized adolescents (of whom approximately 40% were suicide attempters; Goldston et al., 1999) found that the first 6 to 12 months after discharge was the period of highest risk for suicide attempt.

Clearly, more research is needed on the risk factors for repeat attempts in order to improve prediction and target interventions appropriately. For example, Brent and colleagues (1993) found that adolescents who reattempted during the 6-month follow-up period were more likely to have received psychotropic medication and less likely to have received family therapy than their peers who did not reattempt. Cohen-Sandler and colleagues (1982) also noted that adolescents who made a repeat attempt within 18 months were half as likely to have received family therapy as those who did not make a repeat attempt. These two studies provide preliminary evidence that family therapy may be a useful way to decrease repeat suicide attempts among adolescents.

COMPLETED SUICIDE

Adolescent suicide attempters are at a heightened risk for eventual death by suicide. In 1998, 15% of those who committed suicide in the United States were under 25 years old (Murphy, 2000). In adult samples, estimates of eventual completed suicide among suicide attempters appear to be related to the length of the follow-up period (Lester, 1996). Most follow-up studies of adolescent suicide attempters have been conducted over short time periods, with few completed suicides among followed adolescents. Some studies conducted over 5 years after the inital attempt have found relatively high rates of completed suicide. For example,

Nardini-Maillard and Ladame (1980) found that about 4% of 130 adolescent suicide attempters followed at 6 years post-attempt had died by suicide. In another French study (Granboulan *et al.*, 1995), about 4% of 127 patients had committed suicide by the time of the follow-up (mean of 11.5 years). Because some adolescents lost to follow-up in these studies may have been deceased, these rates may underestimate the true incidence of completed suicide.

Thus, studies that review official registries or records have the potential to provide more accurate estimates of the rates of completed suicide. However, even these types of studies may underestimate the true incidence of suicide due to incomplete or inaccurate information listed on death certificates (e.g., Goldacre & Hawton, 1985). Estimates of completed suicide based on this type of data range from 2.2% at 5 years (Kotila & Lönnqvist, 1989) to 4.3% at 10 to 15 years post-attempt (Otto, 1972).

Attention has been paid to identifying critical periods during which adolescent suicide attempters are at highest risk for completed suicide. Although most completed suicides occur within the first year post-attempt, the average time elapsed between a suicide attempt and a later completed suicide is about 3 years (Motto, 1984; Otto, 1972). In one study, about one-quarter of adolescent suicide attempters who subsequently committed suicide did so within the first year (Otto, 1972), suggesting that the first year is a period of particularly high risk.

Follow-up studies of adolescent suicide attempters can help researchers to determine which of these youths are at the highest risk for eventual suicide and can inform interventions and preventive efforts. One of the strongest predictors of completed suicide is a previous suicide attempt. In fact, on average, the annual suicide rate among adolescents with a previous suicide attempt is 14 times higher than the overall annual suicide rate for United States adolescents (Safer, 1997). Approximately 30% of completed suicides among adolescents are the result of a repeat attempt (Shaffer *et al.*, 1988). Adolescents who make multiple attempts are approximately three times more likely to eventually complete suicide than those who make only one attempt (Kotila & Lönnqvist, 1989). The association between past suicide attempts and completed suicide may be related to continued, unrelieved psychological distress or to a tendency to engage in increasingly risky behavior.

There is a robust gender difference in completed suicide among adolescents. Although females are much more likely to attempt suicide than males, male attempters are at far greater risk for eventual death by suicide (e.g., Goldacre & Hawton, 1985; Kotila & Lönnqvist, 1988; Otto, 1972;

Sellar *et al.*, 1990). In 1998, suicide was the third leading cause of death for males ages 15 to 24, and the sixth leading cause of death for females ages 15 to 24 (Murphy, 2000). The rate of adolescent suicide completion, on average, is five times greater for male suicide attempters than for female suicide attempters (Safer, 1997). This gender difference may be even greater during the first 3 months following a suicide attempt (Sellar *et al.*, 1990).

Substance abuse and psychiatric disturbance also heighten the risk of eventual completed suicide among adolescent suicide attempters. For example, psychosis at the time of the initial attempt has been strongly associated with later completed suicide (Granboulan *et al.*, 1995; Kotila, 1992). Kotila (1992) found that low educational level, alcohol abuse, and use of illegal drugs were more common in adolescents who went on to kill themselves within a 5-year follow-up. Moreover, relative to other demographic groups, substance-abusing adolescent males may be at highest risk for eventual completed suicide (DeMoore & Robertson, 1996).

Characteristics of the attempt are also associated with risk for eventual completed suicide. Future completed suicide is more likely if the attempt is by firearm or hanging rather than a more passive method of attempt such as an overdose (Granboulan *et al.*, 1995; Otto, 1972). In a 5-year follow-up study, Kotila (1992) found that adolescents who had died (either by suicide, homicide, or unintentional injury) had an initial attempt that was characterized by clear intent, high lethality, revenge as a motive, or unclear motives.

TREATMENT ENGAGEMENT

Given the evidence for continued psychiatric dysfunction, the relatively high reattempt rate, and the risk of eventual completed suicide, appropriate intervention with these high-risk adolescents is critical. The majority of adolescent suicide attempters are referred for outpatient psychiatric care. Treatment engagement is important because teenagers who drop out of treatment are at a greater risk for reattempt (Litt, Cuskey, & Rudd, 1983). These adolescents may be at greater risk for reattempt because the risk factors associated with their initial attempt remain unaddressed. For example, Pillay and Wassenaar (1995) demonstrated that at 6 months following an attempt, feelings of hopelessness were reduced among adolescents who received psychotherapy, whereas the untreated group remained as hopeless as they had been at the time of the index attempt.

Follow-up studies of these adolescents have typically found poor adherence with outpatient treatment. Although even nonsuicidal adolescents tend to attend relatively few psychotherapy sessions (Tolan, Ryan, & Jaffe, 1988), psychotherapy attendance appears to be worse among those adolescents who have attempted suicide. Trautman, Stewart, and Morishima (1993) found that adolescent suicide attempters dropped out of treatment much more quickly (median = three sessions) than nonsuicidal adolescents (median = 11 sessions).

Treatment adherence rates following an attempt have been reported as low as 23% for patients presenting to a psychiatry emergency clinic (Morrison & Collier, 1969) to 84% for patients seen in a psychiatric hospital (Cohen-Sandler et al., 1982). Some studies have reported that many adolescents fail to attend even one psychotherapy session after their attempt. For example, Pillay and Wassenaar (1995) found that 45% of 40 Indian adolescent suicide attempters in South Africa declined all treatment. In Great Britain, Taylor and Stansfeld (1984) reported that 44% of adolescents failed to keep their initial psychotherapy appointment.

All too frequently, even those suicide attempters who follow through with a psychotherapy referral fail to receive an adequate course of treatment. McIntire and colleagues (1977), for example, found that only about one-third of their sample had treatment for 2 months or more. In an 11-year follow-up of adolescent suicide attempters who had been psychiatrically hospitalized, about one-third did not comply with any post-discharge treatment, and one-fifth attended treatment irregularly or prematurely discontinued treatment (Granboulan et al., 1995). In a review of the literature, Spirito, Brown, Overholser, and Fritz (1989) estimated that about one-half of all adolescent suicide attempters either never receive treatment or attend only one or two psychotherapy sessions.

Adherence to treatment recommendations may vary depending on the setting in which the adolescent is initially treated. In emergency departments (EDs), for example, poor rates of treatment adherence have been documented among adult suicide attempters (see Krulee & Hales, 1988, for a review). Although there are exceptions (Burgess, Hawton, & Loveday, 1998), this is an issue of concern among adolescent suicide attempters seen in EDs as well. Litt et al. (1983) found that of adolescent suicide attempters (n = 14) seen in a general hospital ED and discharged to outpatient care, only one-third received any follow-up treatment. In a sample of minority female adolescents treated in an urban hospital ED for a suicide attempt and referred back to a mental health clinic at the same hospital, 14.5% never attended an outpatient therapy appointment,

38% attended 1 or 2 appointments, and only 32% attended 3 or more appointments (Trautman & Rotheram, 1987). Spirito et al. (1992) found similar rates of treatment attendance in a sample of 78 adolescent suicide attempters seen in a general hospital and discharged to a variety of clinics: 18% never kept an outpatient appointment, 14% went only once or twice, and 23% attended three or four sessions by the 3-month post-attempt. These studies document the extent of treatment nonadherence among adolescent suicide attempters seen in a general hospital ED.

Some studies have shown that adolescents who have been psychiatrically hospitalized after a suicide attempt are somewhat more likely to attend outpatient treatment after discharge than suicide attempters treated in a general hospital and sent home for outpatient treatment (Brent et al., 1993; Spirito et al., 1992). However, treatment engagement is a significant problem in the psychiatrically hospitalized population as well. In fact, Litt and colleagues (1983) found the same nonadherence rate at 1 year among 13 pediatrically or psychiatrically hospitalized adolescents and 14 adolescents discharged to their homes directly from the ED.

Treatment adherence also seems to vary by type of outpatient treatment. King, Hovey, Brand, Wilson, and Ghaziuddin (1997) studied adolescent suicide attempters and ideators following a psychiatric hospitalization. These adolescents were most compliant with their outpatient medication visits (67%), followed by individual therapy (51%), and then family therapy (33%). Less affectionate father-adolescent relationships were related to family therapy nonadherence, whereas maternal depressive and paranoid symptoms negatively impacted individual and family therapy adherence.

Follow-up studies have also provided some important data on the factors characterizing those who are nonadherent with treatment. In one study, socioeconomic status and family size did not discriminate those attempters who attended therapy from those who did attend therapy (Spirito, Lewander, Levy, Kurkjian, & Fritz, 1994; Taylor & Stansfeld, 1984). Characteristics of the adolescent suicide attempter at baseline, such as higher levels of suicidality and depression, are associated with greater likelihood to follow through with the initial psychotherapy visit (Taylor & Stansfeld, 1984). Lack of family cohesion, family conflict, and poor physical health of family members have also been associated with poor treatment adherence (Spirito et al., 1994; Taylor & Stansfeld, 1984; Trautman & Rotheram, 1987).

There is conflicting data in the literature regarding the relationship between treatment adherence and history of previous suicide attempt. In a small sample, Litt *et al.* (1983) found that those adolescents without a history of previous suicide attempts were much more likely to adhere to treatment. However, Trautman *et al.* (1993) found no relation between number of previous suicide attempts and treatment adherence, and Spirito and colleagues (1994) found that a history of prior attempt, alcohol use at the time of attempt, and greater planning of the attempt were all associated with *better* treatment adherence. These factors may have led to a higher level of concern among parents and clinicians, which in turn may have resulted in greater efforts to ensure that these adolescents complied with treatment (Spirito *et al.*, 1994).

SUMMARY AND CONCLUSIONS

Several major conclusions can be drawn from the literature on the follow-up course of adolescent suicide attempters. These studies consistently show a high level of continued dysfunction among adolescent suicide attempters, suggesting that for most adolescents, the suicide attempt is not an isolated problem. Adolescent suicide attempters are also at much higher risk for both repeat attempts and eventual completed suicide than are adolescents without prior suicidal behavior.

Clinicians who work with adolescent suicide attempters should be aware that the first several months following a suicide attempt represent the period of highest risk. Although females are more likely to attempt suicide than males, adolescent male suicide attempters are at greater risk for eventual death by suicide. The risk for future suicide attempts and for completed suicide increases with each subsequent attempt. Other factors that place adolescents at heightened risk include a highly lethal attempt; the presence of an affective disorder, psychosis, or substance abuse; impaired social adjustment or family functioning; and recent losses (such as the death of a loved one or the breakup of a relationship). However, we still have limited ability to predict which adolescents will make repeat attempts or eventually commit suicide. Obviously, adolescent suicidal behavior is a complex outcome with multiple contributing factors, so our predictive power will always be limited, especially for eventual completed suicide.

More information is also needed about factors that may *protect* adolescents from repeat attempts or completed suicide. For example, McIntire and colleagues (1977) noted that among adolescent suicide attempters who moved to an improved living environment (for example, from a foster home to a permanent home), none made a repeat attempt. Other protective factors that have been identified include adequate social relationships (Barter et al., 1968), strong support systems, high educational achievement (Angle et al., 1983), and the use of repression rather than more immature defense mechanisms (Pfeffer, Hurt, Peskin, & Siefker, 1995). Information on protective factors may help to guide new innovations in primary and secondary suicide prevention, as well as bolster treatment efforts for those who have already attempted suicide. For example, schools could develop systems for recognizing loners and assisting these students through social skills development and social programming. Therapists could place greater focus on improving the living situations of their adolescent patients who have attempted suicide. Identifying additional factors that protect against suicidal behavior will be a critical task for our field in years to come.

REFERENCES

Angle, C. R., O'Brien, T. P., & McIntire, M. S. (1983). Adolescent self-poisoning: A nine-year follow-up. *Developmental and Behavioral Pediatrics, 4*, 83–87.

Barter, J. T., Swaback, D. O., & Todd, D. (1968). Adolescent suicide attempts: A follow-up study of hospitalized patients. *Archives of General Psychiatry, 19*, 523–527.

Brent, D. A., Kolko, D. J., Wartella, M. E., Boylan, M. B., Mortiz, G., Baugher, M., & Zelenak, J. P. (1993). Adolescent psychiatric inpatients' risk of suicide attempt at 6-month follow-up. *Journal of the American Academy of Child and Adolescent Psychiatry, 32*, 95–105.

Burgess, S., Hawton, K., & Loveday, G. (1998). Adolescents who take overdoses: Outcome in terms of changes in psychopathology and the adolescent's attitude to care and to their overdose. *Journal of Adolescence, 21*, 209–218.

Cohen-Sandler, R., Berman, A. L., & King, R. A. (1982). A follow-up study of hospitalized suicidal children. *Journal of the American Academy of Child and Adolescent Psychiatry, 21*, 398–403.

DeMoore, G. M., & Robertson, A. R. (1996). Suicide in the 18 years after deliberate self harm: A prospective study. *British Journal of Psychiatry, 169*, 489–494.

Goldacre, M., & Hawton, K. (1985). Repetition of self-poisoning and subsequent death in adolescents who take overdoses. *British Journal of Psychiatry, 146*, 395–398.

Goldston, D., Daniel, S., Reboussin, D., Reboussin, B., Frazier, P., & Kelley, A. (1999). Suicide attempts and formerly hospitalized adolescents: A prospective naturalistic study of risk during the first 5 years after discharge. *Journal of the American Academy of Child and Adolescent Psychiatry, 38*, 660–671.

Granboulan, V., Rabain, D., & Basquin, M. (1995). The outcome of adolescent suicide attempts. *Acta Psychiatrica Scandinavica, 91*, 265–270.

Hawton, K., Fagg, J., & Simkins, S. (1996). Deliberate self-poisoning and self-injury in children and adolescents under 16 years of age in Oxford, 1976–1993. *British Journal of Psychiatry, 169*, 202–208.

Hawton, K., Kingsbury, S., Steinhardt, K., James, A., & Fagg, J. (1999). Repetition of deliberate self-harm by adolescents: The role of psychological factors. *Journal of Adolescence*, *22*, 369–378.

Hawton, K., O'Grady, J., Osborn, M., & Cole, D. (1982). Adolescents who take overdoses: Their characteristics, problems, and contacts with helping agencies. *British Journal of Psychiatry*, *140*, 118–123.

Kerfoot, M., & McHugh, B. (1992). The outcome of childhood suicidal behavior. *Acta Paedopsychiatrica*, *55*, 141–145.

Kienhorst, C. M., deWilde, E. J., Diekstra, R. W., & Wolters, W. G. (1991). Construction of an index for predicting suicide attempts in depressed adolescents. *British Journal of Psychiatry*, *159*, 676–682.

King, C., Hovey, G., Brand, E., Wilson, R., & Ghaziuddin, N. (1997). Suicidal adolescents after hospitalization: Parent and family impacts on treatment follow-through. *Journal of the American Academy of Child and Adolescent Psychiatry*, *36*, 85–93.

Kotila, L. (1992). The outcome of attempted suicide in adolescence. *Journal of Adolescent Health*, *13*, 415–417.

Kotila, L., & Lönnqvist, J. (1988). Adolescent suicide attempts: Sex differences predicting suicide. *Acta Psychiatrica Scandinavica*, *77*, 264–270.

Kotila, L., & Lönnqvist, J. (1989). Suicide and violent death among adolescent suicide attempters. *Acta Psychiatrica Scandinavica*, *79*, 453–459.

Krulee, D., & Hales, R. (1988). Compliance with psychiatric referrals from a general hospital psychiatry outpatient clinic. *General Hospital Psychiatry*, *10*, 339–345.

Laurent, A., Foussard, N., David, M., Boucharlat, J., & Bost, M. (1998). A 5-year follow-up study of suicide attempts among French adolescents. *Journal of Adolescent Health*, *22*, 424–430.

Leon, A. C., Friedman, R. A., Sweeney, J. A., Brown, R. P., & Mann, J. J. (1990). Statistical issues in the identification of risk factors for suicidal behavior: The application of survival analysis. *Psychiatry Research*, *31*, 99–108.

Lester, D. (1996). The mortality of attempted suicides in follow-up studies of male suicide attempters. *Perceptual and Motor Skills*, *83*, 530.

Lewinsohn, P. M., Rohde, P., & Seeley, J. R. (1994). Psychosocial risk factors for future adolescent suicide attempts. *Journal of Consulting and Clinical Psychology*, *62*, 297–305.

Litt, I. F., Cuskey, W. R., & Rudd, S. (1983). Emergency room evaluation of the adolescent who attempts suicide: Compliance with follow-up. *Journal of Adolescent Health Care*, *4*, 106–108.

McIntire, M. S., Angle, C. R., Wikoff, R. L., & Schlicht, M. L. (1977). Recurrent adolescent suicidal behavior. *Pediatrics*, *60*, 605–608.

Mehr, M., Zelter, L. K., & Robinson, R. (1982). Continued self-destructive behaviors in adolescent suicide attempters: Part II-A pilot study. *Journal of Adolescent Health Care*, *2*, 183–187.

Morrison, G. C., & Collier, J. G. (1969). Family treatment approaches to suicidal children and adolescents. *Journal of the American Academy of Child Psychiatry*, *8*, 140–153.

Motto, J. A. (1984). Suicide in male adolescents. In H. S. Sudak, A. B. Ford, & N. B. Rushforth (Eds.), *Suicide in the Young*. Boston: PSG.

Murphy, S. L. (2000). Deaths: Final data for 1998. *National Vital Statistics Reports*, *48*. Hyattsville, MD: National Center for Health Statistics.

Nardini-Maillard, D., & Ladame, F. (1980). The results of a follow-up study of suicidal adolescents. *Journal of Adolescence, 3,* 253–260.

Otto, U. (1972). Suicidal acts by children and adolescents: A follow-up study. *Acta Psychiatrica Scandinavica, 233,* 7–177.

Pfeffer, C. R., Hurt, S. W., Peskin, J. R., & Siefker, C. A. (1995). Suicidal children grow up: Ego functions associated with suicide attempts. *Journal of the American Academy of Child and Adolescent Psychiatry, 34,* 1318–1325.

Pfeffer, C. R., Klerman, G. L., Hurt, S. W., Kakuman, T., Peskin, J. R., & Siefker, C. A. (1993). Suicidal children grow up: Rates and psychosocial risk factors for suicide attempts during follow-up. *Journal of the American Academy of Child and Adolescent Psychiatry, 32,* 106–113.

Pfeffer, C. R., Klerman, G. L., Hurt, S. W., Lesser, M., Peskin, J. R., & Siefker, C. A. (1991). Suicidal children up: Demographic and clinical risk factors for adolescent suicide attempts. *Journal of the American Academy of Child and Adolescent Psychiatry, 30,* 609–616.

Pillay, A. L., & Wassenaar, D. R. (1995). Psyhcological intervention, spontaneous remission, hopelessness, and psychiatric disturbance in adolescent parasuicides. *Suicide and Life-Threatening Behavior, 25,* 386–392.

Safer, D. J. (1997). Adolescent/adult differences in suicidal behavior and outcome. *Annals of Clinical Psychiatry, 9,* 61–66.

Sellar, C., Hawton, K., & Goldacre, M. J. (1990). Self-poisoning in adolescents: Hospital admissions and deaths in the Oxford Region 1980–85. *British Journal of Psychiatry, 156,* 866–870.

Shaffer, D., Garland, A., Gould, M., Fisher, P., & Trautman, P. (1988). Preventing teenage suicide: A critical review. *Journal of the American Academy of Child and Adolescent Psychiatry, 27,* 675–687.

Spirito, A., Brown, L., Overholser, J., & Fritz, G. (1989). Attempted suicide in adolescence: A review and critique of the literature. *Clinical Psychology Review, 9,* 335–363.

Spirito, A., Lewander, W. J., Levy, S., Kurkjian, J., & Fritz, G. (1994). Emergency department assessment of adolescent suicide attempters: Factors related to short-term follow-up outcome. *Pediatric Emergency Care, 10,* 6–12.

Spirito, A., Plummer, B., Gispert, M., Levy, S., Kurkjian, J., Lewander, W., Hagberg, S., & Devost, L. (1992). Adolescent suicide attempts: Outcomes at follow-up. *American Journal of Orthopsychiatry, 62,* 464–468.

Stanley, E. J., & Barter, J. T. (1970). Adolescent suicidal behavior. *American Journal of Orthopsychiatry, 40,* 87–96.

Taylor, E. A., & Stansfeld, S. A. (1984). Children who poison themselves: Prediction of attendance for treatment. *British Journal of Psychiatry, 145,* 132–135.

Tolan, P., Ryan, K., & Jaffe, C. (1988). Adolescents' mental health service use and provider process, and recipient characteristics. *Journal of Clinical Child Psychology, 17,* 229–236.

Trautman, P., & Rotheram, M. J. (1987). *Referral failure among adolescent suicide attempters* (Poster presented at the Annual Meeting of the American Academy of Child Psychiatry). Los Angeles, CA.

Trautman, P. D., Stewart, N., & Morishima, A. (1993). Are adolescent suicide attempters noncompliant with outpatient care? *Journal of the American Academy of Child and Adolescent Psychiatry, 32,* 89–94.

White, H. C. (1974). Self-poisoning in adolescents. *British Journal of Psychiatry, 124,* 24–35.

CHAPTER 13

Case Examples

Anthony Spirito, Jayne Kurkjian, and Deidre Donaldson

Although approximately 8 to 10% of adolescents report in anonymous surveys that they have made at least one suicide attempt, only about 2 to 3% of adolescents receive medical attention following an attempt, and even fewer are psychiatrically hospitalized (CDC, 1998). Developing effective treatments for those who make medically serious attempts is further compromised by the fact that these adolescents are quite a heterogeneous group. For example, our clinical research suggests that these adolescents most commonly fall into one of three diagnostic groups: (1) adjustment disorder, (2) significant mood disorder (major depressive disorder or bipolar disorder), and (3) disruptive behavior disorder with comorbid mood disorder. At the risk of oversimplification, we find these broad categorizations helpful in treatment conceptualization. In this chapter, we have selected case examples to represent each of these three broad categorizations because we have found this approach valuable in developing treatment plans for adolescent suicide attempters. It is important to note that while potentially helpful, these categorizations have not been validated empirically (e.g., by cluster analysis).

Evaluating and Treating Adolescent Suicide Attempters

The three cases presented here are actual cases that we have evaluated in our medical center. Some of the details regarding their presentations have been adjusted to help ensure confidentiality. For each case, we describe the results of a brief, focused assessment battery that we used to evaluate these adolescents. The results of the assessment battery were summarized in a brief clinical report designed to be useful to pediatricians and nurses caring for the adolescent in the hospital. The format for this report can be seen in Table 1. All the measures administered to the three patients have been described in previous chapters.

TABLE 1   Assessment Summary for Adolescent Suicide Attempters

Name:
Date of Evaluation:

REASON FOR REFERRAL
This patient was referred for evaluation as part of a comprehensive psychological assessment of adolescents seen for medical care following a suicide attempt. The evaluation is designed to tap a variety of psychological characteristics pertinent to adolescents who attempt suicide.

SUICIDAL IDEATION
This patient was administered the Suicide Ideation Questionnaire to assess the severity of suicidal thoughts. The scale contains 30 items, rated on a 7-point scale. This patient received a score of _____. Scores greater than 41 suggest significantly elevated suicidal ideation.

SUICIDE SPECIFIC
The patient was administered the Reasons for Overdose scale. The patient endorsed the following items that are checked below:

— Make people understand how desperate you were feeling
— Get relief from a terrible state of mind
— Escape for a while from an impossible situation
— Seek help from someone
— Find out whether or not someone really loved you
— Make people sorry for the way they have treated you; frighten or get someone back
— Try to influence some particular person or get them to change their mind
— Show how much you loved someone
— To die
— Other

(continues)

TABLE 1   (*continued*)

Name:
Date of Evaluation:

ANGER
Anger and angry behavior are often associated with suicidal behavior. This adolescent was administered the State Trait Anger Expression Inventory, which has community adolescent norms. Scores for three subscales were computed:

1. *Anger In*, which reflects personally directed anger including withdrawal and self-destructive behaviors.
2. *Anger Out*, which reflects the outward expression of hostility and anger.
3. *State Anger*, which reflects the level of anger at the time of administration.

Clinically significant subscales based on psychiatric norms are circled above, or none of the subscales was clinically elevated (circle one).

DEPRESSION
This patient was administered the Center for Epidemiologic Studies Depression Scale (CESD), which consists of 20 items designed to measure depressive symptoms in the general population. This patient received a score of _____. Scores of 23 or higher indicate a significant level of depressive symptoms.

HOPELESSNESS
On the Hopelessness Scale for Children, this patient received a score of _____, which falls in the following range: 6 and below (mild), 7 to 10 (moderate), 11 and above (severe). In surveys of high school students, typical teenagers obtain a score of 4 with a standard deviation of 3. The average suicide attempter receives a score of 7 with a standard deviation of 4. A Hopelessness Scale of 11 or above is considered very elevated for adolescents who attempt suicide.

SUBSTANCE USE
Two surveys related to substance abuse, the Adolescent Drinking Index (ADI) and the Adolescent Drinking Questionnaire (ADQ), were administered.
The Adolescent Drinking Index is a 24-item scale that measures the severity of drinking problems among adolescents. The following subscale scores are calculated for the ADI (percentages indicate the frequency of this patient's use compared to same-aged adolescents on each subscale):

1. Self-medicated drinking, which is an indicator of drinking to alter mood: _____%
2. Indicator of aggressive, rebellious behavior related to drinking: _____%

The total score of the ADI was _____. Scores of 16 or above indicate that further evaluation and possible treatment of substance use should be considered.
The Adolescent Drinking Questionnaire examines quantity and frequency of drinking behaviors. This adolescent's response indicates no drinking, a mild drinking pattern, a moderate drinking pattern, or a severe drinking pattern (circle one).

(*continues*)

TABLE 1   (*continued*)

Name:
Date of Evaluation:

PROBLEM SOLVING

This patient was administered the Social Problem Solving Inventory-Revised (SPSI-R). He/She received a total score of _____ on this measure, suggesting no/some/significant difficulties solving problems in his/her life.

In addition, the patient's problem-solving skills were assessed by having him/her respond to three standardized problem vignettes (Means End Problem Solving Measure). His/Her responses suggest:

COPING

The Kidcope was administered to the patient in order to examine his/her coping style. According to the responses, this patient most frequently uses the types of strategies circled below when dealing with life problems:

1. Distraction
2. Social withdrawal
3. Cognitive restructuring
4. Self-criticism
5. Blaming others
6. Problem solving
7. Emotional regulation
8. Wishful thinking
9. Social support
10. Resignation

SOCIAL SUPPORT

The patient was administered the Social Support Scale, which measures the general quality of social support with his/her closest friends.

On this scale, the patient reported a level of social support that is significantly lower than the normal range or within the normal range (circle one).

The Dysphoric Interpersonal Schema Scale is an 8-item scale that assesses adolescents' general expectations about how others will respond to them.

This adolescent's responses suggested that in general, he/she expects others to be emotionally supportive and concerned about his/her needs or not supportive or concerned about his/her needs (circle one).

OTHER SELF-HARM BEHAVIORS

The patient was administered the Functional Assessment of Self-Mutilation Scale. Within the past year the patient reportedly engaged in the following self-harm behaviors (circle all that apply):

— Cutting or carving on skin
— Burning skin
— Tattooing self

(*continues*)

TABLE 1   (*continued*)

Name:
Date of Evaluation:

— Scraping skin to draw blood
— Erasing skin to draw blood
— Hitting self
— Pulling out one's own hair
— Picking at a wound
— Inserting objects under skin or nails
— Biting self
— Picking areas of body to the point of drawing blood

On this scale the patient reported the following motivational reasons for performing the self-harm behaviors listed above (circle all that apply):

— To relieve feeling "numb" or empty
— To punish himself/herself
— To stop bad feelings
— To feel relaxed

PSYCHIATRIC DIAGNOSES280

The patient was administered the Diagnostic Interview Schedule for Children-Child version (DISC-C). This patient **self-reported** the following DSM-IV symptoms. Only the diagnoses listed below were assessed. Because patients were asked to self-report their symptoms, the reader is advised to interpret these results with caution and use clinical judgment.

MOOD DIOSRDERS ASSESSED

Major Depressive Episode: *Meets Full Dx*   _____

A 1.   Depressed/irritable mood   _____
A 2.   Anhedonia   _____
A 3.   Weight loss/gain   _____
A 4.   Sleep disturbance   _____
A 5.   Psychomotor agitation/retardation   _____
A 6.   Fatigue/loss of energy   _____
A 7.   Worthlessness/guilt   _____
A 8.   Poor concentration/indecisive   _____
A 9.   Death/suicide ideation/attempt   _____

PTSD: *Meets Full Dx*   _____

A 1.   Experienced trauma   _____
A 2.   Fearful response   _____
B.   Reexperiencing symptoms
        B 1.   Recurrent recollections   _____
        B 2.   Recurrent dreams   _____
        B 3.   Feeling as if event recurring   _____

(*continues*)

TABLE 1   *(continued)*

Name:
Date of Evaluation:

	B 4.	Psychological distress at cues	_____
	B 5.	Physiological distress at cues	_____
C.		Avoidance or "numbing" symptoms	
	C 1.	Avoids thoughts/feelings	_____
	C 2.	Avoids places/people	_____
	C 3.	Inability to recall details	_____
	C 4.	Less interest in activities	_____
	C 5.	Feels detachment from others	_____
	C 6.	Restricted range of affect	_____
	C 7.	Sense of foreshortened future	_____
D.		Hyperarousal symptoms	
	D 1.	Sleep disturbance	_____
	D 2.	Irritability/anger outbursts	_____
	D 3.	Difficulty concentrating	_____
	D 4.	Hypervigilance	_____
	D 5.	Exaggerated startle response	_____
E.		Duration of symptoms ≥ 1 month	_____

DISRUPTIVE BEHAVIOR DISORDERS ASSESSED

ODD: *Meets Full Dx Criteria*   _____

A 1.   Often loses temper   _____
A 2.   Argues with adults   _____
A 3.   Defies adult requests/rules   _____
A 4.   Deliberately annoys people   _____
A 5.   Blames others for own actions   _____
A 6.   Touchy/easily annoyed   _____
A 7.   Angry/resentful   _____
A 8.   Spiteful/vindictive   _____

CD: *Meets Full Dx Criteria*   _____

Aggression

A1.   Bullies/threatens others   _____
A2.   Initiates physical fights   _____
A3.   Has used a weapon   _____
A4.   Physically cruel to people   _____
A5.   Physically cruel to animals   _____
A6.   Stole while confronting victim   _____
A7.   Has forced sexual activity   _____

Property Destruction

A8.   Set fires with intent to damage   _____
A9.   Destroyed property   _____

(continues)

TABLE 1   (*continued*)

Name:
Date of Evaluation:

Theft/Deceitfulness
    A10. Broke into house/building/car   _____
    A11. Lies to obtain/avoid things   _____
    A12. Stole without confronting   _____
Violation of Rules
    A13. Stays out late at night   _____
    A14. Has run away from home   _____
    A15. Often truant from school   _____

SUBSTANCE-RELATED DISORDERS ASSESSED

Substance Abuse	Alcohol	Nicotine	Marijuana	Other
Meets Full Dx Criteria	_____	_____	_____	____
A1. Substance use interferes with roles	_____	_____	_____	____
A2. Substance use is physically hazardous	_____	_____	_____	____
A3. Substance-related legal problems	_____	_____	_____	____
A4. Continued use despite resulting probs	_____	_____	_____	____
B. Not substance dependence	_____	_____	_____	____

Substance Dependence	Alcohol	Nicotine	Marijuana	Other
Meets Full Dx Criteria	_____	_____	_____	____
A1. Tolerance	_____	_____	_____	____
A2. Withdrawal	_____	_____	_____	____
A3. Substance taken in larger dosage over time	_____	_____	_____	____
A4. Unsuccessful at cutting down	_____	_____	_____	____
A5. Sig. time spent in obtaining substance	_____	_____	_____	____
A6. Decrease in social/recreational activities	_____	_____	_____	____
A7. Continued use despite knowledge of problem	_____	_____	_____	____

FAMILY FUNCTIONING

On the Family Assessment Device (FAD), this patient was asked to answer questions regarding his/her family relationship. The FAD has 7 subscales, 2 of which were administered to this patient:

Problem solving
Global functioning

Those circled above indicate elevated scores, or neither of the subscales was elevated (circle one).

This child's parents also completed the:

Global functioning	Mother	Father
Problem solving	Mother	Father

The subscales that were clinically significant are circled above, or neither scale was clinically significant.

CASE 1: ADJUSTMENT DISORDER WITH DEPRESSED MOOD

Anne was a 16-year-old girl who was evaluated 24 hours after a suicide attempt that resulted in her admission to the pediatric floor of a general hospital. She made the suicide attempt by an overdose of a combination of prescription drugs and over-the-counter medications found in her medicine cabinet at home. With regard to suicide intent, Anne reported no premeditation and took only passive precautions against discovery (i.e., she threw away the pill bottles and went to her room after taking the pills). Anne wrote a suicide note in anticipation of death, which is atypical for adolescents who attempt suicide in response to an acute stressor. The suicide note was brief. Anne wrote that she did not feel that life was worth living because of the stressors she was experiencing at home with her mother and her boyfriend.

Upon interview, Anne described her current stressors as failing grades and a recent breakup with a boyfriend. The acute stressor was an argument with her mother following a minor motor vehicle crash in which Anne had dented her mother's car. Anne reported that her thoughts around the time of the attempt were mainly to escape the stressors that she was experiencing. She was ambivalent about living or dying. However, as reflected in her suicide note, she thought that she might die as a result of this overdose. At the same time, Anne perceived her attempt as reversible.

Other Relevant History

Anne reported never having made a previous suicide attempt and as having no prior contact with mental health professionals. She was living in an intact family with her biological parents and 13-year-old sister. Neither Anne's report nor her parents' report noted any family history of depressed mood, depression, or suicidal behavior. Anne reported a family history of alcohol abuse in maternal grandfather and mother. Anne reported occasional marijuana and alcohol use. With the exception of her recent breakup, her peer relationships were described as supportive and enjoyable. Anne reported several close girlfriends in whom she could confide. She described some family conflict regarding her parents' rules such as curfew.

Assessment Data

Anne was administered a standard battery designed to assess key emotional, behavioral, and cognitive factors related to suicide attempts. The results from Anne's scores on the Suicide Intent Scale (SIS) were compared to a sample of suicide attempters seen in our hospital (Spirito, Sterling, Donaldson, & Arrigan, 1996). Anne's total score on the SIS fell slightly below local norms for other suicide attempters. On the Suicide Ideation Questionnaire, Anne received a percentile score of 60, only slightly above normal for adolescent girls her age.

Anne was administered a self-report measure of depression, the Beck Depression Inventory (BDI). Her score on the BDI was in the moderate range of depression. Her score on the Hopelessness Scale for Children was in the average range for suicide attempters but above average for the general population of adolescents (Spirito, Williams, Stark, & Hart, 1988).

Anne's scores on the various subscales of the State-Trait Anger Expression Inventory (STAXI) were all within the normal range. Her scores did not suggest a particularly angry person, either in her outward expression of anger or in anger turned in upon herself, nor was she particularly angry at the time of the attempt. Family functioning, as assessed via the Family Assessment Device, revealed family problem solving within the normal range but found general functioning to be slightly above the clinical cutoff score.

Anne was also administered the computerized version of the Diagnostic Interview Scale for Children (C-DISC) designed to derive DSM diagnoses. Due to time constraints, Anne was selectively administered modules assessing the psychiatric diagnoses most commonly seen among adolescent suicide attempters: depression, conduct disorder, oppositional behavior, and substance use. Anne did not meet the criteria for any of these diagnoses. She endorsed the most symptoms on the mood disorders module.

Hospital Course and Disposition

By the second day of her admission to the pediatric hospital, Anne was medically cleared. At that time, Anne reported that she was sorry she had made the attempt and was glad to be alive. There was no continued suicidal ideation. When the rationale for continued treatment was presented to Anne, she demonstrated good insight and judgment around the treatment plan and was receptive to follow-up outpatient psychotherapy. Her parents were involved and supportive of the treatment plan. The home environment was assessed as adequate and supportive of the patient. In a family meeting during hospitalization, Anne's parents expressed concern for their daughter and asked appropriate questions in an effort to understand the motivation behind their daughter's suicide attempt. The parents admitted they did not recognize the signs of distress in their daughter that led to the suicide attempt and asked the clinician about signs of future risk. The acute conflict regarding the car crash was also resolved in this meeting. Anne was discharged to outpatient care.

Short-Term Outcome

At three-month follow up, Anne continued to live at home with her parents. She was attending school regularly, and her grades were improving somewhat. Anne reported minor conflicts with her parents and occasional alcohol and drug use, of which her parents were unaware. There was no evidence of any significant oppositional behavior at home. There was no report of further suicidal behavior following discharge. She had been engaged in weekly individual psychotherapy plus occasional family therapy, which Anne deemed as very helpful. Her parents also found the family sessions to be helpful.

Comments

Anne's presentation suggests an impulsive suicide attempt resulting from poor problem-solving in the context of background stressors and precipitated by an acute, common stressor: namely a fight with her mother over a minor car crash. Anne did not report elevated levels of suicide ideation in the weeks leading up to the attempt. She presented as depressed and hopeless but did not meet the criteria for a diagnosis of a mood disorder at the time of the evaluation. Family stressors and conflict were only slightly elevated. Medication treatment did not appear necessary in Anne's case. With the support of her family, Anne responded well to individual therapy and occasional family sessions.

CASE 2: MAJOR DEPRESSIVE DISORDER

Amy was a 13-year-old girl who was evaluated in the emergency department (ED) following a suicide attempt. Amy overdosed on 20 over-
the-counter medications. At the time of the evaluation, Amy reported that
she made the attempt on the spur of the moment, with no evidence of
premeditation detected. She made only very passive precautions against
discovery—that is, after taking the pills, she simply went to her room until
she felt somewhat nauseous then told her mother that she had taken pills.
Amy did not make any last acts in anticipation of death and reported that
the purpose of the attempt was to escape stressors she was experiencing.
Despite what appeared to be a medically insignificant means of attempt,
Amy reported that she wanted to die, and she viewed the act of taking
these over-the-counter medications as lethal. Although she thought
this overdose had the potential to kill her, she did perceive the overdose
as reversible and did not think there was a high probability that she
would die.

Amy reported that the stressor that led up to her suicide attempt was
an argument with her mother. Although reporting that she generally got
along well with her mother, Amy noted that they had been arguing more
lately. School difficulties in particular, along with Amy's irritability, had
resulted in increased conflict with her parents in recent months. Long-
term stressors included rejection by school peers and failing grades in
school.

Other Relevant History

Amy reported that she had made two other suicide attempts prior to this
overdose. Neither of these prior attempts resulted in medical treatment
or referral for counseling. Mother was only aware of one of these attempts
and did not view it as a serious suicidal act. Amy reported the presence
of suicide models in her environment, including high-school classmates
who had attempted suicide in the prior year. Amy also reported engaging in a significant number of risky behaviors, some of which had resulted
in injury. She had no prior contact with mental health professionals. She
was living with her biological parents and her 15-year-old sister. There
was a family history of depression in her father and paternal grandmother.
Amy reported a long history of peer difficulties and rejection that resulted
in limited peer contact outside of school.

Assessment Data

Amy was administered a battery of assessment measures. On the Suicide Intent Scale, Amy's score was above the norm for other suicide attempters. The fact that she made only passive precautions against discovery, that she wanted to die, and that she viewed the overdose as potentially lethal contributed to this elevated score. Her score on the Suicide Ideation Questionnaire was in the 85th percentile for female adolescents her age. This suggests that Amy was experiencing a very high level of suicide ideation in the months preceding the suicide attempt compared to normals.

Most striking was Amy's depressed mood. On the Center for Epidemiologic Studies—Depression Scale (CES-D), Amy obtained a score in the severe range of depression. A sufficient number of symptoms of depression were endorsed on the C-DISC for Amy to meet the criteria for a major depressive episode, including dysphoric mood and irritability, sleep disturbance, appetite disturbance, psychomotor retardation, fatigue and loss of energy, worthlessness, and suicidal ideation. Amy did not meet criteria for any other C-DISC diagnosis. Amy's score on the Hopelessness Scale for Children was more than two standard deviations above the mean for other suicide attempters. Amy's scores on measures of anger (STAXI) and anxiety (Revised Children's Manifest Anxiety Scale) were within the normal range. Her scores on a measure of substance use (Adolescent Drinking Inventory) were within the normal limits. Neither Amy nor her parents reported a significant history of behavior problems or substance use/abuse. Amy's scores on the Family Assessment Device were within the normal range. However, on interview both Amy and her parents reported recent stress and tension between them, often due to Amy's irritability and sullenness.

Disposition

At the end of the evaluation in the ED, which was approximately 5 hours following her admission and more than 10 hours since she had taken the pills, Amy remained quite depressed. Most significantly, she continued to express a wish to be dead. She said she did not feel safe at home, nor could Amy guarantee that she wouldn't attempt suicide again. Similarly, when asked how she would handle any future stressors that might result in suicidal ideation, Amy was not able to report any adaptive coping strategies and at one point said that she might attempt by a more lethal method. Given these concerns, an inpatient psychiatric hospitalization was recommended. Both Amy and her parents were receptive to this plan, and Amy demonstrated good insight and judgment regarding the need for hospitalization.

Short-term Outcome

Amy was admitted to a child psychiatric unit. Despite her willingness to receive inpatient psychiatric care, she became distressed about the hospitalization after several days and left against medical advice. She did follow through with outpatient psychotherapy as well as medication treatment for depression. Nonetheless, within a month she was rehospitalized at a different psychiatric hospital due to continued suicidal ideation and risk of self-harm. During the second hospitalization, which proved more useful to Amy, her antidepressant medication dosage was increased. By 3-month follow-up, Amy's mood had improved significantly. Her overall functioning had also improved, particularly in regard to school performance. She had renewed interest in many of her previously enjoyable activities and had become positively involved with some same-age peers. Amy continued to have weekly psychotherapy, and her medications were closely monitored. There were no reattempts following the second hospitalization for suicidal ideation.

Comments

Although Amy's suicide attempt circumstances were similar to Anne's (Case 1), her history and assessment data were different. Amy's presentation reflects an adolescent with undiagnosed major depression. Her suicidal behavior appeared to result from an interpersonal stressor that amplified her depressive symptoms, including cognitive distortions with suicidal thinking. Amy's depressive episodes may have been biologically based, as reflected in her vegetative symptoms at the time of diagnosis and family history of depression on her father's side of the family. Her initial difficult course following the suicide attempt may reflect the latency between treatment initiation, both psychotherapy and psychotropic medication, and therapeutic response. Her functioning seemed to improve significantly when Amy's antidepressant medication was increased and in turn she probably began to use her psychotherapy sessions more productively.

CASE 3: COMORBID DISRUPTIVE BEHAVIOR DISORDER AND SUBSTANCE USE DISORDER

Allison was a 13-year-old girl who was evaluated one day after a suicide attempt, which resulted in her admission to a pediatric ward of a general hospital. The suicide attempt consisted of an overdose of over-the-counter medications and superficial wrist cutting. With regard to suicidal intent, Allison reported that she made the attempt without premeditation. She did not take any precautions against discovery. Allison did leave a suicide note that left instructions to her family and friends about what to do with her things. Allison reported that the purpose of attempt was to change the environment around her. She did not really want to die, although she perceived her actions, particularly the wrist cutting, as lethal and thought that she would probably die unless she received medical attention.

Allison reported that the acute stressor that led to the suicide attempt was an argument with her mother over her mother's plan to place her in a group home. These actions were the result of a 6-month period of conflict at home due to conduct problems, which included fighting, stealing, alcohol abuse, consistent breaking of curfew, and running away from home.

Other Relevant History

Allison reported, and her mother confirmed, a history of prior suicide attempts, most not medically serious, over the prior year. She endorsed a significant history of self-mutilation, including cutting and burning, on the Functional Assessment of Self-Mutilation scale. Allison lived at home with her mother and a younger brother. She had no contact with her biological father who left the family when she was quite young. Allison also had a history of sexual abuse, which occurred when she was a young child at the hands of a relative. There was a family history of polysubstance abuse in the father and depression in the mother. The mother reported that she had made a suicide attempt when she was 16 years old. Allison reported that a close friend of hers attempted suicide 2 months prior to her suicide attempt and that she knew of a number of friends and acquaintances who discussed suicide attempts and some who had attempted suicide. Allison had a history of short-lived treatment by mental health professionals. Her peer group was composed of teenagers with significant legal and social difficulties as well as substance abuse histories.

Assessment data

Allison was administered a battery of assessment measures. On the Suicide Intent Scale, Allison achieved a score slightly below the norm for other suicide attempters. On the Suicide Ideation Questionnaire, she obtained a score of 83, which is high for the normal population but in the medium range for other adolescent suicide attempters.

On the CES-D, her score approached the clinical cutoff score for depression but did not exceed it. On interview, Allison's reported symptoms did not meet the diagnostic criteria for depressive episode. Similarly, on the C-DISC, she did not meet criteria for depression, although she reported several symptoms consistent with depressed mood including irritability and psychomotor agitation.

With regard to other diagnoses measured by the C-DISC, Allison obtained scores that met the criteria for the diagnoses oppositional defiant disorder and conduct disorder. She also met the criteria for alcohol abuse. She reported regular use of alcohol and marijuana and experimentation with other drugs. Her scores on the STAXI indicated very high levels of externalized anger as well as low levels of anger control. Despite the fact that she did not report being depressed, on the Hopelessness Scale for Children, Allison obtained a score of 12, which indicates a significant degree of hopelessness about the future.

On the Family Assessment Device, Allison was administered three subscales. Her score was in the nonclinical range on the communication subscale. However, her scores on the problem-solving and general functioning scales met the clinical cutoffs and indicated significant family dysfunction.

Disposition

While hospitalized, Allison's behavior was difficult with nursing staff. She was often uncooperative and nonresponsive to requests regarding her routine care. Her interactions with her mother were also conflictual. She was minimally cooperative with interviews by the attending psychiatrist. She did not report continued suicidal ideation but did report wanting to run away and was considered a risk for elopement. Because she was not at imminent risk for suicidal behavior, the treatment plan was to arrange for Allison to be transferred to the group home that had been awaiting her placement prior to the suicide attempt. Arrangements were made for an outside agency to conduct psychotherapy with Allison while living at the group home.

Short-Term Outcome

Allison transitioned to the group home reasonably well. However, as more and more limits were set on her behavior in the group home, she had more difficulty adjusting to these demands. After about 2 weeks she began to threaten to harm herself unless she was removed from the group home. Although the group home attempted to deal with this manipulative behavior, they were not equipped to handle suicidal adolescents. Thus, Allison was discharged from the group home and sent home to live with her mother after 3 weeks. When she returned home, there continued to be a conflict between Allison and her mother. There were also questions regarding level of parental monitoring and supervision of Allison's behavior. Allison's mother admitted that it was difficult for her to enforce limits on Allison, and for that reason she did not set even basic curfews or other rules for Allison.

Allison did return to school and was attending school regularly, although her grades were rather poor. She did not receive any follow-up treatment subsequent to her discharge from the group home. Conflict with mother gradually increased, and by her second month at home, Allison had run away. When she returned home after 5 days, the conflict continued, and Allison made another suicide attempt, which did not result in medical care or further psychiatric follow-up treatment. Allison reported continued suicidal ideation and distress at her circumstances at home. She admitted to being negatively influenced by her peer group, and Allison had joined a gang and become involved in fighting and other risky behaviors. She also reported continued substance abuse, as well as depressed mood.

Comments

Allison's suicide attempt circumstances are similar to both Anne's and Amy's circumstances. In all three cases, a recent fight with their mothers was the acute precipitant to the suicide attempt. However, in Allison's case, the mother-daughter conflict represented significantly more dysfunction in the family. Conduct disorder and substance abuse were accompanied by significant family conflict. The problems that adolescents with conduct and substance abuse disorder encounter may result in depressed mood and in turn suicidal behavior. Sometimes, as in the case of Allison, the depression is not severe, but hope for the future is impaired, which may result in suicidal behavior. The acting-out behaviors displayed by these adolescents make them very difficult to treat, and such adolescents often receive inadequate treatment as they move back and forth between the mental health and legal systems.

CONCLUSION

Based on our clinical experience, we have found it helpful to classify adolescent suicide attempters into one of three subtypes. The first subtype is seen in adolescents who meet criteria for an adjustment disorder most often with depressed mood. Often, these adolescents are reacting to a recent stressor and become overwhelmed by their current problems. The suicidal behavior can range from minor to quite lethal, but all cases should be treated with caution. It is important to avoid blaming the adolescent or minimizing the suicide risk. Even when an adolescent attempts suicide using a nonlethal method, the suicidal act may not reflect the intensity of the adolescent's emotional pain. Fortunately, adolescents with an adjustment disorder are likely to recover quickly. Short-term treatment can help address psychological, interpersonal, and family problems that may have preceded the suicidal act. Follow-up care is helpful but may not need to be overly intensive or prolonged. A medication evaluation is advisable, but psychotropic medication may not be necessary in many cases.

The second subtype reflects adolescent suicide attempters who meet criteria for major depression. These adolescents need a thorough diagnostic evaluation and often inpatient treatment. Major depression may cause impairments in the adolescent's ability to meet daily responsibilities. The suicidal act reflects the desperation and pain that the adolescent is experiencing but is typically triggered by a relatively benign everyday stressor, such as conflict with a parent. Furthermore, many adolescents delay seeking treatment for their depression. By the time they meet with a mental health professional, the depression may have been present for several months. As the depression continues and coping efforts have failed, pessimism and hopelessness are likely to increase. Suicidal adolescents who are diagnosed with major depression will need much more intensive treatment. Psychotherapy can be provided on an inpatient basis and should continue on an outpatient basis. Psychotherapy sessions should target maladaptive coping skills, inadequate problem-solving skills, impaired family functioning, and other areas relevant to the adolescent's needs. Medication is often indicated for these adolescents.

The third subtype is seen in adolescent suicide attempters who present with depression and comorbid disruptive behavior and substance use. In many adolescents, depressed mood is often evident, although this was not so in Allison's case. The adolescents may become suicidal as part of an impulsive reaction to situational problems. Adolescents with conduct disorder or oppositional disorder create frequent conflict with adults. These disruptive tendencies can make psychotherapy more difficult as well. Family involvement will be crucial, but it is difficult to maintain these families in treatment.

The proposed subtypes appear to have clinical utility for understanding the most suicidal behavior in adolescents. This simple classification scheme can help guide the frontline clinician during the triage assessment and initial treatment planning. These three subtypes display different patterns over time. An appreciation of this typology can help clinicians understand the prognosis for different suicide attempters and guide the treatment that will be needed.

REFERENCES

CDC. (1998). Youth-risk behavior surveillance—United States, 1997. *Morbidity and Mortality Weekly Report, 47*, 239–291.

Spirito, A., Sterling, C., Donaldson, D., & Arrigan, M. (1996). Factor analysis of the Suicide Intent Scale with adolescent suicide attempters. *Journal of Personality Assessment, 67*, 90–101.

Spirito, A., Williams, C., Stark, L. J., & Hart, K. (1988). The Hopelessness Scale for Children: Psychometric properties and clinical utility with normal and emotionally disturbed adolescents. *Journal of Abnormal Child Psychology, 16*, 445–458.

CHAPTER 14

Treatment of Adolescent Suicide Attempters

Deidre Donaldson, Anthony Spirito, and James Overholser

The treatment outcome literature on adolescent suicidal behavior is very small. Consequently, there are limited empirical guidelines regarding appropriate treatment for adolescents who have attempted suicide. Managing and treating adolescent suicidal behavior is often anxiety-provoking for clinicians, and the lack of empirical guidelines in this area further compromises the availability of effective treatments for this high-risk group. As in the adult literature, there have been two major approaches to psychotherapy with adolescent suicide attempters: treating the underlying diagnostic condition (e.g., depression; Brent *et al.*, 1997) and addressing the suicidal behavior directly. Although efficacious treatment for the underlying disorder is important, it does not necessarily reduce suicidality (Brent *et al.*, 1997; Harrington *et al.*, 1998). Therefore, this chapter reviews the outcome studies conducted to date and emphasizes the treatment outcome studies and clinical approaches specifically designed for suicidal behavior. Both nonrandomized and randomized trials are included. Clinical guidelines for treating adolescents who have attempted suicide are suggested, drawing on the current literature. The chapter focuses on outpatient treatment protocols, although many of the brief treatment approaches are applicable to inpatient settings. Because no outcome studies of pharmacologic treatments specifically for suicidal behavior have been reported, medication trials are not discussed here.

REVIEW OF TREATMENT OUTCOME STUDIES

Nonrandomized Trials

Several nonrandomized studies have been reported, covering a range of treatment modalities. For example, Ottino (1999) described a short-term, intensive, psychoanalytically-oriented inpatient crisis intervention for adolescent and young adult suicide attempters but did not empirically test it. Pillay and Waasenaar (1995) described a naturalistic study of 40 Indian adolescent suicide attempters in South Africa who received four or five psychotherapy sessions in the community following a suicide attempt compared to a group of adolescents who did not comply with treatment. The type of psychotherapy was not specified. At the time of the 6-month follow-up, hopelessness and psychiatric symptoms had improved significantly in the teens that received treatment compared to teens who did not receive treatment.

Miller, Rathus, Linehan, Wetzler, and Leigh (1997) adapted Linehan's (1993) dialectical behavior therapy (DBT) to be used with suicidal adolescents, including suicide attempters. DBT involves the use of both individual and group therapy modalities to teach problem-solving strategies. The focus of DBT is to improve distress tolerance, emotional regulation, and interpersonal effectiveness. For adolescents, an adult relative participates in the group sessions to model and reinforce positive behaviors at home. The length of treatment was reduced in this adolescent version to cover fewer skills in a simpler format and presentation style. Miller *et al.* (1997) reported that rates of psychiatric hospitalizations decreased and treatment completion improved for adolescents receiving this approach compared to a group of adolescents who received standard care.

Another cognitive-behavioral program (interpersonal problem-solving skills training) included some adolescent suicide attempters in their sample (McLeavey, Daly, Ludgate, & Murray, 1994). In this study, a problem-solving treatment program was compared to a "problem-oriented" control group in which problems were discussed and crises resolved, but patients were not taught specific skills. The group that received the problem-solving treatment (four to six sessions) was significantly better at problem solving and coping at 1-year follow-up than the brief problem-oriented group. There were no differences between the two groups in the level of hopelessness reported. The rate of repeat suicide attempts was lower in the problem-solving group (10.5% versus 25%), but this difference was not statistically significant.

Group therapy has been suggested for use with adolescent suicide attempters. Ross and Motto (1984) conducted a 35-session therapy group with 10 adolescent suicide attempters and 7 suicide ideators. Results showed that none of the adolescents had reattempted or completed suicide within a 2-year period. The major issues addressed in the group sessions included family and peer relationships as well as the management of impulses and negative affect. Aronson and Scheidlinger (1995) described a 12-week psychodynamic group treatment with adolescents who were admitted to an inpatient psychiatric unit following a suicide attempt. Treatment components included problem sharing, male-female co-therapists to provide a "corrective" therapeutic experience, opportunities for peer and therapist feedback about coping patterns, social skills, or dysfunctional cognitions. Unfortunately, no outcome data were reported. Lewinsohn, Rohde, and Seeley (1996) provided a cognitive-behavioral group treatment program for depression for two groups of adolescents: depressed adolescents with a history of suicide attempts and depressed, nonsuicidal adolescents. At the time of the follow-up, both groups had improved, and the suicidal and nonsuicidal depressed adolescents did not differ on measures of depression. However, the investigators did not report on measures of suicidality.

Because of the importance of family factors during adolescence, several family-focused interventions have been examined. A highly structured, six-session outpatient family therapy program called "SNAP" (Successful Negotiation/Acting Positively) reframes the suicide attempt and subsequent family problems in a more positive and less blaming context by focusing attention on the situation rather than on the adolescent attempter. Such reframing can help to defuse a potentially explosive situation. Families are taught problem-solving skills, and then they repeatedly practice solving problems with the help of role-playing, modeling, and feedback. They are also taught new coping and negotiating skills, active listening techniques, and strategies for managing affective arousal (Rotheram-Borus, Piacentini, Miller, Graae, & Castro-Blanco, 1994). Simple strategies such as "feeling thermometers" are used to rate individual level of affective arousal (ranging from *0* for no discomfort to *100* for most discomfort). Preliminary findings indicated that SNAP reduced overall symptom levels among 140 female minority adolescent suicide attempters (Piacentini, Rotheram-Borus, & Cantwell, 1995; Rotheram-Borus *et al.*, 1994).

Many suicidal teens have nuclear families that are isolated from their extended families, have few supportive resources, and sometimes feel powerless to respond to adolescent crises (Gutstein & Rudd, 1990). In an effort to address this situation, Gutstein and Rudd (1990) developed the Systemic Crisis Intervention Program (SCIP) to mobilize and reconfigure the family's kinship network. SCIP crisis teams assemble extended family and friends and meet with them in one or two 4-hour sessions designed to encourage greater cohesion in the kinship network and to begin reconciliation among estranged members. Youth who received the SCIP intervention included attempters in addition to suicidal adolescents who had not attempted. Significant improvements on measures of behavior and family functioning at 1-year follow-up were reported (Gutstein & Rudd, 1990).

Greenfield, Hechtman, and Tremblay (1995) used an outpatient crisis team to follow adolescents seen in an emergency department for a psychiatric crisis. Most of the crises (75%) were due to suicidal behavior, some of which were suicide attempts. The crisis team, which consisted of a clinical nurse specialist and child psychiatrist, conducted a family-focused interview followed by crisis sessions. The number and type of crisis sessions varied according to the clinician's judgment regarding necessity for further treatment. After the crisis was resolved, the patients were referred to community services. This crisis service resulted in a 16% reduction in future hospitalizations, although data specific to suicide attempters were not presented.

Randomized Trials

The use of randomized clinical trials allows for a more sophisticated examination of treatment effects, often controlling for treatment-as-usual, spontaneous remission, and placebo effects. Only three empirical studies of treatments for adolescent suicide attempters are known to have been reported. Rudd and colleagues (1996) devised an experimental program for older adolescents and young adults in a day treatment program who had attempted suicide. Treatment included psychoeducation, problem solving, and traditional experiential-affective techniques. The experimental program resulted in improvements in suicidal ideation and behavior, but the comparison group, which received standard care in the community, had comparable improvement with no difference between groups. Thus, the experimental treatment did not add to the observed benefits beyond the effects obtained from standard treatment.

Harrington and colleagues (1998) provided treatment to 162 adolescents who had attempted suicide by overdose. Patients were randomly assigned to either routine care or routine care plus a four-session home-based family intervention. The family sessions focused on discussion of the suicide attempt, communication in the family, problem solving, and discussion of adolescent developmental issues. The additional home-based intervention resulted in reduced suicidal ideation at 6-month follow-up, but only for adolescents with no major depression. There were no differences in the rate of suicide reattempts. The authors concluded that easy access to treatments is no guarantee of its effectiveness. In further analyses, Harrington *et al.* (2000) examined potential mediators of the family intervention. Improvement in the nondepressed adolescents was not related to changes in family functioning, nor hopelessness, depression, or adolescent problem solving. Harrington *et al.* (2000) suggested that long-term interventions might be necessary to change family functioning.

Cotgrove, Zirinsky, Black, and Weston (1995) provided treatment to adolescent suicide attempters seen in a general hospital. Patients were assigned to either an experimental treatment or standard care in the community. As part of the experimental treatment, patients were given a "green card," allowing them immediate readmission to the hospital if feeling suicidal. Over the course of the next year, 11% of the experimental group used the green card for readmission to the hospital. At 1-year follow-up, only 6% of the 47 adolescents in the experimental group made a repeat suicide attempt. In the comparison group of 58 adolescents who received standard care in the community, 12% made a repeat attempt.

Summary of Treatment Literature

Several treatment modalities have been proposed for use with suicidal adolescents. Results of nonrandomized trials suggest that individual, group, and family treatments may be applicable to adolescent suicide attempters. However, only three treatments for adolescents who have attempted suicide have undergone empirical evaluation. No randomized studies have compared the efficacy of specific treatment modalities or outcome changes (e.g., cognitive-behavioral versus family). All three randomized studies that have been conducted have investigated individual treatment approaches only. Randomized trials of home-based, comprehensive day-treatment programs and randomized controlled trials with adolescent suicide attempters need to clearly describe participant characteristics because adolescent suicide attempters are known to be a heterogeneous group. Research has also begun to differentiate subgroups within this population (e.g., by diagnostic group, number of attempts, adolescents who attempt versus ideate). Unfortunately, we currently do not know which therapy approaches work best for which subgroups of adolescent suicide attempters, the process of change in suicide attempters who improve with treatment, or the stability of improvements over time (Rudd & Joiner, 1998).

CLINICAL APPLICATIONS

Interventions for adolescent suicide attempters have not been well studied. The findings from the randomized trials are modest at best. Nonetheless, practice guidelines based on a combination of the empirical literature and clinical impressions are necessary until more definitive recommendations based on empirical studies are available. Such guidelines, based on those recommended by the American Academy of Child and Adolescent Psychiatry (Shaffer & Pfeffer, in press), are reviewed next.

Post-Attempt Crisis Management

The acute crisis surrounding a suicide attempt includes numerous stressful events that occur several weeks prior to the suicidal act as well as several weeks following the attempt. During this crisis period, the adolescent's personal and social resources are usually drained. The suicidal adolescents and their families are often overwhelmed by external stressors and internal distress. The turmoil and distress disrupt the adolescent's ability to process information and solve problems (Berman & Jobes, 1991). The first goal of therapy is to prevent further suicidal behavior. The therapist must conduct frequent evaluations of suicidal intent (both verbal and nonverbal indicators), continued assessment of access to available means, negotiation (and renegotiation) of a verbal no-suicide contract, and the availability of 24-hour emergency backup services. The therapist must be available as needed and ensure that the adolescent is not socially isolated, either from peers or from family. Clinicians should educate family members regarding the adolescent's suicidal behavior and instruct parents to increase their level of supervision, take all suicidal statements seriously, and restrict access to potentially lethal means, including both prescription and nonprescription medication, firearms or other weapons, toxic household chemicals, and motor vehicles (Berman & Jobes, 1991; Blumenthal & Kupfer, 1986; Brent & Kolko, 1990; Freeman & Reinecke, 1993; Pfeffer, 1990).

When evaluating the negative emotions seen in most suicide attempters, clinicians typically look for and find high levels of depression. However, the emotional distress often includes feelings of hopelessness and anger. Hopelessness and anger should be closely monitored, because these characteristics have been closely linked to suicidal behavior among adolescents. Throughout this assessment, it is important for the therapist to work to understand the emotional pain that is experienced by the adolescent during and after a suicidal crisis. Empathic caring will be essential for building an effective therapeutic alliance.

While managing the crisis, the therapist must establish a working alliance with the adolescent in order to both reduce the risk of further suicidal behavior and maintain the adolescent in treatment (Berman & Jobes, 1991). It is important to elicit the reasons for the suicide attempt. Although some clinicians and most families assume that adolescent suicide attempts often reflect a misguided effort to gain attention, most adolescents report that their suicide attempt was motivated by a wish to die or escape from an intolerable situation (Boergers, Spirito, & Donaldson, 1998). By identifying and better defining the problem, the therapist can appreciate the adolescent's purpose for the attempt and together, therapist and client can begin generating other solutions to future problems instead of resorting to suicidal behavior (Berman & Jobes, 1991).

When working with suicidal adolescents and their families, we have found it helpful to reframe the suicide attempt as a failure in problem solving. Quite often an interpersonal problem acts as a precipitant of the attempt. When discussing the precipitant to the suicidal act, adolescents often display difficulties generating effective coping options and list few alternatives to the suicidal behavior. Even when suicidal adolescents can identify several coping options, they usually anticipate a poor outcome from the responses that are seen as under their control. This pessimism may reflect cognitive distortions, hopelessness, and a negative attributional style. We often summarize the experience using the following types of statements:

"So basically, you felt stuck and decided that the only way you could see to get out of that situation was to hurt yourself. You couldn't think of anything else to do that you thought would be helpful. So you thought you'd solve the problem by escaping it or hurting yourself. What we're going to work on here is how to get yourself 'unstuck' without having to hurt yourself. We're going to talk about problem solving to help get you out of some of those difficult times, and we're also going to teach you some strategies that you can do that help people feel less sad or mad—strategies that can help you when you are feeling the way you did before you hurt yourself."

This conceptualization often helps adolescents and parents feel less blamed or guilty for the attempt. Also, clients may begin to feel more hopeful that something can be done in treatment to prevent future suicide attempts. In addition, Berman and Jobes (1991) have recommended that treatment structuring (i.e., defining short- and long-term goals, the structure of sessions, the number of sessions anticipated, and the process of therapy sessions) be addressed in the crisis or initial phase of treatment because these are likely to improve treatment adherence. Thus, the therapist can work to build an honest relationship with the adolescent by trying to understand the adolescent's recent life problems, the unsuccessful efforts to cope with a difficult situation, and the painful emotions that arise.

Treatment Approaches

After the acute crisis has passed, the exact nature of therapy will vary according to the adolescent's presenting problems, the theoretical approach of the therapist, and the adolescent's preliminary reactions to therapy. Nonetheless, there are a number of principles of psychotherapy with suicidal adolescents that should be observed irrespective of the treatment approach that is utilized. These principles include maintaining an empathic but objective view of the suicidal adolescent and working to thoroughly understand the motives behind the attempt (Blumenthal & Kupfer, 1986). Pfeffer (1990) discussed the need to examine morbid fantasies of death, loss, rejection, and punishment; longing to be with an absent but supportive person; and feelings of alienation from a peer group or family members, which often results in oppositional behavior. Understanding the emotions that accompanied the suicidal behavior helps point the therapist to the specific therapy techniques that could help the adolescent generate more effective ways of coping with life stressors and additional suicidal feelings that may arise in the future.

Rudd and Joiner (1998) describe the next phase of treatment after crisis management as one designed to improve the specific skills that have been found to be problematic in an individual adolescent. For example, therapy may focus on cultivating problem solving, affect management, and impulse control. In this phase of treatment, the goal is to instruct or refine the adolescent's basic coping skills. Most of the therapeutic techniques specifically for suicidal adolescents have been developed for this middle phase of therapy, and several are reviewed next.

Cognitive Therapy

Of the treatment approaches that address suicidal behavior directly, cognitive therapy is frequently advocated because it is highly structured and can address the cognitive distortions that are common among suicide attempters. Occasional booster sessions can be easily incorporated and allow continued contact with the therapist. Similarly, Pfeffer (1990) noted that a cognitive orientation in psychotherapy is useful in the management of impulsive behaviors and confronting biased perceptions of life stress.

Therapists often ask adolescents to monitor the thoughts that lead to angry or depressed moods because both moods can result in suicidal ideation or behavior. Rudd (2000) has outlined the fundamental assumptions of cognitive therapy for suicidal persons. First, suicidality is assumed to stem from maladaptive self-statements regarding one's self, the environment, and the future. These cognitions are described as the suicidal belief system. Second, the relationship between the suicidal belief system and the other psychological/biological systems is interactive and interdependent. Third, although the suicidal belief system varies from individual to individual, hopelessness is a central characteristic of the belief system. Hopelessness in turn consists of three core belief categories (unlovability, helplessness, and poor distress tolerance). Fourth, cognitive vulnerabilities (faulty cognitive constructions) predispose individuals to suicidality, but these vulnerabilities may be different based on underlying syndromes. Fifth, the suicidal belief system exists at the person's core (automatic) conscious and unconscious (metacognitive) levels, but the conscious level is most amenable to change.

Cognitive approaches have incorporated a number of techniques specifically useful for suicidal persons (Freeman & Reinecke, 1993). These include reattribution of blame for the suicide precipitants, "decatastro-phizing," making a list of pros and cons in regard to the circumstances precipitating the suicidal behavior, listing options and alternatives, "scaling" the severity of the events (e.g., from 1 to 100) to prevent the adolescent from conceptualizing everything as "black or white," and thought stopping. Examples are described next.

Questioning of evidence. Suicide attempters often selectively attend to a particular set of evidence that confirms their negative interpretation. In this technique, the therapist helps the adolescent question the evidence that is used to support a negative view. Socratic questions can be useful during this aspect of therapy (Overholser, 1993).

Reattribution. In this technique, the therapist tries to help the adoles-cent change the self-statement "It's all my fault" to a new statement in which responsibility is distributed appropriately, perhaps to friends or parents, chance factors, or negative mood states. The therapist may ini-tially support the adolescent's view that it is his or her fault but then sug-gests it might be worthwhile to look more closely at what the patient contributes to the situation and what other people contribute.

Examination of options and alternatives. In this technique, the therapist agrees with the adolescent that suicide is an option but helps the adoles-cent generate other options. Schneidman (1985) described the use of this technique with a suicidal young adult who was pregnant. After agreeing that suicide is an option to her dilemma, Schneidman had the patient write a list of alternatives without regard to their feasibility (have an abor-tion, put the child up for adoption, raise the child on her own, etc.). Then he had the young woman rank-order the options from the least onerous to most onerous. Although she commented negatively on the options, this procedure helped her to see that there were other options besides suicide and to no longer rank suicide first or second.

Decatastrophizing. In this approach, the therapist helps the adolescent decide whether he or she is overestimating the catastrophic nature of the precipitating event. Questions such as "What would be the worst thing that will arise if _____ occurs?" "If _____ does occur, how will it affect your life in 3 month, 6 months?" "What is the most likely thing to happen here?" "How will you handle it?"

Pros and cons. In this technique, the adolescent is asked to list advan-tages and disadvantages of different options. For example, therapist and client may examine the pros and cons of ending a romantic relationship. It can be useful to create a list of pros and cons because most adolescent suicide attempters view the world in black and white terms and don't typically view issues from both sides.

Scaling the severity of an event. By asking an adolescent suicide attempter to scale the suicidal precipitant or anticipated future stressful events (e.g., on a scale from 0 to 100), the adolescent must view events on a continuum. Scaling the severity of an event provides another useful way to have adolescents not view situations in a dichotomous fashion.

The reader is referred to Trautman (1995) and Overholser and Spirito (1990) for overviews of additional techniques that can be used in a cognitive behavioral treatment protocol with adolescent suicide attempters. The literature on suicidal adolescents consistently shows that this population has significant difficulty in two primary skill areas compared to other same-age peers (even nonattempters with other psychiatric problems): problem solving and affect management.

The deficits in problem solving include limited flexibility, difficulty generating alternative solutions, and limited ability to identify positive consequences of potential solutions. Although there are several different approaches to problem-solving training (e.g., Brent & Kolko, 1990), we developed the "SOLVE" system, described next, which covers the basic steps and has been easily implemented with adolescent suicide attempters. This verbal description is extracted from our treatment manual:

> "We're going to review with you a method for solving problems. We call it the 'S-O-L-V-E system.' Each letter in the word "SOLVE" stands for a different step of the problem-solving process. As you can see on the card, "S" stands for "Select a problem." The first step in solving a problem is to identify what the problem is. The second step is "O" or "Options." After you identify the problem, you need to make a list of ALL of the possible options—not just the ones you think would work. The bigger the list you make, the better the chance you have of solving the problem! The next step in the problem-solving process is "L" or "Likely Outcomes." You need to take the list you made up and decide what might happen when you try each of these "Options." You can rate them in terms of whether you think things would get better or worse with each "Option." Then, you would narrow down your list to one "Option" and pick the "Very Best One" to do. Then you try it out, and at the end, you "Evaluate" or decide whether or not the problem still exists. If it does, you go back to your "Options," weigh them out, and pick the next "Very Best One" to try. You keep doing this until your problem is solved. (Adolescent repeats the steps.) Let's try it."

After problem-solving skills are successfully taught, treatment can address the problems that precipitated the suicide attempt and other subsequent problems using the same system. Often, the adolescent will have initial difficulties generating options. The therapist may need to model the skills in order to help the adolescent learn these new behaviors. Similarly, cognitive distortions may be elicited during "Likely Outcomes" that can then be addressed. An example of utilizing the SOLVE system with a suicide attempt precipitant is as follows:

> *"Think of a problem that brought you here. What was that?"*
>
> *"That's great. You've accomplished the first step in solving a problem, which is to identify what the problem is. Do you remember the second step? (Prompt: "What does it start with? What does 'O' stand for?")*
>
> *"That's right. You need to think of as many things that a person faced with that problem could possibly do in that situation. That includes options you think would work as well as options you don't think would work so well."*

Wait for the adolescent to generate as many options as he or she can, then prompt for more by saying,

> *"You've thought of some already. Keep listing as many as you possibly can."*

When they stop again state,

> *"Great! You actually made me think of one."*

Share another example with the adolescent, being careful to indicate which option you generated versus those that were generated by the patient. Some adolescents will only generate options that they perceive to be workable solutions (a short list). The therapist can prompt the adolescent to generate a minimum of at least two strategies they think would work as well as two strategies they think might not work very well.

> *"You generated several 'Options.' What is the next step?" (Prompt: "What does it start with? What does 'L' stand for?")*
>
> *"That's right. Now you need to weigh each 'Option' and decide whether you think it would or would not be a helpful option. Let's take the first 'Option' you listed (state that here). Do you think this is something that would or would not help in that situation? Rate each one +, −, +/− depending upon how helpful you expect it to be."*
>
> *"What's the next step of solving the problem?" (Prompt: "What does it start with? What does V stand for?")*
>
> *"That's right. You have to pick the 'Very Best One' to do from your list of 'Options.' Which would you pick?"*

When the adolescent responds, ask,

"What is the last step of problem solving?" (Prompt: What does it start with? "What does E stand for?")

"Yes, 'Evaluate' or go back and see how it turned out. If your problem still exists, then you need to go back to your list of 'Options' and pick a different one. If your problem is solved, then you don't have to do anything."

The clinician can also illustrate the attempt as a failure in problem solving using the system:

"What would happen if you only had one option listed and you tried that and it didn't help your problem?"

Cover up all but one option of the list he or she generated and wait for a response.

"Yes. You'd be stuck. That's kind of like what happened when you hurt yourself. You didn't feel like you had many options, you felt pretty stuck, so you picked the only option you thought you had, which was to hurt yourself. That's why we've found 'SOLVE' to be helpful to adolescents who have been in that situation. The more you practice coming up with a big list of options and the more options you have to choose from when you have a problem, and the less likely you'll feel stuck or like the only thing left to do is to hurt yourself."

Cognitive therapy focuses on the relation between cognition and affect. As mentioned previously, adolescents who have attempted suicide have been shown to have significant difficulty modulating sadness and anger. For example, Zlotnick, Donaldson, Spirito, and Pearlstein (1997) found that adolescents admitted for inpatient psychiatric hospitalization following a suicide attempt reported significantly greater problems with affect regulation compared to adolescents admitted for suicidal ideation. Problems with affect regulation were significantly related to frequency of self-mutilation and history of past suicide attempts. Consequently, affect regulation is another important aspect of treatment.

Affect regulation techniques that are used in cognitive therapy include training adolescents to recognize stimuli that provoke negative emotions and learning to reduce physiological arousal via self-talk and relaxation. Feindler and Ecton (1986) developed a system of cognitive mediation techniques and arousal reduction methods to help adolescents with anger control problems. These methods can be helpful in treating suicide attempters. In their system, Feindler and Ecton (1986) use the acronym CALMDOWN to summarize the eight cognitive and behavioral skills taught in their program. Adolescents are first taught **C**ues for identifying anger triggers and to prepare for provocation. Adolescents are then taught to **A**lter the thoughts that lead to the angry feelings. In the next phase of the protocol, the goal is to **L**et the adolescent use self-statements to guide them through angry provocations. Behavioral strategies are also introduced, including relaxation techniques to **M**odulate physiologic arousal. Adolescents also are **D**irected to communicate more effectively and act out assertively, rather than aggressively, in conflict situations. **O**rganization of the anger-control process is taught using problem-solving training. **W**orking through the protocol via modeling and behavioral rehearsal is followed by **N**egotiating a commitment to use the newly taught skills in anger-provoking situations. After receiving this self-instruction training, the goal is for adolescents to repeat calming statements to themselves during interpersonal conflicts and use relaxation techniques to minimize affective arousal.

The following guidelines may be useful for clinicians when incorporating affect management into treatment:

1. Present a rationale for affect management training.

"One thing you have told (or shown) us is that you often feel (e.g., angry, emotionally out of control). This is something that happens to a lot of the adolescents we work with who have hurt themselves. So we're going to help you learn some ways that will help you get better control over your emotions."

2. Introduce the Match and Firecracker paradigm (text adapted with minor modifications from Feindler & Ecton, 1986).

"When a problem comes up it starts two types of reactions at the same time. First, your mind will have certain negative thoughts and feelings about the problem. You might think what's happening to you is unfair, awful, or terrible. You might feel frustrated, annoyed, threatened, irritated, angry, or sad. Second, because of these negative reactions occurring in your mind, your body will start feeling out-of-control. You might experience muscle tightness, butterflies in the stomach, a faster heart rate, sweating, or shortness of breath. You may not even know your body is acting this way! Your mind and body will feed off each other's reactions. The longer you have negative thoughts and feelings about a problem, the more your body will feel out-of-control. So it's not so much the problem that makes you upset, it's actually the way your mind and body react to the problem that makes you upset. Picture your mind and body as if they were a firecracker. A problem acts as the

match that lights the fuse of the firecracker. Your mind is the fuse, and your body is the firecracker. The longer you let the problem last, the longer the fuse burns. This results in more negative thoughts and feelings, a greater risk of losing control of your emotions, for example, feeling really sad or mad. You can put the fuse out quickly by doing things to control your negative thoughts and body symptoms. Remember, the sooner you put out the fuse, the more you can control your body and your actions."

3. Discuss relation between the paradigm and suicidal behavior.

"We have talked about how when problems come up for you, you often feel (describe some of the feelings the adolescent has exhibited or described). For example, you described the match for you being (name the suicide attempt precipitant). Once that lit the fuse, your mind thought (give examples of thoughts the adolescent has shared or reported) and you felt (give examples of the emotions the adolescent has described or exhibited). The fuse burned long enough that it hit the firecracker! In other words, your body felt so out-of-control that you tried to hurt yourself to stop it from feeling that way. What we're going to do is come up with other ways that you can get the fuse to stop burning so that your body doesn't get out-of-control like that again."

4. Complete a Feeling Thermometer (e.g., see Rotheram–Borus *et al.*, 1994).

"Each problem that comes up in our lives makes us feel different. Some problems light the fuse and burn really strong and fast. Other problems light the fuse and burn kind of slow and weak. This thermometer can help us keep track of how bad the problems that happen to you make you feel. For example, fill in the thermometer to show how upset you felt when (the attempt precipitant) happened. The bottom is "0" and the top is "100," or the most upset you could possibly feel."

Emotional dysregulation is the primary focus of dialectical behavior therapy (DBT). In DBT, the suicidal adolescent is presumed to have a biological predisposition to emotional dysregulation, which is exacerbated by the environment. In DBT, four sets of skills are targeted to address emotional dysregulation (Miller, 1999): mindfulness skills to help alleviate confusion about oneself, emotional regulation skills to address emotional instability, distress–tolerance skills to target impulsivity, and interpersonal-effectiveness skills to address interpersonal problems. Mindfulness skills are techniques designed to help adolescents use both natural and emotional input to make more balanced decisions. By helping the adolescent take the time to focus on emotions, the ultimate goal is to teach greater awareness and develop control over emotions. In emotion regulation training, adolescents are taught to identify and label emotions, reduce emotional vulnerability, increase positive experiences, and counteract the current negative emotion by acting the opposite of the distressing emotion. Distress-tolerance skills include crisis survival and acceptance skills. Crisis survival skills include teaching adolescents to distract themselves from emotional pain, to self-soothe, and to generate pros and cons of tolerating versus not tolerating distress. Acceptance skills are designed to inform the adolescent that life involves pain and that by accepting this fact, one can learn the skills necessary to cope with the distress one encounters in life. Interpersonal effectiveness is designed to help the adolescent more effectively manage interpersonal conflict. Assertiveness and interpersonal problem-solving skills help adolescents negotiate their needs while maintaining important relationships.

Depressed mood is also common among adolescent suicide attempters. Therefore, most treatment protocols for adolescent suicide attempters will also use other cognitive and behavioral techniques to further alleviate depressed mood. These techniques include mood monitoring, cognitive restructuring, and scheduling of pleasant activities. Detailed descriptions of these cognitive and behavioral approaches are available in treatment manuals by Brent and Poling (1997) and Clarke, Lewinsohn, and Hops (1990).

Family Therapy

The approaches described here primarily involve working with the adolescent on an individual basis. Individual sessions are useful in addressing several different factors known to contribute to suicidal behavior (e.g., problem-solving deficits, cognitive distortions, affect regulation difficulties). In addition, it is sometimes problematic to access members of the adolescent's family. Even when the family is available, the suicidal teen or other family members may resist working together in treatment. Nevertheless, family functioning is often implicated in the etiology of suicidal behavior, and family sessions are often important in addressing it.

At a minimum, it is important to conduct a family therapy session examining the circumstances surrounding the suicide attempt (Hawton, 1986). If necessary, the therapist should emphasize that suicide attempts are serious, even if the reason for the attempt was not to die. Parent and adolescent explanations for the attempt should be explored, and discrepancies in their explanations can be examined. If differences in perspectives are evident, then the therapist needs to help the parents and adolescent understand and accept each other's explanations of the suicide attempt and work together to prevent future attempts. Wagner, Aiken, Mullaley, and Tobin (2000) interviewed parents regarding their reaction to their adolescent's suicide attempt and found that about one-half of mothers reported angry feelings but were not likely to verbalize this hostility to the adolescent. Wagner *et al.* (2000) has suggested that therapists inform parents about the different emotions experienced following a suicide attempt, examine underlying parental anger, and address this anger in family sessions when indicated.

Family therapy sessions can be used to help shift the focus away from the adolescent and to address conflictual issues that may have contributed to the development of the suicidal behavior (Richman, 1986). The main goals of family therapy typically are to modify communication patterns and negative interactions among family members, support adaptive attempts by the adolescent in separating from the family, and improve the family's problem-solving abilities (Berman & Jobes, 1991). Family therapy programs emphasizing communication and problem-solving skills that have been used with adolescent behavior problems (e.g., Robin & Foster, 1989) are applicable and have been used with families of adolescent suicide attempters (e.g., Rotheram-Borus *et al.*, 1994).

Perhaps the most important areas to address in family therapy for suicidal adolescents are improving family communication and strengthening the parent-adolescent relationship. However, a number of sessions are usually necessary to start to improve communication and relationships within families. If families are able to communicate reasonably well, family problem-solving sessions may be useful. Proponents of such an approach (e.g., Clarke, Lewinsohn, & Hops, 1990) have suggested the following components be addressed:

1. *Introduce active listening skills.* The therapist facilitates discussion about how solving problems together can be difficult because everyone in the family may have different feelings and ideas about the problem. Then "active listening" skills are introduced for use during problem solving when expressing differences of opinion. Clarke *et al.* (1990) presented the three rules of active listening: (a) restate the sender's message in your own words, (b) begin restatements with phrases such as "I hear you saying

that—," or "You said you feel—," and (c) be neutral about the other person's views (think of them as neither good nor bad). Family members take turns restating the therapist's messages using these skills.

2. *Present a problem-solving format for the family to use in addressing family problems.* These skills can be presented in a manner similar to the problem-solving skills that were taught to the adolescent but modified to pertain to all family members.

3. *Discuss rules for defining the problem.* Clarke *et al.* (1990) have suggested that therapists lead the family in using several rules during sessions (and at home). These include focusing on positive occurrences within the family, being specific, describing what the other person is doing or saying that is problematic, avoiding name-calling when describing the problem, expressing feelings in reaction to the problem (not the person), admitting self-responsibility for the problem, avoiding blame toward others, and being brief in providing input.

4. *Develop a contract describing the family's agreement for addressing the problem.* A contract that specifies a plan for addressing problems at home is developed and agreed upon by family members. Components of the contract should include a description of the specific behaviors expected of each person, consequences if family members fail to follow through on the agreement, and the period of time involved (e.g., a 1-week trial period). All family members sign the contract and a copy is given to each member.

Treatment can include the integration of individual and family therapy for adolescent suicide attempters. At the conclusion of a study of treatment for depressed adolescents, Brent and colleagues (1996) noted that many participants who had been randomly assigned to individual therapy requested some family sessions. Similarly, many participants who had been assigned to family treatment desired some individual therapy sessions. Zimmerman and Lasorsa (1995) have suggested that the therapist conduct individual and family therapy concurrently in a flexible manner as needed. For example, difficult issues may be more easily explored initially in an individual therapy session. These issues can subsequently be brought to family meetings where they can be expressed in a controlled environment and managed by the therapist. This approach can help address the resistance among families of adolescent suicide attempters. Unfortunately, the integration of individual and family therapy approaches has yet to be empirically tested.

Treatment Adherence

Chapter 12 summarized the literature indicating high rates of nonadherence with treatment among adolescent suicide attempters. Several investigators have designed interventions to address treatment adherence. Deykin, Hsieh, Joshi, and McNamara (1986) provided a social work outreach intervention for adolescent suicide ideators and attempters seen in a general hospital emergency department (ED). The direct service component of the intervention included providing support, acting as an advocate for the adolescent, helping the adolescent obtain social support and financial assistance, and ensuring that the adolescents kept appointments. Adolescents in the experimental group were more likely to adhere with outpatient treatment recommendations and had fewer subsequent visits to the ED than the attempters who did not receive the special outreach intervention.

Rotheram-Borus and colleagues (1996, 1999) developed an intervention that included training workshops for emergency department staff, an on-call family therapist, and a videotape for families about what to expect in psychotherapy. In a nonrandomized trial, adolescent suicide attempters who received this special intervention attended about three more sessions (on average) than those who received standard care. Rotheram-Borus *et al.* (1999) postulated that their intervention was effective because it impressed upon parents the seriousness of the suicide attempt. At 18-month followup, the mothers of the suicide attempters in the intervention group reported less depression and fewer psychiatric symptoms than mothers in the standard care group. The intervention was most helpful for the mothers of adolescents with high levels of psychiatric symptoms at the time of the attempt.

Brief therapy may facilitate compliance. Donaldson, Spirito, Arrigan, and Aspel (1997) developed a psychotherapy engagement intervention for adolescent suicide attempters that included a verbal agreement between the adolescent and parent to attend at least four psychotherapy sessions and three brief telephone interviews conducted with adolescents and parents over an 8-week period to problem-solve about suicidal ideation and treatment compliance. Preliminary results indicated that only 9% of the suicide attempters who received the intervention failed to attend any treatment sessions compared to 18% of the standard care group. No repeat attempts were reported in the experimental group at 3-month follow-up compared to 9% in standard care.

Given the modest success of prior interventions addressing adherence, we (Spirito, Boergers, Donaldson, Bishop, & Lewander, 2001) randomly assigned 63 adolescents to either standard care or a special psychotherapy compliance enhancement intervention. The special intervention used a problem-solving format, addressed the adolescent's or family's resistance to treatment and misconceptions about psychotherapy, anticipated factors that might impede treatment attendance, and included a verbal contract to attend at least four sessions of treatment. After discharge from the hospital, each participant received four phone call interventions over an 8-week period using the problem-solving approach around two key areas: suicidal ideation and psychotherapy compliance. At 3-month follow-up, the experimental intervention resulted in a greater number of sessions attended (8.4 versus 5.7) after controlling for barriers to service encountered at the mental health centers. The type of service barriers included being placed on a waiting list and problems with insurance coverage. Although the intervention proved effective, service delivery characteristics were the most formidable obstacles to patients in their efforts to obtain treatment. The findings underscore the need to eliminate service barriers for families of adolescents who have attempted suicide and are seeking treatment. This necessitates that clinicians help patients negotiate the mental health system and at times directly assist patients in obtaining access to treatment.

Enhancing Treatment Engagement

As described in the section on initial crisis management, the therapist should address treatment adherence issues at the onset of treatment and continue to address them throughout treatment regardless of the particular treatment approach. The literature suggests individual characteristics (e.g., mood, substance abuse) and family functioning contribute to non-compliance. Other factors seem to be related to the process by which the adolescent and family are referred for treatment, especially with respect to attendance at first appointments. These include factors such as the setting in which the disposition is made, communication across agencies involved (Bassuck & Gerson, 1980), and the specificity of information about the treatment being recommended (e.g., date, time, contact person; Jellinek, 1978). However, of even greater importance to the clinician are those factors that the clinician can influence and address throughout the treatment once the adolescent is engaged in the treatment process.

In our own clinical work, we have found it helpful to focus on the initial engagement in therapy using four basic strategies: (1) education about the specifics of treatment, (2) an attendance contract, (3) identification of potential treatment barriers, and (4) problem solving to address the barriers identified. These strategies were developed based on the available literature on the most common factors affecting psychotherapy compliance. Each of these areas would be addressed ideally prior to the first appointment or when the disposition is reviewed with the adolescent and his or her family. However, after treatment begins, these same issues can be integrated into the session quite easily regardless of the approach.

The following statements illustrate the integration of these strategies in treatment:

> *"We know from our work with teenagers who have been in this situation, that if nothing changes in your life when you leave here, you are at risk for hurting yourself again. In fact, approximately 1 in 10 teenagers try to hurt themselves within 3 months of being in the hospital, so your condition is quite serious. As a result, it is very important that you go to therapy or counseling now that you are out of the hospital. We find that it takes time for counseling to help. Counseling doesn't usually help anyone if they go only one or two times. It takes time for you to get to know the counselor and to feel comfortable with him or her. It also takes time for the counselor to get to know you. Because of this, we recommend that people go to counseling at least six times to increase the chance that it will be helpful. After six sessions, we will discuss whether there is a need for further treatment."*

In reviewing the adolescent's expectations for outpatient treatment, the following questions can be helpful:

> *"What do you think about going to therapy or counseling?"* or *"What do you think usually happens in counseling/therapy?"* or *"When you think about the problems that you are experiencing, how many visits to a therapist or a counselor do you think it would take until things get better?"*

These questions can lead to a discussion of factors that may impede the adolescent's compliance with outpatient therapy. For example,

> *"We know that sometimes things come up that make it difficult for adolescents to go to counseling. What are some things that you can think of that make it hard for teenagers to go to counseling?"*

The adolescent's responses can be utilized either to problem-solve (if barriers are mentioned) or to contract for sessions (if no barriers are elicited). For example,

> *"You're right. Those are the things that teenagers have told us about. Let's say (one of those things) happened. What are all of the things that a teenager could do or say to help them get to counseling?"*

During the initial engagement in therapy, the therapist can provide information such as how treatment visits will be organized (with whom does the therapist meet, how long, content), the expected number of treatment sessions, and how visits will be scheduled. As treatment progresses, it is important to review and update this information and planning. Adolescents should be reminded of the time-limited nature of treatment and the ability to make progress toward the goal of ending treatment. In addition, the therapist and adolescent/family have the opportunity to evaluate treatment progress compared to what they had been told previously and what they expected. This offers the opportunity to allay client anxieties and address any continued potential for treatment resistance.

SUMMARY

Because of the number of existing treatment approaches, the field would benefit most from more definitive investigations of those that are available before abandoning them and generating new treatments. It will be important for follow-up studies to direct more attention to the process and components of treatment that effectively address the negative sequelae of adolescent suicide attempts. Because of the potentially serious consequences of a false negative prediction, we need to provide at least minimal intervention to all adolescent suicide attempters and intensive intervention to some proportion of this group. A comprehensive treatment plan should address a combination of problem areas that may effect the adolescent's suicide risk.

It is important for clinicians to move away from a crisis intervention model and appreciate the long-term nature of therapy for many suicidal adolescents. It can be hard to accomplish much through psychological therapy during a brief inpatient stay. However, outpatient care allows more time to address the factors that precipitated the suicidal act. Thus, therapists should have a plan for different treatment strategies at different times during the therapeutic process.

The central factors during the start of therapy involve preventing self-harm and working to engage the adolescent in therapy. Several strategies have been described that can help the therapist to engage the client and parents in therapy. Also, it is important to develop a therapeutic relationship that is based on trust, flexibility, and collaboration (Overholser & Silverman, 1998). The therapist and family members should avoid critical remarks or attributions that blame the suicidal teen.

When working with suicidal adolescents, therapy often targets the reduction of feelings of depression and hopelessness. The active phase of therapy uses a variety of strategies to reduce cognitive distortions, improve social functioning, and address other risk factors. Cognitive therapy can be used to address the thought processes that underlie both depression and hopelessness, as well as anger. Many adolescents need to learn to reduce the tendency for dichotomous thinking and catastrophizing.

Cognitive-behavioral therapy can also help the suicidal adolescent develop a wide range of adaptive coping skills. Useful coping skills can include directly confronting a problem situation instead of indirectly avoiding a difficult situation, learning to focus on desirable solutions instead of complaining about life's problems, and encouraging persistence, hopefulness, and a sense of personal control when struggling through a challenging situation (Overholser, 1996b).

A central component of the adaptive coping skills involves creative problem-solving skills. When helping clients to improve their problem-solving skills, the therapist can help clients learn to define problems in terms of specific and realistic goals, generate a variety of response alternatives, learn to make rational decisions, and implement a specific coping plan (Overholser, 1996a).

Because interpersonal problems can play a major role in depression and suicide risk, it is important for therapy to focus on helping adolescents improve their social functioning. Therapy may focus on increasing the frequency of pleasant social activity, improving the adolescent's basic social skills, reducing interpersonal conflict with family or friends, and reducing social isolation (Overholser, 1995). Family meetings can help improve communication within the family (Harrington *et al.*, 1998) and increase support provided by family members (Gutstein & Rudd, 1990). As social functioning improves, adolescents often report less depression and reduced risk of suicidal behavior.

Finally, it is important to keep a focus on relapse prevention issues. Even after therapy has been successful, adolescent suicide attempters remain vulnerable to a sudden resurgence of suicidal feelings. The therapist can forewarn the adolescent and parents so that any resurgence of suicidal feelings does not come completely unexpected. Instead, therapy can help to identify low levels of sadness or pessimism that can be confronted and managed before they reach unmanageable levels. In this way, the adolescent can gain a sense of mastery, learning how to cope effectively with stressful life events, negative mood states, and pessimistic expectations. It is hoped that by the end of treatment, suicidal adolescents can move away from their reliance on maladaptive coping strategies and can learn how to manage difficult situations more effectively.

REFERENCES

Aronson, S., & Scheidlinger, S. (1995). Group treatment of suicidal adolescents. In J. K. Zimmerman & G. M. Asnis (Eds.), *Treatment approaches with suicidal adolescents.* New York: John Wiley & Sons.

Bassuk, E., & Gerson, S. (1980). Chronic crisis patients: A discrete clinical group. *American Journal of Psychiatry, 137,* 1513–1517.

Berman, A. L., & Jobes, D. A. (1991). *Adolescent suicide: Assessment and intervention.* Washington, DC: American Psychological Association Press.

Blumenthal, S. J., & Kupfer, D. J. (1986). Generalized treatment strategies for suicidal behavior. *Annals of the New York Academy of Sciences, 487,* 327–340.

Boergers, J., Spirito, A., & Donaldson, D. (1998). Reasons for adolescent suicide attempts: Associations with psychological functioning. *Journal of the American Academy of Child and Adolescent Psychiatry, 37,* 1287–1293.

Brent, D., Holder, D., Kolko, D., Birmaher, B., Baugher, M., Roth, C., & Johnson, B. (1997). A clinical psychotherapy trial for adolescent depression comparing cognitive, family, and supportive treatments. *Archives of General Psychiatry, 54,* 877–885.

Brent, D., & Kolko, D. (1990). The assessment and treatment of children and adolescents at risk for suicide. In S. Blumenthal & D. Kupfer (Eds.), *Suicide over the life cycle: Risk factors, assessment, and treatment of suicidal patients* (pp. 253–302). Washington, DC: American Pychiatric Press.

Brent, D., & Poling, K. (1997). *Cognitive therapy treatment manual for depressed and suicidal youth.* Pittsburgh, PA: University of Pittsburgh, Services for Teens at Risk Center.

Brent, D. A., Roth, C. M., Holder, D. P., Kolker, D. J., Birmaher, B., Johnson, B. A., & Schweers, J. A. (1996). Psychosocial interventions for treating adolescent suicidal depression: A comparison of three psychosocial interventions. In E. D. Hibbs & P. S. Jensen (Eds.), *Psychosocial treatments for child and adolescent disorders: Empirically based strategies for clinical practice* (pp. 187–206). Washington, DC: American Psychological Association Press.

Clarke, G., Lewinsohn, P., & Hops, H. (1990). *Adolescent coping with depression course.* Eugene, OR: Castalia Publishing.

Cotgrove, A., Zirinsky, L., Black, D., & Weston, D. (1995). Secondary prevention of attempted suicide in adolescence. *Journal of Adolescence, 18,* 569–577.

Deykin, E. Y., Hsieh, C., Joshi, N., & McNamara, J. J. (1986). Adolescent suicidal and self-destructive behavior: Results of an intervention study. *Journal of Adolescent Health Care*, 7, 88–95.

Donaldson, D., Spirito, A., Arrigan, M., & Aspel, J. W. (1997). Structured disposition planning for adolescent suicide attempters in a general hospital: Preliminary findings on short-term outcome. *Archives of Suicide Research*, 3, 271–282.

Feindler, E., & Ecton, R. (1986). *Adolescent anger control: Cognitive-behavioral techniques*. New York: Pergamon Press.

Freeman, A., & Reinecke, M. (1993). *Cognitive therapy of suicidal behavior*. New York: Springer.

Greenfield, B., Hechtman, L., & Tremblay, C. (1995). Short-term efficacy of interventions by a youth crisis team. *Canadian Journal of Psychiatry*, 40, 320–324.

Gutstein, S. E., & Rudd, M. D. (1990). An outpatient treatment alternative for suicidal youth. *Journal of Adolescence*, 13, 265–277.

Harrington, R., Kerfoot, M., Dyer, E., McNiven, F., Gill, J., Harrington, V., Woodham, A., & Byford, S. (1998). Randomized trial of a home-based family intervention for children who have deliberately poisoned themselves. *Journal of the American Academy of Child and Adolescent Psychiatry*, 37, 512–518.

Harrington, R., Kerfoot, M., Dyer, S., McNiven, F., Gill, J., Harrington, V., & Woodham, A. (2000). Deliberate self-poisoning in adolescence: Why does a brief family intervention work in some cases and not in others? *Journal of Adolescence*, 23, 13–20.

Hawton, K. (1986). *Suicide and attempted suicide among children and adolescents*. Beverly Hills, CA: Sage.

Hawton, K., Arensman, E., Townsend, E., Breminer, S., Feldman, E., Goldney, R., Gunnell, D., Hazell, P., van Heeringen, K., House, A., Owens, D., Sakinofsky, I., & Traskman-Bendz, L. (1998). Deliberate self-harm: Systematic review of efficacy of psychosocial and pharmacological treatments in preventing repetition. *British Medical Journal*, 317, 441–447.

Jellinek, M., (1978). Referrals from a psychiatric emergency room. Relationship of compliance to demographic and interview variables. *American Journal of Psychiatry*, 135, 209–213.

Lewinsohn, P., Rohde, P., & Seeley, J. (1996). Adolescent suicidal ideation and attempts: Prevalence, risk factors, and clinical implications. *Clinical Psychology Science and Practice*, 3, 25–46.

Linehan, M. (1993). *Cognitive behavior therapy of borderline personality disorder*. New York: Guilford.

McLeavey, B., Daly, R., Ludgate, J., & Murray, C. (1994). Interpersonal problem-solving skills training in the treatment of self-poisoning patients. *Suicide and Life-Threatening Behavior*, 24, 382–394.

Miller, A. (1999). Dialectical Behavior Therapy: A new treatment approach for suicidal adolescents. *American Journal of Psychotherapy*, 53, 413–417.

Miller, A., Rathus, J., Linehan, M., Wetzler, S., & Leigh, E. (1997). Dialectical behavior therapy adopted for suicidal adolescents. *Journal of Practical Psychiatry and Behavioral Health*, 3, 78–86.

Ottino, J. (1999). Suicide attempts during adolescence: Systematic hospitalization and crisis treatment. *Crisis*, 20, 41–48.

Overholser, J. C. (1993). Elements of the Socratic method: I. Systematic Questioning. *Psychotherapy, 30*, 67–74.

Overholser, J. C. (1995). Cognitive-behavioral treatment of depression, Part II: Techniques for improving social functioning. *Journal of Contemporary Psychotherapy, 25*, 205–222.

Overholser, J. C. (1996a). Cognitive-behavioral treatment of depression, Part IV: Improving problem-solving skills. *Journal of Contemporary Psychotherapy, 26*, 43–57.

Overholser, J. C. (1996b). Cognitive-behavioral treatment of depression, Part VII: Coping with precipitating events. *Journal of Contemporary Psychotherapy, 26*, 337–360.

Overholser, J. C., & Silverman, E. (1998). Cognitive-behavioral treatment of depression, Part VIII. Developing and utilizing the therapeutic relationship. *Journal of Contemporary Psychotherapy, 28*, 199–214.

Overholser, J., & Spirito, A. (1990). Cognitive behavioral treatment of suicidal depression. In E. Feindler & G. Kalfus (Eds.), *Adolescent behavior therapy handbook* (pp. 211–231). New York: Springer.

Pfeffer, C. R. (1990). Clinical perspectives on treatment of suicidal behavior among children and adolescents. *Psychiatric Annals, 20*, 143–150.

Piacentini, J., Rotheram-Borus, M. J., & Cantwell, C. (1995). Brief cognitve-behavioral family therapy for suicidal adolescents. In L. V. Creek, S. Knapp, & T. Jackson (Eds.), *Innovations in clinical practice: A source book* (Vol. 14, pp. 151–168). Sarasota, FL: Professional Resource Press.

Pillay, A. L., & Waasenaar, D. R. (1995). Psychological intervention, spontaneous remission, hopelessness, and psychiatric disturbance in adolescent parasuicides. *Suicide and Life-Threatening Behavior, 25*, 386–392.

Richman, J. (1986). *Family therapy for suicidal people.* New York: Springer.

Robin, A. L., & Foster, S. L. (1989). *Negotiating parent-adolescent conflict: A behavioral-family systems approach.* New York: Guilford Press.

Ross, C. P., & Motto, J. A. (1984). Group counseling for suicidal adolescents. In H. Sudak, A. Ford, & N. Rushforth (Eds.), *Suicide in the Young* (pp. 367–392). Boston: John Wright.

Rotheram-Borus, M. J., Piacentini, J., Miller, S., Graae, F., & Castro-Blanco, D. (1994). Brief cognitive-behavioral treatment for adolescent suicide attempters and their families. *Journal of the American Academy of Child & Adolescent Psychiatry, 33*, 508–517.

Rotheram-Borus, M. J., Piacentini, J., Van Roosem, R., Graae, F., Cantwell, C., Castro-Blanco, D., & Feldman, J. (1999). Treatment adherence among Latina female adolescent suicide attempters. *Suicide and Life-Threatening Behavior, 29*, 319–331.

Rotheram-Borus, M. J., Piacentini, J., Van Roosem, R., Graae, F., Cantwell, C., Castro-Blanco, D., Miller, S., & Feldman, J. (1996). Enhancing treatment adherence with a specialized emergency room program for adolescent suicide attempters. *Journal of the American Academy of Child and Adolescent Psychiatry, 35*, 654–663.

Rudd, M. D. (2000). The suicidal mode: A cognitive-behavioral model of suicidality. *Suicide and Life-Threatening Behavior, 30*, 18–33.

Rudd, M. D., & Joiner, T. (1998). An integrative conceptual framework for assessing and treating suicidal behavior in adolescents. *Journal of Adolescence, 21*, 489–498.

Rudd, M. D., Rajab, M. H., Orman, D. T., Stulman, D. A., Joiner, T., & Dixon, W. (1996). Effectiveness of an outpatient intervention targeting suicidal young adults: Preliminary results. *Journal of Consulting and Clinical Psychology, 64*, 179–190.

Schneidman, E. (1985). *Definition of suicide.* New York: John Wiley & Sons.

Shaffer, D., & Pfeffer, C. (in press). Practice parameters for the assessment and treatment of children and adolescents with suicidal behavior. *Journal of the American Academy of Child and Adolescent Psychiatry*.

Spirito, A., Boergers, J., Donaldson, D., Bishop, D. & Lewander, W. (2001). An intervention trial to improve adherence to community treatment by adolescents following a suicide attempt. *Manuscript submitted for publication*.

Trautman, P. (1995). Cognitive behavior therapy of adolescent suicide attempters. In J. K. Zimmerman & G. M. Asnis (Eds.), *Treatment approaches with suicidal adolescents* (pp. 155–173). New York: John Wiley & Sons.

Wagner, B. M., Aiken, C., Mullaley, P. M., & Tobin, J. J. (2000). Parents reactions to adolescents' suicide attempts. *Jorunal of the American Academy of Child and Adolescent Psychiatry, 39*, 429–436.

Zimmerman, J. K., & Lasorsa, V. A. (1995). Being the family's therapist: An integrative approach. In J. K. Zimmerman & G. M. Asnis (Eds.), *Treatment approaches with suicidal adolescents* (pp. 174–188). New York: John Wiley & Sons.

Zlotnick, C., Donaldson, D., Spirito, A., & Pearlstein, T. (1997). Affect regulation and suicide attempts in adolescent inpatients. *Journal of the American Academy of Child and Adolescent Psychiatry, 36*, 793–798.

CHAPTER 15

Working with Suicidal Teens: Integrating Clinical Practice and Current Research

James Overholser and Anthony Spirito

The goal of this book has been to examine suicidal behavior in adolescence. Throughout the different chapters, we have attempted to summarize the current research on adolescent suicide by examining different risk factors that have been identified. This chapter summarizes our views on the issues related to the assessment and treatment of suicidal behavior in adolescents. We strive to integrate clinical practice with findings from recent research.

Suicidal urges can take a variety of forms. Perhaps the most basic level involves a desire to die, when an individual feels that life is so filled with problems that it will never improve. The desire to die underlies various forms of suicidal activity, including suicidal ideation, suicide attempts, and completed suicide. Suicidal ideation can range from vague thoughts of death that occur infrequently to persistent and detailed plans for when and how the death should occur. Suicide attempts can range from non-lethal forms of self-injury to highly lethal acts that might result in death unless medical treatment is provided. Completed suicide involves the deliberate act of killing oneself. Fortunately, most adolescents do not attempt suicide, and very few adolescents actually complete it. More research has been conducted on adolescents who have attempted suicide than on adolescents who have died by suicide. Thus, we know much more about suicide attempters than completers. These two groups overlap in many but not all ways, and both groups display many of the risk factors that have been examined in this book.

In general, research that has attempted to predict suicidal behavior has failed. Because of the low base rate for suicidal behavior in the general population, statistically, one would never predict that a given individual would make a suicide attempt or complete suicide in the near future. However, such statistical guidelines fail to help frontline clinicians when confronted with an adolescent in crisis. The best strategy for managing suicide risk may involve identifying and protecting high-risk groups during high-risk times. High-risk groups include adolescents diagnosed with certain psychiatric disorders, such as depression, as well as gay, lesbian, and bisexual youth, homeless and runaway youth, and incarcerated youth. Within these high-risk groups, certain factors can increase vulnerability to suicidal behavior, such as an impulsive cognitive or behavioral style, weak or rigid problem-solving skills, frequent family discord, or inadequate social support. High-risk times are often triggered by a stressful life event and can involve the breakup of a romantic relationship, family stress, or recent relocation or incarceration.

Stressful life events play an important role in suicidal behavior. Recent stressors often provide the situational trigger that activates the actual suicide attempt. For many people (including the adolescent, family members, and the therapist), stressful life events only partially explain why the adolescent became suicidal. Most adolescents are capable of enduring the same stressor without becoming suicidal. Hence, stressful life events do not explain "Why?" the adolescent has become suicidal, but they may help explain "Why now?" It is most likely that the stressful event has pushed a vulnerable adolescent toward suicidal behavior by creating a feeling that the problem is overwhelming and insurmountable. It can be useful to discuss the stressful event in session. The adolescent may be less likely to feel threatened by discussions that focus on external factors instead of internal vulnerabilities. However, therapy can be more effective when it looks beyond the stressor and examines vulnerability factors that underlie the adolescent's difficulties coping with problems.

Stressful life events often trigger a variety of emotional reactions. The three most prominent negative mood states are depression, anger, and anxiety. Often, suicidal teens will report a mixture of these moods. Negative mood states appear to play a central role in suicidal tendencies, and it is unlikely that we could find a suicidal teen who does not admit to at least one of these negative mood states. However, these emotions provide a nonspecific clue to suicidal behavior. In fact, most adolescents (suicidal and nonsuicidal) experience a range of negative emotions, especially when forced to confront life's difficulties. Hence, negative mood states are usually quite visible in suicidal adolescents, but probably do not play a causal role in suicidal behavior. More commonly, emotional distress is a natural and common reaction to problems encountered by adolescents. Nonetheless, because a strong negative mood state reflects inner turmoil and difficulties coping with social or environmental problems, it can serve as a nonspecific risk factor for suicidal behavior.

Substance abuse can predate and lead to emotional distress or be viewed as a maladaptive reaction to stressful life events. In adults who present with substance dependence, biological and genetic aspects of addiction may play an important role. However, in adolescents, we are more likely to deal with the early stages of substance abuse. Substance abuse has been found to occur more often in suicidal adolescents than nonsuicidal controls and can increase the risk of suicidal behavior several ways. First, some substances are toxic and can cause injury or death through deliberate or unintentional overdose. Second, when intoxicated, the adolescent may not think clearly. Impulsive or aggressive acts are more likely to occur while the adolescent is under the influence of various drugs. Finally, substance abuse may reflect a more general pattern of emotional distress or social discord that underlies suicidal behavior. An adolescent who has become addicted to alcohol or other drugs may have a family life characterized by chaos or discord. The adolescent may be treating recreational drug use as a means of suppressing negative emotional reactions or gaining acceptance from a deviant subculture. Whatever the reason, drug abuse during adolescence reflects an important nonspecific risk factor for suicidal behavior. When substance abuse and depression are both present in the adolescent, a lethal combination can develop. The comorbid presence of substance abuse and depression reflects a higher degree of risk for suicidal behavior and completed suicide than observed when either factor is seen alone.

Impulsive and aggressive behavior have been related to suicide risk. Actually, many suicidal acts can be seen as impulsive behaviors that were triggered by a recent stressful life event. Impulsive behavior is hard to measure when construed as a long-standing personality trait. However, impulsive suicide attempts typically differ from premeditated attempts.

Impulsive attempts rely on a range of methods, using whatever is readily available. Premeditated attempts are more serious and potentially more dangerous. In some adolescents, aggressive acts may reflect a stable form of pathology sometimes seen in conduct disorder. A suicide attempt may at times be viewed as an act of aggression directed toward the self. In other adolescents, aggressive acts may reflect a time-limited period of crisis and turmoil. In both cases, aggressive acts reflect a disregard for the health or safety of others. The more often an adolescent harms someone or something, the easier it may become to harm himself or herself.

Cognitive factors have been found important in understanding suicide risk. Research on adults has found that cognitive factors, such as hopelessness, can be predictive of suicide risk even years later. However, the research on adolescents has been less clear. Most adolescents do not look to the future in the same way as adults. Hence, hopelessness may not be as important with suicidal teens. Nonetheless, it may be useful to treat hopelessness and pessimistic attitudes that appear during the course of therapy. Other cognitive factors, such as coping style and problem-solving skills, should also be considered in suicidal teens. Suicide attempters often use maladaptive or passive coping strategies, such as wishful thinking, when under stress. Adolescent suicide attempters also appear to have negative expectations about their ability to solve problems. This lack of confidence in their ability to solve problems must often be addressed as a preliminary step in the therapeutic process.

Family factors may play a central role in suicide risk during adolescence. For most teens, adolescence is a period of amazing growth combined with difficult adjustments. Teenagers often struggle to gain independence from family rule. Nonetheless, parents still control most important aspects of the adolescent's life, which may lead to conflict between the adolescent and parents. In many ways, the adolescent fights against the family structure. Despite the conflict, adolescence is a period of life when teens need as much affection and support from their parents as they did in childhood. Deviant behavior (e.g., substance use, aggressive acts) can trigger major family conflict. The adolescent may not be equipped to handle the conflict and potential rejection. Family therapy can be essential for helping adolescents learn to express emotional distress in an open, direct, and constructive manner, and helping the parents learn to manage their teenager during a difficult period of adjustment.

As the adolescent struggles for independence from the family, peer relationships become prominent. Peer relationships are important for growth, adjustment, and maturity. Without adequate peer relationships, the teen will experience social isolation and loneliness. Also, peer relationships provide a sense of social support that can help to buffer the negative impact of stressful life events. Suicidal adolescents often report that a close relationship has recently ended or became filled with conflict. Therapy may help these adolescents learn to resolve conflict in their close relationships. Also, some teens need guidance in developing relationships or expanding their range of social activity in order to have a satisfying interpersonal life.

Suicide can be viewed as a process that develops over time. Suicidal behavior is likely to be the result of a combination of the factors. A stressful life event serves as the situational trigger for the suicidal crisis. The stressful event does not act in isolation but is most likely acting on preexisting vulnerabilities in the adolescent. After an adolescent has attempted suicide, the suicidal crisis does not necessarily subside quickly. The acute crisis may subside, and family support may provide an important period of relief from the ongoing conflict. However, it is naive to assume that the risk of future suicidal behavior will resolve with brief crisis management strategies. After a suicide attempt it may take time for changes to occur in the adolescent or the family. The adolescent who has attempted suicide may remain at risk for future suicidal acts. The period of risk will depend on the type and quality of treatment and the number of risk factors that were present at the time of the suicide attempt. A comprehensive treatment plan should try to identify and modify those risk factors deemed most problematic for a particular suicidal adolescent. It is unfortunate that many suicidal adolescents and their families to do not follow through with their referrals for outpatient care after discharge from the hospital.

We believe that most suicidal teens can be treated effectively. The treatment of suicidal adolescents should address a variety of factors that have pushed the adolescent toward suicidal behavior. Although many treatment modalities may be relevant, we endorse a cognitive-behavioral model. In this model, the therapist can conduct a comprehensive assessment of the adolescent and the family, and identify risk factors that may underlie the suicidal urges. Then, specific strategies can be used to help the adolescent and parents make specific changes in their lifestyle. A central focus on cognitive distortions and problem-solving skills appears useful. Suicidal teens can learn new ways of approaching the problems they encounter, learning to confront and overcome problems instead of being overwhelmed by the stressors encountered by most adolescents. Throughout this therapy process, the adolescents develop courage and confidence in their coping abilities. Emotion regulation strategies may be equally useful in these adolescents.

The process of therapy is not easy. Many adolescents are not very forthcoming about their perceived weaknesses and inadequacies. It may be difficult for them to share their emotional distress with an adult. However, we believe that psychotherapy can help most suicidal teens. The therapist needs to use a calm but confident style, working with the adolescent to understand recent problems and the emotional distress that developed. The therapist may use recent problems as examples of the adolescent's difficulties in coping. Together, the therapist and the adolescent can explore various coping options using a collaborative problem-solving format. The Socratic method (i.e., systematic questioning, inductive reasoning, universal definitions) can be useful in protecting the therapeutic alliance while allowing the therapist to confront sensitive issues with the adolescent. It is hoped that the suicidal teen can view the therapist as a supportive ally and wise confidant.

When working with suicidal adolescents, interdisciplinary collaboration should be encouraged. Suicide is a complex problem that requires a comprehensive approach. Although the use of psychotropic medication has not been discussed in this book, a biopsychosocial model is important for incorporating many different factors related to suicide risk as well as different modalities of treatment. Psychologists, psychiatrists, social workers, and other professionals can contribute to and benefit from a biopsychosocial model. The treatment of suicidal adolescents raises many challenges for the clinician, and supportive teamwork among mental health professionals is very important. A comprehensive model helps each professional respect the limits of one field and encourage collaboration among colleagues.

Subject Index